Forgotten Englishman

Forgotten Englishman

Thomas Stephens and
the Mission to the East

Nicholas Fogg

Foreword by William Dalrymple

GRACEWING

First published in England in 2021
by
Gracewing
2 Southern Avenue
Leominster
Herefordshire HR6 0QF
United Kingdom
www.gracewing.co.uk

No part of this publication may be reproduced, stored in a retrieval system, or transmitted in any form or by any means, electronic, mechanical, photocopying, recording or otherwise, without the written permission of the publisher.

The right of Nicholas Fogg to be identified as the author of this work has been asserted in accordance with the Copyright, Designs and Patents Act 1988.

© 2021 Nicholas Fogg

ISBN 978 085244 852 6

Typeset by Gracewing

Cover design by Bernardita Peña Hurtado

To my dear friend Willi Vossenkuhl
Whose talents are made for mighty deeds.

Contents

Contents vii

Illustrations xi

Foreword xiii

Preface xv

1 Wiltshireman and Jesuit 1
   England and India 1
   Wiltshireman and Jesuit 2
   Douai 16
   'The Chair of the Fisherman' 17
   'His Sighs, his Prayers and Desires' 20
   The Spiritual Exercises 23
   Christopher Clavius 28
   The English College 30
   Sir Thomas Stukeley 35

2 The Voyage of the São Lourenço 41
   Thomas Pounde in the Marshalsea 41
   'Towards Japponia' 44
   Accommodation 47
   'Imprisonment for the Faith's Sake' 52
   From out of the Flaminian Gate 54
   'No Hope of Life nor Comfort' 60
   'Roma do Oriente' 68

3 Golden Goa 83
- Francis Xavier 88
- Goencho Saib 93
- The Inquisition 96
- Roma do Oriente 113

4 Conversion and Coercion 131
- The Royal Hospital 132
- St Paul's College 136
- Garcia de Orta 139
- At the Court of Akbar 141
- Come Rack, Come Rope 163

5 'Had it not Pleased God' 173
- Mar Abraham 173
- The Union of Crowns 177
- A Pressing Need 179
- The Martyrs of Cuncolim 180
- Bernardo 190
- 'Our Troubles have been so Great' 194

6 Of a very good Talent for Conversions 211
- Matteo Ricci 211
- The Mirror of Holiness 217
- 'A Wonderful Kind' 221
- Back in Goa 223
- One of the 'Professed' 226
- The Synod of Dampier 231
- Jan Huygen van Linschoten 241
- To Agra 248

7 'An Apostle and a Saint'..251
Roberto de Nobili 251
'A Word from your Fraternity' 258
Pyrard de Laval 262
Bassein..276
'The Highest Efforts of the Poet's Genius' 277

Bibliography..293
Manuscripts..293
Letters and Papers 293
Jesuit Sources 293
Bibliography 294
Books 294
Articles and Essays 296
Theses..298

Index of Persons..299

Index of Places..323

Illustrations

Winchester College in 1404 3

St Edmund Campion, National Portrait Gallery 1631 print ..11

Fr Everard Mercurian, the General of the Jesuits at the time that Thomas Stephens joined the Order, British Library 19

Fr Christopher Clavius, 16th century engraving after a painting by Francisco Villamena 29

Fr Robert Persons, scanning of an engraving in *Gallerie illustreé de la Compagnie de Jésus*, 1893 30

Fr Alessandro Valignano, 17th century engraving 48

Harbour scene by depicting Portuguese ships preparing to depart from Lisbon. Engraving by Theodor de Bry c1593 57

Plan of Goa, 1750, from *Histoire general des voyages* 69

Goa Market, 1599 from Hugo van Linschotten's *Navigatio in Oriente* 74

Akbar leads the Mughal Army during a campaign, 16th century manuscript 161

Coat of Arms of the King of Portugal at the entrance to the Rachol Seminary 183

Fr Matteo Ricci, painted in 1610 by the Chinese brother Emmanuel Pereira (born Yu Wen-hui), who had learned his art from the Italian Jesuit, Giovanni Nicolao 212

The Saviour of the world church at Loutolim 229

Aleixo de Menezes, Archbishop of Goa, 1595–1612 232

Portrait of Jan Huygen van Linschoten from H. Kern (1910),
Het Itinerario van Jan Huygen van Linschoten 1579-1592 242

Bom Jesus Church, Falko Berges 247

Roberto de Nobili, etching by Alfred Hamy, *Galerie illustrée de la Compagnie de Jésus*, 1893 (1656 date on etching) 252

Foreword

Thomas Stephens' life took him from Reformation Oxford to Borgia Rome and hence Eastwards to 'Golden Goa' at the peak of the Portuguese Empire. Here, as one of the very first Englishmen to play a part in Indian history, and certainly the first to write in an Indian language, he composed an extraordinary *Christian Purana* in Marathi. Encompassing tales of martyrdoms, shipwrecks, colonialism, kidnapping and piracy, Nicholas Fogg's *Forgotten Englishman* tells the story of a fascinating life, brilliantly illuminated by dogged research in the archives.

William Dalrymple
28 September 2021

Preface

I cannot recall when or how I first encountered the name of Thomas Stephens. This is surprising, since I have devoted so much time to him subsequently. I did write an article about him for *Wiltshire Life*, the magazine of the county in which he was born, but while researching this man and his times, I have done lots of other things, including writing a biography of William Shakespeare. Perhaps surprisingly, there are links between the poet and the priest in that smaller world of Elizabeth's England. There is circumstantial evidence that both men were familiar with three future saints of the Catholic Church: Thomas Cottam, Edmund Campion and Robert Southwell. Thomas Stephens would almost certainly have encountered the infant Henry Wriothesley, a cousin of his fellow Catholic evangeliser Thomas Pounde. As the third Earl of Southampton, he was to become Shakespeare's patron. Yet, to the biographer, there are issues other than that of who knew whom. 'The past is a foreign country,' L. P. Hartley wrote. 'They do things differently there.' Hartley, of course, was writing of a period (1900) within living memory when his book *The Go-Between* was published in 1953. They did things very much more differently in the Elizabethan era.

In an age long before the emergence of the mass media, there was less interest in personalities. Every major aspect of William Shakespeare's life can be traced, but much of the information reads like programme notes, recording the author's dealings and endeavours, but telling little of his character. This was a man who was truly noted, at least among his immediate contemporaries. It is surprising, then, that in some ways we probably know more of Thomas Stephens than we do of William Shakespeare. No letter written by the poet survives, whereas there are extant three important ones written by the priest. Even so, the task of tracing such shadowy figures represents a conundrum for the biographer. It is rather like building a picture for a police artist. Certain details stand out clearly, while others are more shadowy. The only way to pick out the picture as a whole is to attempt to illuminate the world in which the subject dwelt. In the case of Thomas Stephens, this is not one world but several. We find him rooted in a Catholic England that is passing away, when people were being challenged to choose between secular or spiritual loyalties. He was in the rare group who chose the latter. Many of those who did so paid a high price. Men like Edmund Campion, Robert Southwell and Thomas Pounde could have risen high in Church and state. Instead they faced humiliation and carried it as the ultimate bond of their faith. Such men were crucial to the faith of Thomas Stephens and were truly bound to him, so it is important to follow their lives and witness, as he would have sought to do from afar.

As a Jesuit, Stephens would have been bound to obey a call to the English Mission and would almost certainly have shared the fate of his companions in the Society. Instead, he was directed to the Mission to the East, as the only Englishman to serve there: indeed, as the first Englishman to make a significant impact in India. The contrast between the two missions could not have been greater: the one struggling to keep the flame of its faith alive, in a society whose objective was its complete obliteration; the other serving in a milieu in which great things could be attained. Amongst other achievements, the Jesuits brought the printing press to India, and Western science and astronomy to China. They compiled the first dictionaries and grammars of Asian languages and even brought the silk trade to Japan. This was a process in which Thomas Stephens would play a considerable part. Yet even this contrast is not as simple as it appears. The Jesuits in England were operating in a culture with which they were familiar because it was their own, despite the aberrations that they believed and hoped would be temporary. Robert Southwell directed his poetry, and men like Campion and Persons their polemics, towards an audience with which they were intimately familiar. The basic language of faith was the same. In his missionary days in England

Preface xvii

with Thomas Pounde, Thomas Stephens played a part in that too, so he uniquely links the two worlds.

In the east, the Jesuits were operating in an unfamiliar culture and this carried its own dilemmas. The caste system in India, and the Japanese belief that a man's outward appearance reflected his innate worth, may have struck faint echoes with the Western class system, but they were in essence the reverse of the Jesuits' own social perspectives, so the issue became how such societies should be addressed: whether an attempt should be made to impose Western values and practices, as the Portuguese colonisers certainly did; or whether an 'accommodation' should be made with local cultures, incorporating such aspects of them as did not contradict Catholic belief. Of course, as Francis Xavier had warned, such approaches had their perils. In the latter process, the essence of Christianity might be diffused into a wider potpourri of beliefs, or even lost altogether. Yet there was clear precedent for such practices. The early Church had 'Christianized' Roman feasts and festivals and even changed the meaning of secular language, so that its main function became doctrinal and liturgical. In such a process, Thomas Stephens played a significant part. In his *Christian Purāṇa* he provided Indian converts with an anchor to their cultural roots. He also recognised that much of the Catholic language of faith was inexplicable to Indians and attempted to infuse the existing language with Christian concepts.

Just as the original sources for accounts of individuals may be sparse, so can they be for the wider world they inhabited. There are only two surviving accounts of the doings of the Inquisition in Goa; the official records have largely been destroyed. There is nothing sinister in this. The interest of posterity has rarely (or at least not until comparatively recently) been a factor in the retention of historic records. The two accounts are in some ways complementary. Indeed, one may be, in some ways, dependent on the other, but they give very different pictures. The Inquisition, with its terrible reputation (partly, but not entirely, created by subsequent novels of Gothic horror), is a subject on which it is difficult to be objective. Suffice it to say that, in the wider context, it was part of a world in which, in general, toleration of conflicting views was uncommon. It is the task of the historian to present these issues as objectively as possible and for the reader to make his or her own judgements. Although some issues may appear more obscure, they may have continued meaning for today. The Jesuit approach of 'Accommodation' has clear relevance to modern issues in a multicultural society, for example.

In one respect at least, the people of the sixteenth century demonstrated an interest that is still with us—that of a growing fascination with travelogues. This interest was shared by William Shakespeare who based *The Tempest* on several accounts of the wreck of Admiral Sir George Somers's ship the *Sea Venturer* on the coast of Bermuda in 1609. Several such accounts permeate the pages that follow this preface—those of Pyrard de Laval, Jan Huyghen van Linschotten, Pietro della Valle and Ralph Fitch among them. Collectively, they add to a fascinating picture of the Goa that was the backdrop to the world of Thomas Stephens: a world of contrasting colours, of piety and vice and of tension between cultures. To this may be added the recorded journeys of the Jesuits themselves, notably those of the missions to Akbar the Great, travelling in hope to attempt to convert the greatest ruler in India. The accounts of the Moghul Emperor and his Court give wonderful insights into an empire whose power and grandeur matched anything in Europe.

The letter by Thomas Stephens to his father, with its account of his voyage to India in a Portuguese *nau*, as he became the first Englishman to sail round the Cape of Good Hope, stands among the best of the *journals de voyage*. This brave venturer into a world beyond his previously known horizons sees creatures whose names are unknown to him and describes the hazards of a journey that many of those embarking did not survive. It comes as no surprise that Richard Hakluyt incorporated Stephens's letter in his monumental *The Principal Navigations, Voiages, Traffiques and*

Discoueries of the English Nation. It was an inadvertent part of a process that was changing the world. For centuries, European perspectives had extended little further than the borders of the Roman Empire. The sea was a barrier rather than a gateway. The western extremities of Europe were also its fringes. Now, with the voyages westwards of Columbus and his ilk and eastwards of the Portuguese navigators, the perspective was becoming worldwide. When Thomas Stephens voyaged, Portugal had created the first empire on which the sun never set. Her naval might dominated the Indian Ocean. Trade was the impetus that drove this huge surge. The colonial power and the Society of Jesus had an objective in common (to make Christians), but their approaches were very different. The Portuguese saw this process as one of establishing a base of Indian Lusitanians, a policy that has left its mark on the sub-continent. The Jesuits, through the policy of Accommodation, sought to build an indigenous Indian Catholicism (a policy that has also left its mark).

Acknowledgments

I would like to thank the following for their help and support: the Revd. Dr Paul Haffner, William Dalrymple (for the Foreword), Kathy Hamilton, Mark Allen, James Paterson, Martha Fogg, Suzanne Foster, Helen Redfern, Rebecca Volk and Prof. Wilhelm Vossenkuhl.

Note on proper names

Wherever practical I have sought to render people's names in the form they would have used themselves. There are exceptions to this. The names of Philip II and Francis Xavier are so familiar that to refer to them as 'Felipe' and 'Francisco' might be confusing. The word used occasionally by the Jesuits for their policy of cultural integration is 'Adoptionism' (*adoptio*) and it is used when appropriate in this text. This is not to be confused with the second-century heresy that bears the same name.

1

Wiltshireman and Jesuit

England and India

In England (but not in India), the name of Thomas Stephens is almost forgotten. It should not be, if only because he was the first Englishman to sail round the Cape of Good Hope, leaving a fulsome account of his voyage. It has been claimed that he was the first Englishman who is certainly known to have visited India, but this is not the case. During the siege of the Portuguese island fortress of Diu in 1546, the Moslem attackers blew up the bulwark of St John. A list was made of ninety-eight survivors 'blown up and still alive', which includes 'Lançarote Barbudo, an Englishman much burnt in his legs' and 'Estevan Lopez, Englishman, often wounded and therefore in bad condition'. These are obviously the names by which their fellows knew them—*barbudo* means 'the bearded one'.[1] A much earlier possibility is contained in the Anglo-Saxon Chronicle, which says that in the year 883, King Alfred the Great sent two courtiers, Sighelm and Aethelstan, with alms to Rome 'and also to India and St Thomas and St Bartholomew'.[2]

William of Malmesbury, writing in the twelfth century, expands the account further. Sighelm makes the journey to India and visits the shrine of St Thomas. On his return to England, his grateful King makes him Bishop of Sherborne where the Treasury of the Cathedral held the sundry jewels and spices with which he had returned. This story is probably true, but even if it is false, it demonstrates that, as early as the ninth century, Englishmen were not only aware of an overland route to India, but knew that there were Christians there and even a shrine of St Thomas.[3]

Christianity had come to India at much the same time as it arrived in Europe. A powerful tradition says that it was brought by St Thomas the Apostle in AD 52. The indigenous Christians were known as St Thomas Christians or Syrian Christians, and they were in communion with the Nestorian Patriarch in Mesopotamia. Tradition states that St Thomas died a martyr at Antmodar, a mountain close to Mylapore. There were two caves there to which he would retire for prayer and meditation. One day as he was at prayer in one of the caves, a Brahmin thrust a spear through a cleft in the rock that let in the light and gave him a mortal wound. The saint had just enough strength to get to the other cave, where he died embracing a stone on which was carved a cross.[4]

The legend of St Thomas is soundly based on practicalities. In Apostolic times, there was a flourishing trade between India and the Middle East, both by land and sea. Pliny in his *Natural History* records the existence of a thriving sea route to India and states that in the monsoon winds of July, a ship would take forty days to reach the Malabar coast.

Wiltshireman and Jesuit

Thomas Stephens was born in 1549 at Bushton Manor in the parish of Clyffe Pypard in North Wiltshire, the son of a wealthy merchant (also called Thomas Stephens) and his wife Jane Prator.[5] In 1533, St Swithun's Priory in Winchester had granted a repairing lease of the manor to Richard Stephens, Thomas the elder's father. At the dissolution of the monasteries in 1549, the property was surveyed by the Receiver of the Crown, Sir John Thynne. The house possessed a chapel, named fields and common grazing for 200 sheep. The Steward of the monastery made a yearly visitation to inspect the property. The tenant was obliged to find him meat, drink, a good bed stuffed with wool and provender on two days in the year.

Wiltshireman and Jesuit

Bushton was an isolated hamlet, situated along the back road that ran between Clyffe Pipard and the village of Lyneham, between Devizes and Swindon. At the dissolution of the monasteries, the ownership of the manor was transferred from the Bishop of Winchester to Thomas Seymour, Lord Sudeley, who was executed on the orders of his brother, the Lord Protector, in March 1549. The freehold of the property was sold to one William Richmond in 1553.[6]

Winchester College in 1404

Thomas Stephens had at least one sibling, an elder brother, who entered Winchester College in 1553 at the age of 13, as Richard Stephens of Bushton. In 1564, Thomas followed him to Winchester. The College had been founded in 1382 by William of Wykeham, Bishop of Winchester and Chancellor to King Richard II. It was endowed for seventy poor scholars, a warden, a headmaster and an usher, ten priest-fellows, three chaplains, three lay-clerks, ten commoners and sixteen 'quiristers', who were given free education in return for their singing. Grammar was to be taught according to the methods of Donatus, whose *Ars*

Grammatica predated the foundation of the College by a millennium. This was a standard work in schools and, with the invention of the printing press, it had been produced in its thousands. The first part, or *Ars Minor*, covered the eight fundamental parts of speech: noun, pronoun, verb, adverb, participle, conjunction, preposition and interjection. Part two, or *Ars Major*, listed stylistic faults and graces such as metaphor, synecdoche, allegory and sarcasm.

The boys were roused each morning at five o'clock and would be in full voice in the chapel at six. Following the dissolution of the monasteries, the College was in a chaotic state. Many of the clergy had left and for a number of years, there was no-one to teach the 'quiristers'. In 1560, the College Statutes declared that a master for reading, writing and music must be found for them. Such a pedagogue was duly obtained in the person of Christopher Johnson, who was a physician by profession. A noted Latin poet, he versed his pupils in the comedies of Plautus and introduced a full-scale study of poetry and rhetoric. He had a particular penchant for Latin epigrams. As well as making pithy translations, his students would be urged to devise their own.[7]

After leaving Winchester, according to his contemporary, Richard Hakluyt, Thomas Stephens was 'sometimes of New Colledge in Oxford'. Although there is no record of his graduation, this is almost certainly the case. Hakluyt was writing around 1598 and would almost certainly have known Stephens's father. New College had also been founded by William of Wykeham and Winchester was a feeder school for it. Stephens's subsequent career marks him out as a university man.

When Thomas Stephens signed the Book of Novices on his entry into the Society of Jesus in Rome on 20 October 1575, he stated that he had done his 'humanities' privately, This accords with the notion that he had studied at New College, but that his religious scruples had inhibited him from taking a degree. Robert Persons, a fellow novice, declared that Stephens had been at Oxford, where he had known Edmund Campion, the Latin

Orator. The dates fit very well. In 1568, Persons was appointed a Fellow and tutor of Balliol College. He resigned in 1574 and joined the Jesuits in Rome a few weeks before Stephens. Edmund Campion was one of the most brilliant scholars of his generation. When Mary Tudor had entered London as Queen, he was the scholar of Christ's Hospital chosen to give the Latin salutary. In 1557, at the age of seventeen, he became one of the first Junior Fellows at St John's College, Oxford, recently founded (in 1555) as a Catholic institution (Queen Mary was then on the throne) by a London merchant, Sir Thomas White. A colleague at the college in this first intake was Gregory Martin, a brilliant scholar and linguist, who became his lifelong friend. Campion had been appointed the University's Latin Orator in 1564 and in that position had welcomed Queen Elizabeth to Oxford two years later. It was at this time that Lord Chancellor Burghley described him as 'one of the diamonds of England'. He was a cult figure at the university: his erudition, charisma and charm caused his students to imitate his mannerisms and style of dress. They were proud to call themselves 'Campionists'.

Oxford University was in a state of great spiritual turmoil. Two Acts of Parliament had been passed in 1559 which made it, to put it mildly, difficult to be both a loyal Catholic and a loyal subject of the Queen. The Act of Supremacy abolished papal authority over the Church in England and imposed an oath obliging any person taking public or ecclesiastical office to swear allegiance to the monarch as 'the only supreme governor of this realm'. Most Catholics would have had no difficulty in accepting that as an expression of the Queen's secular authority, but the next phrase defined this authority as being 'in all spiritual or ecclesiastical things or clauses'. Some Catholics sought to equivocate on the oath by declaring that it could not be a sin to swear an invalid oath, but for men of conscience the situation was impossible.

It was possible for Catholics to avoid the oath, simply by being elsewhere when it was administered or avoiding any kind of office that required the oath to be taken. The oath was supported, however, by an Act of Uniformity that instituted a progressive scale of penalties to be imposed on those failing to attend Anglican services or found to be attending Catholic ones. These began with a fine of one shilling, but could end in a charge of high treason. The Act of Uniformity made Mass an illegal form of worship and restored the 1552 Book of Common Prayer. It was deliberately vague about the significance of the Eucharist. The idea that Christian doctrine could be formulated by compromises in Parliament would have been anathema to any devout Catholic who would recognise an apostolic continuity with the faith of the early fathers of the Church. The matter was eloquently expressed by Edmund Campion in his speech from the dock after he was condemned to death. 'In condemning us, you condemn your own ancestors. You condemn all the ancient Bishops and Kings. You condemn all that was once the glory of England.'[8]

A century-long orgy of destruction was taking place, which could be described, in terms of the modern parallel, as a 'cultural revolution'. England had been a Catholic country for a thousand years. Now the 'Elizabethan Settlement' sought to revive the work that had been begun in the reign of Edward VI to abolish all trace of Catholicism from the fabric of English life. The stone altars that expressed the Sacrifice of the Mass were broken up and replaced by communion tables that represented the new theology. Rood screens and reredoses were demolished: altarpieces and vestments burnt, wall-paintings whitewashed, stained glass smashed and chalices melted down. At New College, the magnificent stained glass only survived because the fellows claimed they had no money to replace it. The great processions on the Feast of Corpus Christi, with their Exposition of the Blessed Sacrament, were banned—as were the many local festivals in honour of the patronal saint. An entire culture was lost. Whereas Catholic Europe has a rich heritage of medieval art, in Britain it is all but gone.

Equally devastating was the destruction of the social structure that had brought dignity to all men. Historically, the Church had provided an educational system of surprising universality: the surest path into the upper echelons of society for young men from poor backgrounds was through her hierarchy. The monastic system had provided sustenance to the poor and the destitute in their need. Now the resources of these philanthropic communities were plundered for the rich and powerful. The number of people living in abject poverty was increasing. Thus, it became necessary to enact no less than five Poor Laws between 1563 and 1601, detailing the treatment of the impoverished.

The question has to be asked concerning the motivation of the Elizabethan authorities in inflicting such traumas on the English people. Without a doubt there was a strong and sincere Protestant party within the nation, who must have regarded their ideology as an idea whose time had come. The more extreme variety of this manifestation—the Puritans—at best saw Elizabeth's Settlement as an interim stage towards the Rule of the Saints. In their millennium there would be no bishops and a congregational system of church government. Ironically, it was this group that ultimately represented the greatest threat to the survival of the monarchy and the Catholics, who were amongst its most loyal supporters. The Puritan view was at least theologically based. It is difficult to see the Elizabethan church establishment as anything other than an attempt to suborn the spiritual power of the Papacy towards the monarchy: the emergence of a state system that reserved all powers for itself. To further this end, a vast network of agents and spies was established to provide information on the activities of their fellow countrymen, who, in most cases, were loyal and respectable citizens.

This move towards authoritarianism was not restricted to England. The often not-fully-understood theory of the divine right of kings was ensuring a similar process in France, where authoritarian power was to be seized by the monarchy. It was also true that Elizabeth's political instincts, which led to a ferocious persecution of individuals, led her to back away from confronting powerful groups, so frequently the religious adhesion of the Catholic nobility was tolerated. The subordination of the Church of England to the functions of the state was to prove a frustrating experience for many clergy and led to occasional bursts of revivalism that sought to restore a more spiritual dimension—whether it was Archbishop Laud's 'Beauty of Holiness', the non-Jurors, the Clapham Sect or the Oxford Movement.

When Elizabeth visited Cambridge in 1564, some members of the University, thinking to please her (they didn't) staged a burlesque of the Mass. One of them, posing as a dog, cavorted about the stage with a host in his mouth.[9] The sacrament was called by such derisive nicknames in pamphlets and broadsheets as 'Round Robin', 'Wormes Meat' and 'Jack in the Box'. The net result that the prevalent religion of Englishmen became what might be described as 'anti-Catholicism'. Its long-lasting effects were seen by Flora Thompson in her hamlet in North Oxfordshire three centuries later:

> On Catholicism at large, the Lark Rise people looked with contemptuous intolerance, for they regarded it as a kind of heathenism, and what excuse could there be for that in a Christian country? When, early in life, the end house children asked what Roman Catholics were, they were told they were 'folks as prays to images', and further enquiries elicited the information that they also worshipped the Pope, a bad old man, some said in league with the Devil. Their genuflexions in church and their 'playin' wi' beads' were described as 'monkey tricks'. People who openly said they had no use for religion themselves became quite heated when the Catholics were mentioned.[10]

There was considerable resistance to the new religious legislation at Oxford University and several heads of colleges were dismissed for failing to conform. It was said that fewer than one in twenty Oxford men would take the Oath of Supremacy. Since the university was basically a monastic foundation, this is hardly surprising. Many men quit it at this time, including Gregory Martin, who became tutor to the children of the Catholic Duke of Norfolk (one of them was the future martyr Philip Howard). It is likely that Thomas Stephens, then aged around twenty, was amongst those who decided to leave the university. He would have foregone taking the degree that might have necessitated him taking the oath. It was the hope of the authorities that Edmund Campion would embrace the new faith and at first, this appeared likely. He took the Oath of Supremacy after the Queen and her favourite, the University chancellor Robert Dudley, visited Oxford in 1566, and took deacon's orders in the Church of England soon after. Yet, his conscience was troubled. Gregory Martin wrote to him, warning that his integrity was being undermined by his ambition and urging him to leave the university. This he did when his Proctorship ended in 1569, traveling to Dublin, where he hoped to participate in the founding of a university.

In 1563, it had become a capital offence for a Catholic priest to say Mass, although in practice this sentence was not carried out. The priest, on first conviction, was liable to be imprisoned for six months: at the second, to a year's imprisonment and, on the third, life imprisonment. Anyone whose premises harboured a Mass was fined a hundred marks in the first instance; four hundred in the second; and, for the third, he could have his entire property sequestered and be imprisoned for life. All this changed in February 1570, when Pope Pius V issued the Bull *Regnams in Excelsis*, excommunicating Queen Elizabeth. The Queen was an apostate from the Catholic faith and her government was doing all in its power to suppress it. Yet, the decision was a further disaster for English Catholics. The Bull declared that any subject of Elizabeth who was loyal to her was also excommunicated. This compelled many Catholics to choose between their religious and secular allegiance, transforming them in the eyes of the authorities from undesirable religious dissidents to potential enemies of the state. Catholics who continued to practice their faith faced traumatic dilemmas.

The response of the English government was swift and ferocious. John Felton, a wealthy Catholic layman who was married to Queen Mary Tudor's maid-of-honour, obtained copies of the Bull in Calais and brought them to London. In the early hours of 25 May, he nailed one to the Bishop of London's door, challenging him to declare whether his allegiance was to the Queen or the pope. The answer was obvious. He was arrested the next day, tortured on the rack in the Tower of London and hanged, drawn and quartered in St Paul's Churchyard on 8 August.[11] Felton's offence was not his challenge to the Bishop, but it had been made an act of high treason to bring into the country 'any bull, writing or instrument from the Bishop of Rome'. He was the first Catholic martyr of Elizabeth's reign. Many would follow.

The hand of Elizabeth's vengeful government extended overseas. In the same month that Felton was executed, the 67 year-old Dr John Storey was kidnapped by English agents, who had lured him to Bergen-op-Zoom in the Netherlands. A former Head of College, he had been the first Regius Professor of Civil Law at Oxford University. As a Member of Parliament he had been imprisoned for opposing the Bill of Supremacy, so incurring the wrath of the Queen. He had escaped from the Marshalsea Prison and fled to Antwerp, seeking the protection of the Spanish Crown, where he was given the honorary post of Inspector of Customs. Now he was brought back to the Tower of London and ferociously tortured.[12]

In Dublin, Edmund Campion had thought through his doctrinal position. Although he was still technically a deacon of the Church of England, his clear and unswerving adhesion to the Catholic faith made him a marked man. He only escaped arraignment by the Protestant forces in Dublin because of the protection of friends in high places. Now his resolve was clear. He slipped back to England under an assumed name. In London, he may have attended the show trial of John Storey in Westminster Hall, which must have given him a foretaste of the fate that awaited him. As a former Professor of Law, Storey mounted a skilled defence, claiming that he had taken Spanish citizenship and therefore could not be arraigned for treason. Nevertheless, he was condemned to be hanged, drawn and quartered, a sentence that was carried out three days later. Campion 'was animated by that blessed man's example', wrote the Jesuit, Robert Persons, 'to any danger and peril for the same faith for which the Doctor died.'

St Edmund Campion

Recognising his true vocation, Campion crossed the Channel and sought refuge in the newly-founded English Catholic seminary at Douai in Flanders. Two years later, he set off as a barefoot pilgrim to Rome, where he was received into the Society of Jesus. At some point, Richard Stephens, who had taken Anglican orders, also had a change of heart. Perhaps he was influenced by his younger brother. He had appeared destined for high things in the Established Church and served as secretary to John Jewell, the Bishop of Salisbury and then to Matthew Parker, the Archbishop of Canterbury, but in 1573, he too entered the seminary at Douai where he became a Professor of Theology.[13] Thomas Stephens, on the other hand, had become a proselytising Catholic by 1571. He had become associated with Thomas Pounde of Belmont House at Farlington in Hampshire, the nephew of the first Earl of Southampton. A fellow Wykehamist, born in 1540, some ten years the senior of Thomas Stephens, he possessed, in Stephens' words, 'a tall and handsome figure, a flowing beard and a pleasing countenance'. In an age of eloquence, he was noted for his eloquence. He became a student of Lincoln's Inn on 18 February 1560. He succeeded to Belmont on the death of his father in the same month. Soon after, Queen Elizabeth created him an 'Esquire of the Body'. This gave him an important role at Court. He played the part of Mercury in George Gascoigne's royal masque, enacted before the Queen at Kenilworth in 1566. He exiled himself from the Court after an unfortunate incident when he fell over while dancing an intricate step in front of Queen Elizabeth during the Christmas revels in 1573. 'Rise, Sir Ox', ordered the Queen. '*Sic transit Gloria mundi*', muttered the humiliated Thomas and left the Court for ever. He spent the next two years in hiding in the house of a relation—almost certainly the second Earl of Southampton—atoning 'for his past life in pious reading, in watchings, and prayers'.[14]

Pounde and Stephens concluded that the survival of Catholicism in England depended on the continuing adhesion of the nobility on their estates. This turned out to be a correct analysis. The maintenance of the Faith by the great Catholic families—the Howards, Talbots, Throckmortons and the like—was a major factor in its survival. Pounde and Stephens accordingly commenced a mission to families whose adhesion appeared to be wavering. Pounde travelled under various aliases—Duke, Harrington, Gallop and Wallop. Stephens posed as his servant. There was a dual purpose behind this.

> Both because this better suited my means, as well, and chiefly, by way of a blind to the inquisitive Protestants. Yet indoors I lived as his guest in common, excepting, however, the austerities which his more fervent desire of living to God, led him to exercise upon himself.[15]

The traditions of hospitality in great houses meant that it was possible to pass from place to place, as John Aubrey did a century later.

> ...1670, 1671: at what time providence raised me (unexpectedly) good friends—the right honourable Nicholas, Earl of Thanet, with whom I was deliscent lying hidden at Heathfield in Kent near a year; Sir Christopher Wren; Mr Ogilby; then Edmund Wyld esquire FRS of Glasely Hall, Salop, took me in...[16]

Aubrey's purpose was, of course, survival. Pounde's was reflected in his austere life-style. Stephens recalled that he 'used no bed, but slept on the ground.

> He would spend an hour at midnight in prayer, following this with spiritual reading till daybreak. He would then resume his prayer, following this with spirited reading till daybreak. He would then resume his prayer for two, three, or four hours, and devote the rest of the day to reading the Fathers, again devoting two or three hours to prayer in the evening... He was always striving to reconcile enemies, to convert heretics to the true faith and schismatics to a sincere profession of Catholic belief and practice.[17]

One 'heretic' who was so converted was Thomas Cottam, the Master at a London grammar school. He came from a Protestant family in Lancashire. His brother John had been appointed as the schoolmaster in Stratford-upon-Avon in 1579 and may have taught William Shakespeare. After priestly ordination at Soissons, he became a Jesuit novice at Sant'Andrea a Montecavallo (now Sant'Andrea al Quirinale) in Rome at almost exactly at the time that Thomas Stephens was departing for his mission in Goa.

On his visits to London, Thomas Stephens would have seen his father, who was still living at Bushton in 1571, when he was assessed on the Lay Subsidy Rolls. The assessment of 1576, however, contains a note indicating that he was not actually resident there. He was certainly living in the capital by 1581. After two years of incessant travel, during which they were briefly imprisoned in Ludlow, the two men sought the protection of Pounde's cousin, Henry Wriothesley, the second Earl of Southampton. Stephens described the Earl as 'the most illustrious and leading Catholic in England, and a great supporter of the faithful'. He had been imprisoned in the Tower for allegedly plotting to put Mary, Queen of Scots on the English throne.

At this time, the Wriothesley family was in residence at Cowdray House, the home of Lady Southampton's father, Anthony Browne, the first Viscount Montague. This great house covered an entire acre within a six-hundred-acre park. Had the two men sought the safety of Cowdray, they would have approached the house along the great causeway, lined with a double row of trees that ran the four hundred yards from North Street in the village of Midhurst and crossed the River Rother fifty yards from the great gateway. It was here that Southampton's son and heir, another Henry, was born on 6 October 1573. This is the future third Earl, patron of William Shakespeare to whom the poems *Venus and Adonis* and *The Rape of Lucrece* were dedicated. His father had been released from captivity before his birth. Thomas Stephens would have been aware of this toddler. At some point the Wriothesleys moved back to their mansion at Place House, Titchfield, with their new heir. Pounde and his 'servant' are likely to have accompanied them. Religion aside, Pounde's kinship would have assured him of a seat at the table in the great hall.[18]

In 1573, the year of Southampton's release from the Tower, a ship was driven ashore in Southampton Water. A Jesuit, Fr Henry Alvarez, was amongst those on board. He sought refuge with the Earl of Southampton. While at Titchfield, he told Pounde and Stephens about the Society of Jesus and showed them letters from Jesuits serving in the eastern missions. As a result, Pounde conceived a lasting passion for the Society and a desire to lead a group of young men to Rome to seek to join it. He converted all his available assets into cash. It was arranged that Thomas Stephens should go on ahead and he would join him. Although it was comparatively easy to find a ship that would take him across the Channel from the little harbours along the Solent near Titchfield, he may have accompanied Pounde to London and voyaged from there. Wherever it was from, at some point in 1574, Thomas Stephens took his leave of England forever.[19]

Before he could join his friend, Thomas Pounde was betrayed by a 'heretic' he was hoping to convert and arrested on the orders of an official of Edwin Sandys, the Bishop of London. He was flung into the Marshalsea Prison. While there, he was in the habit of dressing 'most handsomely, thinking thus to inspire Catholics with greater courage and possibly conciliate authority'. He was released six months later following another intervention by his kinsman, the Earl of Southampton. The Calendar of State Papers on 7 December 1585 records that he was bound in the sum of a hundred marks to remain at the house of Ellen, his mother, at her house at 'Kennyton in the counties of Surrey'.[20] He was forbidden to propagate the Faith, but, with reckless courage, continued to do so, addressing letters to the Privy Council and such prominent courtiers as Sir Christopher Hatton, the Queen's godson and one of her chief favourites, who had been a friend of Pounde's since his days at Court, where he too was noted for his skill at dancing. He was strongly Protestant and deeply loyal to Elizabeth—he was to be a strong advocate for the execution of Mary, Queen of Scots—but was consistent in his efforts to help his old friend.

Inevitably, Pounde was rearrested together with a fellow Hampshire Catholic, George Cotton, eighteen months later on the orders of the Bishop of Winchester. He was confined in Winchester Prison for two months before being transferred back to the Marshalsea. He was to spend most of the next thirty years behind bars. During his brief period of liberty, he had become linked to the Catholic Association founded by George Gilbert, a wealthy young layman. The members undertook to live an austere existence propagating the Catholic faith wherever possible.[21] In his prison cell, Thomas Pounde heard of the activities at Douai, perhaps from Thomas Stephens. He wrote of 'a true English Bible which is coming forth'.

Douai

Although there is no record of it, it is probable that, once he had crossed the Channel, Thomas Stephens made his way to Douai. His brother Richard was there and it would have been the obvious place to rendezvous with Pounde and any others he had persuaded to make the journey. It was for Douai that Edmund Campion had also made once he had arrived on the continent. Over the previous decade, the town had developed into a kind of unofficial capital of English Catholicism. Now in the Nord department of France, it was then in the Spanish Netherlands and the prevailing language was a dialect of Flemish.

Philip II had founded a university at Douai in 1560–62. Avowedly Catholic in character, it had five faculties: Theology, Canon Law, Civil Law, Medicine and Arts. The new institution was modelled on the ancient university at Louvain and the majority of its first professors were drawn from there, but its foundation coincided with the presence in the Low Countries of large numbers of Catholic exiles from England. Quite a number of these were distinguished scholars who had fled from Oxford University and now they gained important posts at Douai. The first Chancellor was Dr Richard Smith, a former Fellow of Merton College. There were two former Fellows of New College, with whom Thomas Stephens was probably already acquainted: Dr Owen Lewis was a former Regius Professor of Canon Law who now took on the equivalent post at Douai and the first Professor of Civil Law was Dr Richard White. The presence of the exiles and their role in the University, prompted William Allen, a former

Fellow of Oriel College, to lease a house at Douai on Michaelmas Day 1568 for the purpose of founding a seminary to train English priests. It was the hope of Elizabeth's ministers that, with the ordination of Catholic priests in England at a standstill, English Catholicism would simply die out within a generation. It was to prevent such an occurrence that Allen founded his seminary, which opened in 1569. He was convinced that the Elizabethan Settlement was a mere aberration and that England would soon return to the Catholic fold, as it had done under Queen Mary, and he wanted to ensure that there was a body of learned clergy ready to return. The English College was the first of the seminaries ordered by the Council of Trent. Allen, after taking his doctorate at Douai, became its Regius Professor of Divinity.

Richard Stephens had entered the seminary a year before his brother's probable arrival there. The Prefect of Studies was Richard Bristow, a former Fellow of Oriel College. Campion's friend Gregory Martin was also in residence. The two men were part of a team working on a translation of the New Testament, which was published in 1582 as part of the constant stream of Catholic literature that could not be printed in England. Lack of means prevented the publication of the Old Testament until 1609 when the entire volume was issued under the name of the Douay Bible, two years before the Anglican Authorised Version. The English College at Douai experienced periodic difficulties in its relations with the university and the town. These necessitated the College's removal to Reims in 1578 whence it remained until 1593 when it returned to Douai. Richard Stephens would have gone with it.[22]

'The Chair of the Fisherman'

At some point Thomas Stephens redirected his feet towards Rome, probably arriving in the early months of 1575. On his arrival, he would have climbed the Quirinal Hill, overlooking the city. There stood the house and church of Sant'Andrea a Montecavallo, which had been donated to Francesco Borgia,

Vicar-General of the Society of Jesus, by Andrea Croce, Bishop of Tivoli, in 1567. It became the church of the Society's novitiate. It would be a century before it was replaced by Bernini's Baroque masterpiece. One thing that cannot have escaped Thomas Stephens' notice was the feeling of universality that pervaded the city. As the French essayist, Michel de Montaigne, commented during a visit in 1580:

> The sovereign of Rome embraces all Christendom and makes laws for all. At his court it matters nothing whence men come. At Venice the independence of the Government and commercial interests attracts many foreigners, but they are there in the house of a stranger. Here, everyone is at home.[23]

Perhaps like Edmund Campion in a letter to Gregory Martin, Thomas Stephens was inspired by the sight of Rome to reflect on the *sic transit* theme and to glory in the resilience of his faith.

> Make the most of Rome. Do you see the corpse of the Imperial City? What can be glorious in life, if such wealth and beauty have come to nothing? But who has stood firm from these wretched changes—what survives? The relics of the Saints and the chair of the Fisherman.[24]

It is inconceivable that Thomas Stephens had not sought the encouragement of the Superior General, Everard Mercurian, to travel to Rome to seek admission into the Society. He had probably written from Douai and travelled after receiving a suitably positive reply. As a candidate for the Society, he would have had to apply in person to the Novice Master, the Roman nobleman Fabio de Fabii. It is highly likely that he would also have had conversations with the Superior General. His first ten days in residence would have been as a guest to enable him to test his commitment to his perceived vocation. He would then have been referred to four of the senior fathers. Strict scrutiny of his fitness to join the Jesuits would have been made of his talents, his background and his former life. The fathers must have found him an impressive candidate, although he had the rigours of his noviciate still to come. He possessed sufficient scholarship to meet the rigorous intellectual standards of the Society and had demonstrated his commitment by his escape from England and journey to Rome. Doubtless his mission to the Catholics of England with Thomas Pounde would have been discussed, and the fact that at least one of his converts had sought admission to the Society. He was found to be eligible and was received into the novitiate on 20 October 1575, at the Church of Sant'Andrea a Montecavallo.

Fr Everard Mercurian

Another contemporary English novice, Robert Southwell, was to recall his own feelings on this, the threshold of a religious life.

> You have come like an outlaw from the world, all torn and filthy with sin: you have come into religion like a beggar,

> having no other place to fly to and take refuge from your enemies ... and God in calling you thus from the world has made this clear to you: that while before you were his servant, he is now asking more of you: henceforward, you are the servant of his servants. He made this very clear to you when on the threshold of religious life he gave you this keen desire: to be forgotten and ignored by all and put to work at all the meanest tasks.[25]

'His Sighs, his Prayers and Desires'

On arrival in Rome, Thomas Stephens must have written with his news to his friend. Thomas Pounde must have been elated that his friend had achieved what they hoped to accomplish together, which was now unlikely to happen for him. In his prison cell, he now conceived an extraordinary scheme. In 1575, he wrote to his friend in Rome asking him to request that he could be received into the Jesuits as a novice. Thomas Stephens accordingly wrote to Claudio Acquaviva, the Provincial Superior of Rome, praying him not to refuse the petition because the applicant was 'far away and unknown, seeing that whilst God had called him to the Society, though known to him only by report, he had at the same time given him reasons for choosing it.'[26] This was an unprecedented request. The scrutiny to which an applicant to join the Society was subjected was intense; now here was a candidate asking to forgo the entire procedure. The first petition was rejected on these grounds, but Thomas Stephens made a second on 4 November 1578, hoping that the Father-General would give regard to

> His sighs, his prayers and desires, now for these four years daily poured out before God, and would persuade yourself (which is most true) that Thomas Pounde has been so disposed towards the Society for the past seven years, that he would esteem all labours light to him were he but admitted to it.[27]

'He has not done his philosophy', he wrote of his friend's intellectual achievements, 'but is well-versed in the humanities and most devoted to the study of the Fathers.' This time the petition was successful. It was decided that the case was exceptional and that, under normal circumstances, Pounde would have been admitted. His intense desire to become a Jesuit and his sufferings for the faith would have counted in his favour. On 1 December 1578, the Superior-General Everard Mercurian wrote to him in Marshalsea Prison. The letter was given to Campion and Persons as they embarked on their mission to England.

> Thomas Stephens, our very dear brother in Christ, relates many things to us of your constant piety and faith, which are most grateful to us, but especially that you have now for many years aspired with great desire to our Society. Therefore, although our Institute rules that we admit no one amongst our members unless he hath been well proved by many trials, yet nevertheless, moved by the very clear testimony, both of Stephens and others, and accepting as a long probation your labours and sufferings of so many years, we are induced to yield to your pious desires.

> Wherefore, by virtue of that authority which God our Lord hath deigned to bestow upon us, though unworthy, we now already embrace you as a son and brother, we receive and admit you to our Society, and as a true member engrafted into the whole body, and we do also at the same time make you a sharer and participant in all our works, our labours, and our merits. But we hope the mercy and infinite goodness of God will at some future time be so propitious to you, that as we greatly desire, delivered from these troubles, we may be permitted to enjoy your company and presence : but should the providence of God for any cause deprive us of this opportunity, we nevertheless wish that this thought should console you, that, after a few days of this brief life, we shall be so united together in that eternal immortality (which we should all look forward to,

and keep before our eyes), that nothing may be able then to separate us.

As for the rest, although I know that your virtue, which I hear is truly worthy of a Christian man, requires no confirmation, yet as a most dear son, I will briefly admonish you in the words of the Apostle, that you may be mindful to be a spectacle to God, to Angels, and to men; to God indeed as the bestower of eternal rewards for the smallest labours; to Angels as strengthened by their presence; to men also that you may greatly inflame them, as hitherto you have done by your example, to true piety, and to encourage such as need it to undergo dangers with alacrity for Christ. Which thing, however, we wish may be so prudently and cautiously conducted by you, that you neither run into open danger without cause and fruit: a course which is held to be, not courage, but rashness nor that you destroy your health and strength by immoderate abstinence and fastings, to which we hear you are abundantly addicted; but rather, as the Prophet saith, that you take care to preserve your strength for God—fortitudinem suam ad Deum custodire.

May our Lord, however, to Whom it always belongs to protect and defend innocence and integrity, especially when brought into any danger in His own cause, be so propitious to you, that He may either totally drive away from you all these troubles, or, should He deem it to be more expedient for you otherwise, may He increase in you fortitude, constancy, and salutary patience to endure them. At least we never cease, both ourselves, as also all of ours, to pray and beseech our Lord in this behalf.

Mercurian was aware of how many of the English faithful deeply desired martyrdom as a sure path to Heaven. He urged discretion and caution on his new lay member. He clearly felt a desire to preserve his flock from the consequences of their impetuosity.

This one thing, however, I greatly desire of you, that you publish to no-one this your determination regarding our society, neither by habit or dress, nor by discourse, but that you keep your secret to yourself until better times beam forth, when this your desire, by the grace of God, may be openly followed out.[28]

It says much for Thomas Stephens and the respect in which he was already held within the brotherhood that he was able to persuade the General to accept Pounde's imprisonment in lieu of his entry into the noviciate. It also says much for Everard Mercurian that he appreciated the rigours of the English Province and sought to divert his flock there from acts of rashness.

The Spiritual Exercises

Pope Pius V had died on 1 May 1572 and Ugo Buoncompagni, the Secretary of Papal Briefs, had been elected in his stead twelve days later as Pope Gregory XIII. The new Pontiff did not possess a stainless past. A late vocation, he was the father of an illegitimate son, whom he fully acknowledged, born of an unmarried woman while he lectured in jurisprudence at the University of Bologna. He had a reputation for worldliness and a love of display but took his new responsibilities with great seriousness. After his election he lived an austere life, determined to put into practice the decrees of the Council of Trent and cracking down severely on ecclesiastical abuses.

Although Gregory XIII campaigned steadfastly to depose Queen Elizabeth, it may have been the influence of the growing number of English Catholics in Rome that caused him to temper the tone of *Regnams in Excelsis*. Realising the pressure that the Bull put on English Catholics, the Pope issued a clarification in 1580 explaining that as long as the Queen remained the *de facto* ruler, it was lawful for Catholics to obey her in civil matters and to co-operate with her in all just things. It was this that enabled

Catholic martyrs like Edmund Campion to declare their loyalty to her on the scaffold.

This atmosphere of struggle against corruption, venality and spiritual lassitude accorded well with the feelings of the English novitiates arriving in Rome. The Society of Jesus was an institution that was in full sympathy with the pontifical outlook. It had been founded on 15 August 1534 at Montmartre by a Basque nobleman and former soldier, Inigo (Ignatius) Lopez de Loyola. The original intention was to found a mission in Jerusalem, but this was forestalled by the outbreak of war between the Ottoman Empire and the Venetian Republic. Instead, it was decided to add a fourth vow to the traditional commitment to chastity, poverty and obedience—to go without questioning wherever the Pope might send them. There were six other founder-members of the Society, all fellow students at the University of Paris. One of them was a fellow Basque, Francisco (Francis) de Jasso y Azpilcienta, who would take his name from his birthplace, the Castle of Xavier near Pamplona. The constitution of the Society was confirmed in 1540 by Pope Paul III. It was placed under a hierarchy at the top of which was a Superior General whose control was absolute.

From the earliest days of the Society, the *Spiritual Exercises* devised by Ignatius Loyola formed an essential part of its being. Over a four week period participants engage in silent and directed meditations on the life of Christ, meeting regularly with a Spiritual Director who helps them interpret whatever call or message God appears to have offered them. The penitent is required 'to spurn everything that the world loves and embraces: to allow and long for, with the whole heart, whatever Christ Our Lord loved and embraced...

> ... so much so, that if it could be without any offence to the Divine Majesty and without any sin on the part of another, we should desire to suffer insults and calumnies and violence, to be held for fools and posted as such (but without ourselves giving any occasion for it), because of this great longing we have to be in some sort of way con-

> formed and assimilated to Jesus Christ Our Lord and
> Creator, and to put on his garments and livery.²⁹

This clear call to martyrdom was not one for which Thomas Stephens was destined, but it was one of which he would have been conscious. It was to be the fate of many of his present and future colleagues. The fourth week of the Spiritual Exercises, *Contemplation to Attain Love*, has a feel to it that almost presages the ecological obsessions of the late twentieth century.

> I will consider how God dwells in creatures; in the elements, giving them existence; in the planets, giving them life; in the animals, giving them sensation; in human beings, giving them intelligence; and finally, how in this way he dwells also in myself, giving me existence, life, sensation and intelligence.

The Society was undergoing a number of spiritual traumas at the time that Thomas Stephens arrived in Rome. The fourth Superior General, Everard Mercurian, who came from Marcourt in Luxembourg, was struggling to contain what he perceived as divisive forces within. These were largely centred around Balthasar Alvarez, SJ, who was the Spiritual Director of the Spanish mystic, Teresa of Avila. Mercurian was highly suspicious of what he saw as a potentially disruptive movement within the Society and was using all his powers to restrain Alvarez. This is one of those controversies that appeared deeply serious at the time, but does not strike many modern readers as significant. It concerned the nature and methods of spiritual contemplation, but, at least in Mercurian's view, it was an issue that could affect the entire cohesion of the Society. He believed that the rule of obedience imposed an obligatory conformity to its rules and to the use of the Spiritual Exercises. The problem centred around the fact that Alvarez had formulated a meditative system built around a discipline of silent contemplation rather than the didactic approach of the Spiritual Exercises. He also had a curious way of attempting to instil humility into novices by keeping them waiting for appointments for several hours. In contrast to the strong spiritual relationship that Alvarez had established with Sister Teresa, the constitution of the Society stated that Jesuits should not generally undertake the direction of souls, especially as regular confessors or as spiritual directors of female religious. This was to enable a Jesuit to fulfil his promise to go wherever and whenever the Society bade him. He saw Alvarez, a worthy, even a saintly man, as a threat to the discipline under which Thomas Stephens was about to place himself.[30]

As a novice Jesuit, Thomas Stephens was received into the House of First Probation. Here his motivation and determination to remain within the Society of Jesus were to be proven. He would have been forbidden all outside contact. His qualities would have been relentlessly scrutinised, especially that of obedience. Once he had reassured his superiors on these points, he would have passed to the House of Second Probation. After a period of confession and meditation—Father Mercurian had made it a rule that all novices should make the Spiritual Exercises in their entirety—Stephens embarked on a course of service in hospitals, ministering to the poor and at the bedsides of the sick. He was then required to live the life of a mendicant, begging for bread from door to door, living on the coarsest food and sleeping on the hardest bed. He worked in the latrines, doing any humiliating task required of him. Robert Southwell cast a wry eye at this assuagement of vanity.

> God knows your talents are made for mighty deeds. He knows your gifts of nature and of grace. He has examined them thoroughly and considered them from every angle and he has come to the conclusion that the kitchen is the place that suits you best—at least for the moment, though, of course, there may be needs in the future for which he will provide a different set of circumstances.[31]

Thomas Stephens was part of a remarkable intake of Englishmen into the Society, which included three future heads of the English

Mission in Robert Persons, William Weston and Henry Garnet, and, later, the poet Robert Southwell and William Shakespeare's former schoolmaster, Simon Hunt. At some part, when the assessment had been completed, each novice was assigned to a particular Province of the Society. Allocating Thomas Stephens to the forthcoming English Mission must have been considered, but it was decided that his talents would be best employed elsewhere. He was apportioned to become, as Fr Persons put it, 'a painfull and fruitfull labourer in ye east Indies'. The decision must have been partly based on his long desire to serve there, but this would not have been the only factor. His great gift for languages would have been noted. For the Jesuits, evangelisation in native languages and cultures was an essential part of their mission.

The Province of India is the third-oldest in the Society of Jesus. Francis Xavier was appointed as its first Provincial in 1549. On his death in 1552, he had sixty-four Jesuits under his direction, including nineteen priests.[32] These numbers increased in the next quarter century, but there could never be enough to cover an area that extended over all the lands east of the Cape of Good Hope. This urgent need for priests would have made Thomas Stephens' desire to serve there seem a godsend.

Once Thomas Stephens' course of service had ended, he was ordained deacon and embarked upon a new role, giving instruction and pastoral help to the faithful and preaching. After two years, he was required to present himself before the Superior furnished with certificates from those who had overseen the six rigorous programmes to which he had been subjected. This hurdle passed, he could now commence the rigorous intellectual training that characterised the Jesuits. At this point he made the threefold vow of poverty, chastity and obedience. He would be required to renew this every six months. He now became one of the approved scholars (*scholastici approbati*) and entered upon a course of study more rigorous than that in any contemporary university. He entered the Roman College, which had been founded by Ignatius Loyola and Francesco Borgia in 1551 as a seminary for missionary priests. In the same year Ignatius had written his vision of the creation of an education system that would fit the Jesuit for a host of potential disciplines.

> From among those who are now merely students, in time some will depart to play diverse roles. One to preach and carry on the care of souls, another to the government of the land and the administration of justice, and others to other callings.

The Society had made its greatest impact in the field of education. By 1579, the Jesuits administered 144 colleges. At the apex of these foundations stood the *Collegio Romano* with over a thousand students. To house this soaring influx, Pope Gregory XIII opened a grand new building in 1584, which was henceforth known as the Gregorian University.

Christopher Clavius

Thomas Stephens's education at Winchester and Oxford may have given him some advantage in the study of the classics but in his first year he would have been involved in intense theological and philosophical studies. In 1578, Thomas Stephens was in his second year of philosophy at the *Collegio Romanum*, studying logic, ethics and metaphysics and studied physics and mathematics under the Bavarian Jesuit, Christopher Clavius. Clavius was a mentor of the great astronomer Galileo Galileo, who was familiar with his textbooks and visited him in Rome in 1577. He was the inventor of the decimal point and had been almost single-handedly responsible for the adoption of a rigid mathematical curriculum at a time when the subject was belittled by many philosophers and theologians. The *ratio studiorum* of the *Collegio Romanum* is clear about this: the mathematics tutor should first teach the first six books of Euclid, followed by the study of *De Sphaera*, the basic account of spherical geometry composed in the thirteenth century by Johannes de Sacrobosco.

The name is believed to be a Latinised version of that of an English mathematician and astronomer, John of Holywood.

Clavius determined that 'to the end that mathematical studies be held in higher esteem', his scholars should gather once a month to hear him enunciate on the propositions of Euclid. Thomas Stephens would have been part of this group. He could have had no better tutor for the cosmology and astronomy that formed a further part of the course. Under Clavius, he would have studied the Alfonsine Tables that listed the positions and movements of the planets.[33] In the same year that Thomas Stephens became his student, Clavius was appointed by Pope Gregory XIII to his Commission to revise the calendar, seeking to arrest the process whereby the Church's festivals were drifting out of season due to flaws in the Julian calendar.

Fr Christopher Clavius

The English College

The letters of Fr Robert Persons reveal that the English seminarians in Rome constituted something of a collective, of which Thomas Stephens would have been a part. In recognition of this, in 1575, when the number of students at the English College in Doaui had reached 120, Pope Gregory XIII summoned William Allen to open a similar institution in Rome. He converted the ancient and moribund English Hospice into a seminary. The first students arrived from Douai in 1577 and included the twenty-seven-year-old Ralph Sherwin, an Old Etonian who had been a Fellow of Exeter College, Oxford. A contemporary, Anthony à Wood, described him as an acute philosopher.

Fr Robert Persons

From the first, the seminary was beset by difficulties.[34] A Welshman, Dr Morys Clynnog, was appointed its perpetual warden in 1578. The English seminarians accused him of favouring his compatriots' interests over theirs. It is probable that linguistic and cultural divisions also contributed. Clynnog regarded the heresy and apostasy that permeated the English nation as long predating the Protestant Reformation; indeed, it stretched back to the Anglo-Saxon and subsequent Norman French invasions. Wales was the one repository of true Catholicism on the island. In 1575, he had submitted to the Pope a plea for the invasion of his homeland, a region he described in glowing terms.

> This region is nearly one third of the Kingdom of England where scarcely a single man in a thousand will be found to be a heretic. The British people indeed is the original stock of that island, which to this day retains the ancient British language (which the English do not understand since they are of Saxon descent) and the ancient, the ancestral Catholic faith.

The main cause of the friction was a profound difference of opinion concerning the purpose of the seminary. Clynnog saw the College as a home for exiles: a place where the Catholic traditions of England and Wales could be maintained until the nation returned to the fold. To this end, the students were encouraged to learn Italian so that they could take up positions in Italy until the happy day of the restoration of the hierarchy in England. In this policy, Clynnog appears to have enjoyed 'the resolution and purpose of his contrymen in the colledge.'[35] By contrast, the majority, if not all, of the English students felt passionately that the Catholic cause in England would be placed in jeopardy if the College 'should continue in that sorte under Mr Morrice his government, whom they avouched to have no care for making men for England, nor sending them thither...'

Allen had ensured that there was a strong Jesuit element in the College from the first and this became the focus for a profoundly different view. This faction shared the missionary ideals of their Society—that their nation was becoming as pagan as the lands beyond the seas and that only the blood of sacrifice could restore it. Ralph Sherwin, who had joined the Jesuit noviciate, was a leader of this party. 'While here in Rome', it was recalled, 'the news of the inflictions and tortures which his Catholic fellow-countrymen were made to suffer, far from daunting, rather fired him with more intense longing... to fly to the help of his wretched country.'[36] The two groups circulated pamphlets and petitions and even sought Pope Gregory's support for their cause. Finally, Clynnog was replaced, on a temporary basis, by Robert Persons on 19 March 1579. Although Thomas Stephens would doubtless have supported Sherwin's party, by this time his vocation was taking him on a very long journey.

From the first, the English College was an institution that gave any Englishman traveling to Rome a warm welcome but this seeming strength was also a weakness. The place was permeated with spies, sent by Elizabeth's government to report on the seminarians. One such was eighteen-year-old Anthony Munday, a London draper, poet and playwright, who arrived at the seminary posing as the son of a prominent English Catholic. He was treated with great kindness by Dr Clynnog and sent regular reports to his masters in London. Clearly no detail was considered too trivial to recount. From his account, it would appear that its residents included Jesuits. Even if these did not include Thomas Stephens, the solidarity felt by his countrymen in Rome would have certainly made him a part of its fellowship. The reports occasionally possess inadvertent charm:

> As for their fare, trust me, it is very fine and delicate, for euery man has his owne Trentcher, his Manchet, knife, spoone and forkc layde by it, and then a fayre white napkin couering it, with his glasse and pot of wine set dainti by him. And the first messe, or antepast (as they call it) that is brought to the Table, is Englishe, some fine meat to vrge them to haue an appetite: as sometime the Spanish An-

chouies; and sometime stued Prunes and Raysons of the Sun together, hauing such fine tarte sirope made to them, as I promise you a weake stomacke would very wel digest them. The second, is a certaine messe of potage of that Countrey manner, no meat sod in them, but are made of diuers thinges, whose proper names I doo not remember: but me thought they were both goode and wholesome. The third is boylde meat, as Kid, Mutton, Chickin, and such like: euerie man a pretie modicum of eche thing. The fourth is rested [roasted] meat, of the daintiest prouision that they can get, and sometime stewde and bakte meat, according as pleaseth Maister Cooke to order it. The first and last is some time Cheese, sometime preserued conceytes, some time Figges, Almonds and Raysons, a Limon and Sugar, a Pomegranate, or some such sweet geere, for they know that Englishmen loueth sweete meates.[37]

Such pleasant diversions were for many, a lull before the storms to come. Ten of the seventy students attending the English College would die martyrs' deaths and twenty more would be broken by imprisonment. Their potential fate was well known in Rome. Philip Neri, a friend of Ignatius Loyola and founder of the Congregation of the Oratory, lived at S. Girolamo della Carità opposite the College. Each morning he greeted the students with the words: *Salvete flores martyrum*—'Hail flowers of the martyrs.'[38] The severity of the system of penitence was a preparation for the fate that many of the Collegians were destined to suffer. Public humiliations described by Munday included kneeling in the hall during dinner while saying the rosary.

> Or to stand vpright and haue a dish of potage a dishe of potage before him on the grounde, and so to bring vp euerie spoonful to his mouth: Or to loose, either one or two or three of his dishes appointed for his dinner: Or to stand there all dinner time, & eate no meate.

More severe were the private penances 'appointed by the ghostly Father at Confession, which are hilfilled [fulfilled] without publique knowledge of the cause.'³⁹ Seven or eight of the penitents were confined to their chambers. One would be appointed to perform an act of public self-flagellation over dinner.

> When they are all set at the Tables, he commeth in, cloathed in a Canuas vesture downe to the grounde, a hood of the same on his head, with two holes where through he hath sight, and a good bigge round place bare, against the middest of his backe: in this order he goeth vp and downe the Hall, whipping him selfe at that bare place, in somuch that the blood doth trickle on the ground after him.

Other penitents flagellated themselves in their chambers, 'either before a Crucifix or the image of our Ladie, turning their backes when they bleede towarde the Image, that it may see them'. This Munday declined to do. One of the Jesuits took him into his chamber.

> Saying, I should see (because I was so fearful) what he would inflict vpon his own body. So when he was vnapparelled, he tooke a whip, the Cords whereof was wier, & before the Picture of our Lady, he whipped himself very greeuouslly.

The Jesuit said a flagellator's version of the *Ave Maria—Sancta Maria mater Dei, accipe Flagiiium meum. Etorapro me, nunc et in hora mortis.* The objective of the self-scourging was to share some part of the suffering of Christ. This was the view taken by those who would suffer in England of their martyrdom. 'Why should you feare to put your body to any torment, to recompense him who hath done so much for you?' asked the Jesuit. Munday translated his further prayer into English.

> O egregious Jesus be thou entreated by that glorious virgin thy mother, who I am sure maketh intercession to thee for me. The remembraunce of thy whipping, bloody sweat, Crosse, death and passion, maketh me do this, in so much as thou hast suffered ten times more for me.

Other penances included fasting, wearing a hair shirt, 'trudging to the seuen Churches, lying vpon ghostly bare boardes, going into the darke vautes vnder the ground, or traueling on Pilgrimage'.

Sir Thomas Stukeley

The best-known Englishman in Rome in Thomas Stephens's time there was Sir Thomas Stukeley. It is highly probable that they encountered each other. The knight was well known to the little English community there, if only because of his habit of crawling penitently through the streets, bare-legged and barefoot. When word of this got back to Ireland, the Protestant Lord Deputy Sir William Fitzgerald was so incensed that he wrote a letter, warning the Pope that this English adventurer had performed the same self-publicising routine in Waterford in 1570 while he waited for winds to carry his ship to England. Then, instead of fulfilling his declared intention, he had sailed to Vimeiro in Portugal and offered his services to the King of Spain, who had rewarded him lavishly and agreed to support his project of an invasion of Ireland. Why Stukeley did this is uncertain: he may have decided that his credit with Queen Elizabeth was low and he would fare better elsewhere. In 1563, he had persuaded the Queen to support an expedition to establish an English colony in Florida. She had financed and equipped a fleet of six ships, but instead of sailing for the Americas, he had established himself as a privateer off the coast of Munster, preying on French, Portuguese and Spanish ships. Understandably irate, the Queen sent an expedition, which arrested him at Cork, but through the intervention of Hugh O'Neil, the powerful Earl of Tyrone, he was pardoned.

Tiring of waiting for Philip II to act, Stukeley proceeded to Rome the following year, where Don John of Austria appointed him to command three galleys in his fleet that decisively defeated the Turks at the Battle of Lepanto. His military credit high, Stukeley returned to the Spanish Court, where Philip II again agreed to support an invasion of Ireland. Again tiring of delays, he went back to Rome in 1575, probably arriving there at much the same time as Thomas Stephens. His arrival must have caused a sensation. This hero of Lepanto was a Devonian from the same wild school of gentlemen adventurers as Humphrey Gilbert, Francis Drake and Walter Raleigh, yet here he was offering his sword in the papal cause. The intrigue grew with the arrival of James Fitzmaurice Fitzgerald, brother of the Earl of Desmond, who was also seeking to raise a force for an invasion of Ireland that would coincide with an uprising by the Earls of Desmond, Kildare and Tyrone. He made common cause with Stukeley, so Rome must have resounded with rumours of plots and counter-plots.

Gregory XIII agreed to support the expedition and Stukeley raised and equipped a force of 2,000 men for his service. As was the custom with mercenary armies, these were mainly highwaymen and robbers who had signed up on the promise of an amnesty. The expedition sailed in rotting ships from Civitavecchia in March 1578. In April, it arrived in Cadiz, but the ships were declared to be too perilous to proceed. Philip II was again sympathetic but indecisive. Thomas Stukeley dubbed himself the Marquis of Leinster (a title he claimed to have received from the Pope) and whiled away the time by issuing a magnificent passport to any Irishman he encountered. He decided to go to Lisbon to obtain shipping from the King of Portugal, but Sebastian I was preparing an expedition against the Sultan of Morocco and invited him to take a command in his army and enlist in his motley force instead. Stukeley immediately dropped his plan to invade Ireland, declaring that he knew the country as well as any and that there were only 'hunger and lice' to be got there. Morocco turned out to be an even worse prospect. On landing, Stukeley advised the King against marching immediately against the vast army of Moors and derided both the quality of his forces and his tactics. He was killed when a cannon ball scythed off both his legs at the Battle of Alcácer Quibir on 4 August 1578. In death, Thomas Stukeley became something of an English folk hero. At least two plays about his exploits were performed on the London stage and ballads were composed in his honour.[40]

The King died in a melee on the same day; his death would lead ultimately to the end of his royal line and the union of the crowns of Spain and Portugal, which would have an effect on the future of Thomas Stephens's intended destination of Goa.[41]

Notes

1. This episode was first discovered by Fr G. Schurhammer, *Oriental* (Lisbon: Centro de Estudos Históricos Ultramarinos, 1963), pp.307–8.
2. B. Thorpe (ed.), *The Anglo-Saxon Chronicles* (London: Rolls Series, 1861).
3. J. A. Coles, *William of Malnesbury's Chronicles of the Kings of England* (London: George Bell and Sons. 1904), p. 118.
4. S. Neil, *A History of Christianity in India*, Vol 1 (Cambridge: Cambridge University Press, 1984), p. 29.
5. C. J. Pereira, *An English Jesuit in Goa*, unpublished paper, on http://hku-hk.academia.edu/CliffordPereira [accessed 21 May 2019]
6. *A History of the County of Wiltshire: Volume 8, Warminster, Westbury and Whorwellsdown Hundreds* (London, Oxford University Press, 1965), pp. 23–43.
7. A. F. Leach, *A History of Winchester College* (London: Gerald Duckworth, 1899), pp.258–273.
8. R. Simpson, *Edmund Campion: a Biography* (London: Williams and Norgate, 1867).
9. J. A. Froude, *History of England from the Fall of Wolsey to the Death of Elizabeth*, Vol 2 (New York: Screbner, Armstrong and Co., 1873), p.92.
10. F. Thompson, *Lark Rise to Candleford*, (London: Oxford University Press, 1947), p. 210.
11. Dom B. Camm, *Lives of the English Martyrs*, Vol 1 (London: Longmans, Green and Company, 1914),p.2.
12. 'Blessed John Story', *The Catholic Encyclopaedia*, Vol 8 (New York: Robert Appleton Company, 1910).
13. T. M. McCoog, SJ, 'The English Jesuit Mission and the French Match' in *The Catholic Historical Review*, Vol 87/2, (2001), pp.186–213.

14. 'Poiunde, Thomas', *Oxford Dictionary of National Biography* (online edition), 2019.
15. H. Foley, *Jesuits in conflict, or, historic facts, illustrative of the labours and sufferings of the English mission and province of the Society of Jesus, in the times of Queen Elizabeth and her successors* (London: Burns and Oates, 1873), p.29.
16. J. Aubrey, *Brief Lives*, Vol 1, ed. by A. Clark (Oxford: Clarendon Press, 1898).
17. Stonyhurst MSS, Collectio Cardwelli (MQ.i) p. 16 et seq., Stonyhurst Collections, Stonyhurst College, Lancashire, England.
18. G. R. V. Akrigg, *Shakespeare and the Earl of Southampton* (Cambridge, MA: Harvard University Press, 1968).
19. Letter of Thomas Stephens, Stoneyhurst MSS, Collectio Cardwelli (f.15), Stonyhurst Collections, Stonyhurst College, Lancashire, England.
20. *Calendar of State Papers Domestic: Elizabeth, 1581–90*, ed. Robert Lemon (London, 1865), accessed via *British History Online* http://www.british-history.ac.uk/cal-state-papers/domestic/edw-eliz/1581–90 [accessed 21 May 2019].
21. 'Gilbert, George', Oxford Dictionary of National Biography (online edition), 2019.
22. 'Douai', *The Catholic Encyclopaedia* (New York: Robert Appleton Company, 1913).
23. L. von Pastor, *History of the Popes*, Vol 20 (London: George Routledge & Sons, 1930), p. 559.
24. R. Marie, 'The Diamond of England: the Mission and Martyrdom of Edmond Campion', published in *The Fellowship of the King: A Catholic Literary Magazine* (https://thefellowshipoftheking.net/2015/12/01/the-diamond-of-england-the-mission-and-martyrdom-of-st-edmund-campion/) [accessed 21 May 2019].
25. C. Devlin, *The Life of Robert Southwell* (London: Sidgwick and Jackson, 1967), p. 42.
26. H. Foley SJ, *Jesuits in Conflict* (London: Burns and Oates, 1873), pp. 37–38.
27. *Ibid.*, p. 49.
28. *Ibid.*, pp. 50–54.
29. Devlin, *The Life of Robert Southwell*, p.85.
30. A full account of the dispute is given in S. M. Lewis, SJ, 'Balthazar Alvarez and the Prayer of Silence' in *Spirituality Today* vol 41/ 2 (1989), pp. 112–132.

31. *Ibid.*, p.41.
32. J. F. Raj, SJ, *Jesuit Mission in India*, www.goethals.in/felixrayarticles/Jesuitcontibution.htm [accessed 22 May 2019]
33. 'Collegio Romano', on www.galileo.rice.edu/gal/romano.html [accessed 21 May 2019]
34. These are described by Robert Persons in his manuscript *A Storte of Domesticall Difficulties in the English Catholike Cause* (1600).
35. Quoted by J. M Cleary, 'Dr. Morys Clynnog's Invasion Projects of 1575–7', *Recusant History* vol. 8/6 (1966), pp. 300–322.
36. www.angelusonline.org [accessed June 25th 2020]
37. Anthony Munday, *The English Romayne Life (1582)* (London: Bodley Head, 1925), pp. 17–29.
38. 'Our History: A Synopsis', on https://www.vecrome.org/history1.html [accessed 21 May 2019]
39. Munday, *The English Romayne Life*, pp. 17–29.
40. R. Simpson, *The School of Shakspere:* (London: Chatto and Windus, 1878).
41. J. C. Levinson, *The Famous History of Captain Thomas Stukeley, 1605* (Manchester: Malone Society Reprints, 1975).

2

The Voyage of the São Lourenço

Thomas Pounde in the Marshalsea

Security in the Marshalsea Prison was relatively lax. As far away as Rome, a seminarian at the English College commented on this, somewhat injudiciously, to the government spy Anthony Munday.

> You might have gone to the Marshalsea', he told him, 'and enquired for Maister Powde ... for sometime walk en, under ye habites of Gentlemen, Serving-men, going into or what apparel they imagine most convenient, preestes do daily resorte unto him, where they confesse him and give him such hallowed things as are sent him from Papistche Rome, as Agnus Dej, Grana benedicta and other things.

Clearly, the Elizabethan spy system was not as efficient as might be supposed.

On his arrival in London in June 1580 as the leader of the first Jesuit mission, Robert Persons, disguised as a soldier, visited Pounde in his cell and discovered how to make contact with George Gilbert. Presumably he delivered the letter from the Superior General. Another labourer in the cause, Edward Brooksby, was visiting Pounde when Persons called. He guided Persons to the safehouse in Chancery Lane that George Gilbert had taken. He had established a network of lay people who would assist priests on their arrival in England. Previously, they had been on their own and so much more vulnerable to capture.[1] Through such contacts, a secret press was established at East Ham. Pounde was able, either through bribery or laxity, to come and go from his prison virtually as he pleased. In June 1580, he met Edmund Campion, who had arrived in London disguised as 'Mr. Edmunds', a jeweller. The Jesuit mission was highly successful, confirming many Londoners in their Catholic faith. Nevertheless, the authorities were closing in and it was decided that it was judicious for Persons and Campion to leave London to continue their work in the provinces. On the first stage of their journey, they stayed in Hoxton, then a village just outside London. Pounde was able to secure a horse and ride out to join them. He suggested to Persons and Campion, that in the event of their arrest, imprisonment and execution, it would be valuable to have their spiritual testaments, which could be circulated to counterbalance any false claims made by the authorities. The Fathers agreed and sat down to write their credos.

Returning to the Marshalsea, Pounde copied and circulated Campion's document to his fellow prisoners. Visitors to the prison took away copies to circulate around the country. Thus the credo, which had been intended as a vindication of the mission, became its testament. This ensured that the profile of the Jesuits and their cause was raised considerably, but it also increased the determination of the authorities to apprehend them. Campion's statement became known to his detractors as his *Brag*. Like many derogatory names, it stuck and became an ornament.

Inspired by the success of his mentor's credo, Thomas Pounde wrote his own *Sixe Reasons*,

> to show that it is no orderly way in controversies of faith to appeal to be tried only by Scripture (as the absurd opinion of all the Sectaries is), but to the sentence and definition of the Catholic Church by whom as by the Spouse of Christ, always inspired with the Holy Ghost, the Holy Scripture is to be judged.

This too was circulated widely. Copies came into the hands of Henry Tripp, the Anglican Chaplain to the Marshalsea and the Bishop of Winchester, in whose diocese the prison was situated. From as far away as Wiltshire, the High Sheriff sent the document to London, with the comment that it constituted 'Certain Papistical reasons set down for the withdrawing of men to come to the church.'[2]

A response to Pounde's pamphlet came from Robert Crowley, a stationer and printer who had become a clergyman and held the living of St Lawrence Jewry. He was a curious choice as the defender of Anglican orthodoxy. An archetypal Puritan, he had been imprisoned in 1566 for refusing to allow his choir to wear surplices, which he described as the 'conjuring garments of popery'. A tract he wrote on the topic has been described as the 'first distinct utterance of Nonconformity'. The title was decidedly long-winded and reveals that he failed to grasp the point of the argument.

> An aunswer to six reasons, that Thomas Pownde, Gentlemen and prisoner in the Marshalsey, at the commaundment of her Maiesties Commissioners, for causes Ecclesiasticall: required to be aunswered. Because these reasons doo moue him to think that controversies and doubts in religion, may not be iudged by the Scriptures, but that the scriptures must be iudged by the catholique Church ...[3]

Given the fact that others whom the Commissioners investigated ended up being hung, drawn and quartered, it is curious that Pounde was able to get away with so much. It can only be concluded that he continued to have powerful friends in high places: Christopher Hatton may well have been one of them. Nevertheless, the authorities felt that action must be taken to curb this unofficial Jesuit seminary that was emerging in the Marshalsea.

On 18 September 1580, 'for his own good and peace of mind', Pounde was transferred to the 'lonely' castle at Bishop's Stortford on the orders of John Aylmer, Bishop of London. While there, he wrote to Christopher Hatton, describing the terrible conditions in the prison.

> It is nothing but a large varst room, cold water, bare walls, noe windows, but loopholes too highe to loke out at, nor bedstead nor place very fit for any; the homeliest things a high pair of stockes, such a pair of virginalls all athwart my cold harbour and nothing else but chains enough, which yet I am not worthy of.[4]

Pounde's letter to his powerful friend may have had some effect. Within six months he was returned to the Marshalsea. Apart from one brief spell of freedom, he would remain incarcerated for more than two decades.

'Towards Japponia'

After his intense academic induction, Thomas Stephens would have achieved the status within the Society of Jesus of a 'formed scholastic', one whose path was regarded as being towards the priesthood. It was a position in which he could remain for at least two and up to fifteen years. At this point, his superiors decided that the time had come to grant his desire to join the mission of Portuguese India. 'I thinke I have the less need at this time to tell you the cause of my departing', he wrote to his father, 'which neverthelesse I may conclude, if I do but name obedience.'[5] The decision must have been a formality. There was a desperate shortage of priests in the mission to the East and a vast area to cover. It is virtually certain that Brother Stephens would have anticipated permission being granted by learning Portuguese. He had never set foot in that country, but he demonstrated fluency in the language from the time he arrived in India. His probable tutor was Antonio Francisco, a Portuguese fellow Jesuit.

Thus it was arranged that Thomas Stephens should complete his studies in Goa. Sometime after 19 March, 1579, Robert Persons wrote to a fellow English Jesuit, Fr William Good.

> Missions since your departure hath byn dyvers of importance namely two or three to the East Indyes where hence, and especially from Japonia, we have had letters of great

consolation which are newly printed. And among these Missions was one English-man, that is Thomas Stephens, a yong man of great fervour and a reasonable talent, whome I would have diverted towards a certayne North India, but the latt you shall know after.[6]

In stating that he would have diverted Thomas Stephens towards North India, Fr Persons is not referring to a geographical location, but a treasured project of the Jesuits—to attempt to reach and convert the greatest ruler in all India, Jalahidedin Muhammad Akbar, whose name has passed to posterity as 'Akbar the Great'. The Mughal Emperor was known to have a great interest in religion. If he could be converted to Christianity, his vast empire might convert along with him. In 1576, two Jesuits, Fr Antonio Vaz and Fr Peter Dias, who had arrived in Bengal at the request of the Bishop of Cochin, rebuked some Portuguese merchants who had defrauded the Mughal treasury of legitimate taxes and persuaded them to make retribution. Word of this reached Akbar. He was deeply impressed with their conduct and became curious about this religion, which demanded such high moral standards. He sent for Fr Gil Eanes Pereira, the Vicar-General of Bengal, who arrived at his court at Fatehpur Sikri in 1578 and suggested that the Emperor invite a Jesuit mission from Goa to engage in debate with his Moslem scholars. The news caused great excitement in Rome and an eight-volume Bible produced in Antwerp by the great printer Christoffel Plantijn was dispatched to Goa for presentation to the Emperor. Francesco Borgia, the third Jesuit Superior-General, had obtained permission from Pope Pius V to have copies made of the Borghese Madonna in the Church of Santa Maria Maggiore in Rome. One of these was probably dispatched eastwards together with a picture of Jesus. The Society's missionaries were aware of the power of Christian art to fortify their message and took paintings with them over the globe, so is likely that the intention was to present a copy of the Borghese Madonna to the Emperor.[7]

That Robert Persons considered Thomas Stephens suitable for the mission to the East demonstrates the esteem in which he was already held within the Society. Participants in this extraordinary project would require qualities of physical endurance, moral steadfastness, diplomacy, linguistic abilities and intellectual rigour. Fr Persons also mentioned Thomas Stephens' departure in a letter to Edmund Campion. 'One English of good learning is presently now herehence sent towards Japponnia.'[8] It seems curious that Persons thought that Stephens was bound for Japan when he was never to go within three thousand miles of that land. It is likely that Fr Alessandro Valignano, the Visitor of the Missions in the Indies, had requested him, once he had completed his studies and ordination, for his forthcoming mission to Japan. The young English-man was certainly in the mould of the kind of missionary that he would have been seeking to recruit.

Other Jesuits destined for the Indian Province that Thomas Stephens would have known in Rome epitomised the fact that the Society transcended nationality and class. Rodolfo Acquaviva was a member of one of the most illustrious noble families in Italy. The fifth child of the Duke of Atri in the Kingdom of Naples, his abilities were recognised early. His uncle, Claudio Acquaviva,[9] was Chamberlain at the Court of Pope Pius V—a post that the Duke wished his 17-year-old son to assume after his uncle resigned to join the Jesuits in 1567, but his mind was set on the same course. It took several months to gain his father's consent before he was received into the Society on 2 April, 1568.[10] Matteo Ricci was another Jesuit from a noble family. He was born in the Papal States in 1552. He went to study law and mathematics at the Sapienza University of Rome in 1568, but, much to the chagrin of his father, who forbade any talk of religion in his house, he joined the Jesuit noviciate in 1571. In 1577, he offered himself for service in the Indian Province and that year embarked for Goa in a party of Jesuits that included Rodolfo Acquaviva.[11] Antonio Francisco also joined the Society in Rome in 1571. He was a poor student from the first Jesuit College at Coimbra in Portugal.

Finally, Pietro Berno was born in Ascona, a Swiss village on the shores of Lake Maggiore, the son of a fruit merchant. He started to study for the priesthood in his own diocese, but, when his father moved to Rome, he went with him and continued his studies in the German College. He was received into the Jesuit novitiate at Sant' Andrea on 2 July 1577.[12] When a man joined the Order, he did not lose his own culture, but became part of an organisation that transcended it. This supranational quality would bring the Society into conflict with colonial rulers.

Accommodation

Alessandro Valignano was a seminal figure of the Catholic missions in the East. He was born in the Kingdom of Naples in 1539. After a brilliant career at the University of Padua, he joined the Jesuits in 1566. A man with a fiery temper, this clever lawyer's commanding presence was increased by his great height, which was enough to 'turn heads in Europe and draw crowds in Japan'.[13] In Rome, he was put on what would now be known as a 'fast-track', for he made his profession of the Fourth Vow—that of complete obedience to the Pope in undertaking any mission required of him—after only seven years in the Society. In 1574, he embarked for Goa. En route to Lisbon, he recruited to the Eastern Mission Alphonso Pacheco, a Spanish Jesuit from a noble Castilian family, who was studying at the University of Alcala. The two arrived in Goa in September 1574, where Pacheco was ordained and made assistant to the Rector of St Paul's College.[14]

Valignano embodies one side of the dilemmas and the disputes that are perhaps inevitable in the mission field. He undertook his first mission to Japan in 1579. On arrival in Nagasaki, where the mission was based, he was shocked by what he considered to be the condescending cultural practices which prevailed. He wrote that the Superior, Francisco Cabral, and many of the other Jesuits, regarded

> Japanese customs as abnormal and invariably speak disparagingly of them. When I first came to Japan, our

people (the crowd usually follows the leader) showed no care to learn Japanese customs, but were continuously carping about them, arguing against them, and expressing their preference for our own ways to the great chagrin and disgust of the Japanese.

Fr Alessandro Valignano

Valignano's first official act was to ensure that all new missionaries in the province spent two years learning Japanese. He formulated the policy that became known as 'Accommodation' (*Accommodacio*) or 'Inculturation'—the incorporation of such aspects of the local culture's prevailing practices as did not clash with Catholic values. The idea was not new. A great missionary priest, Fr Gaspar Vilela, who had known Francis Xavier, had learnt Japanese, shaved his head and beard and clothed himself in a kimono.[15] Cabral, who possessed the rigidity typical of the former soldier, took the view that Japanese converts must adapt to Western modes of thought. Under his regime, Japanese seeking to join the Society were restricted to becoming Brothers. Now Valignano opened the possibility of the priesthood to all members.[16]

While the course followed by Valignano seems reasonable, it was not without its difficulties. It is one thing to adopt certain external customs in order to assuage hostility (his Jesuits were not unsuccessful in doing this), but quite another to enter the mindset of a nation. He realised this and wrote of the dilemma that must have confronted every intelligent and sensitive missionary: 'The longer I am in Japan, the less confident I am in writing about this country and judging its problems.'

Cabral, whose mission had not been without its successes, had noted that Japanese culture stressed the suppression and concealment of emotion. To reveal secret thoughts and activities to another (as in the confessional) was perceived as a serious violation of social norms. His assessment of the chances of foreign Jesuits becoming fluent in Japanese—or even gaining much understanding of the language—frequently proved correct, but there was surely no other way forward. Fr Vilela had been told by the older Christians in Miyako, on whose experience he had to depend, that the Japanese judged people by their external appearance and dress. The feudal lords that the priests would meet regarded it as an insult if anyone appeared before them in everyday dress with no regard to their great dignity.

Francis Xavier, while being an adherent of the policy of 'Accommodation' had warned that it could lead to Christian doctrine and practices being simply absorbed into the local culture. Valignano appears to have been aware of this danger, insisting that convert ordinands learn Latin—and made no attempt to diminish the liturgical life of the Japanese Church. He did, however, model the hierarchy of his mission on the grades of Zen Buddhism.

From the very first, the missionaries had realised that a key to the conversion of the masses was the conversion of the feudal lord, the *daimyo*, who possessed absolute power. If he embraced Christianity, his entire district would follow. If he proscribed it, all but those who held the true faith in their hearts would despise it. Cabral was conscious of the hazards of the cheap grace obtaining from such mass conversions and tended to shun them. Valignano shared his view, but did not eschew the prospect, rather seeing the necessity of establishing instruction for converts in the faith after their baptism. A number of the *daimyo* had indeed converted during the thirty-odd years of the mission. The process was not entirely disinterested. In embracing Christianity, they gave themselves greater independence and through the missionaries, they could establish relations with foreign Heads of State, receive embassies and establish profitable trade. Such may have been the case when Samitada, the *Daimyo* of Omiro, became a Christian. On 9 June, 1580, he presented the Society of Jesus with the port of Nagasaki, which was situated within his fiefdom. The place was then little more than a fishing village with a single street and a population of around 1,500, mainly fisher-folk and farmers. A contract was drawn up. The *Daimyo* would have a share of any profits arising from the venture and continue to exert the political jurisdiction, which Jesuit priests were forbidden from exercising by Canon Law and their own constitutions.

If the *daimyo* was hoping that the Jesuits would bring him prosperity, he was not disappointed. Fr Valignano proved a shrewd businessman. Conscious that the scope of the mission was restricted by its poverty, he had already entered into an arrangement with the Portuguese merchants in Macao to take a share of their trade with Japan. Now the Society became active in the silver trade to Canton, importing Chinese silk in exchange.

A monopoly was established on customs dues for all imported goods and Nagasaki grew into an international port to rival Goa or Macao. The resulting new-found prosperity caused the population to expand rapidly to 40,000—all of them ostensible Catholics. News of the venture reached Rome, where the Superior-General expressed disquiet about Jesuits engaging in commercial ventures and ordered that their control of the trade should cease, but Alessandro judiciously chose to stretch his vow of obedience and ignore instructions from so far away. After all, he was the man on the spot who had been given license to order the missions as he saw fit. He could point to the success of the mission, newly-funded by the commercial windfall. Jesuit schools and two seminaries to train Japanese priests had been built. A printing press had been established. Two hundred churches were served by eighty-five Jesuits, who included twenty Japanese brothers and a hundred acolytes. Nor was worship neglected. On Holy Thursday, Fr Valignano washed the feet of twelve poor Christians. Penitents flagellated themselves on Good Friday, while on Easter Day a great procession wove through the streets.

More Jesuits were clearly needed to reap the rich harvest of souls. It is most likely that it was around this time Valignano summoned Father Sebastian Gonsalves from Bassein, the Portuguese outpost in India, He was accompanied by one of his young students, Gonsalo Garcia, son of a Portuguese father and a Canarese mother. He became fluent in Japanese and was active as a catechist, but for some reason his dream of becoming a Jesuit was not to be fulfilled, so he later settled in the Philippines as a trader and lay missionary.[17] If Thomas Stephens was chosen for the Japanese mission by Alessandro Valignano, it is a mark of his shrewd judgment of character. The Englishman, with his gift for languages and his interest in the policy of Accommodation, would have been a great asset. It was not to be, however. His great talents would be of value elsewhere.

'Imprisonment for the Faith's Sake'

It is clear that the authorities could never quite determine what to do with Thomas Pounde. He was questioned on several occasions by Richard Young, an agent of Sir Francis Walsingham, the Queen's Principal Secretary. Twice he was brought before five or six Commissioners. On another occasion he was brought before a great assembly of persons, loaded with fetters, and remanded to Newgate. This was the prison from which the condemned were drawn on hurdles for hanging and quartering at Tyburn. Despite the ordeal that this and other prisons represented, he never lost his sense of humour, even when it came to discussing his own desire for martyrdom.

> The gaoler, as though I was already a condemned criminal, tore off both my hat and cloak, but what was equally a source of regret to him, as it was to myself, he left my head safe upon my shoulders. As I went along with uncovered head ... the mob cried out 'Crucify Crucify him'.[18]

That the other inmates of this dreadful place actually shouted this is questionable. Doubtless there was vicious verbal abuse, but Pounde's use of the word 'crucify' is probably reflective of what he regarded as his imminent martyrdom. The gaolers could not wait to get hold of him. 'They liberally bestowed upon me the alms of the widow of Newgate,' he wrote, '(a certain kind of instrument of torture called the widow s mite).' After this ordeal, he awaited the sentence of the judges, which would be delivered that afternoon. Suddenly, to his astonishment, his manacles and chains were removed and his hat and cloak restored. He was taken to the hall of Lincoln's Inn, 'where I formerly lived when studying the law'. Five commissioners awaited his arrival. One was the notorious Richard Topcliffe, described by Pounde as 'the Prefect of the Examinations'. Topcliffe was a sadist, a relentless torturer of Catholics, described by Fr John Gerard, as 'old and hoary and a veteran in evil'.[19] The very sight of him must have struck terror into the heart of the most fervent would-be martyr. The Commissioners told him why they had summoned him before them.

> They had it in command from the Queen to recall me from my course of life, either by threats or by blandishments; but all was in vain. They urged upon me that, if I would prove myself faithful to the Queen and her loving subject, it was necessary that I should disclose the names of those with whom I was accustomed to consort, and the places of resort.[20]

It is significant that the Queen seems to have become actively involved in Pounde's case. Perhaps she realised that it was her incautious remark that had been the catalyst for his strong adherence to the Catholic faith. Pounde replied that it was not appropriate to his faith, his rank and education, or the dictates of his conscience, that he should bring 'innocent and friendly men into danger by disclosing their names'.

> Finding that they could gain nothing from me by their coaxing words, they remanded me back to my prison. After two days, Topcliffe (that most unrelenting persecutor of Catholics) came to me with the governor of the prison. They endeavoured to shake my constancy by every kind of means; but they accomplished nothing ; they deplore my condition; this specially grieves them but in which I greatly glory the faith, and my imprisonment for the faith's sake.

What became known as the 'good cop bad cop' routine was not unknown to the Elizabethans:

> After they were departed came Young again, who asked me what Topcliffe had been doing with me? The man (truly urban[e] and affable!) feared lest Topcliffe, severe and rough as he was, should have done anything rude towards me. With the most winning manner of voice, he endeavoured to coax me to betray my friends, and to disclose any secret which might, perhaps, serve his wicked ends. Finding that he could gain nothing from me, he

> urged me to write a letter to the Lord Chancellor, asking for favour. I did so, indeed, but in such a manner that they could get no handle against me, and with such effect that from thence forth they cared less about me, deeming me an obstinate fellow, and of all Catholics the most dangerous to the public safety of the realm that is, the most hostile to heresy.

Pounde's view of Young was confirmed in his report to Walsingham, in which he describes the prisoner as a 'dangerous fellow'. He seems to have gained more information than Pounde supposed, for he reported that Pounde had been committed as a layman, but was, in reality, a professed Jesuit. Communication between the various Catholic prisoners of the State was possible, as Pounde's concluding remarks, addressed to his fellow sufferers, demonstrate.

> Therefore here I am, secluded from the company of all the rest, without hope of a freer custody, unless by chance I am summoned again to the next sessions of Newgate, to answer the charge of my duty to God and defence of the Catholic faith. This I have to warn you of, O my companions in chains! that you believe not any sinister reports about me; and I would exhort you, with all my heart, to that perseverance in the faith I desire for you. Farewell!

From out of the Flaminian Gate

Sometime in late February in 1579, Thomas Stephens rode out of the Flaminian Gate in Rome on the first stage of his long journey. He was accompanied by other Jesuits bound for the Indian mission and probably followed the same route taken by Alessandro Valignano six years before through Viterbo, Siena, Florence, Bologna, Modena, Parma, Picenza and Milan. At Siena and Florence they would have found hospitality in Jesuit colleges and at Bologna they were probably entertained by Cardinal Paleotti, the Bishop. One of the architects of the Council of Trent, he was one of the first bishops to thoroughly augment the Tridentine reforms.

It was *de rigueur* for those bound for the mission field to call on Carlo Borromeo, the Archbishop of Milan, in his great palace. Valignano had done so in 1573 and Campion, Sherwin, Persons and their companions would do so on their way to England the following year. Evelyn Waugh described the scene they experienced:

> That huge and princely establishment was well accustomed to visitors of every degree; it numbered over a hundred members of the regular household; there were Chamberlains, Almoners, Stewards, Monitors, Oblates, Discreets of the Confraternity, Prefects of the Guests Chambers, all maintained and graded in hierarchic order under the Praepositus, the Vicar and the Auditor-General. Three hundred guests a month, on average, passed through these hospitable courts; there all the ways and passages of the vast, ecclesiastical labyrinth seemed to intersect, and in the centre of it all, living in ascetic simplicity amongst the lavish retinue, eating his thin soup, sleeping on his folding bedstead, wearing his patched hair shirt, moving with halting gait, chilly even in the height of summer, speaking in a voice so subdued that it was hardly audible, grave and recollected as a nun, was the dominating figure of the great Cardinal. The pilgrims were received, entertained, blessed and sent on their way, and the immense household went about its duties; in its splendour and order and sanctity, a microcosm of the Eternal Church.[21]

Carlo Borromeo was born in 1539 into an aristocratic family. He was the nephew of Pope Pius IV and the outstanding interpreter of the spirit of the Counter-Reformation, epitomising the reforming zeal in the Church in the light of the Council of Trent. He reorganised ecclesiastical structures, imposed severe moral principles and fought heresy. In these tasks he saw a vital role for the Society of Jesus. He stressed the pastoral functions of a Prince of the Church, visiting every parish in his Archdiocese. He founded innumerable charitable institutions, including the Confraternity of Christian Doctrine, an organisation that would now be called a Sunday School. When Milan was visited by plague two years earlier, he worked incessantly to relieve suffering. He avoided no danger and spared no expense in fighting the epidemic.

Borromeo's reforms met much opposition from vested interests. On 29 October 1569, four members of the somewhat misnamed Order of the Humiliati attempted to assassinate him while he was at prayer. The bullet, fired from close-range, failed to penetrate his body. His escape was hailed by some as miraculous, a confirmation of his future sainthood. There is no doubt that the great Cardinal represented a role model for many a young priest, including Thomas Stephens.[22]

Leaving Milan, and its inspiring source of strength for his mission, Thomas Stephens would have followed in Fr Valignano's footsteps to Genoa, where he was due to take ship for Spain, but there were considerable delays, perhaps due to the contrary winds of March. When his ship did sail, he must have despaired of reaching his destination on time. Disembarking at Alicante, the party would have ridden post-haste across Spain, passing through Madrid on its way to Lisbon. He must have pondered his future within his chosen mission if he missed the boat, both in the literal and metaphysical sense, but in late March he entered Lisbon, the hub of the vast Portuguese empire, through one of the walled city's thirty-eight gates. Fortunately for Thomas Stephens, the departure of the fleet from Lisbon had been delayed by what he described as 'weighty matters', but more probably by bureaucratic maladministration. This was to have severe consequences on the subsequent journey.[23] The authorities had nominated other passengers to go in the Jesuits' places, who now missed the chance of the voyage. In fact, it was eight days before they set sail and Thomas Stephens was able to write a (now lost) letter to his father in England, describing his journey from Rome.

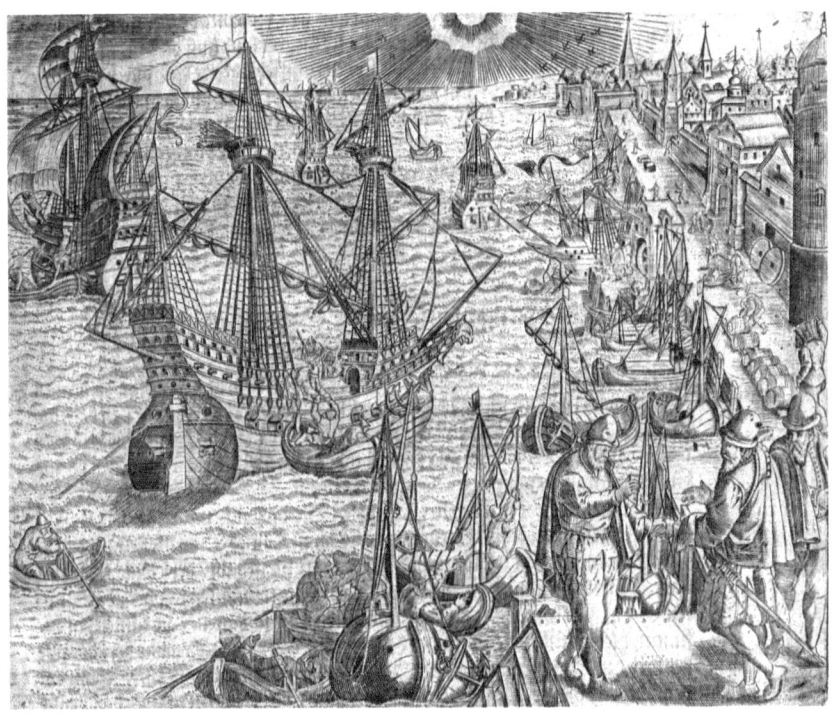

Harbour scene engraving, depicting Portuguese ships preparing to depart from Lisbon.

Once they had confirmed the voyage, Fr Stephens and his companions made for the Jesuit College of Santo Antão. In 1540, two of Ignatius Loyola's closest companions, Simon Rodriguez and Francis Xavier, had come to Lisbon, intending to embark for the Indies. Their preaching and devotion so impressed King John III that he invited them to stay. He wanted the Society to be a force for education in his realm and vast empire. Xavier voyaged on to fulfil his mission, but Rodriguez and other Jesuits founded a college at Coimbra, endowed by the King. A base was established in Lisbon in 1542 in the Hospital de Todos-os-Santos, later relocated to the College of São Antão. The College built up a strong reputation as a place of learning, particularly in the field of mathematics, where the influence of Christopher Clavius, who had spent four years in Portugal, was strong. The companions would have visited the Church of São Roque, which was to be the ecclesiastical base of the Society in Portugal. After Lisbon was ravaged by plague in 1505, a cemetery for the victims was established beyond the city walls. King Manuel I sent to Venice for a relic of San Roch (Roque), the patron saint of plague victims, to be housed in a shrine in the cemetery. The shrine was dedicated in 1515 and the Confraternity of São Roque founded to support it. A 'Plague Courtyard' for the burial of victims was dedicated in 1527. When the College failed to match the Jesuits' desire to build a church worthy of their mission, the king arranged with the Confraternity that it would be built around the shrine of São Roque. The Society took possession on 1 October 1553 at a ceremony at which Fr Francisco Borgia, SJ (later the third Superior General of the Society) preached. When Thomas Stephens arrived in Lisbon, the church was still under construction, but the shrine within it was a place of veneration.

When the time came to sail, Thomas Stephens and his companions were conveyed by land or water the short distance to Belém, a port situated near the mouth of the River Tagus. Hundreds of people would be waiting to embark aboard the flotilla of five ships under the command of João de Soldanha. On the harbourside was the impressive monastery of Our Lady of Bethlehem. King Manuel I had begun its construction on the site of an earlier chapel, in 1501, as thanks for the epic voyage of Vasco da Gama to India in 1497. He established there a community of monks of the Order of St Jerome, who were also known as Hieronymites. It was their purpose to pray for the soul of the King and to provide spiritual comfort to voyagers, who would spend the night in prayer. Twelve confessionals in the monastic cloister served the needs for absolution of those embarking with no certain prospects of return.

The monastery was well-nigh completed and its nautical location and vocation was reflected throughout its structure. The ornate side entrance has a statue of Our Lady of Bethlehem

(*Santa Maria de Belém*). The most prominent of the many other carved figures is that of Prince Henry the Navigator. It was he who had set in motion what would be known as 'the Age of Discoveries'. The third son of King John I, he had commissioned the development of the fast and manoeuvrable carrack for ocean voyages, the type of ship on which Thomas Stephens was about to sail. Prince Henry sponsored the voyages that led to the discovery of the islands of Madeira, the Azores and the *Voto do Mar*—'the Turn of the Sea'. This was the understanding that by beating due west out into the Atlantic, navigators could pick up favourable winds that would carry them past the treacherous, shoal-ridden Cape Bojador, on the west coast of Africa, considered for centuries to be the limit of the known world. Even more importantly, this route (a closely guarded secret) would enable them to return and gave Portugal dominance of the eastern seas for a century.

The ornate portal is surmounted by the cross of the Royal Military Order of Christ, of which Prince Henry became the Grand Master in 1417. The Order was founded in 1318, as a continuation of the Order of the Knights Templar, which had been suppressed by Pope Clement V. It was regarded as having done great service in the liberation of Portugal from the Moors and was granted a share in the revenues emanating from the colonial empire. It was ambivalent about its monastic role. The vow of celibacy for the knights was amended to one of conjugal chastity and the vow of poverty was dispensed with altogether. Eventually, the threefold vow was only applied to priests and religious within the Order. Nevertheless, its monastic and crusading origins and its influence over the voyages of trade and discovery would ensure that Portuguese overseas enterprise always saw evangelisation as one of its prime purposes.

'No Hope of Life nor Comfort'

On 4 April, 1579, Thomas Stephens was one of twelve priests who embarked aboard the annual fleet that sailed to Goa and from thence to other Portuguese outposts in the Indies. The departure was most impressive. 'The setting forth from the port I need not tell you how solemn it is with trumpets and shooting of ordinance', he wrote. The ships were also carrying 'The Orphans of the King' (*Ortãs do Rei*), young orphan girls of marriageable age who, since 1545, had been despatched by the Crown to the Indies as wives for the Portuguese settlers. Their fathers were soldiers who had been killed in his service. Thomas Stephens sailed aboard the *São Lourenço*, a *nau*, as the Portuguese called a carrack. This three or four-masted vessel possessed a high mounted stern with an aftcastle, a forecastle and a bowsprit. Conditions aboard were extremely cramped: she was packed with passengers, soldiers and crew. There were five other Jesuits on board. One was his former fellow novice in Rome, the Swiss, Pietro Berno, who had completed his noviciate in Lisbon.

The ships were towed into mid-stream and then drifted down the Tagus on the ebbing tide. As the fleet passed the Belém Tower that marked the entrance to the Tagus, Thomas Stephens may have been moved to offer a prayer to the Blessed Virgin, whose statue adorned a richly-carved niche on the side of the fortress. Beyond lay the open sea. As the mainsail was unfurled, bearing its red cross of the Order of Christ, many voyagers must have felt a sense of despair at leaving their familiar world for the unknown. No such traumas would have been felt by Fr Stephens, who had determined his destiny seven years before at Cowdray House. Now it was being fulfilled.

The Dutch voyager Jan Huyghen van Linschoten, who sailed to Goa in 1583 to take up the position of the Archbishop's secretary, gave details of the ships' complement and cargo.

> The shippes are commonlye charged with foure or five hundred men at the least, sometimes more, sometimes less,

> as, there are souldiers and saylors to be found. When they go out, they are but lightly laden, only with certaine pipes of wine and some small quantitie of Marchendize, other things they have not, but balist, and victuals for the company.[24]

Stephens sent his father a warm and extensive account of the voyage. It seems incredible that a letter could be conveyed from Goa to England. Once there, it must have been handed round in great wonder. The letter opens with appropriate filial sentiments: 'After most humble commendations, these shall be to crave your daily blessing with like commendation unto my mother, and withal, to certify you of my being, according to your will and my duty.'[25] Thomas Stephens seems to have suffered from seasickness when the ship hit the open swell, but he noted that the 'great number of children… in the seas beare out better than men and no marvell, when that many women also pass very well.' He is sparing on detail about the awful conditions that the voyagers had to suffer. His reticence was not shared by his fellow Jesuit, Giovanni Pietro Maffei, who compiled an account of such voyages as part of his history of the mission to the Indies.

> Most of the travellers lie [down], if no cruel winds were blowing, on the open deck… but if the cruel storms require the sailors to run forward and backwards as the sudden commands are given, these poor men are driven, frightened and wet below deck, where, since the air is stale and the heat great, the pestilential smell of the bilge and the bad odour and the dirt afflict the bodies and make them rotten.

> The large ships contained usually a population of 600, 800 and sometimes 1,000 persons. Since commercial goods took the largest part of the ship, the poor passengers had to keep heaped upon each other in the narrow space, which was left free. The wealthier ones bought, at a high price and for a short time, the use of the few cabins available on the ship.[26]

The Jesuits would certainly not have had the resources to hire such cabins. Jan Huyghen van Linschoten, gave details of the shipboard diet.

> All the officers and other persons which sayle in the ship, which have for their portion every day in victuals, each man a like, as well the greatest as the least, a pound and three quarters of Biskit, halfe a Can of Wine, a Can of Water, an Arroba, which is 32 pounds of salt flesh the month. Some dryed fish, onyons and garlicke are eaten in the beginning of the voyage, as being of small value, other provisions, as Sugar, Honny, Reasons [i.e. raisins], Prunce [i.e. prunes], Ryse and such like, are kept for those which are sicke: yet they get but little thereof, for that the officers keep it for themselves.[27]

After six days sailing, the *São Lourenço* had lost the rest of the fleet and came in sight of Porto Santo in the Madeira Islands. Just before they entered harbour an English ship, 'very faire and great', opened fire on them with a few shots 'that did no harm, but after that, our ship had laid out her greatest ordinance, they straight departed as they came.'[28] The English ship was probably a privateer, for the two countries were not yet at war. 'I was sorry to see [her] so ill-occupied' wrote Fr Stephens, 'for she went roving about, so that we saw her again at the Canarian Iles, unto which we came the thirteenth of the sayd moneth.' Just as Christopher Columbus had replenished his stores in the Canaries in preparation for his long voyage, so did the Portuguese navigators. Thomas Stephens was impressed by the islands: 'Good leisure we had to woonder at the high mountaine of the Iland Tenerif, for we wandred betweene that and great Canaria foure dayes by reason of contrary windes.' These same winds almost proved their downfall; he wrote, 'Such evill weather we had untill the fourteenth of May, that they despaired to compasse the Cape of Good hope that yeere.'

The navigators could work out the latitude of the ship, but it would be many years before the discovery of longitude enabled the determination of a precise position. 'You know that it is hard to saile from East to West, or contrary', wrote Thomas Stephens to his father, 'because there is no fixed point in the sky.' Proceeding southwards, the *São Lourenço* ran into what was called 'the burning Zone'—the Guinea coast that had already been colonised by the Portuguese. Here they were again forestalled by adverse winds for thirty days. The heat was unbearable, as he wrote:

> The atmosphere on the greatest part of this coast [is] not cleare, but thicke and cloudy, full of thunder and lightening and raine so unholesome that if the water stand, all is full of wormes and, falling on the meat which is hanged up, it maketh it straight full of wormes.

Progress was very slow ('We found so often calmes that the expertest mariners wondred at it'). This was a product of the late departure, which ensured they missed the vital trade winds. Thomas Stephens also noted the sharks during these torpors.

> There waited on our ship fishes as long as a man which they call Tuberones. They come to eat such things as from the shippe fall into the sea, not refusing men themselves if they light upon them and if they finde any meat tied in the sea, they take it for theirs... The Mariners have in time past have eaten of them, but since they have seen them eate men their stomacks abhorre them. Nevertheless they draw them up with great hooks and kill of them as many as they can, thinking they have made a great revenge.

The sharks had 'waiting on them six or seven small fishes (which never depart),

> With gardes blew and greene round about their bodies, like comely serving men, and they go two or three before him and some on every side. Moreover, they have other fishes which cleave always unto their body, and seems to take such superfluities as grow about them, and they are sayd to enter into their bodies also to purge them if they need.

The Portuguese had named to the wildlife 'according to some property which they have'. He describes a Portuguese Man o' War, although he knows no name for it.

> All along that coast we saw a thing swimming upon the water like a cocks combe (which they call a ship of Guinea) but the colour much fairer, which combe standeth upon a thing almost like a swimmer of a fish in colour and bignesse and beareth underneath in the water strings which save it from turning over. This thing is so poisonous that a man cannot touch it without great peril.

> The neerer we came to the people of Afrike, the more strange kinds of fowles appeared, inasmuch that when we came within no lesse than thirty leagues (almost an hundred miles)... as good as thousande fowles of sundry kindes followed our ship.

The flying fish were 'as big almost as a herring, which hath wings and flieth... together in great number.

> These have two enemies, the one in the sea, the other in the aire. In the sea, the fish which is called the Albicore, as big as a salmon, followeth them with great swiftnesse to take them. The poor fish, not being able to swim fast, for he hath no fines, but swimmeth with mooving of his taile, shutting his wings, lifteth himselve above the water and flieth not hie. The Albacore seeing that, although he have no wings, yet he givetth a great leape out of the water, and sometimes catcheth him, or else he catcheth him, or els he keepeth himself under the water going that way and when the fish being weary of the aire, or thinking him-self out of danger, the Albacore meeteth with him, but sometimes his other enemy, the sea-crow, catcheth him before he falleth.

He saw albatross, but he did not know the name for them. They were 'so great that their wings being opened from one point to the other contained seven spannes...'

Thomas Stephens was intrigued by the way the ship tacked against the adverse winds. He admired the experience and skill of the sailors and their ability to navigate by reading the signs in nature. There was not 'a fowle that appeareth, or signe in the aire, or in the sea' that those who had made the voyage before could not interpret. The sailors were pleased to see birds they called 'Velvet sleeves because they have wings the colour of velvet and bowe them as a man boweth his elbow.' Their presence signified that the *San Lorenzo* was approaching the Cape of Good Hope. 'With these and like sights', he wrote, 'but always making our supplications to God for good weather and salvation of the ship, we came at length unto the point, so famous and feared of all men, but we found there no tempest, only great waves.'

The conditions misled the Captain who, thinking he had 'winde at will', pulled closer to the shore. All at once the wind turned to the south, driving the ship nearer the shore in fourteen fathoms of water, just six miles from the Cape.

> There we stood as utterly cast away, for under us were rocks of maine stone stone so sharpe and cutting that no ancre could hold the ship, the shore so evill that nothing could take land and the land itselfe so full of Tigers and people that are savage and killers of all strangers that we had no hope of life nor comfort, but onely in God and a good conscience.

After the ship had lost several anchors, the Captain, convinced they were doomed, made the desperate decision to hoist the sails in the forlorn hope of beaching her on a more hospitable section of the coast. Suddenly the wind turned from the north and they were saved. Thomas Stephens thanked God for their deliverance.

The experience of the sailors who had made the voyage before bore fruit next day on a rich fishing ground: 'So many they tooke that they served the ship for that day and part of the next'. One of the sailors pulled up a lump of coral 'of great bignesse and price. For there they say ... that the corals doe grow in the maner of stalks upon the rocks in the bottome and waxe hard and red.' There were two routes that the navigators could follow to India. The most appealing was 'within the Ile of S. Laurence, which they take willingly because they refresh themselves at Mosambique, a fortnight or a moneth, not without great need.' After a further month's sailing, they would arrive in Goa.

The normal time for a voyage from Lisbon to Goa was five months and the *Sao Lourenço* had taken four just to reach the Cape. Thus, they were obliged to take the shorter route. This involved passing to the east of the Isle of St Laurence, as the Portuguese called Madagascar. 'They go heavily', wrote Thomas Stephens, 'because in this way they take in no port.' The passengers and crew were aware of the implications of this decision. The passage to the east of the island was full of hidden rocks and quicksand and the ship hoved to at night rather than risk such hazards. Worse still were the terrible effects of scurvy.

> By reason of the long navigation and want of food and water, they fall into sundry diseases, their gummes waxeth great and they are faine to cut them away. Their legges swell and all the body becometh sore and so benummed that they cannot stirre hand nor foot and so they die for weaknesse. Others fall into fluxes and agues and die thereby.

More than 150 people fell sick, of whom 27 died, 'which losse they esteemed not much in respect of other times.' The crew considered that Stephens, whose vocation made him appear less physically vigorous than many of his fellow passengers, was almost certain to perish, but, amidst the sick and dying, he remained healthy.

It was nearly seven months since they had made their last landfall on the Canaries. Because of corruption and theft in Lisbon, food supplies were running low. Ships bound for India were obliged by royal decree to carry sufficient provisions for seven months but the *San Lorenço* was only supplied for five. The prospect of starvation was real, but after they had crossed the Equator for the second time, a huge shoal of fish followed the ship, 'whereof we caught so many that for fifteene days we did eate nothing else'. Fish contain small amounts of vitamin C, so the cumulative effect of such a lengthy diet would have been highly beneficial, and protective against scurvy. The ship was approaching the latitude of her destination. There was great rejoicing when two hawks—land birds—were taken. The seas were running high and, once again, they were in danger of being driven ashore. Their anguish increased when a great wind blew up and drove them across the open seas for ten days. Gradually their error dawned on them. The ship was running westwards, so they could not have been off the coast of India. Prevailing currents and faulty compass readings had brought them close to the desolate island of Socotra, at the entrance to the Red Sea. Ironically this placed the *São Lorenço* on the route she would have followed had she called at Mozambique.

Under the circumstances, Thomas Stephens's criticisms of the navigational standards were comparatively mild.

> These running seas be so perilous that they deceive the most part of the governours and some be so little curious, contenting themselves with ordinary experience, that they care not to seeke out any meanes to know when they swarve, neither by the compasse, nor by any other triall.

With the sighting of birds that the crew knew to be of India, they gave thanks for their deliverance. Soon after, branches of palm and stalks of sedge floated by and snakes were seen swimming in the water. Next day, 'to our great joy', land was sighted—and not a moment too soon, for the water and victuals were close to running out. The *São Lorenço* reached Goa on 24 October after a voyage of 213 days—over a month longer than normal. It was clearly feared they had been lost. They were greeted with 'passing great charity'. The rest of the fleet with which the *São Lorenço* had embarked from Lisbon must have arrived at Goa some time before. Thus relief at their deliverance would have increased 'the rejoicing and merriment' and the tolling of bells of the many churches that greeted the arrival of a ship from Lisbon. Francisco Rodrigues da Silveira, a Portuguese soldier in India between 1585 and 1598, considered such a welcome superficial because,

> those unfortunate soldiers who had escaped from the jaws of shipwreck, scurvy and pestilent infection received no welcome and were abandoned after disembarking in Goa. Those poor soldiers arrive, mostly without a single coin which would buy them a meal on that first day... those who did not carry some letter of recommendation to some friend or relative, would spend that first night under the eaves of the churches, or inside some vessel anchored on the riverside, with such misery and mishap as if... the sea had thrown them in some part or land of enemies. Thus the soldiers spent the first or second day, pawning or selling a cape or their sword... And they go, four or six together, living in little hovels... consumed by hunger and so many get sick and die.[29]

'Roma do Oriente'

The colony had become known as *Goa Dourada* (Golden Goa) or *Roma do Oriente* (the Rome of the East). Its bustle was a new world for Thomas Stephens. The city was huge (as large as London) and the bells of three hundred churches pealed forth daily. The Se' Cathedral of Santa Catarina, which was to be the biggest church in Asia (bigger than any in Portugal), was rising in the main square. When Thomas Stephens arrived at Goa, the city was at the peak of its power and prosperity. The houses of the rich were built of fine stone and painted red and white. Instead of glass, their windows were made from thin polished oyster-shells set in lattice work. 'The whole of this land', wrote the Italian traveller Pietro della Valle, 'is thickly covered with villas and pleasure walks, and the banks of the rivers particularly are studded with houses and other buildings, emblasoned in delicious gardens and palm groves.'[30] The island abounded in corn, rice, mangoes, pineapples, plantains and coconuts.

Plan of Goa in 1750

In the great hall of the Viceroy's Palace, Portugal's naval might was expressed in pictures of every ship that had ever come from Lisbon to Goa, with the name of her captain and details of her ordinance. The Italian artist and engineer Plăcido Francesco Ramponi, who was commissioned by the Grand-Duke of Tuscany to install the mausoleum of St Francis Xavier, was filled with admiration at the sight of the arrival, every eight or ten days, of fleets of twenty to thirty ships.

> One with a load of linen, another with raw or spun cotton, a third with pepper, a fourth with large quantities of drugs; these goods were being loaded and dispersed: some, to one part of India, some to another. And the city shops! Full of merchandise. And among the streets that of "Baniani", which is very long, where on both sides, one could see ships, all full of great chests, piled high with linen, turbans and coloured cloth, and cloth for Brazil, for the ships that return to Lisbon from Goa, touch at Brazil.[31]

Merchandise from all over the East was displayed in the bazaar. Each street was dedicated to a particular commodity: pearls and coral from Bahrain, Chinese porcelain and silk, Portuguese velvet, drugs and spices from the East Indies. Plăcido Francesco Ramponi was lost in admiration for the imports from China.

> Many of the graceful things which come from China are so elegant that they grace the European cities. First and foremost there are the trinkets of porcelain of every kind, every quality, colour and size, draperies and brocades with gold leaves and other fine materials, contadori', that is cabinets, varnished, in different colours and scented and with locks picked out in different colours; screens about three arms high, made of strips of finest silk and various other gallantries and merchandise. But, what is even more admirable, each year they vary their inventions in all types of work from porcelain vases to 'contadori', from the quality of draperies to linen.

The Chinese traders refused to bargain over prices. If the goods on offer failed to reach the asking price, they refused to sell. 'A man who has been in Goa', wrote the French traveller François Pyrard de Laval,

> can assure himself of having seen the greatest curiosities of the Indies, that town being the most famous and renowned for the traffic of all the Indian nations. For that they carry thither all that their own country can produce, as well manufactures as produce, and other commodities, all of which are to be found there in plenteous store. You will see arriving there more than a thousand vessels laden with all goods.'[32]

Three days before the fleet departed for Lisbon, the merchants known as *Guseratti* arrived, carrying little sacks full of precious stones: diamonds, rubies, emeralds, topaz, cat's eye and other items. Placido Francesco Ramponi was so overwhelmed that he wrote that 'for this sight alone, I would wish to return'. He also admired the local pottery:

> The way in which the Canerin [i.e. the Konkani: the local inhabitants] mould the earth of red clay into jars and jugs which they call 'Gurgulettas' and other jars, for holding water, worked like fine porcelain, is curious. They give them the colour of carmine with the juice of grasses. The workmen are real artists and their method of work is quite different from ours.

Beef and pork constituted the diet of the Portuguese. One was an anathema to Hindus, the other to Muslims, which must have increased the disdain in which the Portuguese were held. Fowl was also available, but despite the city's location near the sea, fish was scarce. Most of the native converts to Christianity consequently changed their diet. They tended to wear European clothing and, at baptism, acquired Portuguese Christian names, which further distinguished and alienated them from their former co-religionists. Jan Huyghen van Linschoten noted that the owners of the shops were 'commonlie the Bramenes, which serve likewise for Priests and idolatrous Ministers, and have their shops throughout the Cittie. In every place and corner and under prentices, whereby everyman may have to serve him at his need.'[33]

Huge gambling saloons were licensed by the municipality. Compulsive punters lodged in them for weeks together. François Pyrard de Laval was impressed by the attention given to personal hygiene amongst the local women, although how he obtained such intimate information must be a matter of speculation: 'The Portuguese, Meriços and Indian women and girls bathe and wash the private parts daily, as also do the other Indian women who are not Christian.'[34] He found no sense of personal decorum among Christian men, however. Presumably, he was mainly referring to the Portuguese:

> One thing I remarked throughout all India, that the Gentiles [Hindus] and Mahometan, at their washing and bathing, never uncovered their private parts, but always kept them covered with a cloth. It was only the Christians that had no shame in the matter and even took pleasure in exposing themselves in a vile and disgusting manner.

Thomas Stephens looked on the local population with a cool Jesuit's descriptive eye.

> The people here are tawny, but are not disfigured in their lips and noses, as are the Moors and Kaffirs of Ethiopia. They that be not of reputation, or at least the most part, go naked, save an apron of a span long and as much in breadth before them, and a lace two fingers broad before them, gilded about with a string, and no more.[35]

His anthropological knowledge was somewhat lacking: Moors and Kaffirs lived at opposite ends of the continent from Ethiopia. Since he had never set foot in Africa, it can only be concluded that he had seen African slaves, with their pierced and be-ringed noses and lips, in Goa.

Jan Huyghen van Linschoten, was disturbed by the sensuality of the scantily-dressed women.

> The women go altogether naked onely with a cloth before their privie members, which openeth chewing all they have, which is by them ordayned to the ends that by such means it should tempt men to lust after them and to avoid the most abominable and cursed sin of Sodomie ...[36]

In Linschoten's view, this intense sensuality was caused by the hot climate, but he saw a positive aspect to it, suggesting that it helped curb the homosexuality that was apparently common practice in at least some sections of Goan male society. He shared the long-prevailing view that excessive sexual intercourse caused debilitation and even death:

> The stone, gravel and rupture raigneth much, specially amongst married men by reason of the great quantitie of water that they drink, being given to all pleasures and riotousnes, enjoying what their hearts desire, always with their bellies open in their shirts in gallerie, recreating themselves with the wind that cooleth them.

Linschoten was also aware of the practices of certain of the indigenous population as they related to sexual initiation.

> There are among the natives those that doe sowe up the privie member of their female children as soon as they are born, leaving them but a little hole to void their water. And when she marrieth the husband cutteth as great or as little as he will ...

There was also a custom whereby

> the bride is brought to the pagoda which is made of ivory and by force they take the bride's maidenhead so that the blood remaineth still upon the image and then after other devilish superstitions and ceremonies bring the bride home, where she is delivered to the bridegroom who is

joyful and proud that the pagoda hath honoured him so much and eased him of so much labour...

Goa- Market, 1599

The native women had 'many devilish practices which they devise to make nature more lively...

> They doe use to eat those betteles, arreques and chalk and in the night it standeth by their beds. They eat whole handfuls of cloves, pepper, ginger and a baked kind of meate they call chachunde ... all to increase their lechery ... and they are not content therewith but give their husbands a thousand hearbes for the same purpose to eat, they not knowing thereby to fulfil their pleasures and to satisfy their desires ...

In the 1960s, Goa became notorious as the centre of a hippy drug culture. There was nothing new in this. The great physician Garcia de Orta described how Indian women used opium to make their lovers perform more slowly and satisfyingly. He also heard that many women took cannabis to give them confidence when they wanted 'to dally and flirt' with men.[37] Pyrard de Laval heard that the native women used

> An hearbe called Deutrea which beareth a seed whereof bruising out the sap they give it to their husbands eyther in meate or drinke and presently therewith the man is as though he were halfe out of his wits and without feeling or else drunk, laughs and sometimes it taketh him sleeping like a dead man, so that in his presence they will and take their pleasure with their friends and the husband never know of it.[38]

Even the palanquins, the Indian equivalents of sedan chairs in which upper class women were carried by attendants, could be places of sensuality. In 1602, the Provincial Council forbade that they should be curtained from the world to prevent illicit affairs occurring within them. There was an inevitable sequela to such license. 'Concerning syphilis' [*vérole*] wrote Pyrard de Laval:

> it is in no way infamous to contract it a few times. They even make a virtue out of it. They cure it without sweating with

the *bois de chine*. [China wood] This illness exists only amongst Christians and they prefer it to fever or dysentery.³⁹

This last statement is not as unlikely as it sounds. According to Davinder Mohan Thappa, the evidence suggests that syphilis, at least, was unknown in India before the early sixteenth century. The fact that it was known as the 'Portuguese disease', or *firangi roga*, indicates its perceived origins. It seems probable that the Portuguese introduced it to India. It did not take long to spread among the native population.⁴⁰

Like the other European maritime powers, the Portuguese sponsored the slave trade. The actual traffic was largely in the hands of the Arabs. Indeed, it long predated the Portuguese. It was endorsed in the Books of the Law of both Hinduism and Islam. The French traveller François Pyrard de Laval, cast a lascivious eye over the slave market, which was situated on the main street, the *Rua Direita*.

> You see there very pretty and elegant girls and women from all countries of India, most of whom can play upon instruments, embroider and do all kinds of work, such as the making of sweetmeats, preserves, etc.. All these slaves are very cheap, the dearest not being worth more than 20 or 30 pardos. Girls that are virgins are sold as such and are examined by women, so that none may dare any trickery. They deem it no sin to have intercourse with their slaves... so long as they are not married: for a girl's master being the man who marries her, she may not be so used after a man has pledged his troth to her. Some of these girls are very pretty, fair and comely, others are olive-coloured, brown and of all colours. But the ones to whom they are usually most attracted are the Caffre girls of Mozambique and other places in Africa, who are wondrously black skins, with curly hair.
>
> In this market there are a great number of other slaves that are not for sale, but themselves bring the work they have done, such as tapestries, embroideries and needlework; as

also preserves, fruits Others earn money by fetching and carrying anything required. The girls deck out in fine style for this purpose, so as to be more attractive and to sell their goods the better, Sometimes the men call them into their houses to see them there talk to them of love, whereto they, being nothing loth, yield at once, the men giving them something. Often too, they manage love affairs for their mistresses in whose service they are, and never play a contrary game.[41]

The author of the *Luciados*, Luis Vaz de Camôes, fell in love with one such market girl, a negress called Luisa Barbara, who he described as 'the gentle slave who serves and adores'. He had been left penniless by a shipwreck and she took pity on him, giving him dishes of food and gifts of money. Later, she appears to have followed him to Portugal where she cohabited with him.[42]

Slavery, or rather emancipation from it, was used by the Portuguese as an aggressive means of conversion. A royal decree of Dom João III in 1533 granted freedom to the slaves of non-Christians who converted, while Decree 16 of the first Provincial Council of Goa in 1567 declared that the slaves of 'infidels' who converted should be freed without compensation to their owners.[43] 'The slaves of Goa—their number is infinite', wrote Pyrard de Laval:

> They are of all Indian nations, and a very great traffic is done in them. They are exported to Portugal, and to all places under the Portuguese dominion. The Portuguese carry off the children, seducing them by fair speeches, and leading them away and hiding them, both little and big, and as many as they can, yea, even though they be the children of friendly races, and though there be a treaty of peace whereby they are prohibited from taking them for slaves; for all that, they cease not to kidnap them secretly and to sell them.

Male slaves mainly performed menial or construction jobs, especially the vital task of carrying drinking water from the

Bangany spring outside the city to their households. Others carried the grand parasols of the elite. Female slaves generally worked in the household. The more attractive ones sold food and handicrafts in the street or worked as prostitutes on behalf of their owners. If slaves despaired and ran away, unless they could flee the area of Portuguese rule, they were liable be captured and punished by the official Slave Retriever employed by the city. The authorities made some attempt to curb the excesses of owners against their slaves. A Royal Decree of 1 January 1599 sought to prevent this 'great scandal' of 'so many homicides and such inhumanity'. The Viceroy was ordered to compile an annual list of owners who had killed their slaves while punishing them. Such cases would be investigated by the *Mesa de Relaçao* (Supreme Court). 'True it is, wrote Pyrard,

> that slaves are so maltreated by their master and mistresses, who lord it over them cruelly, that it is nothing strange that they should have their revenge. One day at Goa, I saw one aged eighteen or nineteen years, that cast himself into a well and was killed, to escape the fury of his master, who was running after him to chastise him.

As a good Jesuit, Thomas Stephens took more interest in the local fauna and flora than the women. He was amazed that the only plant he recognised in India was the grapevine. He was obviously interested in its fruits, for he recorded that it grew 'to no good purpose, so that all the wines are brought out of Portugall.' The vines must have been brought to India aboard Portuguese ships. Goa's presence in Portugal's empire ensured the introduction of over three hundred species of flora, including sweet potatoes, tapioca, tomatoes, pumpkins, cashews, papaya, tobacco, guavas, pineapples, and that essential ingredient of a curry, chillies. Thomas Stephens was also amazed by the versatility of the uses of the palm.

> We have here a tree oftener seen than the elm or the vine, called the palm on account of the likeness to it, or perhaps

because it is really so, if you admit that palm is a generic word and consists of two species. It gives oil, liquor (vinum) toddy (lac), syrup (mel), sugar and vinegar. Coir rope is also made from it to tie with and its branches are used to protect huts from rain. It gives fruit all the year round. One type bears nuts rather than dates, resembling a man's head. When the exterior rind has been removed, they equal the size of two fists. Inside the fruit contains water like light beer and good to quench one's thirst. It is so plentiful that after drinking from one fruit you would not look for another. In the interior of the nut is a kernel, lining it all over like a covering and forming a prized article of food. The shell furnishes the blacksmith with charcoal. Those that live near the sea not only load their boats under the tree, but also utilise it for making ropes and sails.[44]

The palm even provided a form of paper. 'You will hardly find any piece of writing except on its leaves', wrote Fr Stephens. 'Those that live on land invariably make use of them to shelter themselves from rain.'

Notes

1. C. Devlin, *The Life of Robert Southwell* (London: Sidgwick and Jackson, 1967), p. 91.
2. T. M. McGoog, 'Pounde, Thomas (1539–1615)' *Oxford Dictionary of National Biography* (Oxford: Oxford University Press, 2004).
3. R. Crowley, *An aunswere to sixe reasons...* (London: John Charlewood and John Kingston, 1581).
4. F. J. A. Skeet, in *Herts and Essex Observer* (3 June 1905), cited in *A History of the County of Hertford* vol.3 (London: Victoria County History, 1912), p. 69.
5. J .L. Saldanha, *The Christian Puranna of Thomas Stephens: Biographical Note* (Mangalore: Simon Alvares, 1907), pp. xxvi-xxx. A copy of the original is in the National Library of Brussels: ms 3353–61. f. 6fr-63v.
6. L. Hicks (ed.), *Letters and memorials of Father Robert Persons, S.J.* (Leeds: Publications of the Catholic Record Society, 1942), pp. 156–7.

7. E. Maclagen, *The Jesuits and the Great Mogul* (London: Burns, Oates and Washbourne Ltd., 1932), pp. 23, 24.
8. E. L. Taunton, *The History of the Jesuits in England* (London: Methuen & Co., 1901), p. 39.
9. He was to become the fifth Superior-General of the Society of Jesus.
10. 'Acquaviva—Familia Napolitan', *Dizionario Biografico degli Italiani*, vol. 3 (Rome: Istituto dell'Enciclopedia Italiana, 1960).
11. J. Brucker, 'Ricci, Matteo', *The Catholic Encyclopaedia*, vol. 13 (New York: Robert Appleton Company, 1912).
12. The Jesuit Singapore Website: www.jesuit.org/.../saints.martyrs/july/berno.and.aranaq.html (accessed 22 Nov. 2019).
13. J. B. Hoey III, 'Alessandro Valignano and the Restructuring of the Jesuit Mission to Japan, 1575–1582', in *Eleutheria, A Graduate Student Journal*, vol. I/I (2010).
14. The Jesuit Singapore Website: www.jesuit.org/.../saints.martyrs/july/alphonsus.pacheco.html (accessed 22 Nov. 2019).
15. M. Ribeiro, 'Gaspar Vilela, Between Kyushu and the Kinai' in *Bulletin of Portuguese-Japanese Studies*, vol. 15 (December 2007), pp. 9–27.
16. Hoey, 'Alessandro Valignano', p. 13.
17. A. De Mello, 'St. Gonsalo Garcia, the 1st Indian Saint' in *The Times of India* (8 October 2008).
18. H. Foley, *Jesuits in Conflict, or Historic Facts* (London: Burns and Oates, 1873), pp. 56–61.
19. As cited in A. Stewart, *The Oxford History of Life Writing, vol.2* (Oxford: OUP, 2018), p. 22.
20. Foley, *Jesuits in Conflict*, pp. 56–61.
21. E. Waugh, *Edmund Campion: Jesuit and Martyr* (London: Penguin Books, 1923), p. 39.
22. 'St Charles Borromeo', Catholic Encyclopedia: www.newadvent.org/cathen/03619a.html.
23. Saldanha, *The Christian Puranna*, pp. xxvi-xxx.
24. A. Cole Burnett (ed.), transcription of the 1598 English translation of *The Voyage of John Huyghen van Linschoten*, vol. 1/1 (London: Hakluyt Society, 1885), pp. 10–14.
25. R. Hakluyt, 'Thomas Stephens' Letter to his Father' in *The Principal Navigations...* vol. IV (London: J.M. Dent, 1927), p. 234.
26. G. P. Maffei, *Le istorie dell' Indie Orientali del P. Gio. Pietro trodotte di*

Latino in lingua Toscano da M. Serdonati, vol. 1 (Charleston, NC: Nabu Press reproduction, 2012), p. 139.
27. Cole Burnett, *The Voyage*, pp. 13, 14.
28. Hakluyt, 'Thomas Stephens' Letter', p. 236.
29. F. R. Silveira, *Memórias de um Soldado da India*, compiled from a manuscript in the British Museum by A. de S.S. Costa Lobo (Lisbon: Nacional-Casa de Moeda, 1987), p. 21.
30. E. Gray, *The Travels of Pietro della Valle in India from the English Translation of 1664* (London Hakluyt Society, 1892), p.154.
31. F. P. Ramponi, 'Old Goa Yesterday' (www.gogoa.net/old_goa.htm).
32. A. Gray and H.C.P. Bell (trans) *The Voyage of François Pyrard de Laval to the East Indies...* vol. II, Pt. 1 (London: Hakluyt Society, 1887), p 105.
33. Cole Burnett, *The Voyage*, p. 235.
34. Gray and Bell, *The Voyage*, p. 118.
35. Saldanha, *The Christian Puranna*.
36. Cole Burnett, *The Voyage*, pp. 244–249.
37. G. de Orta, *Colloquies on the Simples and Drugs of India*, ed.. F. l. de Melo Breyner, tr. Sir C. Markham (London: Henry Sotheran, 1913), p.246.
38. Cole Burnett, *The Voyage*, p. 114. Datura grows wild in Goa. It resembles an eggplant and bears thorny fruits. This is the sedative that Pyrard calls 'Deutrea'. 'If anyone takes of it', wrote Thomas Stephens, 'he is out of his mind for twenty four hours, in such a way that you would not be able to tell if he was drunk or utterly abandoned.'
39. S. Greenblatt and others, *Cultural Mobility: A Manifesto* (New York: Cambridge University Press, 2010), p. 48.
40. D. M. Thappa, 'Evolution of Venereology in India', *Indian Journal of Dermatology. Venereology and Leprology*, vol 72/3 (2006), pp. 187–96.
41. Gray and Bell, *The Voyage*, pp. 65, 66.
42. A. de Mello on Luis de Camoens www.colaco.net/1/AdmCamoens4.htm.
43. L. de Sousa, *The Portuguese Slave Trade in Early Modern Japan* (Leiden: Koninklijke Brill: 2019), p. 482.
44. Saldanha, *The Christian Puranna*.

3

Golden Goa

On July 8, 1497, a flotilla of four ships sailed out of the Tagus in a bold bid to succeed where Christopher Columbus had failed and open a sea route to the Indies. After Vasco da Gama's successful expedition, the Portuguese dominated the lucrative spice trade for the next century. The island city of Goa on the Mandovi River was established as the centre of their empire in the east after its capture by Afonso de Albuquerque in 1510. He laid siege to the city, which was then part of the dominions of Sabaio (Sultan) Yusuf Adil Shah of Bijapur. Adil Shah had devised a formidable system of defence, but on 17 February, Albuquerque took the city and gave safe conduct to the Moorish defenders. When Adil Shah counter-attacked, they rose up against the Portuguese and, on 23 May, Albuquerque had to abandon Goa. He attempted to recapture it a few months later, with the help of Timoji, a Hindu chieftain. He could not have timed his attack better, for Adil Shah had just died. As the Portuguese fought their way into the city on 25 November, St Catherine's Day, they made 'prodigious execution', in revenge for the perceived treachery. Two-thirds of the 9,000 defenders perished and their corpses were fed to the alligators in the river. The Portuguese had lost fifty men. The surviving Moslem defenders were expelled from the city, but the Hindu inhabitants were spared.[1]

The Portuguese intended the city to be more than a trading post and it became the first European colony in Asia. It was always the intention that it should be not just Portuguese territory, but an outpost of Portugal itself. To this effect, Albuquerque engaged a number of his men to marry native women and settle in Goa as farmers, traders and artisans, giving them marriage portions of 18,000 reis and sequestered land and houses on which to settle. He was cognisant of the Indian custom that the wife should assume the religion of her husband, but according to Pietro della Valle, the arrangements did not always go as planned.

> On one night when some of these marriages were celebrated, the brides became so mixed and confused together that some of the bridegrooms went to bed with those who belonged to others. When the mistake was discovered next morning, each took back his own wife, all being equal in regard to the point of honour.[2]

The offspring of these matches were known as *mestiços* or 'mixed'. They set the pattern for Portuguese colonialism worldwide which was very different from the later British policy since it aimed to integrate the local populace into Portuguese culture. The women and children that Fr Stephens records as being aboard the São Lourenço were part of this process.

Religion was undoubtedly an arm of Portuguese strategy: Vasco da Gama had said that the aim of his explorations was to seek spices and Christians. As early as 1510, Dominican friars had arrived in the city and a Franciscan mission was established in 1517. In 1534, Pope Paul III, by his Bull *Auquum Reputamus*, designated Goa a suffragan bishopric under the suzerainty of the geographically distant Bishop of Funchal in Madeira. The church of St Catherine was raised to the status of a cathedral in the same year. In 1557, an Archbishopric of Goa and Damão was created, with a jurisdiction stretching from the Cape of Good Hope to Macão. Its incumbent bore the title of 'Primate of the East'.[3] In 1541, the Franciscan Friar Diogo de Borba established the Confraternity of the Holy Faith, with the assistance of senior officials, including the Governor Dom Estãvão da Gama and the Vicar General Miguel Vaz Coutinho. That year, the *Seminário de Santa Fé* (Seminary of the Holy Faith) was founded for the education of boys aged 13 to 15 at their admission 'of all Asian nationalities: Canarese, Decanis of the north, Malabaris, Sinhalese, Pegus, Malays, Javanese, Chinese and Abyssinians, so that the torch of Faith may be taken to the whole East'.[4] Clearly, the institution was intended to provide for converts who might follow a vocation to the priesthood from the whole of the oriental Portuguese Empire. The church was dedicated on 25 January 1543—the Feast of the Conversion of St Paul. By then, there were 60 seminarians enrolled. The seminary was originally situated in the Market Place in Goa and Goa was amongst the first dioceses to pioneer such seminary education for the training of secular priests. Only after the Council of Trent in 1578 was seminary education made compulsory for all dioceses.

The division between the sacred and the secular was narrow. In 1540, the beleaguered Pope had given the Portuguese kings the right to appoint bishops, but the division remained. The Society of Jesus, like other religious orders, was a truly international body that owed allegiance to no secular power. This was a major reason for its ultimate expulsion from many countries, but not the only one. Albuquerque did not interfere with the Hindu religion a great deal, although he abolished the terrible practice of *sati* (the burning of widows on their husbands' funeral pyres), and his successor as Viceroy, Dom Lopo Soares, abolished the custom of killing children born under what astrologers deemed to be unlucky stars. Both practices would have horrified the Portuguese.

Central to the Hindu faith is a belief in reincarnation—that an individual soul continues in successive bodies until it finally wins release from the cycle of birth and death through union with the universal soul; a belief in *karma*—that the merits and demerits of an individual's actions in the current life are imprinted on the current soul; and that a person's life in each incarnation should be guided by a set of rules appropriate to his or her caste status. Hindu society was rigidly divided into castes or *varnas*. The system was sanctified in the religious code called the *manu-*

smriti that defined each person's position and role. Caste rules governed a person's diet, dress, social behaviour and relationships. There are four basic caste divisions, but many sub-divisions within them. The *Kshatriya* are the warrior and ruling class. Even more powerful are the Brahmin, so called because they possess *Brahma*—the power inherent in spells, prayers and rituals. Things don't happen because the gods make them happen, therefore, but because the Brahmins make the gods make them happen. Because they claim this immense power over all creation, the Brahmins occupy the highest position in the caste system. Next in the caste hierarchy come the *Vaishyas*. These are farmers, merchants, artisans and the like. The first three *varnas* are called the 'twice born', which has nothing to do with reincarnation, but means that they are eligible for initiation into the inner body of the religion. The fourth *varna*, the *Śudras*, the caste of labourers and menial workers, are only once-born. The *Śudra* has no right even to listen to the *vedras*, or sacred scriptures. The murder of a *Śudra* by a Brahmin was considered equivalent to killing a cat, a frog, or a cow. Yet, although the *Śudras* were placed at the very bottom of the caste system, there were those (the *Dalits*, or Untouchables) whose place in society was even sorrier. Translated from the Hindi, the term means 'crushed', 'stepped on' or 'oppressed'. These are people who historically work in those occupations regarded as ignominious, polluting and unclean, but that are nevertheless vital for the maintenance of society. These tasks not only made the *Dalits* unclean, but also made their uncleanliness contagious to anyone who came into contact with them. If the shadow of a *Dalit* was cast over a Brahmin, he was obliged to ritually purify himself.

This all seemed bizarre to the Portuguese. When the Navigators first arrived in India, they were asked to which caste they belonged. Their behaviour was closely scrutinised: how many times they washed daily; how they treated women; and their diet, which included eating beef, the product of the Hindu sacred cow. All their habits (social and cultural), their language and their dress, defined their otherness. It was concluded that the Portuguese observed no caste rules and were therefore ranked with the *Dalits*, or Untouchables. The implications of this were severe. The Indians had admired the great bravery of the Portuguese. Indeed, if a caste system were imposed upon them in Hindu terms, then the likes of Albuquerque were *Kshatriya*; the Catholic priests, Brahmins; the merchants who thronged the markets, *Vaishyas*; and the common soldiers, *Sudras*. Although the Portuguese had a class-system, their Christian beliefs admitted of no such fundamental inequalities between men. This was reflected in the Church, which was a sure vehicle for advancement for able men from poorer homes. Thus, the Indian religion seemed barbaric, idolatrous and bizarre—and not just to the Portuguese. 'They have a very strange order among them, they worshipe a cowe...' wrote Ralph Fitch, an early English venturer in India, with clear incredulity '...and they be great idolators. And they have their idols standing in the Woods, which they call Pagodes. Some be like a Cowe, some like a Monkie, some like Buffles, some like peacocks, and some like the devil.'[5] Their idols', wrote Francis Xavier, with equal derision, in a letter to the Society in Rome in 1543, '...are generally so rubbed over with oil as to smell detestably, and seem to be as dirty as they are ugly and horrible to look at.'[6]

It was unlikely that many Brahmins would be open to conversion. Christianity could hardly compete with the status of being able to manipulate the actions of the gods. However, the *Sudras* and the *Dalits* were more obvious targets for evangelisation. Conversion would free them from the caste system, but, ironically, their lowly status made them an essential part of it. The Brahmins avoided any contact with the Portuguese, who they called 'the polluted *firangana*'. The word had reached India at the time of the Crusades. The Arabs called the crusaders *Franj*, because most of them came from France. By the time the soubriquet reached India, it had been corrupted to *Faranjis* or *Firangana* and had become pejorative. The potential for a clash of cultures was intensified in 1543, when the colony was expanded by the annexation to the Portuguese Crown of the outlying areas of Bardez and the peninsula of Salcete, each of which contained many Hindu villages and temples.

Francis Xavier

In 1542, one of the great figures of Catholic missionary history became associated with Goa. Francis Xavier, aged 36, had the impressive credentials of a Papal Nuncio and a Plenipotentiary of the king of Portugal, but he almost never used this status except against those who attempted to thwart his mission. After he arrived in the colony on May 6, he spent five months preaching, ministering to the sick, comforting the dying and visiting prisons. He would go through the streets ringing a little bell and inviting the children to hear the word of God. When he had gathered a crowd, he would take them to a church and explain the catechism. After Sunday Mass, he took the sacraments to the Leper Hospital of St Lazarus on the outskirts of the city. It was reported that,

> he did everything with great joy... and cheerfulness... always very joyful and pleasant with a smile on his face; in this manner he used to deal with all, whether good or bad... always smiling with everybody, especially those who lived badly.[7]

Like many others, he was appalled by the degenerate society he found in Goa, and dismayed by the brutality with which the Portuguese soldiers and settlers treated the native population. He considered that their lifestyles did not commend their nominal faith and that his work in the evangelisation of the native peoples was thus severely retarded by their bad example. He wrote a bold letter of protest to King João III.

> It is possible that when our Lord God calls your Highness to His Judgement that your Highness may hear angry

words from Him. 'Why did you not punish those who were your subjects and owned your authority and were enemies to me in India?'[8]

In October, Xavier set out for the Fishery Coast, where he undertook a highly successful mission to the Paravas, the Tamil pearl fishermen. He adopted a method of instruction that was indigenous to the local culture. He wrote verses in the Malabar language, setting out the truths of the Christian faith, and set them to catchy music. His doggerel was extremely popular and was sung everywhere. By contrast, in the Americas, the Spanish and Portuguese colonists had undertaken a policy of the forcible conversion of the native peoples. Realising that this went against the basic spirit of Christianity, Francis Xavier had formulated his alternative strategy based on 'Accommodation', the process of absorbing local traditions and culture wherever they were not in contradiction to Catholic doctrines. This was to have a profound effect on the Jesuit missions. Francis Xavier's proselytising amongst the poor fisherfolk led, inevitably, to a clash with the Brahmins, for whom he developed an intense distaste. He expressed his disapproval in a letter to the Society in Rome in 1543.

> We have in these parts a class of men who are called Brahmins. They keep up the worship of the gods, the superstitious rites of religion, frequenting the temple and taking care of the idols. They are as perverse and wicked a set as can anywhere be found, and I always apply to them the words of the holy David, "from an unholy race and a wicked and crafty man deliver me, O Lord!" They are liars and cheats to the very backbone. Their whole study is, how to deceive most cunningly the simplicity and ignorance of the people. They give out publicly that the gods command certain offerings to be made to their temples, which offerings are simply the things which the Brahmins themselves wish for, for their own maintenance and that of their wives, children and servants. Thus they make the poor folk believe that the images of their gods eat and

> drink, dine and sup like men, and some devout persons are found who really offer to the idol twice a day, before dinner and supper, a certain sum of money. The Brahmins eat sumptuous meals to the sound of drums, and make the ignorant believe that the gods are banqueting. When they are in need of any supplies, and even before, they give out to the people that the gods are angry because the things they have asked for have not been sent and that, if the people do not take care, the gods will punish them by slaughter, disease, and the assaults of the devils. And the poor ignorant creatures, with the fear of the gods before them, obey them implicitly.

Xavier's disapproval and his view of the Brahmin economic and social dependence on the maintenance of the caste system would be echoed in many European assessments of India, notably those of the later British colonialists, yet he does not even mention that Brahminism was a caste of learning and scholarship.

> These Brahmins have barely a tincture of literature, but they make up for their poverty in learning by cunning and malice. Those who belong to these parts are very indignant with me for exposing their tricks. Whenever they talk to me with no one by to hear them they acknowledge that they have no other patrimony but the idols, by their lies about which they procure their support from the people. They say that I, poor creature as I am, know more than all of them put together.

Xavier's antipathy to the Brahmins was partly based on their strong interest in the status quo, which made them resist strongly the idea of conversion to Christianity, for both themselves and the other castes in Indian society. 'If it were not for the opposition of the Brahmins', he wrote, 'we should have them all embracing the religion of Christ.' The French traveller Pyrard de Laval took a different view of the caste system, regarding the Brahmins as a 'Most noble race, honoured and respected of all the others.'

They have their peculiar habits of life, and practice a more religious and austere observance of their faith; they have their peculiar habits of life; they have this peculiarity, that they never eat flesh or fish, or anything that has had life, or drink aught but water, but they preserve this austerity from father to son for all generations, never mingling or allying themselves with other people. They preserve an inviolable rule that the daughters of Brahmins never marry but with Bramenis, and the same with the men, who never marry a second time. Their habit is a frock of cotton cloth, with a turban on the head, and red slippers on the feet ... The only mark distinguishing them from other people is a cord of three strands of cotton, which they wear next to the skin. It is a kind of order given to them at their temples, with great display and solemnity; and one could not do a Brameny a greater injury than to break his cord; in that case he would have to get another with like ceremony, otherwise he would no longer be a Brameny. So also if one is punished, he is first degraded and his cord removed; likewise, if he intermits any of his ceremonies he is deprived of it, and is then no longer of this order. ... It was necessary for the Brahmins to continuously identify themselves, to avoid contact with inferior castes.

When they go about the town with their Cabaye, or white cotton garment, and meet some stranger, they at once tell who they are and their race, in order to be acknowledged for what they are (for their cord, being worn next to the skin, is not seen) ... When a Brameny would swear, he puts his hand on his cord, and then he must be believed. However poor they may be they maintain their rank and rules of life, and other folk in passing salute them by bowing their head as a mark of respect.[9]

Nobody seems to have taken a neutral view of the Brahmins. The Florentine traveller Filippo Sassetti described them as being 'as subtle as the Jews, or more so, vile like them and lacking spirit', although he did regard them as possessing 'the swiftest intellects.' His opinion of most of those he met in India was not high. He was contemptuous of the Portuguese; Hindus in general were 'a miserable people who live on betal and Arcca'; and he described Muslims as 'dogs'.[10] Both Pyrard and the Dutch traveller van Linschoten observed a curious habit of the Hindus.

> The first thing they meet when they go out of their houses, whether birds or quadrupeds, they honour and worship the whole day, and ask of their priests and sorcerers, in whom they put their trust, what they have to tell of these things.[11]

Pyrard also noted the strict Hindu food laws.

> All these Gentiles abstain from the flesh of the cow, just as the Mahametans from pork; and they are so bound to this superstition, that most of them, when they become Christians, enter into a bargain that they shall not be compelled to eat it. Nor do they eat the flesh of oxen, bulls or buffaloes.

He was justifiably sceptical about the authenticity of such conversions.

> They dislike also to quit their own style of dress, and this they are allowed to keep, along with many other superstitions; which leads to the belief that they are not by any means good Christians—and the fact is, most of them become Christians of necessity.

If a Hindu man became a Christian and his wife did not, she was obliged to 'act in all respects as if her husband were dead, except she does not burn herself alive; she only cuts her hair, separates herself from all society, and lives out the rest of her days in solitude.' Pyrard acquired some knowledge of the Hindu belief in the transmigration of souls, although the idea that it came from Pythagoras must have been his own speculation.

They believe that after death their souls pass into the bodies of cows, buffaloes or bulls, and that when the cow or bull dies, they take to other bodies; and I believe that to be the reason why they will not eat the flesh of these, viz., on account of their notion of the passage of souls from one body to another. They have received this from the ancient tradition of the Brachmanes and Indian Gynosophists, who were instructed in the doctrine of Pythagoras, for he was the first author of this Metempsychosis. They have places of retreat for wandering beasts, and are mindful to give food and drink to birds and all other animals. They would not for anything in the world willingly permit the slaughter of any animal, and would sooner redeem it with money.[12]

Goencho Saib

It may have been the influence of Francis Xavier that led Rome to take an irenic line with the Christians of St Thomas, who were reckoned to number some 30,000 families—perhaps 250,000 people—along the Malabar coast. As espousers of Nestorian doctrine, they were technically heretical in Catholic eyes. India's noted ability to absorb cultures into herself had had its effects. The caste system was even more intricate in south India than in the north and the Thomas Christians had been assigned a high place within it, as honorary *nagars*, a sub-division of Brahmins. The St Thomas Christians were a warrior race, famed for their martial exploits in the service of the local rajas. They shared many customs with the Brahmins. They bestowed sacred threads (to which a cross was added) upon their infants and adorned them with gilded mongoose teeth and panther toes. Their marriage rites were similar to the Hindus. Most of all, they observed the niceties of the caste system, including shunning *Dalits*.

On his return to Goa, Xavier learned that a papal decree of 27 September 1543 had approved the creation of the missionary order of the Society of Jesus (he had been one of its seven founders eight years before). Soon after, he embarked on his great mission to the East, visiting Malacca, the Moluccas and possibly the Philippines, before returning to Goa to deal with the affairs of the Society. In 1547, both Miguel Vaz and Diogo Borba died and the future of the Seminario de Santa Fé was plunged into doubt. The Governor, Royal Secretary and Bishop realised that only one body could ensure its survival. After approval granted by Ignatius Loyola and King João III, the College was handed over to the authority of Francis Xavier, who accepted it on behalf of the Society of Jesus. It was the first Jesuit seminary in India. Xavier realised the importance of training a native priesthood, noting that, '[m]any, many people hereabouts are not becoming Christians, for one reason only: there is nobody to make them Christians.' As he could not hope to have from Europe either the number or quality of missionaries he needed, he determined to train missionaries of his own. Accordingly, he wrote to Portugal, asking that a worthy Rector be sent for what had become known as St Paul's College.

Simon Rodriguez, the Provincial, sent a young Jesuit father, Antonio Gomez, who arrived with his letters of appointment while Francis Xavier was away in the South. Although Gomez was a scholarly and ascetic priest with a reputation as a compelling preacher, many of his qualities were the antithesis of much of what Xavier represented. He was a product of the noted University of Coimbra in Portugal and regarded it as the model on which all other universities should be based. He wanted to raise the status of St Paul's College to that of a university and recruited the sons of the Portuguese officials and magnates throughout the Orient. He began his tenure as Rector by drawing up rules on eating, drinking, sleeping and recreation, spiritual duties and work that were based on practices in European institutions and largely unsuited to life in the tropics. Such was his hostility to the indigenous students that, by 1550, 200 of them had absconded from the seminary. Francis Xavier realised that he must find Gomez another appointment outside Goa. In his stead, he summoned a Dutch Jesuit for whom he had a great admiration, Fr Gaspar Baertz. He wrote of his strong feelings to the Provincial in Portugal.

> As you know well, the office of Superior is very dangerous for one who is not perfect. I ask you therefore to send as Rector and Superior of the brethren in India, one to whom this office will do no spiritual injury. Antonio Gomez does not possess the necessary qualifications.[13]

Gomez used all the resources in his power to resist his reallocation, including the influence he had established with the Viceroy and the Bishop. As a result, it was Fr Gaspar who was sent elsewhere (to Ormuz) not Fr Antonio. Scarcely had Xavier sailed for Japan than Gomez had dismissed many of the native students and replaced them with Portuguese. Many of these were put on a fast track to ordination, which was adduced by Gomez as evidence of the success of his policy. Hearing of this in Japan in November, 1551, Xavier felt that he had no choice but to make the long journey back to Goa. At Malacca there was a letter awaiting him from the Head of the Society, Ignatius Loyola: the first he had received for four years. Loyola had also been having trouble with Simon Rodriguez, who as the Provincial of Portugal had authority over the Mission to the East. Loyola could not send physical help to Xavier, but he could make decisions that would transform the situation. He constituted India and the East as an independent Province of the Society and appointed Xavier as its first Provincial.

Armed with this power to impose his will, Xavier sailed for India. At Cochin he learned that much of his work in the south had been undone. Fr Antonio Criminale, the trusted Italian priest he had left there, had been murdered by Moslem raiders. He was the first Jesuit martyr in India. Along the Fishery Coast, everything had been thrown into confusion. The local customs that Xavier had conceded were not antipathetic to Catholicism, Antonio Gomez had banned. Francis Xavier arrived back in Goa in February 1552 and immediately exercised his new powers. He sent Gomez to Diu with instructions that he should be returned to Portugal with the next fleet. Simon Rodriguez had clearly realised that Gomez was on the way out but does not appear to have grasped that he no longer possessed authority over the Indies, for he sent out a priest to replace him. 'What qualities do you possess that fit you to be a Rector?' Francis Xavier is supposed to have asked Fr Melchior Nunez on his arrival. 'Six years of philosophy and three of Theology' came the reply. 'Would you had six years of experience,' Xavier answered, and sent Nunez to Bassein to gain it. Father Gaspar was finally appointed to his allotted place.

Returning to Japan, Xavier embarked on his last mission: to spread the Gospel in China, then a forbidden nation. He died on an offshore island before he could reach the mainland. After several months, during which his coffin was moved from place to place, it was discovered that his body showed no signs of decay. Hearing of this, the Viceroy of the Indies ordered that it should be conveyed to Goa. The body of Goencho Saib, as he was known to the Indians, arrived on 16 March 1554 and was conveyed to St Paul's College, where it was exposed for the veneration of the faithful for three days. A team of priests and doctors examined the body and pronounced it uncorrupted.

The Inquisition

In May 1545, Francis Xavier had written to King João III, requesting that the Inquisition be established in Goa, only five years after it had been installed in Portugal. The request was not granted till 1560, when the Regent, Cardinal Henrique, dispatched the secular canons Aleixo Dias Falcão and Francisco Marques with orders to set up the Holy Office in Portugal's Asian empire. They established themselves as Inquisitors in the old palace of Sabaio Adil Shah. After the conquest, it had become the residence of the early Viceroys, but it had been empty for six years after the 70-year-old Viceroy Dom Pedro de Mascarenhas, had become unwilling to climb its two flights of stairs and moved the Viceregal Palace elsewhere. In 1565, the Inquisition in Goa employed a mere five staff, all Dominicans.

Xavier's motivation seems to have been twofold. He was repelled by the debauchery and corruption of Goa, but also concerned that Indian converts from Hinduism retained many of the customs of their old faith. 'There are many', he wrote to the King, 'who live according to the Jewish law, and according to the Mahomedan sect, without any fear of God or shame of the world.'[14] Thus, the ostensible purpose of the Goan Inquisition was to prevent Christian converts from other religions from reverting to previous religious practices. It was not concerned with the practices of Moslems, Hindus or Jews per se, with just two provisos: those who dissuaded or otherwise hindered those who might convert to Christianity and those who attempted to persuade such converts towards apostasy. Such measures as were taken against these indigenous religions were amply handled by the secular arm. In 1557, even before the institution of the Goa Inquisition, the Governor Fransisco Barreto barred Brahmins and other 'infidels' from various public offices. A decree of King Dom Sebastião I in March 1559 declared that the orphans of Hindus in Goa, who were left without grandparents or other relations 'and are not of an age at which they can have understanding and judgement' should be placed in the care of 'the Judge of the Orphans and handed over to the Jesuit College of St Paul' to be 'baptised, educated and indoctrinated' in the Catholic faith. The official known as the *Pai de Cristâos*, or 'Father of Christians' had the task of finding such unfortunates and removing them, if necessary by force. Presumably, it was considered that, because they were minors, the reluctance of the religious orders to engage in forcible conversions did not apply.[15] It must be considered that the attitude towards the native population on the part of the missionaries was that the process of conversion would save their souls. To most of them, Hinduism was a primitive religion of idol-worshippers, permeated by barbaric practices such as infanticide and the immolation of widows. Certainly, these orphans would be materially and socially better off under the care of the Jesuits than as street children.

Part of the process of making Indians into Lusitanians concerned nomenclature. Renaming converts was part of a supposed cultural break with their past. A decree of the Provincial Council of Goa in 1567 ordered that Goan Catholics should no longer be permitted to use their Hindu names. Converts typically adopted the surname of the priest or their godfather at their baptism and thus names like Fernandes, Menezes, Dias, Soares, de Souza and Rodrigues became the norm. The *Pai de Cristâos* was the official—almost always a cleric—charged with ensuring the welfare of the converts to Christianity. 'There [was] another house', wrote Pyrard de Laval, 'called Catechumens for catechizing and teaching the New Christians. They are fed and supplied with clothing there, until such time as they are instructed and baptised.'[16] Usefully for the converts, the *Pai* could recommend them for employment in government service. He also organised their training in skills like carpentry, tailoring and tool and die-making.[17]

In the years 1560 and 1563, the Viceroys Dom Constantino de Braganza and Dom Fransisco Coutinho issued orders, banishing large numbers of Brahmins. In February 1575, the Governor, Antonio Moniz Barrera, ordered that, if any of these Brahmins re-entered the colony without official authorisation, their estates would be forfeited and the money so realised would be used to provide clothing for converts. In 1567, the first Ecclesiastical Council held in Goa declared that all religions, other than Catholicism as defined by the Council of Trent, were intrinsically wrong and harmful. It declared that the Portuguese Crown had the 'inescapable duty of spreading the faith and should use the secular power of the Church for this purpose', but it also stated that conversions should not be made by force or threats of force, since no-one came to Christ, 'unless he is drawn by the Heavenly Father with voluntary love and prevenient grace.'[18] No such relative tolerance was apparent in the decree of December

1567 by Dom Sebastião I, which banned from his dominions (particularly Goa) Muslim 'Kajis', Hindu preachers, 'Joshis', sorcerers, 'Gurous', and any other person holding a Hindu religious office. Those failing to leave would be pressed into service at the *Ribeira*, the Royal Dockyards of Goa. The decree also ordered that Hindus living in Goa be compelled to attend sermons by a priest specially chosen for that duty. In 1585, the third Provincial Council recommended that Hindus should be forbidden to wear the sacred thread or to initiate their sons into the practice. However, there is no evidence that these orders ever became law. Indeed, it would appear that many of the enactments which were generally promulgated from afar, did not have much impact on the daily life of the colony.

The Inquisition is a topic on which it is difficult to be factual, let alone objective. It was never the single monolithic office that featured in later myths. In the Middle Ages, inquisitors travelled to give support to the local ecclesiastical courts in trials for heresy. Generally speaking, church courts had the (deserved) reputation of being more lenient than their secular equivalents. Famously this was one of the causes of the contention between Henry II and Thomas à Becket. Later, particular circumstances led to tribunals of the Inquisition being established in several countries. Most of them were independent, only coming under the nominal control of the Papacy (the Roman Inquisition was an obvious exception). Their existence was dependent on secular political support and the strength of alternate sources of judicial procedures. Generally, the Inquisitor was a member of one of the mendicant orders, usually the Franciscans or Dominicans. The Jesuits were rarely, if at all, involved. Indeed, Ignatius Loyola had himself appeared before tribunals eight times on suspicion that he might be an Illuminist, a believer in the forms of enlightenment that pertain through advancement in the ranks of a secret society. Pope Gregory IX gave the Inquisition the power to use torture as a 'free faculty of the sword against enemies of the Faith'. As in Elizabeth's England, its use was subject to various restrictions and it was rarely resorted to, but that does not diminish its terror and inhumanity when it was. In the light of a considerable number of unsubstantiated statements about the use of instruments of torture and public burnings against Hindus by the Inquisition, it is necessary to iterate that the institution was not formed to deal with 'pagan' beliefs, but behaviours that were perceived as Christian heresy and malpractice.

It would have been normal practice in virtually every country in Europe—irrespective of denomination—to have tribunals that sought to ensure orthodoxy and root out perceived heresies amongst the populace. The architects of the Elizabethan Settlement who equated what they defined as heresy with treason were following the example set by various Papal Bulls in the Middle Ages. It was almost always the case that the church was seeking to persuade rather than enforce. Yet it was recognised that when these efforts had failed, stronger measures were required. Public confession of fault was a frequent sentence. This was an aspect of ecclesiastical discipline that was retained within the Consistory Courts of the Church of England until the mid-nineteenth Century. The predilection of such tribunals to try offences against the sexual code gave them the popular name of 'Bawdy Courts'. The Inquisition, however, does not seem to have been overly concerned with trying cases concerning sexual morality. Had it done so, the prevailing licentiousness characterising much of contemporary Goan society would have represented a formidable task. An exception occurred in 1644, when the Goa Inquisition enquired of its parent body in Portugal as to whether women accused of lesbian acts should be prosecuted. The Portuguese Inquisition sought expert advice and came to a similar conclusion to the view famously and probably erroneously attributed to Queen Victoria: '[s]uch business is highly dubious' ('*Sendo a material duvidsa*').[19]

On admission or conviction of minor offences, a mild rebuke was the most common sanction, but the Inquisition could order the standard penances of the confessional: the recitation of prayers, fasting, almsgiving, catechetics and pilgrimages. Wearing of a yellow cross, imprisonment and flagellation were imposed for more serious heresy. Life imprisonment was the most extreme penalty that the Inquisition could impose. The death sentence was not an option for the tribunals: only the secular authorities possessed the power to execute people, so those whose actions the Inquisition deemed beyond their powers of punishment were handed over: those who refused to recant, or who lapsed after previous censure for severe heresy. The tribunals would have been fully aware of the consequences of the referral. A relatively small number of charges ended in capital punishment. Geoffrey Parker estimates that, in the whole of the vast Spanish Empire, of some fifty thousand cases dealt with by the Inquisition between 1540 and 1700, around seven hundred led to a death sentence.[20] Of course, most (if not all) of these would be unacceptable to the modern sense of justice, but it was certainly proportionately far less than what religious dissentients suffered under the various regimes in England in the same period.

Since virtually all the records of the Inquisition in Goa have been destroyed (although certain lists naming the accused and giving a brief summary of the case have survived), it is impossible to assemble precise and reliable factual evidence of how it operated in the colony.[21] It would be reasonable to assume that duties were undertaken with different degrees of enthusiasm during different periods of its lengthy history. The situation is further complicated by the fact that it was normal to impose a vow of silence on those released by the Inquisition as to their treatment. If what a French traveller, François de la Boullaye-le-Gouz, wrote around 1650 was correct, the Inquisition did not bother with 'such infidels as were Dutch, English, Danes, foreign Jews, Hindus or Moslems', because they were neither born Catholics, nor had they made a profession of faith. However, its jurisdiction extended over all Catholics, even the Viceroy. If the Inquisitor chose to examine a suspect, there would be no news of them and it would be forbidden to intercede for them on pain of excommunication. Only when those so charged made public confession of their faults would their supposed offence be known.[22]

It appears that the Inquisition could be used as a vehicle to settle scores. This was the case with Charles Gabriel Dellon, a 24-year old French physician, who broke the vow of silence, presumably on the basis that he could not be bound by something that had been involuntarily imposed. He also seems to have been an exception to the practice of not indicting foreigners, although he was a Catholic. Dellon sailed to India in 1668 with the newly-formed French *Compagnie Royale des Indes Orientales*. He spent some time in the French outposts in southern India, embarking on a number of journeys on behalf of the *Compagnie*. In January 1672, he arrived at Goa and provided his Company not only with fulsome accounts of the local topography, but also precise descriptions of the city's major fortifications, its trade, sailing times, governmental structure and the location of the noted *Casa da Póllora*, or gunpowder factory. On his return to Surat, he resolved, in a spirit of adventure, to travel to China, so he resigned from the Company and, in 1674, arrived at the Portuguese stronghold of Damão in northern India. There, the Governor of the city, Manuel de Mendonça Furtado, persuaded him to stay and practice medicine. According to the French prelate and traveller, the Abbé Barthélemy Carré, as well as becoming a much sought-after practitioner, 'he had other qualities to commend him, which soon gave him an entrée into Portuguese society. He was young, good-looking and intelligent.' According to Dellon's own account, it was these very qualities that led him to disaster: he incurred the jealousy of the Governor over his 'frequent but innocent' visits to a woman that Furtado himself admired, a Mme Vidal. On the evening of 24 August 1673, Dellon was accosted by the Criminal Judge of the city, who commanded him to follow him to the prison, 'without deigning to acquaint me by what authority until I entered... When my conductor told me it was by order of the Inquisition, my astonishment was so extreme that I was for some time motionless.'

Since the Tribunal took little interest in sexual matters, there had to be a doctrinal justification for proceedings. According to Dellon, this was provided by an Indian Dominican, who was Secretary to the Holy Office. Again, according to Dellon, this priest also lusted after Mme Vidal, who had told him that he 'had repeatedly solicited her to gratify his infamous passion.... On noticing my attentions, he became as jealous as the Governor, and although he had hitherto been on friendly terms with me, and I had even done him some important services, he eagerly joined with Don Manuel Furtado in oppressing me.'

The priest claimed that Dellon had expressed heretical views on baptism. It was also claimed that he had failed to show due reverence to the alms boxes common in Portuguese India, which bore images of the Virgin Mary and the saints. 'I for some time refused to kiss the cabinet, whence it was concluded ... that I despised it and was consequently heretical.'[23]

Dellon was held in the prison at Damão for several weeks. On Christmas Eve, he was visited by the Abbé Carré. 'Knowing how dangerous the Inquisition was... ', he wrote, 'I pretended I had great repugnance at visiting this young Frenchman, and that I was only doing so out of consideration for his parents.' He had agreed to take a letter from Dellon to his family back to France. To the Abbé's amazement, the other prisoners begged him not to try to secure Dellon's release because local families had been sending food and clothing to him, which he had shared with his fellow unfortunates.[24] On 1 January 1674, Dellon embarked for Goa, arriving there two weeks later. Pending his initial examination by the Inquisitor, he was held in the *Aljeuvar*, the common prison, which he described as,

> more foul, dark and horrible than any one I had seen ... The stench was excessive; for there was no other place for the necessities of the prisoners than a well sunk in the floor, in the midst of the cavern, which it required some resolution to approach; from which cause part of the odure [*sic*] remained on the brink, and the greater part of the prisoners

did not even go so far, but made their evacuations all around. When night approached, I durst not lie down for fear of the swarms of vermin which everywhere abounded, but I was constrained to recline against the wall.[25]

On the morning of 16 January, an officer arrived with orders to take Dellon before the Grand Inquisitor, Francisco Delgado Ematas, a secular priest aged around forty. After a brief interview, during which Dellon claimed that he was not made aware of the charges brought against him, the *Alcaide* (gaoler) took him to a long corridor, where an inventory was taken of his possessions and everything was taken from him except his rosary, his handkerchief and some gold pieces that he had secreted in one of his garters, He was told that his things would be restored to him on his release, but he claimed that nothing of value was ever returned. He was then locked in small cell and saw no-one until his supper was brought to him. He requested books but was told they were not permitted.

Over the next two years, he was brought before the Inquisitor on several occasions, each time hoping to be discharged. He stated that what seems to be an absurdly lengthy incarceration without a verdict being delivered was due to the practice of retaining prisoners until there were enough to make the *Auto da Fé* procession a sufficiently compelling spectacle: Fryer reveals that the *autos da fé* were held annually on the feast day of 'St Iago' (St James), 25 July, but he did not witness one himself.[26] It may be the length of this incarceration that caused François de la Boullaye-le-Gouz to believe that those arraigned by the Inquisition simply disappeared.[27] Dellon considered that the prisoners of the Inquisition were 'tolerably well kept...' There were three meals daily. Breakfast was at six, dinner at ten and supper at four. Breakfast 'for blacks is generally cange (water mixed with rice) and their other meals consisted of rice and fish.' White people were 'treated more delicately. In the morning they receive a soft roll, weighing about three ounces with fried fish and fruits'. On Sundays and sometimes on Thursdays, they were given a sausage.

'The sick receive every necessary attention', he wrote. Rich prisoners were treated in exactly the same way as the poorer ones; indeed, they were obliged to contribute towards the upkeep of their less affluent fellows.

It was the 'perpetual and rigid silence' combined with the solitary confinement that Dellon found most distressing. He claimed to have 'succombed [sic] to despair' and 'attempted to put an end to my existence' on at least two occasions. After each attempt, the Inquisitor ordered that he should be put on a special diet and placed in a cell with a companion.

Eventually, Dellon claimed to have been brought before the Tribunal of the Inquisition with a large number of others. They wore the *sambenito* or penitential hood, which reflected the nature of their offence and they were arraigned in the order of the severity of their alleged transgressions. They were then marched barefoot to the Franciscan church, where a sermon was preached. Two were then taken to the riverside, where they were burnt at the stake. Those who professed the Christian faith were strangled before this ordeal. Even the dead, he wrote, were not immune from the attentions of the Inquisition: the bones of those considered guilty of offences when living were disinterred and their estates were forfeited.

Dr. John Fryer, an English visitor later in the seventeenth century saw some of those who had been sentenced by the Inquisition for a specific offence.

> As we rowed by the Powder Mills, we saw several the Holy Office had branded with the names of Fetisceroes, or Charmers, or in English, Wizards, released thence to work here, known by a Yellow Cope, weed, or Garment, like our City poor Pensioners, Sleeveless, with a Hole for their Neck only having a Red Cross before and behind.[28]

Dellon and the other remaining prisoners were ceremonially pronounced excommunicate. He was then sentenced to five years serving on the galleys. Unlike the others, he was taken to Portugal, where he was released after one year of servitude, following an appeal from the French authorities.[29] Dellon's account of his experiences, *Relacion de l'Inquisition de Goa*, published in 1688, reveals the terrible ordeal of incarceration in a contemporary prison but it can scarcely be said that he suffered the worst excesses attributed to the Inquisition; nor did he appear to suffer any lasting ill-effects. Ever the romantic, he dedicates his book to one Mlle du Cambaut de Coislin, stating that it would be wrong to complain of his treatment, since it gave him the opportunity to dedicate his book to her.

Dellon recounts the stories of some other prisoners and their fates. Fr Hyacinth was a Dominican priest who had lived a 'dissolute' life at Surat. After the death of the woman who had borne him several children, he resolved to reconcile himself to his Order. He travelled to Diu where the Order reinstated him but he was obliged to report to the Inquisition, which imprisoned him and sequestered all his worldly goods before releasing him.[30] Joseph de Pereira de Meneses was a Fleet Commander who was ordered in 1668 to take a force to relieve Diu, which was under siege by the Arabs. His expedition was delayed by hostile winds and the city fell. On his return to Goa, he was charged with cowardice and paraded through the streets by the public hangman. Worse followed as an enemy persuaded his servants to accuse him of sodomy with his page. He was sentenced to death, but the Inquisitor decided to question the witnesses separately. Such was the discrepancy in their testimonies that Pereira, who never ceased to protest his innocence, was acquitted and the perjurers were sentenced to periods of exile in Africa.[31] In a third case a soldier in Damão made friends with two young sailors. They travelled to Goa together and he got married in Damão before embarking. In Goa he saw the chance to make an advantageous match and wed again, calling on his friends to certify before the priest that he was a bachelor. When he returned to Damão to visit his wife, the second wife's brother became suspicious and denounced him to the Inquisition. Despite protesting that they knew nothing of his first marriage, the two sailors were sentenced to three years exile on the coast of Africa, while the bigamist received seven years of exile after which he was to return to his first wife (she appears to have had no choice in the matter).[32]

In these cases, the Inquisition's responses were unexceptional. An ecclesiastical tribunal was bound to take a dim view of a promiscuous priest who had contravened his vows of celibacy and poverty. In having his worldly goods removed, Fr Hyacinth may be deemed to have got off lightly. Sodomy was universally an offence at the time that Dellon was writing and was punishable by death in many countries: the death sentence remained on the Statute Book in England until 1861 and in Scotland until 1887. The actions of the Inquisitor in probing into the case demonstrates that pains were taken to ensure that justice was done in this case. Bigamy remains an offence in all countries that retain the traditional commitment that marriage should be a monogamous condition.

Dellon's account of his treatment was what anti-clerical Europe wanted to hear and certainly contributed to the growth of what became known as 'the Black Legend'. Fifteen editions were published in Amsterdam, London, Lyons, Paris, Cologne and Rotterdam between 1688 and 1709. It set the pattern that was to be incorporated into the Gothic horror genre of the next century and tts continuing popularity is demonstrated by the fact that a translation was published in Pittsburgh as late as 1819. The only other contemporary accounts of the proceedings of the Inquisition predate Dellon's and contrast with it greatly. They concern a French Capuchin friar, Fr Ephrem de Nevers, who travelled overland to Surat in 1641. He visited the newly established English outpost of Fort St George in Madras. He founded the small church of St Andrew on the invitation of an official of the East India Company and ministered there for the next eight years. Outraged by the excesses of Portuguese priests in the town, he wrote a letter of complaint to Manuel de

Mascarenhas, the Captain Major of São Tomé de Meliapore (Mylapore), the Portuguese territory that surrounded the English colony. As a result, he was seized by Portuguese officials, placed in irons and shipped to Goa, where he arrived on 15 January 1650 and spent the next 18 months as a prisoner of the Inquisition.

As with all the records of the Inquisition in Goa, there are no surviving official records of Fr Ephrem's trial, but two accounts of it exist. One is by Niccolao Manucci, a Venetian merchant who was a friend of his. In his *Storia do Mogor*, he details the proceedings 'to the public just as I learnt it from the father himself'.[33] The second account is provided by a French dealer in gems, Jean-Baptiste Tavernier. The two accounts, although almost certainly produced independently of each other, have much in common. Each regards Fr Ephrem's arrest as the product of malignant acts of jealousy and give similar accounts of the conditions of his confinement. The accounts agree with Dellon's claim that the treatment of prisoners was 'tolerable'. The cell in which Fr Ephrem was confined was small, but very clean. Regular healthy meals were provided. He was allowed access to reading material to help him prepare his case and a Father Commissionary of the Franciscan Order was appointed to defend him. Yet, curiously, he was not allowed to go to confession, receive communion or to attend Mass during Holy Week and he was denied a Missal or a Bible. Perhaps those under scrutiny by the Inquisition were regarded as excommunicate until proven otherwise. Fr Ephrem faced several charges, including the absurd allegation that he was a Calvinist. He was also charged with saying that Anglican priesthood possessed some validity. He would not be the last Catholic priest to suggest that.

A fellow Capuchin, Fr Zenon de Beaugé, journeyed to Goa to make representations for Fr Ephrem. On arrival, he was visited by friends who were aware of the purpose of his journey, and who warned him not to advocate for Fr Ephrem

> [u]nless he wished to keep him company in the Inquisition. Every one knows the strictness of this tribunal, and not only is it not permitted ... to speak for one whom they hold prisoner, but moreover they never confront the accused with those who give evidence against him, nor even allow him to be acquainted with their names.[34]

Eventually Fr Ephrem was released after agreeing to read a mild public acknowledgement of his errors from the pulpit of the Se Cathedral. Dellon knew of the accounts of Fr Ephrem's treatment by the Inquisition. Indeed, apart from the horrors he alleges about the *Auto da Fé*, the stories are very similar, so the question arises as to what extent he might have used the material about the cleric to colour his own version. There are also discrepancies in Dellon's account. He appears to believe that people professing religions other than Christianity came under the remit of the Inquisition, but this was not the case. He writes of the huge crowds that the *Auto da Fé* attracted 'from all parts of India', so it is surprising that few other accounts of this ceremony survive.

The secrecy that surrounded the Inquisition contributed to the sparsity of first-hand accounts, but also to the terror with which it was regarded. Secrecy breeds rumour and there can be no doubt that, severe though it might have been, there were exaggerated accounts of its dealings. Few of the foreign visitors who wrote of sixteenth-century Goa encountered the Inquisition or even mention it. Indeed, van Linschoten noted that while Hindu ceremonies of cremation and marriage were forbidden in Goa, the Portuguese dwelt

> in the towne among all sorts of nations, as Indians. Heathens, Moores, Iewes, Armenians, Gusarates, Benians, Bramenes, and all Indian nations and people, which doe al dweil and traficke therein, everie man holding his owne religion without constrayning any man to doe against his conscience.[35]

The Florentine merchant Filippo Sassetti conveys a different perspective. In a letter to his friend, the scholar Bernardo Davanzati, in 1585, he complains that writing about local customs has been made 'difficult and almost impossible by the absolute rule the Portuguese have exercised over this island of Goa' (a remark that, paradoxically, he clearly managed to get past the censor). He also succeeds in transmitting his views on the economic decline of the colony, which he detects as early as the 1580s. This he attributes to what would now be called a 'brain drain': '[t]he best part of the Gentiles [Hindus]', he comments, 'who had resided there, who were many and very learned, since this was a seat of learning', had moved away.

> The cause for the departure of these people was the request that they should convert: yet, since they were forbidden to read their scientific books, to perform their sacrifices and devotional acts; since their temples were destroyed and they were forbidden again to cross over from here to the mainland to carry out their ceremonies as they were used to, the best amongst them went to live in other places.[36]

Pyrard de Laval considered that the Inquisition was a means of seizing the goods of the better-off New Christians. 'The first time they are taken before the holy Inquisition, all their goods are seized at the same time. They are seldom arrested unless they are rich'. Yet he gives only one specific example—that of 'a Hollander jeweller or lapidary',

> That had resided there five and twenty years and was married to a Portuguese *metice*, by whom he had an exceedingly pretty daughter of marriageable age, and had amassed goods to the amount of thirty or forty thousand crusados. Being at that time on bad terms with his wife, he was accused of having the books of the pretended religion [presumably his previous religion, or even Protestantism], whereupon he was arrested and his goods seized. One half was left to his wife, the other to the

Inquisition. I know not what befell him, but I am inclined to believe that he was put to death, or at the least, lost all his property.[37]

Here is another manifestation of the effects of the obsessive secrecy imposed by the Inquisition. Laval writes of the Dutchman, but is unaware of his fate. If he were indeed a Dutch Protestant he would have been, in theory at least, beyond the official remit of the tribunal. Laval does record another persistent theme, however, that anyone could be denounced to the Inquisition without reasonable cause and the person making the allegations would remain anonymous, suggesting again that the tribunal could be used as a vehicle for revenge or envy.

There may have been a further and more fundamental reason for the arraignment of Dellon, Fr Ephrem and the unnamed Dutchman by the Inquisition. Portugal's eastern empire was coming under increasing threat from other European maritime powers. Dellon had been in the employ of the Compagnie Royale des Indes Orientales and had, on his own confession relayed information of strategic importance back to the Company. His presence in Damão may well have been viewed with suspicion by the authorities, as might his association with the Abbé Carré, who was on his return journey to France bearing important dispatches from Louis XIV's Viceroy in India. He was to entitle his account of his journeys *Le Courrier du Roi en Orient*. Fr Ephrem was certainly no foreign agent, but he had placed himself under the patronage of another rival body, the East India Company. As well as being, on occasions, a means to settle old scores, the Inquisition could, therefore, appear as an expression of Portuguese paranoia about foreign encroachment.

The Inquisition would have held little fear for the Jesuits. It did not interfere with the universities a great deal, although it had the power to ban or amend books. Doubt was cast on the prevailing view of the Spanish Inquisition as cruel and invasive by Julián Juderías as early as 1914.[38] Modern documentary research indicates that the Inquisition was no more cruel than most other contemporary European judicial systems: certainly not that of England.[39] Of course, the original purpose of Francis Xavier in calling for the establishment of the Inquisition in Goa had been to control the tendency of New Christians to revert to aspects of their old religion under cultural pressures and it appears that this remained its primary purpose until its abolition in 1812.

Fátima da Silva Gracias records the fourteen cases that appeared before the Goa Inquisition in two of its sessions, in April 1784-March 1785 and March 1790-March 1791. Ten involved men and four, women. All were ostensibly Catholics. The cases demonstrate that traditional Hindu medicine and 'superstition' continued to exercise its hold over at least some Goan Catholics. Only one of the cases is not concerned with a reaction to a medical condition and concerns a breach of Catholic practice: that of Salvador, a tailor, who appeared before the Tribunal 'for eating meat on forbidden days and making a mockery of the ban'. He was reprimanded and ordered to perform spiritual penance. Many of those who turned to traditional healing methods seem to have done so in desperation. Barthelemeo, a farm labourer, sought help for the safe delivery of Antonia, his wife, while Antonio, who worked at the Mint, did the same on behalf of a sick relative. Manoel, another farm labourer, sought 'the help of the temples to find out if the disease he was suffering was due to witchcraft', while Nicholao, a third, was ordered to perform spiritual penance 'for allowing a woman to perform superstitious rituals in his house for the cure of his son'. The sad case of Feliciana who was presented 'for permitting a non-Christian to perform superstitious rituals' for her sick husband, demonstrates that even the placebo effect could be ineffective. She is described as the 'widow of Antonio Miguel de Azavdo'. Two other elderly widows described as 'midwives', appeared before the tribunal in 1790. Catherina Boteli, aged sixty-six, was presented for attending superstitious rituals. Clearly the Inquisitor took a stern view of quack medicine. She was reprimanded and ordered to practice her trade no longer. The other 'midwife', Anno Pinto, aged seventy-five, was presented 'for attributing the illness of her child to witchcraft and for advising superstitious remedies'. She was ordered to spend two years in exile, in Rachol. Presumably this was at the seminary, which by this time was under the auspices of the Oratorians following the expulsion of the Jesuits from Goa in 1759. Although the general sentence of spiritual penance appears mild, the tribunal could exile miscreants to a place within the colony as a potentially more severe sanction, presumably reserved for repeat offenders. Four others were given this sentence: Feliciana, a superstitious widow from Cuncolim, was sent to Varca, site of the Church of Our Lady of Gloria, for two years, while Domingo, the fourth farm labourer to be presented during this period, who had been 'caught at mid-day while making offerings at a temple on a hillock in the company of other Christians for the cure of a sick person', was ordered to do spiritual penance at Raia, the site of the Church of Our Lady of the Snows. The most severe sentence of exile was passed on Miguel de Souza, who sent to the *Casa de Polvora*, the gunpowder factory at Panelim, for five years. Only one of those presented was not a nominal Christian. Polpotto Naique, a sailor, was accused of bringing a fellow non-Christian across the border to perform rituals at night in a temple 'for the health and happiness of some Christians who were in attendance'. The Inquisition took a dim view of those who sought to divert the flock from the ways of righteousness and despite being aged seventy, he was sentenced to being lashed in the street before being sent to the prison at Ponda for three years.[40]

Roma do Oriente

Goa was the capital of the whole Portuguese empire in the East, which included Mozambique, Ormuz, Ceylon, Malacca, Macao, East Timor, Nagasaki and the various Indian enclaves. The city held the same civic privileges as Lisbon. Its senate and city fathers maintained direct contact with the king and paid a special envoy to represent their interests at court. In 1563, the governor even proposed making Goa the seat of a parliament, in which all parts of the Portuguese East would be represented, but the project was vetoed by the king. The city did possess an elaborate form of local government, with a municipal council of various officials, known collectively as *Officials de Camara*. They had to be Old Christians and could not be, at least openly, of Jewish descent. They were elected triennially under a complicated system of balloting. The *Camara* could convene as a court and it supervised the leasing of municipal land, fixed the price of commodities, licensed street traders, checked the quality of merchandise and was responsible for public works and sanitation.

Whenever a new Viceroy of India arrived, he would be greeted by the Senate at the gateway facing the Mandovi River—one of the four erected by Adil Shah. In 1597 the Viceroy, Francisco da Gama, the grandson of Vasco da Gama, built an impressive 'Arch of the Viceroys' on the site. A small statue of Vasco Da Gama, fully dressed in royal uniform, stands on the top of the arch, on the side facing the Mandovi River. At the time of Thomas Stephens's arrival, Dom Luis de Ataide, Count of Atougaia, had been serving as Viceroy since August 1577. This was his second term in the office. He had been Commander in Chief of the Portuguese forces but the impetuous young king, Sebastiáo, grew frustrated with his prudent advice and reappointed him to India as a means of removing him. As soon as he had arrived in Goa, he began to fit out a mighty fleet to wage war on Ali Adel Shah, the Sultan of Bijapur, but peace had been concluded by the time of Thomas Stephens' arrival. Every year at the beginning of September, the Viceroy would order the assembling of a large fleet of a hundred galiots and three or four galleys. Half of this fleet, the *Armada do Norte*, was then sent northwards as far as Diu or Cambay, to prevent any trade that had not been sanctioned by the Portuguese. The second fleet, the *Armada do Sud* or *do Malavar* ('of Malabar'), went south as far as Cape

Comerin, partly for the same purpose and partly to purge the seas of Malabar pirates.

Almost all manual labour in Goa was done by slaves. Slavery would have been a new phenomenon to Thomas Stephens: it did not exist in England, or indeed in those countries that constituted historic Christendom. The paucity of surviving records does not enable the precise delineation of the Jesuits' attitudes towards the institution in Goa, but the doctrinal pronouncements of the Church and the attitudes of the Society in missions elsewhere make it very likely that they would have opposed it. Fr Peter Claver SJ, who was born the year after Thomas Stephens, worked for thirty-five years to alleviate the suffering of slaves in the New Kingdom of Granada[41] and declared himself 'the slave of the negroes forever'. Such Jesuits were often the only force between Native Americans and slavery. They were frequently seen as interfering with the legitimate colonial enterprises of the royal governments and this, without a doubt, was a contributory factor in their ultimate suppression and expulsion.

In the thirteenth century, St Thomas Aquinas had written that slavery was in opposition to Natural Law, deducing that all 'rational creatures' were entitled to justice. The issue was largely academic in Catholic Europe, but the growth of the plantation system in the colonies would turn all the major maritime powers, both Protestant and Catholic, into slavers. Three major pronouncements were made against slavery by Pope Paul III in 1537, but the aegis of the church could be limited by the bounds set by the civil power. Thus, the Society was neither consistent nor uniform in its approach. At the worst extremity, the Society in Maryland would become a slave-owner itself. Yet in all cases, Catholic theological thought insisted on the obligation of the slave-masters to provide for the spiritual welfare of the slaves. By contrast, in the USA, some Protestant church leaders were uncomfortable with the idea of bringing Christianity into the slave quarters. It would be true to say, however, that it was the Christian vision of the fundamental value of every human being that would do most to fuel the abolitionist movements.

The luxury and ostentation of Goa's rulers had become a byword. Francisco Rodrigues Silviera was disillusioned by what he called the 'organised robbery within the administration', which anticipated the nabobs in the early days of British India.

> It seems a shameful thing, and scandalous to see, what many Viceroys profit from their three-year term. It is not known nor understood, the amount of money they pocket if it weren't for persons who with secret curiosity knowingly observe the five hundred or six hundred thousand cruzados, which in exchange of so much discredit of the royal authority, blood and lives of their fellowmen, they pocket.[42]

Luis Vaz de Camôes described Goa as 'that grave of honest poverty'. 'Of this land', he wrote in 1555, 'I can tell you that it is the mother of despicable villains and stepmother of honest men. For it's always those who set out to make money here that float on the water like inflated bladders.'[43] Fr Alessandro Valignano, the Jesuit Provincial, wrote a careful letter from Goa in 1575 in which he described a governmental system so bad that the Jesuits hesitated to hear the confessions of civil and military officials. He depicted a society of badly-paid soldiers, poorly-armed forts, shabby fleets and a vilely unfair system of justice.

'Each public official', noted Jan Huyghen van Linschoten, 'tried to make the most money possible doing this term of three years.' He considered that only those with 'neither wealth nor practice in Portugal' ventured there.[44]

François Pyrard de Laval noted the many impoverished soldiers in Goa who spent the day seated in the doorways of their shacks, playing the guitar and singing. Passers-by would sit down to chat and tell jokes. These common soldiers often assumed high-sounding titles. According to Pietro della Valle, they had

> no sooner passed the Cape of Good Hope than they all become Fidalgos or gentlemen and add Dom to the simple

name of Pedro or Jeronimo by which they were known when they embarked. This is the reason they are commonly called in derision 'Fidalgos of the Cape of Good Hope'.

According to Pyrard, they never walked out together round the city, 'but only in twos and threes, because often they don't have enough clothing to serve ten or twelve.' Instead they pooled a few silken cloaks, a silken umbrella and a common manservant, so that each of them could take his turn to parade the streets, fashionably attired and with a proper escort.[45] Pyrard also described *'La grande différence d'honneur'*—the subtle nuances of status that defined colonial society, which he compared with the Indian caste system. Most esteemed were the *Portugais de Portugal*, i.e. those who had been born in the home country, followed by those born in India of Portuguese parents, who were called *castiços*. Lower down the order were the *mestiços,* or those of mixed race.[46]

The Portuguese had adopted many customs from the Indians, who, as Pyrard recorded, 'never change theirs'. They drank, Indian-style, from a *gargaleta*, an earthenware vessel with a spout that enabled liquid to be poured into the mouth from a distance, avoiding direct contact with the flask. To be inept in its use marked a person as a *reinol*, or 'griffin', fresh from Europe. Jan Huyghen van Linschoten reveals that women customarily went to church in palanquins, the Indian version of the sedan chair, which permitted modest concealment. Although he describes these women as 'Portuguese', they were most likely to have been the secret Indian wives of Portuguese officials.

The Italian scholar Pietro Della Valle attended the wedding on 19 May 1624 of 'Ventura da Costa, a Native of *Canara*... a domestick servant of Sig. Alvaro da Costa, a Priest and our Friend, Lord of a village near Goa.'[47]

> I and some other friends went thither to accompany the Bride and the Bridegroom to the Church of San Biagio, a little distant in another Village, which was in the Parish of the Bride, where the Ceremonies were perform'd in the

evening for coolness' sake. The Company was very numerous, consisting of many Portugal gentlemen, such, perhaps as few other Canarins have at their weddings. The Bride and Bridegroom came under Umbrellas of Silk, garnish'd with silver and in other particulars the Ceremonies were according to the customs of the *Portugals*, onely I observ'd that, according to the use of the Country, in the Company before the Married Persons there marched a party of fourteen, or sixteen men oddly cloth'd after the Indian fashion, to wit naked from the girdle upward, and their Bodies painted in a pattern with white sand and adorned with bracelets and necklaces of Gold and Silver, and also with flowers and turbans upon their heads, in several gallant fashions, and streamers of several colours hanging down behind them ...

These danc'd all the way both going and returning, accompanying their dances with chaunting many verses in their own Language, and beating the little sticks which they carry'd in their hands ...

The marry'd Couple being return'd from Church to the Bride's House, we were entertained with a handsome Collation of Sweet-Meats in the yard, which was wholly cover'd over with a Tent and adorn'd with trees and green boughs, and the Company sitting around, and the marry'd Couple, on one side at the upper end, upon a great Carpet, under a Canopy. After which we all return'd home, and the Husband stay'd that night to sleep in his Wife's House.[48]

The Patronal Festivals of the many churches created a carnival atmosphere around the city. One of the great events was the Feast of Sao Joao Baptista on June 24th as a thanksgiving for the arrival of the monsoon. The Viceroy would ride out of his palace, accompanied by a procession of gentlemen, all wearing masquerading dress, but without masques. They rode two or three abreast, each duo or trio attired alike and bearing Moorish lances. After hearing Mass in the church, they proceeded to La Carriera de

Cavall, the finest open space in Goa. Many companies of Goan Christians would then march by with banners, drums and arms. Many leapt about, making passes with unsheathed swords. The horseman then divided to embark on a formal ride: one section went down the hill and back up it: the other, up the hill and back down. They then rode in column back down to the piazza of the Viceroy's Palace, where they took their leave of each other.

The local people were known to the Portuguese as Canarins, a distorted form of the name of the language that they spoke, Konkani. They wore long white gowns, which Pyrard considered 'Not at all convenient, because the soil of Gaza is red … insomuch that, whether in summer or winter, the dust or mud stains and soils all their garments. They change them, however, every day, and sometimes oftener.' For footwear they wore *alparcas*, a kind of sandal with several leather soles and gilded straps. Jan Huyghen van Linschoten stated that they wore them 'like antiques with cut toes, and fastened above upon their naked feete'. All Indian men, whether Hindu or Moslem, rubbed sandalwood oil over their bodies. Pyrard found the women of Goa 'very pretty and of good figure'. In complexion, some were as fair as the Portuguese. They were heavily bedecked with jewellery. Their pierced noses were adorned with 'trinkets of gold, silver and jewels' and their fingers covered with trinkets and rings, with rings of gold and silver on their toes. In their ears they wore plates of gold and silver, as large as small saucers, which were studded with gems. On their arms, from their hands to their elbows, they wore what they called *manile*, a word derived from the Portuguese word for bracelet, *manhilas*, made of gold, silver and glass. Much prized were those made of tortoiseshell, worked into all kinds of colours and patterns. Rich women wore massive gold collars, 'of two or three fingers width', which were studded with diamonds.[49] On the death of their husbands, Hindu women 'first take off their trinkets and give them to whom they will'. This was in preparation for their immolation on the funeral pyre, the custom known as *sati* that so shocked the Europeans.

The most eminent of the Brahmins and the 'other Gentiles' always went abroad with a large escort:

> One carries the parasol, another a silver box full of betel, a third, a silver flagon of water for washing. After obeying the calls of nature they wash the private parts; they also carry some water in their palanquins... None of them eat ere they have washed and bathed; and then they use simply a cloth to cover their private parts, leaving off the rest of their clothes while they eat. Their food must be prepared by those of their own race, or even by themselves, no matter how great folks they be; for after food is touched, whether cooked or during the cooking, none durst touch the man who has or carries it; if they had to die, they would not eat anything that had been touched by a man or a woman who was not of their race and faith.[50]

Despite Portuguese efforts to strengthen their hold on the hinterland, the territory was under continual threat. 'The City Goa is sctuate in the kingdome of *Dialacam*, a King of the *Mores*,' wrote the Venetian traveller, Cesare Federici,

> Whose chiefe citie is op in the countrie 8 dayes jorney and is called *Bisapor*. This kinge is of great power, for when I was in *Goa* in the yeere of our Lord, 1570, this king came to give assault to *Goa*, being encamped neere unto it by a River side with an armie of 2 hundreth thousande men of war and he lay at this seige 14 monaths in which time there was peace concluded, & as the report went amongst his people, there was great calamitie and mortality which bred amongst them in the time of Winter, and also killed very many elephants.[51]

Being in the horse trade, Federici could not resist expressing satisfaction at the potential commercial advantage that the death of so many elephants brought. The trade was encouraged by the authorities. The normal dues payable by a ship arriving at Goa was 8% of the value of the cargo, but a ship bringing twenty horses or more paid nothing.

On his arrival in Goa, Thomas Stephens immediately resumed his studies, but they were interrupted by a serious illness—perhaps a reaction to the rigours of the voyage, as suggested by Jan Huyghen van Linschoten, who considered that the variations in the climate caused much of the prevailing sickness.

> The sicknesses and diseases of Goa and throughout India which are common come most with the change of the times and the weather. There reigneth a sickness called mordexijn[52] which so stealeth upon men that it weakneth a man and make him cast out all that he hath in his body and many times his life withal. The bloody flux is very common and dangerouse as the plague with us. They have many continall fevers which are burning agues and consume men whereby within four or five days they are whole or dead. This sickness is very common and hath no remedy for the Portugales but letting of blood but the Indians and Heathens doe cure with hearbes and other such ointment wherewith they ease themselves. This sickness consumeth many Portugales every year, some because they have little to eat and less to drink of that which is nourishing and use much company of women because ye land is natural to provoke them thereunto... Pockes and piles with other secret diseases, they are very common and not concealed. They heal them with the root China. The plague hath never been in India... but poysoning, witchcraft and suchlike whereby some lose their lives is their daily exercise.[53]

Thomas Stephens took a more benign view of things.

> The climate is not painful. The heat, which was formerly said to render the earth uninhabitable, is so much tempered by refreshing winds that it is milder than Italy or Spain... Winter in this country is distinguished from the summer only by rain, and not by cold, so that the greenness of the fields would make you think that it was

summer... For though the forests are scorched by the sun from October to May, the leaves on the trees are still green all the year round.[54]

As a celibate Jesuit, Thomas Stephens would not have been vulnerable to the

> stone, gravel and rupture [which] reigneth much among married men by reason of the great quantitie of water that they drink, being given to all pleasures and riotousness, enjoying what their hearts desire, sitting always with their bellies open in their shirts in gallerie, recreating themselves with the wind that cooleth them...

This situation was exacerbated by the fact that, due to the hazards of the voyage to the east, there were few European physicians in Goa: only those with few prospects in Portugal ventured there. Van Linschoten was impressed by the Indian physicians, who were treated with great respect by the native population, even to the extent of being provided with the protection from the sun accorded to those of high standing.

In 1563, the Viceroy, Dom Francisco Coutinho, ordered that all non-Christian physicians should leave Goa within a month. The decree was clearly more honoured in the breach than the observance, because four years later, the first Provincial Council of Goa banned non-Christian physicians from treating Christian patients, 'on account of the many evils arriving therefrom both to faith and morality'. Further decrees were issued in 1585, 1582 and 1606. Van Linschoten reveals that these decrees were also largely ignored even by those who must have pronounced them.

> There are in Goa many Heathen phisitians [physicians] which observe their gravities with hats carried over them for the sunne, like the Portugales, which no other heathens doe, but [onely] Ambassadors or some rich Marchants. These Heathen Phisitians doe not onely cure their owne nations [and Countriemen] but the Portugales also, for the Viceroy himselfe, the Archbishop and all the

> Monkes and Friers doe put more trust in them than in their owne countriemen, whereby they get great [store of] money and are much honoured and esteemed. The contrimen [in the villages] round about Goa and such as [labour and] till the land are most Christians: but there is not much difference [among them] from the other heathens, for that they can hardly leave their heathenish superstitions, which in part are permitted them, and is done to draw other heathens [to be christened], as also that otherwise they would hardly be persuaded to continue in the Christian faith.[55]

François Bernier, a French physician who visited Goa in the 1560s, revealed that the Indian physicians possessed 'a great number of small books, which are rather collections of recipes than regular treatises. The most ancient and the most esteemed is written in verse...' The practice of the native physicians differed from that of the Europeans in that it was based on set principles.

> A patient with the fever requires no great nourishment; the sovereign remedy for sickness is abstinence; nothing is worse for a sick body than meat broth for it soon corrupts in the stomach of one afflicted with the fever; a patient should be bled on extraordinary occasions and when the necessity is most obvious as whenever there is reason to apprehend brain fever, or when an inflammation of the chest, liver, or kidneys has taken place.

'Whether these modes be judicious', he concludes, 'I leave it to decide. I shall only remark that they are successful in Hindostan...' He did not find it surprising that the native physicians understood nothing of anatomy.

> They never open the body either of man nor beast and those in our household always ran away with amazement and horror whenever I opened up a living goat or sheep for the purpose of explaining the circulation of the blood...'[56]

In the next century, John Fryer, a Fellow of the Royal College of Surgeons, proffered an explanation for this reluctance on the part of the Hindu physicians.

> They are unskilled in anatomy, thinking it unlawful to dissect human bodies, whereupon phlebotomy is not understood, they being ignorant of how the veines lie, but they will worry themselves martyrs to death by leeches, clapping on a hundred at once, which they know not how to pull off until they have fulfilled themselves and drop off of their own accord. Chirurgery is in as bad a plight.... Pharmacy is in no better condition, apothecaries being no better than perfumers or druggists at best...[57]

The French physician Charles Dellon was highly critical of 'the pagan physicians', or 'Pandites', whom he also regarded as 'a sort of people without learning or any knowledge or insight into anatomy':

> All their skills are applied to a certain number of receipts that they have learned from their ancestors. These they apply promiscuously without making the least alteration as often as they meet with a patient afflicted with the same distemper, without making the least reflection upon the different age, sex, constitution or strength of their patient. They are very timorous and rather will let a patient perish than run the hazard of a remedy, which, as they believe, not being sufficiently approved by experience, appears doubtful to them, though they judge the distemper to be mortal or incurable without it.

Yet, he gave credit where it was due:

> Nevertheless it is observed that by their long experience they have made such observations concerning certain distempers peculiar to those countries, that they practice with better success than the most learned foreign physicians, who upon certain occasions must follow their footsteps if they expect to succeed, in their cures in this climate. They allow their clients afflicted with fever in the

> Indies, neither meat nor eggs nor broth... They allow them no other drink but fair water and for the rest of their sustenance they give them a Cange (made of rice, salt and pepper). The Cange, besides that it nourishes well, serves also to quench the thirst... Letting of blood is much used amongst the Indians and with good results.[58]

Neither European nor native medical practitioners possessed much idea of the source of most of the frequent epidemics that raged through the territory. Both cultures tended to ascribe the frequently occurring fevers to 'bad air'. In 1570, several epidemics broke out simultaneously, including a particularly virulent outbreak of cholera that affected around nine hundred people, of whom around a third died.[59] The Society of Jesus made a positive response to the emergency, preparing lists of the sick, distributing food and medicines and fumigating the worst affected area—the Ward of the Potters—with aromatic herbs. The Jesuits' careful tending of the sufferers and the risks that involved to themselves aroused great admiration. People were astonished, not only 'at our familiarity with the sick given that the disease was contagious', but also that no Jesuit fell sick.

Although the Jesuits were not affected by the cholera—they must have had a purer source of water—they were much stricken by the simultaneous outbreak of fever, which must have inhibited their humanitarian efforts. That the Jesuits discussed the possible causes of the cholera outbreak is revealed in a report written by Duarte Leitão. Different causes were put forward for the source of the disease: the majority said it was due to corrupted air because of the presence of a dead elephant in the nearby Carambolim Lake.

> And they let it rot without removing it and the foul smells corrupted the air and provoked this penitential disease. In the beginning, it started with fever and then swellings appeared and the sick became yellow and dropsical, and in the end diarrhoea killed them in a few days.[60]

Finally, an outbreak of bubonic plague also occurred around this time, killing several people. According to van Linschoten, it was a disease that had 'never been in India. Neither is it known to Indians.' It must have been brought by the rats on Portuguese ships. Some indication of this is given by the fact that in Goa it was known as *Firinghi Rog* ('European disease'). That so many epidemics occurred simultaneously was not merely coincidental. The Sultanates of Murtaza Nizam Shah of Ahmednagar and Ali Adil Shah of Bijapur had joined forces in an attempt to oust the Portuguese from India and the city was under a year-long siege by a vast army. Doubtless the resultant cramped conditions and lack of hygiene had contributed greatly to the series of epidemics, but the very factor that had escalated Goa's problems also proved its salvation. Bogged down in the surrounding swamps, the invaders also succumbed to the cholera and were forced to withdraw.

The Jesuits realised that a major contributory factor to the spread of ailments was the unhygienic situation of the city of Goa in its dank, marshland setting. To remedy this, they bought a property on the *Monte do Rosario*, which was regarded as a healthier site. From 1578 onwards, the old building was abandoned progressively as classes were transferred to the new one. The old buildings continued for a while to house the Novitiate, but that too was later transferred elsewhere. The new complex consisted of two buildings connected by a corridor: the *Seminario* and the *Colégio de São Paulo*, and was named the *Colégio de São Roque*.

Notes

1. H. Morse Stephens, *Rulers of India: Albuqueque* (Oxford: Clarendon Press, 1892), pp. 74–87.
2. E. Grey, *The travels of Pietro della Valle in India: from the old English translation of 1664 by G. Havers* (Chapel Hill, NC: University of North Carolina Press, 1976), p. 178.

3. A. Pinto Lobo, *Memoria Historico-Eclesiastica da Arquidiocese de Goa* (Nova Goa: Archdiocese of Goa and Daman, 1933), p. 275.
4. *The Life of Francis Xavier from the French of Father Dominic Bouhours* (Philadelphia: Eugene Cumminsky, 1841), p. 88
5. R. Hakluyt, *The Principal Navigations, Voyages and Discoveries of the English Nation*, vol. 2, Pt. 1 (London: G. Bishop, R. Newberie & R. Barker, 1599), p. 250.
6. H. J. Coleridge (ed), *The Life and Letters of St. Francis Xavier* (London: Burns & Oates, 1890), pp. 151–1.
7. Georg Schurhammer, S.J., *Francis Xaviet, His Life and Times, India 1541–1544* (Rome: Jesuit Historical Institute, 1973), p. 224.
8. *Ibid.*, p. 81.
9. A. Gray and H. C. P. Bell (trans), *The Voyage of François Pyrard de Laval to the East Indies*, vol. II (London: Hakluyt Society, 1887), p. 339.
10. N. Scott Baker and B. J. Maxson (eds), *Florence in the Early Modern World* (Abingdon: Routledge, 2019).
11. A. Cole Burnett (ed.), transcription of the 1598 English translation of *The Voyage of John Huyghen van Linschoten*, vol. 1, pt. 1 (London: Hakluyt Society, 1885), pp. 10–14.
12. Gray and Bell, *The Voyage*, p. 115.
13. A. Goodier, *Saints for Sinners* (San Francisco: Ignatius Press, 1993), p. 77.
14. G. J. Ames, 'Acts of Faith and State: the Goa Inquisition and the French Challenge to the Estado da India'. *The Portuguese Studies Review*, 17.1 (2009), p. 15.
15. C. R. Boxer, 'A Note on Portuguese Missionary Methods in the East', *The Ceylon Historical Journal* (1965), pp. 84–85.
16. Gray and Bell, *The Voyage*, p. 101.
17. G. J. Ames, 'Religious Life in the Colonial Trenches: The Role of the Pai dos Christos in Seventeenth-Century Portuguese India', *The Portuguese Studies Review*, 1.2 (2008), p. 13.
18. Grace that exists prior to and without reference to anything human beings may have done.
19. F. Soyer, *Ambiguous Gender in Early Modern Spain and Portugal* (Brill: Leiden and Boston, 2012), p. 45.
20. G. Parker, 'Some Recent Work on the Inquisition in Spain and Italy', *Journal of Modern History*, vol. 54.3 (September, 1982).
21. According to Dr F. da Silva, the *Conselho Geral do Santo Oficio* in Por-

tugal contains loose bundles of material concerning the Goa Inquisition, with lists of *Actos de Fe*, decrees, accounts and correspondence between the Government and the *Inquisidor General de Goa*.
22. *Les Voyages et Observations du Sieur de la Boullaye le Gouz* (Paris: Gervais Clousier, 1653), pp. 203, 204.
23. G. Dellon, *An Account of the Inquisition at Goa*, trans. A. Bower (Pittsburg: R. Patterson & Lambdin, 1819), p. 25.
24. Lady Fawcett (trans), Sir C. Fawcett (ed.), *The Travels of the Abbé Carré in India and the Near East*, vol. III (London, Hakluyt Society, 1948), pp. 750–760.
25. Dellon, *An Account*, chapters IX, X.
26. T. Roe and J. Fryer, *Travels in India in the Seventeenth Century by Sir Thomas Roe and Dr John Fryer.* (New Delhi: Asian Educational Services, 1993), p. 382.
27. Dellon, *An Account*, chapter XIV.
28. However unpleasant their fate, the 'wizards' of Goa certainly fared better than their counterparts at Salem or at Pendle in Lancashire.
29. *Ibid.*, chapter XXXII.
30. *Ibid.*, chapter XXXVII, pp. 150–153.
31. *Ibid.*, chapter XXXVIII, pp. 153–158.
32. *Ibid.*, chapter XXXIX, pp. 159–161.
33. N. Manucci, *On Mogul India, 1653–1708*, trans. W. Irvine (London, J. Murray, 1906), pp. 407–453.
34. Dr V. Ball (trans), *Travels in India by Jean Baptiste Tavernier* (London: Macmillan & Co., 1889), pp. 220–234.
35. Van Linschoten, *The Voyage*, p. 181.
36. E. Narcucci (ed.), *Lettere di Filippo Sassetti* (Florence: Le Monnier, 1855), pp. 341–351.
37. Gray and Bell, *The Voyage*, p. 93.
38. J. Juderías I, *La leyenda Negra y la Verdad Histórica* ['The Black Legend and Historical Truth'] (Madrid: Tip de la Revista de Archives, 1914).
39. In his book *The Marrano Factory* (Leiden 2001), A. J. Sarrava estimates that between 1561 and its temporary abolition in 1765, 16,202 people were tried before the Portuguese Inquisition, of whom it is known that 57 were sentenced to death and executed and 64 were burned in effigy.
40. F. da Silva Gracias, *Health and Hygiene in Colonial Goa*, Appendix 6-A (New Delhi: Concept Publishing Company, 1994).

Golden Goa

41. The modern Columbia: Peter Claver was canonised in 1888 and is the patron saint of slaves.
42. F. R. Silviera, *Memoirs of a Soldier in India*: quoted by A. de Melo in *On Luis de Camoens,* p. 2. www.colaco.net/1/AdmCamoens2.htm
43. Luis Vas de Cameons: letter of 1555, quoted by M. Mullin in *Trade and Romance* (Chicago: University of Chicago Press, 2014), p. 128.
44. Van Linschoten, *The Voyage,* p. 219.
45. Gray and Bell, *The Voyage,* p. 3.
46. C.R. Boxer, *Race Relations in the Portuguese Colonial Empire, 1415–1825* (Oxford: Clarendon Press, 1963), p. 63, n. 18.
47. Presumably the servant had adopted his master's surname.
48. G. Havers, *The Travels of Pietro della Valle in India from an old English translation of 1664,* vol II (London: Hakluyt Society, 1887), pp. 427–429.
49. Gray and Bell, *The Voyage,* p. 113.
50. *Ibid.,* p. 247.
51. T. Hickock (trans), *The voyage and travaille of M. Caesar Frederick, merchant of Venice into the East Indies* (London: Richard Jones and Edward White, 1588), p. 8.
52. 'A Species of colic, which comes on in those countries with such force that it kills in a few hours; and there is no remedy discovered. It causes evacuations by stool or vomit, and makes one burst with pain. But there is a herb proper for the cure…' F. Carletti, *My Voyage around the World:* tr. H. Weinstock (New York: Pantheon, 1964), p. 227.
53. Van Linschoten, *The Voyage,* p. 115.
54. J. L.Soldanha, *Biographical Note* (Mangalore: Simon Alvares, 1907), pp. xxvi-xxx.
55. Quoted by S. Desouza in *Health Practices and People's Identity* published in Lusotopie 7 (Aix-en-Provence: Institute d'Ethnologie, 2000), p. 456.
56. Quoted by Dr S. K. Pandya in 'Medicine in Goa—A Former Portuguese Territory', *Journal of Postgraduate Medicine,* 28 (1982), p. 123. This is some half a century before Sir William Harvey's *De Motu Cordis,* which is erroneously and frequently cited as the first work on the circulation of the blood. In fact, Harvey's work produced a greater understanding of its function, rather than discovering it.
57. Anonymous, 'John Fryer, M.D., F.R.C.S., British Traveller of the Seventeenth Century and his Impressions of Modern Medicine in India', published in the *Bulletin of the Department of the History of Medicine,* 2 (Hyderabad: Osmania University, 1964), pp. 241–250.

58. I. G. Zupanov, 'Drugs, Health, Bodies and Souls in the Tropics: Medical Experiments in Sixteenth-Century Portuguese India' *The Indian Economic and Social History Review*, Vol. XXXIX, No. 1 (January–March, 2002), pp. 1–45.
59. *Report to the members of the Portuguese Province, Goa. Nov. 16, 1570* (Bibioteca Nacional Lisboa: Funde Geral. 4532.f82v).
60. *Ibid.*, ff.81v–82r.

4

Conversion and Coercion

Portuguese hegemony of trade and her naval might extended over the Indian Ocean, Mozambique, Goa and the other Indian enclaves, as well as Ceylon, Malacca, Timor, Ormuz, Macao, Japan and the Moluccas. Civil and military administrations were established. The Viceroy, based in Goa, had authority over all these possessions. A vital contribution to the infrastructure of the Portuguese Empire was made by the religious congregations of the Catholic Church, which established the facilities in education, health and welfare required for social sustenance. In the *Estado da India*, the Society of Jesus was the most significant of these, although it always set itself apart from the colonial power. By the late sixteenth-century, the Jesuits were responsible for a huge administration, covering schools, hospitals, seminaries and colleges. Churches and chapels were constructed. Native builders created a distinctive style of local architecture, which, advertently or otherwise, coincided with the policy of 'Accommodation'. Agriculture was developed, notably in the cultivation of palm plantations, the native tree whose diverse usage had amazed Thomas Stephens on his first arrival in India. The cost of the enterprise was huge and required administrative skills of the highest order. Large enabling grants were obtained from the Portuguese Crown, but there was always a shortfall, which was made up through alms-giving, bequests large and small, and a measure of commercial enterprise. There may be an element of truth in the allegations made by Jan Huyghen van Linschoten in the 1590s:

> The Jesuits are so cunning in trade, they traffic in bills of exchange and such-like, that they surpass all the secular merchants, so that in all India there is no place where there is something to be gained but they have a hand in it, so that the other orders and religious bodies and also the ordinary people are starting to murmur greatly about it, and to loathe their ways and avarice.[1]

There is little or no evidence that the Jesuits as a whole reneged on the spirit of their vows or ceased to be conscious of their God-given duties. Yet there can be no doubt that the sheer scale of the Society's social enterprises that led to such accusations. Two institutions alone were astonishing in their scale, scope and organisational capacity: the Royal Hospital and St Paul's College.

The Royal Hospital

The colony of Goa was one of the first places where the state had an input into welfare and medicine. The *Santa Casa da Misericorda*, or Holy House of Mercy, was a publicly-supported institution that worked with the needy, providing them with food, clothing and healthcare. There are references to it from as early as 1510. It was run by a confraternity of lay brothers and was closely modelled on its mother house in Lisbon. It was a flourishing organisation that began with a hundred brothers, swelling to four hundred by 1595 and six hundred in 1609. Welfare was a form of proselytising: the institution was only for Christians. It provided homes for widows, orphans and 'fallen women', dowries for the female orphans in its care and jobs for the men prepared to marry them.

The most likely institution for Thomas Stephens's convalescence after his voyage was the *Hospital Real*, the Royal Hospital on the banks of the Mandovi River near the Se Cathedral. Founded by Alfonso de Albuquerque shortly after the conquest, it had grown from small beginnings into one of the best hospitals in the world. It was handsomely supported by the Kings of Portugal, who subscribed 25,000 pardoes a year towards its upkeep. The hospital was for men only and constituted one of the earliest examples of state-funded medical treatment, with the Government of Goa contributing large sums towards its upkeep. Under canon law, priests and religious are not permitted to practice medicine without a papal dispensation. The activities of the Society of Jesus in the mission field would have been inhibited without one and the Papal document *Unigeniti Dei Filii* granted this faculty in 1576, but it was only to be employed if there was no secular doctor available. The injunction did not apply to Temporal Coadjutors, Jesuit Brothers who were not ordained to the priesthood. Such a one was the noted surgeon Pedro Afonso, who began working in 1560 at the hospital that Padre Paolo Camerto had founded in 1551. Every day, scores of out-patients waited patiently for him outside the front door of the hospital. The demand for his services was huge. 'From time to time', he commented, 'I run out of paper for writing prescriptions'.

The Society was extremely reluctant to become involved in running the Royal Hospital. The Superior General Claudio Acquaviva considered that the administration of such an institution was in breach of the Society's constitution. More practically, it may have been considered a strain on limited resources. With the arrival of each new Viceroy, the Jesuits attempted to relinquish their charge, without success.[2] From the point of view of the authorities, the Society's discipline and dedication made it ideal for the task. After an epidemic caused many deaths in the hospital in 1578, the Provincial Ruy Vicente, SJ, agreed to accept the charge on behalf of the Society on a temporary basis, after which responsibility for its administration was to be transferred to the *Santa Casa da Misericordia*. Unfortunately, this arrangement did not work out and in 1591, the Viceroy Matias de Albuquerque ordered the Jesuits to take over again. Order was immediately imposed in the form of a written *Regimenta* to which patients and staff had to adhere, 'because the life and health of the sick depends on a good cure, and on its order'. The day began at 5am with Mass, which all who were capable of so doing were obliged to attend. Breakfast was at seven o'clock, lunch at ten and dinner at five.' Chamber pots were emptied at 11am, and 3pm. All bed-linen was thoroughly washed three times a week and the air of all the rooms was to be purified by the burning of aromatic substances.

The Royal Hospital had a large staff, including the *Mordano* or Jesuit Superior, physicians, surgeons, chaplains, secretaries, a buyer, cooks, washermen, barbers and slaves. The apothecary lived on site and his shop was well-stocked. Each ward had its own orderly, who was in charge of security. He was responsible for enforcing the times when silence was to be maintained and was obliged to provide the Hospital Bursar with a regular stock-take. It must be regarded as indicative of practices in other medical institutions that it was considered noteworthy that the Bursar kept an inventory of everything, 'even of the sick, their names, and of the days of their arrival and departure.'[3] All the staff were paid, except for the *Mordano* and the Chaplain. The scale ranged from twenty-five xerafins a month for the physician to two-and-a-half for menial labourers, who were given their food and half a litre of *urraqua* (locally produced alcohol) per day.[4]

As well as the hour-to-hour running of the hospital, the regulations laid down an annual timetable. In March and April, rice and sugar arrived from Bengal. In April and May, spices like cinnamon and cloves, and medicines like *pâo de China* (china root) and *benjoim* (benzoin) were imported from the Portuguese outposts at Malacca and Macao. In June and July, the Royal Hospital was refurbished with new beds and linen, in preparation for the arrival of ships from Europe in September and October, carrying large numbers of sick people. These ships also brought wine, olives and vinegar to be bought by the hospital. All the wards were to be whitewashed for Easter, Christmas and the Feast of the Assumption. Finally, the Hospital Chapel was to whitewashed annually for its Patronal Feast of the Holy Spirit.[5]

There were generally around forty patients, but this number rose sharply when ships arrived from Portugal after their long,

Conversion and Coercion

unhealthy voyage. 'It is verily a royal hospital', wrote the Frenchman Francois Pyrard de Laval, who was a patient, 'excellent and magnificent in all respects, where the sick, both rich and poor, are served with the utmost care, propriety and kindness'.

> Viewing it from the outside, we could hardly believe it was an hospital. It seemed to us a grand palace, saving the inscription above the gate: HOSPITALE DIL REY NOSTRO SEIGNORO. The beds are beautifully shaped and lacquered with red varnish: the sacking is of cotton; the mattresses and coverlets are of silk or cotton, adorned with different patterns ... pillows of white calico.

The patient was provided with a nightgown, cap, slippers, a bedside table on which there was a fan, drinking water, a clean towel and handkerchief, and a chamber pot under the bed. Each patient was served with a complete fowl and the plates, bowls and dishes were of Chinese porcelain. Pyrard continues, 'In the evening they brought us supper at the appointed hour: to each a large fowl roasted, with some dessert, so we were astonished at the good cheer we received'. On admission, the patient was given a haircut and a wash and issued with bedclothes. There was even an out-patient facility: 'He that will not lie there, and hath any woundes or privie diseases may come thether twice every day and be drest, and goe his way againe, without any question or denial.'[6] The food was excellent, as the Jesuits purchased provisions from all over the region.

As was characteristic of contemporary European medicine, bleeding of patients was frequent, but during the seventeenth century, Indian practices began to creep in. The most disturbing of these, at least for newcomers to the sub-continent, was the insistence that, before they could be discharged, they must drink three glasses of *pissant de vache* each day, in the morning, at midday and in the evening. Pyrard notes that this was to help them 'recover their colour and get themselves in perfect health'. Unsurprisingly, many patients were somewhat reluctant. 'The convalescent swallows as little of it as possible, however much he may desire to recover his health', but he was not allowed to leave until he had partaken in full.

If regulations reflect the necessity to curb abuses, then the Royal Hospital did not always run as smoothly as intended. A *proviso* (decree) by the Viceroy of 25 May 1595 forbade too many relations or friends from visiting the patients at any one time and bringing food that had not been approved by the physician or the surgeon. At times of silence, all visitors were barred and the door was kept firmly locked. Weapons were banned: it appears that some visitors had taken the opportunity to settle old scores with the patients. Patients were not permitted to receive letters from women other than their mothers, wives or sisters and even these were censored. It appears that many patients were so disturbed by the contents of the letters that they received from lady friends that their condition deteriorated.

Once he had recovered from his illness, Thomas Stephens was rapidly advanced to Holy Orders as 'there was a vast number of souls to be harvested and extremely few labourers'. Many of these who so laboured were already known to him. Pietro Berno had travelled to India with the same fleet, possibly also on the *São Lourenço*: Matteo Ricci had arrived in Goa the year before, together with Rodolfo Acquaviva, Nicolas Spinola, Francisco Paolo and Michele Ruggieri. In 1588, an Italian Jesuit, Fr Lazzaro Cattaneo, arrived in the colony. After four years in Goa, he joined Matteo Ricci's mission in China, becoming the first missionary in Shanghai in 1608.

St Paul's College

After ordination, Thomas Stephens went to complete his studies in Systematic Theology at the *Colegio de Sao Paulo dos Arcos* (St Paul's College of the Arches). It had been founded as the *Seminario de Santa Fé* at Goa and grew to be one of the largest colleges in India. Such was its association with the Jesuits that members of the Society in Asia were often referred to as

'Paulistas'. Following an ordinance from King Dom João III in 1556, a wide range of secular subjects was offered to degree and higher degree level, including Music, Latin, Theology, Philosophy and the Arts and Sciences. A letter of 1560 describes the development of the curriculum:

> Philosophy began to be read for those who had finished their lessons in logic: to three lay brothers of the house and to the boys of the college, eleven of whom are Malabaris and three external students. Father Francisco Cabral lectures on medicine every morning from 7 to 9.[7]

In 1560, the foundation stone of the collegiate church of St Paul was laid by Antonio de Quadras, the Provincial of the Society in India. He oversaw the work until its completion fourteen years later. By 1568, some three thousand students from India and other parts of Asia were enrolled at the College. They were educated free of charge, so, together with the Royal Hospital, the building of numerous and colleges and charitable works, the financial and administrative burdens on the Society were huge. The financial pressure was offset by government grants and donations large and small, but the administration remained a huge task.

The College possessed a hospital and a large library. The first printing press in Asia was established there. It had been intended for a mission in Abyssinia, but had arrived in Goa by mistake. From small beginnings, as Francisco de Souza noted, the College 'so grew in shape, in amplitude of structure, in the number of disciplines as well as in the exercise of knowledge and virtue that it can be compared to all of Europe's colleges'. It was at St Paul's College that *Santos Passos*—the penitential procession on Good Friday characterised by public self-mortification—was introduced into Asia. First-aid posts were erected along the route and the tradition of throwing flowers on the Feast of Our Lady of Mount Carmel on 16 July also originated there.

Pyrard de Laval noted that the students were occasionally entertained with theatrical performances and participated in mock fights in which they were divided between foot soldiers and cavalry and arrayed in order of battle. They attended Mass before their studies began and returned in groups to their lodgings at the close of the college day, singing sacred songs through the streets. Every Sunday morning they formed into groups according to their classes and processed to the Church of Bom Jesus, carrying crosses and banners and chanting hymns.[8]

It is surprising that only one Indian was admitted to the Society of Jesus during its mission in India until its suppression in 1773, perhaps reflecting suspicions about the integrity of native converts. Pero Luís Bramane was born a Brahmin in a village in Kerala in around 1531. Around the age of fifteen, he converted to Christianity. He was extremely useful to the Jesuits as an interpreter of the Malayalam and Tamil languages. He began studying at St Paul's College and, in 1559, wrote to Diego Laínez, the second Superior General of the Society in Rome, seeking to become a Jesuit. His wish was granted and he was admitted as a novice at St Paul's College in 1561, and ordained priest in 1575.

As a seminarian, Fr Stephens studied Philosophy under Rodolfo Acquaviva, who had arrived in India the year before in the party that included Matteo Ricci, who also joined St Paul's College. He had brought to India mathematical and astronomical instruments and a considerable library that included the works of his old mentor, Christopher Clavius, and the first six volumes of Euclid's Elements. Clearly, the name Thomas Stephens would have been a tongue-twister for the locals, whether Portuguese or Canarin. Accordingly, one of the names by which he became known was Padre Estevam. According to Dodd's Church History of 1742, he was also known as Stephen de Buston or Bubston. Perhaps when he was asked where he came from and replied "England", the reply would be, "but whereabouts in England?", to which the answer was, "Bushton!"

Garcia de Orta

Garcia de Orta had an infinite curiosity about oriental medical practices. Born into a Spanish family of Jewish origin at Castelo de Vide in Portugal, he was educated at the Universities of Salamanca and Alcalá de Henares, where he studied under the renowned classical scholar and botanist Antonio de Nebrija. After practising medicine in his hometown for seven years, he was nominated to the Chair of Moral and Natural Philosophy at the University of Lisbon in 1530. He became a member of the University Council in 1533.

At some point, Garcia de Orta encountered a national hero. Martim Afonso de Sousa had founded the first two Portuguese settlements in Brazil in 1532 with five ships and four hundred men. The following year, he was appointed Captain-Major of the Indian Ocean. He persuaded Garcia, who was then in his mid-thirties, to accompany him to India as his Chief Physician. The invitation must have been irresistible for a doctor with a fascination for exotic travel and Eastern learning. On his arrival in India in 1534, one of de Sousa's earliest acts was to conclude a defensive alliance with Bahadur Shah I, the Sultan of Gujerat, against the Mughal Emperor Humayun. The treaty gave the Portuguese possession of the island fortress of Diu. Garcia de Orca accompanied de Sousa on his various diplomatic missions and military campaigns. Bahadur Shah also appointed him as his consultant physician. He had what may have been his first encounter with the effects of cannabis when Bahadur Shah told him that, 'when at night he wanted to go to Portugal, Brazil, Turkey, Arabia or Persia, he only had to take this *Bhangus*'.[9] This was made up into an electuary with sugar and spices and was called *Maju*.

After de Sousa was recalled to Portugal in 1538, Garcia de Orta settled in Goa, where he established a lucrative practice. His garden was stocked with medicinal herbs. He became consultant physician to successive Viceroys. In 1542, de Sousa returned as Viceroy and reappointed him as his physician. Around 1543,

Garcia married a Portuguese lady called Brianda de Solis, who bore him at least two daughters. He became a close friend of the poet Luis Vaz de Camôes, who praised him in a sonnet.

Martim Afonso de Sousa was again recalled to Portugal in 1544. His successor as Viceroy, Pedro Mascarenhas, granted de Orta a long lease on a property at the southern end of the island of Bombay. He spent several months there each year, living in some style with a large retinue of servants. The English physician Dr Fryer, who spent some time in the city in the next century, described de Orta's garden, filled with medicinal plants, fruit trees and vegetables, as 'the pleasantest in India'.[10] Dr de Orta delighted in discussions with native herbalists and physicians, the Hindu *vaidyas* and the Muslim *hakims*. His *Colóquios dos simples e drogas da India*, published in 1563, was dedicated to de Sousa. It was the earliest treatise on the medicinal plants of the country and the third book to be printed in Goa. It is written as a series of dialogues between the author and a Spanish colleague called Dr Ruano, an Aristotelian traditionalist, and further conversations between a slave girl called Antonia and Malapa, a Hindu physician. Although these characters were fictional, they were probably based on real people. The book gave information on 57 drugs, some of them unknown to Western medicine, including tamarind. He observed that there are two varieties of galangal, one from China (smaller and more potent) and one from Java (thicker and less aromatic). He gave the first description of Asiatic cholera and performed the first autopsy conducted on a victim of the disease. He was intrigued by the use of *bhang* (cannabis), whose use was so prevalent that there was 'no mystery about it'. He explained how a spicy drink was prepared from it and noted its effects. 'The profit from its use is for the man to be beside himself and to be raised above all cares and anxieties, and it makes some break into a foolish laugh...' When de Orta discovered that some of his servants were taking cannabis, he questioned them on its effects. They told him that 'it made them so as not to feel work, to be very happy and to have a craving for food'. Many Portuguese told him that they had experienced the same symptoms when they had taken it, 'especially the female partakers'. He did not, however, regard it as having any medical value.

At the Court of Akbar

In September, 1579, the great project that had caused such excitement in Rome came to fruition. The Mughal Emperor, Akbar the Great, sent an Ambassador called Abdullah to Goa asking for learned priests to be sent to his Court at Fatehpur Sikri. In 1575, he had begun a series of religious discussions in which Muslim scholars debated with representatives of other faiths in the *Ibadat Khana*, his 'House of Worship'. In 1579, he proclaimed himself the supreme arbiter of all religious issues.

Abu'l Fath Jalal ud din Muhammad Akbar was the greatest ruler in India. He had been raised far from the splendours of the Court, in the rugged country of Afghanistan, where he had learnt to hunt and fight, but not to read or write. Despite this, he was as knowledgeable as the most learned of his scholars, having books read to him by his courtiers. He was a great patron of architecture, art and literature. His court was rich in culture as well as in wealth. He was familiar with the practical aspects of artistic creativity, designing and crafting beautiful Persian carpets. Akbar was only thirteen years old when he succeeded Humayun, his father, as Mughal Emperor in 1556. He proved as ruthless a ruler as his forebears. Within weeks of his accession, he ordered the beheading of the Hindu General, Hemu, who had been defeated in battle. When the city of Chittor in Gujerat was taken in 1567, according to Abul Fazl, his vizier, some thirty thousand Rajput prisoners were massacred. 'A monarch should ever be intent on conquest", he declared, "otherwise his enemies rise up in arms against him.'[11]

Akbar was a brilliant administrator of his vast empire. He was an absolute ruler who delegated his powers wisely. His decisions were carried out by four ministers, for financial, judicial, religious affairs and household matters. He built great public works, including roads and canals, and devised fair and efficient methods of taxation.

His policy of religious tolerance extended towards his many wives. As well as Muslim women, he married Rajput princesses to reconcile this warrior people to his rule, and Hindu women for the same purpose. Mughal Emperors had previously used the marriage-bed as an arm of diplomacy, but the wives were obliged to convert to Islam, whereas Akbar encouraged them to maintain their own religious adherence.

With his gift for languages, the Provincial Fr Ruy Vicente may have considered Thomas Stephens for this important mission. However, it was necessary for him to complete his studies, so the expedition was led by his tutor, Fr Rodolfo, who would be accompanied by Fr Francisco Henriques, a convert from Islam, to act as interpreter. He was born in 1538 and educated at Ormuz, joining the Society at Bassein in 1556. The third member of the party was Fr Antonio Monserrate, who was asked by his superiors to keep a journal recording the mission, which he did assiduously.[12] The Jesuits set out on the long journey from Goa on 17 November 1579. They travelled to Surat where they stayed for a month. They then joined a caravan of merchants carrying Chinese silk and other wares. They passed through Gwalior and arrived at Akbar's capital on 28 February 1580, after a journey of forty-three days. Akbar had started to build the city a few years before. It was said that the Emperor, who was heirless at the time, had made a pilgrimage over the 26 miles between Agra and the village of Sikri to visit the renowned Sufi holy man, Shaykh Salim Chishti, who lived there in a hilltop shack. He told Akbar that he would have three sons. In 1569, his Rajput Queen, Maryam Zamani, gave birth to a son, whom he named Salim after the seer and later reigned as the Emperor Jahangir.

Shaykh Salim was a follower of Moinuddin Chishti, who had founded the *Chistiyya* Order in India in the twelfth century. He had propounded the doctrine of *Wahdat-al-Wujud* or Unity of Being, which preached tolerance and respect for religious differences. This was to have a profound effect on Akbar. He made another pilgrimage on foot to Ajmer, the city where this seer had lived. It appears that Akbar's main reason for building the city was nothing more than the fact that Salim Chishti had lived there. Perhaps he felt that the presence of the holy man would sanctify it. He added the name Fatehpur to that of Sikri—'the city of Victory'—because he had just concluded a successful campaign against the Gujerats. Shaykh Salim Chishti died in 1570 and Akbar erected a magnificent tomb on the site where he had sat in meditation in his hermitage. It is one of the finest examples of marble work in India.

The Jesuits must have been astonished by what they saw. The approach to the city was described by Ralph Fitch, who visited it five years later.

> Betweene Agra and Fatepore are 12 miles, and all the way is a market of victuals and other things, as full as though a man were still in a towne and so many people as if a man were still in a market. They have many fine cartes, and many of them carved and gilded with gold, with two wheeles which be drawen with two little Buls about the bignesse of our great dogs in England, and they will runne with any horse, and carie two or three men... they are covered with silke or very fine cloth, and be used here as our Coches be in England. Hither is a great resort of marchants from Persia and out of India, and very much marchandise of silke and cloth, and of precious stones, both Rubies, Diamants, and Pearles...[13]

The city was two miles long and a mile wide and it was built in the brilliant local red sandstone. From afar, a great panorama of domes and pinnacles astounded the eye. As they rode in through the great gates that led into the royal complex, the Jesuits were greeted with the spectacle of a capital city on the scale that befitted the greatest ruler in the East. Building works were still proceeding, with hundreds of masons, carpenters and labourers going about their tasks.

Had they possessed the great gift of foresight, they would have realised from the style of the architecture that the prime purpose of their mission—to convert the Emperor—was unlikely to be successful. The place was an amalgam of influences, incorporating Islamic, Hindu, Jain and even Christian styles, reflecting Akbar's ultimate desire to create a synthesis of various religions. The effect was breath-taking. As they passed through the great gate, the dome and minarets of the *Jama Masjid* (the Friday Mosque), which was one of the largest in India, soared above them. People carrying floral offerings were making their way towards the *dargah* or tomb of Salim Chishti. It had become a place of pilgrimage for Muslims and Hindus alike. Groups of men sat in the courtyard by the tomb, playing their instruments and singing the *quwwals* or songs of devotion, as part of a *sama* or musical assembly. These occasions formed one of the nine principles of the *Chistiyya* order. The pilgrims tied cotton threads to the *jails*, the exquisitely carved marble screens that surrounded the tomb, in the hope that they too would be blessed with offspring. Those participating in this engaging ritual would not have realised that disapproval of miraculous feats was another of the nine principles of *Chistiyya*.

Fatehpur Sikri was a city of elaborate palaces, formal courtyards and translucent pools. Akbar's senior wives had separate residences. The Place of *Jodha Bai* was the *zenana* or harem for his Hindu, wives while the *Panch Mahal* or Palace of Five Storeys housed more of his wives and concubines. He was reputed to have eight hundred in total. Both buildings were zealously guarded by the royal eunuchs. The Emperor granted public audiences and heard the entreaties of the populace in the *Diwan-I-Am*, the great Hall of Public Audiences, seated on a raised platform, elaborately carved in Hindu style that protected him from potential assassins. Everything about Akbar's court was on a grand scale. He possessed a thousand elephants and thirty thousand horses with which to go to war. Fourteen hundred deer grazed in his parks and his menageries contained a huge variety of beasts, including snow leopards, tigers and buffalo.

The Jesuits reported their arrival at the *Naubat Khana* or Drum House near the gate, where important arrivals were announced to the populace. On their way to their audience with the Emperor, the Jesuits passed through his *Parcheesi* court: a huge square marked out as a board on which Akbar played the game, using slave girls clad in different colours as live pieces. Like the great monarch he was, Akbar was available to his subjects. 'It is hard to exaggerate', wrote Fr Antonio, 'how accessible he makes himself to all who wish to have audience of him.' Almost every day he created opportunities for anyone who wished to see him, to do so, whether peasant or nobleman.

> He endeavours to show himself pleasant and affable, rather than severe, to all who come to speak with him. It is very remarkable how great an effect this courtesy and affability has in attaching to him the minds of his subjects.[14]

Akbar received the Jesuits in his House of Private Audience, the *Diwan-khan-I-khas*. In the centre of the audience chamber was a profusely carved column supporting a colossal bracketed capital. The Emperor's throne surmounted this structure. Four narrow causeways ran from the centre to each corner of the room and his four ministers sat at the end of these when their presence was required. The Jesuits were impressed by Akbar's royal bearing and presence. 'This Prince is of a stature and of a type of countenance well-fitted to his royal dignity', wrote Fr Antonio, so that,

> one could easily recognise, even at first glance, that he is the King. He has broad shoulders, somewhat bandy legs well-suited for horsemanship, and a light-brown complexion. He carries his head bent towards the right shoulder. His forehead is broad and open, his eyes so bright and flashing that they seem like a sea shimmering in the sunlight. His eyelashes are very long. His eyebrows

are not strongly marked. His nose is straight and small, though not insignificant. His nostrils are widely opened, as though in derision. Between the left nostril and the upper lip there is a mole.

Akbar had a limp in his left leg, which must have been from birth, for he had never been injured there. He was well-built, 'neither too thin, nor too stout'. When he laughed, his face became 'almost distorted'. His expression was 'tranquil, serene and open, full also of dignity, and when he is angry, of awful majesty'. Akbar greeted the Jesuits with extraordinary warmth. When they presented him with the Bible and the two holy portraits that had been dispatched to Goa, he received them with great reverence, holding them until his arms ached. As a cradle Muslim, Akbar would have been familiar with the figures of Mary and Jesus. The Blessed Virgin is the only woman mentioned in the *Q'uran* and one of its eight chapters is named after her. The Emperor's own mother bore her Arabic name, Mariam. The virgin birth of Jesus betokened that he was the last and greatest of the prophets, but not, as in Christian belief, divine.

> Some time later, a nobleman, a relative of Akbar, asked the officer in charge of the royal furniture for the picture of the Virgin. He placed it on a bracket on the wall of the balcony at the side of the royal audience chamber. Thinking it would please Akbar, he surrounded it with hangings of cloth and gold and embroidered linen. The Emperor was delighted. This gave great pleasure to the priests, who, as Fr Antonio notes, perceived that the non-Christians were worshiping and reverencing the picture, and—as if compelled by the unaided force of the truth—were not denying veneration to the image of her whom the morning stars extol, and whose beauty amazes the Sun and Moon.

Akbar assigned his court artists to study painting with the Jesuits. They were ordered to attend catechism classes and to paint what they heard. Thus they recorded the pageantry of the liturgy and learned European techniques of perspectives and light. Akbar gave the Jesuits permission to convert a room in the palace into a chapel. When they asked that this should be put in writing, he replied that this was unnecessary, since his presence was living writing. Fr Francisco Henriques created a chapel that was 'well-appointed, with its perfumes and fragrances'. He bought oil lamps that were supposedly from Mecca in the bazaar. The Jesuits had had a copy made in Goa of a picture illustrating the legend that St Luke painted the Virgin and Child: a popular subject of the period. As good as his word, Akbar visited the chapel. On entering, he removed his turban and knelt on the ground with great devotion. There is a sign of the Emperor's desire for a fusion of religions in Father Montserrate's description of the scene:

> He prayed before the picture of Christ and of the Virgin. Venerating thrice, once in our manner, the other in that of the Moslems and the third in the Hindu fashion, that is to say, prostrate, saying that God should be worshiped with every form of adoration.

Akbar extolled the pictures to his retinue, who were waiting outside, before returning to the chapel with his chief courtiers and his many excellent court painters. They were all struck with wonder and 'could no longer contain their great joy at seeing the Infant Jesus in his Mother's arms. They declared that there could be no better artists or paintings than these.' While gratified by the devotion shown by Akbar and his officials, the Jesuits were at pains to explain that the icons were not objects of worship *in themselves*, addressing a letter of explanation to the Emperor.

> Sire, we do not venerate the images for what they are, because we are well aware that they are merely paper or canvas with pigments. It is because of those whom they represent. Just as with your fermans [decrees]. You do not touch them to your forehead because they are papers covered in ink, but because you know that they contain your order and will.

The religious discussions (the purpose for which the Jesuits had been summoned to Fatehpur Sikri) continued late into the night. Their intellectual rigour came to the fore. According to Pierre du Jarric, the first dispute ended in the complete discomfiture of the Mullas and Caziques, who, unable to find any answer to the arguments of the Fathers, took refuge in silence. Another dispute took place three days later, 'concerning the paradise which the Mahometan law promises to its followers':

> The Fathers assailed the infamous and carnal paradise of Mahomet with arguments so clear and convincing that the Mullas blushed for shame; not knowing what to say in reply. The King, seeing their perplexity, essayed to take up their cause; but he was as little able as they to disprove the incongruities that had been pointed out.
>
> On the following Tuesday, the disputants met for a third time. The Jesuits took the argument to the Mullahs, dealing with 'Mahmet's pride... and the irregularities of his life; All of which with the humility and purity of life of Jesus Christ; and in a like manner they contrasted the truth of the Christian doctrine; which a thousand miracles has confirmed, and the holiness of those who have proclaimed it to the world, with the fables and inconsistencies of the law of Mahomet, which has been spread abroad by means of the sword. In this dispute the Mullas were again put to confusion; and they never, from that time, had the hardihood to meet the fathers in debate. The latter, however, were treated by the King with the same kindness as before.[15]

As their stay at Akbar's Court lengthened, the Jesuits became familiar with its routine. At dawn, when the cocks crowed, a 'barbaric din' was kept up for a full hour on trumpets, bugles, rattles, bells and anything that was to hand. Everything that occurred in the palace was regulated by a highly-ingenious clock. It consisted of brass vessels filled with water that filtered into a bronze cone that took exactly a quarter of an hour to fill through a small hole in the bottom. It was overseen by orderlies who would strike the time on bronze gongs.

Fatehpur Sikri was far from complete. New buildings were rising at an astonishing rate. Akbar built a very large peristyle, two hundred feet across and surrounded by colonnades, in just three months, and circular baths three hundred feet in circumference, complete with dressing-rooms, private apartments and many water channels, in six months. He did not care for the din that the works engendered, so he had all the parts of the structure precisely fashioned elsewhere and then brought to the site and fitted together. The priests were fascinated by this process and reflected on the Biblical story of the building of the Temple in Jerusalem, which states that no iron instruments of the builders were heard. The example of Fatehpur Sikri made them realise that the story was not necessarily an account of the miraculous. Such was the enthusiasm of Akbar for his building works that he sometimes gave a hand with the quarrying himself. He amused himself by learning artisan trades and built workshops near the palace, which contained studios that Fr Antonio describes as 'for the finer and more reputable arts, such as painting, goldsmith-work, tapestry-weaving, carpentry, curtain-making and the manufacture of armaments'. He found it relaxing to watch the artists at work.

Akbar had appointed around twenty Hindu chieftains to assist in the task of governing his empire and controlling the royal household. Fr Antonio notes that:

> They are devoted to him and are very wise and reliable in conducting public business. They are always with him, and are admitted to the innermost parts of the palace, which is a privilege not allowed even to his Mughal nobles.

When Akbar was deliberating on important decisions, he would ask each of his councillors privately for his view and then decide on the course which seemed to be supported by the largest number and the most experienced. He even asked their advice on matters on which he had already made up his mind, saying,

"This is what I think should be done. Do you agree?" They would reply "Salaam, O King"; whereupon he said, "Then let it be carried out". If anyone did not agree with him, he listened patiently, and sometimes altered his opinion. The Emperor was astute enough to grasp that economic control was tantamount to political control. When princes who had been driven from their dominions appealed to him for protection, he would furnish them with troops and resources—on the condition 'that they shall employ only his own weights and measures and money coined by himself.'

Part of the means to finance the governance of his great empire came from Akbar's almost perpetual state of war, which gave him the spoils of the kings and chieftains he subdued. He seized their treasure and exacted great levies on his new subjects, many of whom were ruined by the financial burdens. 'The King,' recorded Fr Antonio,

> exacts enormous sums in tribute from the provinces of his empire, which is wonderfully rich and fertile both for cultivation and pasture and has a great trade both in exports and imports. He also derives much revenue from the hoarded fortunes of the great nobles, which by law and custom all come to the King on their owners' death. He also engages in trading on his own account, and thus increases his wealth to no small degree; for he eagerly exploits every possible source of profit.

Akbar allowed no bankers or money-changers to operate in his empire. Gold, silver and copper coins could only be exchanged at the royal treasuries, a huge monetary market that generated enormous profits. He made a quarterly public display of his great wealth in which sacks of copper money were piled in a heap ten feet wide and thirty feet high. The superintendents and tellers of the Treasury sat beside it and paid out those to whom money was owed, after subtracting the amount that would have been deducted if it had been deposited in a bank. Each sack held about four thousand coins. The officers, secretaries, and paymasters who administered the royal supplies and granted safe-conducts, passes and contracts were accommodated in a very large hall.

> This secretariat is presided over by a chieftain of great authority and ability who signs the royal 'farmans'. These are eight days afterwards signed by one of the queens, in whose keeping is the royal signet ring and also the great seal of the realm. During the eight days interval every document is most carefully examined by the confidential counsellor and by the King himself, in order to prevent error and fraud. This is done with especial care in the case of gifts and concessions conferred by the royal favour.

Akbar's palace was approached through four great gates, each with its custodian, namely the Chief Executioner, the Chief Doorkeeper, the Chief Trainer of Gladiators and the Chief Dispatch Runner. The dispatch runners carried messages to and from all parts of the empire. Some of them could run as far in a day as a horse ridden at full speed. It was said that they had their livers removed in infancy in order to prevent shortness of breath. To strengthen their leg muscles they trained in shoes made of lead, or stood on each leg alternately and pressed their heels against their buttocks. 'Base-born' prisoners were handed into the custody of the Captain of the Dispatch Runners or the Chief Executioner, who kept them in irons but did not imprison them. Princes sentenced to imprisonment were sent to the gaol at Gwalior, 'where they rot away in chains and filth'. Noble offenders were handed over to other nobles to determine their punishment.

As in contemporary Europe, the punishment of malefactors could be cruelly severe. 'Those who are guilty of a capital crime', wrote Fr Antonio, 'are either crushed by elephants, impaled or hanged'. The Chief Executioner was a figure who inspired some awe around the palace, for obvious reasons. Fr Antonio noted that:

> [He was equipped], even in the palace and before the King with many instruments of punishment, such as leather

thongs, whips, bow-strings fitted with sharp spikes of copper, a smooth block of wood used for pounding the criminal's sides or crushing to pieces his skull, and scourges in which are tied a number of small balls studded with sharp bronze nails (this latter weapon must I think be the one called by the ancients the Scorpion).

To the relief of malefactors, no-one was actually punished with these terrifying instruments, 'which seem to be intended rather to inspire terror than for actual use'. The same applied to the variety of chains, manacles, handcuffs and 'other irons' that the Chief Executioner hung on the gate in his charge. Akbar was extremely strict with officials who proved corrupt or incompetent. Hence they all strived to do as he desired. Muslim *Sharia* law applied in most court cases, but the most important ones, including all those involving capital charges, were conducted before Akbar himself. To allow time for fair reflection, the guilty in cases that he had tried were not punished until he had given the order for the third time.

Akbar greeted ambassadors with great courtesy, unless they seemed insufficiently aware of his status as a great emperor and appeared to be attempting to manipulate him. Such was the case when envoys arrived from the Turkish Viceroy of Arabia Felix[16] sent in an attempt to persuade him to make war on Philip II. They behaved so arrogantly that the embassy 'vanished in a cloud of smoke'. Akbar did not fear the consequences of putting the chief ambassador in irons and banishing him for a long period to Lahore, whilst his attendants made good their escape.

Akbar employed a body of scribes, with four or five on duty every day. Their task was to note the orders he gave and the business he transacted. They took down everything he said 'with such speed that they appear carefully to catch and preserve his words before they can fall to the ground and be lost'. They reminded Fr Antonio of the chroniclers in the courts of the old Persian kings who are mentioned in the Books of Daniel, Esdras and Esther. Akbar's court was what would now be called a meritocracy. 'Men of low birth', wrote Fr Antonio, upstarts, and (as the Mongols say) 'men who have risen', together with those of alien birth, are given posts in the royal household if the King finds them capable and efficient, and are gradually promoted. But if such men practice mean and contemptible tricks or intrigues, he bids them always carry about with them the tools of their original handicraft, lest in their vulgarity and insolence they ever forget the low station from which they have sprung.

Akbar was a great patron of learning, also. Fr Antonio tells us that,

> [h]e always keeps erudite men around him, who are directed to discuss before him philosophy, theology and religion, and to recount to him the history of great kings and glorious deeds of the past. He has an excellent judgement and a good memory, and has attained a considerable knowledge of many subjects by means of constant and patient listening to such discussions. Thus he not only makes up for his ignorance of letters (for he is entirely unable either to read or write), but he has also become able clearly and lucidly to expound difficult matters. He can give his opinion on any matter so shrewdly and keenly, that no one who did not know that he is illiterate would suppose him to be anything but very learned and erudite—and so indeed he is, for in addition to his keen intellect… he excels many of his learned subjects in eloquence, as well as in that authority and dignity which befits a King.

Akbar was devoted to hunting, riding elephants, camels and horses. He drove a two-horse chariot, on which he appeared 'very striking and dignified'. He loved singing, concerts, dances, conjuring tricks, and 'the jokes of his jesters, of whom he makes much'. Yet the burden of his huge responsibilities was never far away: Fr Antonio notes that, '[a]lthough he may seem at such times to be at leisure and to have laid aside public affairs, he does not cease to revolve in his mind the heavy cares of state'. Except when he held public banquets, the Emperor generally dined alone, reclining on a couch covered with silken rugs and cushions stuffed with fine down. 'His table is very sumptuous', wrote Fr Antonio:

> Generally consisting of more than forty courses served in great dishes. These are brought into the royal dining-hall covered and wrapped in linen cloths, which are tied up and sealed by the cook, for fear of poison. They are carried by youths to the door of the dining hall, other servants walking ahead and the master-of-the-household following. Here they are taken over by eunuchs, who hand them to the serving girls who wait on the royal table.

Akbar rarely drank wine, but this was not in obedience to Quranic injunctions against alcohol. His favoured drink was 'post', an alcoholic beverage made from the poppy. When he had drunk 'immoderately' of it, he would sink back, 'stupefied and shaking'. Similarly, there was a carnal side to the great Emperor. In his *zenana* he had thirteen wives and hundreds of concubines. His Grand Vizier Abul Fazl was censorious of his other moral foibles.

> His Majesty has established a wine shop near the palace ... The prostitutes of the realm collected near the shop could scarcely be counted, so large was their number ... The dancing girls used to be taken home by the courtiers. If any well-known courtier wanted a virgin they should have first His Majesty's permission. In the same way, boys prostituted themselves and drunkenness and ignorance soon led to bloodshed... His Majesty called some of the prostitutes and asked them who had deprived them of their virginity. This was the state of affairs during Akbar's rule, where alcoholism, sodomy, prostitution and murderous assaults were permitted by the king himself. The condition of civic life during Akbar's life is shocking.[17]

Yet part of Akbar's greatness was his ability to listen to criticism. When Fr Rodolfo reproved him sharply for his licentious relations with women, instead of resenting the priest's audacity, he blushingly excused himself. The Jesuits were equally shocked by the Islamic practice of polygamy, which they regarded as little more than licensed prostitution. 'Muhammad', wrote Fr Antonio,

> invented and introduced among the Musalmans two forms of marriage.

> First that with regular consorts, who may number four, and second, with those who are merely called wives, and who may be as numerous as a man's resources allow. Musalman kings employ this sanction and license of the foulest immorality in order to ratify peace and to create friendly relationships with their vassal princes and/or neighbouring monarchs. For they marry the daughters and sisters of such rulers. Hence Zeldanus[18] has more than 300 wives, dwelling in separate rooms in a very large palace.

Despite his huge entourage of women, Akbar did not possess great fecundity. When the priests were at his court, he had only three sons (as Shayk Salim Chishti had prophesied) and two daughters.

It may seem a contradiction, given this huge entourage, that Akbar should have possessed a deep 'hatred of debauchery and adultery', but this is to miss the point. Women who had been debauched, however innocent they may have been, were almost certainly condemned by the prevalent social mores to prostitution from that point on. This is why Akbar made a habit of asking prostitutes who had deprived them of their virginity. The severity with which he regarded those who had dishonoured eligible maidens is demonstrated by his treatment of his Chief Trade Commissioner. Although he was married, the man had violently debauched a well-bred Brahmin girl. Antonio writes, 'The wretch was by the King remorselessly strangled. Although Muhammed did not forbid unnatural crime, yet Zeldanus punished those who are guilty of such crimes by savage scourging with leather thongs.'

According to Fr Antonio Monserrate, the prince's literary education was, 'according to Persian custom', in the hands of 'learned old men of a spurious value (but really their character is as wicked as that of the most abandoned amongst these Muselmans), and of an empty and ostentatious kind of piety.' They also had instructors in the use of weapons and coaching from riding-masters. Akbar gave great care and attention to the education of his two daughters, who were rigorously excluded from the sight of men. They were taught to read and write, and trained in other ways, by selected matrons. Akbar also gave 'a liberal education' to many noble boys and youths who had lost their fathers. Fr Antonio considered that 'in this he might well be imitated by other princes'. Such was the esteem that Akbar developed for the Jesuits that he appointed Fr Antonio as tutor to his son, Murad. The Emperor's opinion was reciprocated by the Jesuits. 'Akbar looks the part for royalty', wrote Fr Monserrate, 'so much so that you can tell he's the King at first glance.'

The Jesuits were not the only religious group to influence Akbar. A Jain delegation persuaded him to renounce hunting, abstain from eating meat for most of the year and to drastically limit the number of days on which animals could be slaughtered. The Jains were involved in Akbar's interfaith discussions late into the night, together with the Jesuits, Sunni and Shi'ite Muslims, and Hindus. To the consternation of the *Ulema*, or Islamic scholars, Akbar was drifting away from Islam. It need hardly be said that the esteemed and vital roles that Akbar bestowed on his Hindu councillors were a cause of disquiet. As early as 1563, he had abolished the tax levied on Hindus when they gathered for their festivals. He instituted a number of measures in direct contravention of *Shari'ah* law, giving permission for adherents of non-Islamic faiths to build places of worship and decreed that Hindus who had been forcibly converted to Islam should be permitted to apostatize (the prescribed Islamic penalty for this is death). He also forbade the forced conversion of non-Muslim slaves. He ceased sponsoring caravans for those desiring to make the *hadj* to Mecca. A famous Sunni ascetic, Shaikh Ahmad Sirhindi, accused him of the heresy of *shirk*, or polytheism. It may well have been the Jesuits who brought this upon him because it was a charge levelled against Christians—that in worshiping Christ as divine, they were associating a lesser being with God.

Akbar was unfazed by this. He was undoubtedly developing a messianic belief in his own destiny. It was rumoured that those entering his harem were obliged to declare 'There is no God but Allah and Akbar is his messenger.' Fr Jerónimo Xavier, who led a third mission to the Imperial Court in 1595, recorded the bizarre fact that he posed as a prophet, wishing it to be understood that he could work miracles. The sick were invited to be healed by drinking the water in which he had washed his feet. Whether the invalids were coerced, suitably pious or desperate goes unrecorded. In 1582, Akbar fulfilled the worst fears of the *Ulema* by founding his own religion, the *Dīn-i Ilāhī* (Faith of the Divine). This was in essence a personality cult, dissolved quickly after his death. The goal of the soul was union with God and, to this end, it incorporated elements of Islamic Sufism, the *Bhakti* or devotional cults of Hinduism, Christianity, Zoroastrianism and Jainism. Anyone adopting the Divine Faith was permitted to continue practicing another religion.[19] The new religion called for alms-giving, the ending of cruelty to animals, permitting widows to remarry, the prohibition of child marriage and the outlawing of *sati*. Akbar also repealed the law prescribing the death penalty for apostatising Muslims. It would not have escaped the attention of the *Ulema* that, to them, he was guilty of this himself.

That Islam sat lightly on Akbar's shoulders is demonstrated further by his interest in figurative art and artists. Muslim traditions did not allow for painting or sculpture. 'Those who make these pictures will be punished on the Day of Resurrection', goes one *hadith* or saying of the Prophet, 'and it will be said to them, "Make alive what you have created."' The response of the Islamic establishment was an oblique challenge to Akbar's authority. In 1578, Abdul Nami, the Chief Imperial *Qazi*,[20] sentenced to death a Brahmin accused of insulting the name of Mahomet. The sentence was carried out despite Akbar's express disapproval. It must have become clear to him that the *Ulema* had to be curbed or he would become impotent as a ruler. His response was twofold, firstly issuing an Imperial Edict that declared that he was assuming the authority of the *Khalifa* in succession to the Ottoman Sultanate which had possessed the title since 1517[21] and the power of arbitrating all disputes within Muslim scholarship and jurisprudence. He pressurised eminent Islamic judges into signing the document. Secondly, Akbar appealed beyond the Islamic establishment to his Hindu subjects, whose elevation as the Emperor's closest advisers was already causing friction with the *Ulema*. Within the scope of *Shari'ah* law, non-Muslims were granted restricted rights. Christians and Jews, who were not exactly numerous in Akbar's domains were regarded as 'people of the book', or *dhimmi*. Others, such as Hindus and Buddhists, who were numerous in Akbar's empire, were generally regarded by Muslims as *kuffar*, or infidels. Unlike the *dhimmi*, they were predestined to the torments of hell unless they embraced Islam. All non-Muslims were obliged to pay a graduated property tax called the *jizyah*. In 1579, the same year in which the Jesuits came to his Court, Akbar abolished this tax. This poured oil on the flames of Islamic disaffection because it abolished the privileged role of the religion within the empire and the supremacy of *Shari'ah* law.

Akbar must have known that his actions could lead to open rebellion. Indeed, he may well have calculated that it would bring his enemies into the open where they could be eliminated. In 1580, Mullah Muhammad Yazdi, the Shia *Qazi* of Jaunpur, pronounced a *fatwa* that declared that Akbar had ceased to be a Muslim and the people should rise up against him. Akbar sent for him and for Muiz-ul-Mulk, the Chief *Qazi* of Bengal, where there was also considerable unrest, and had them both drowned. By this time there was also open rebellion in the Eastern provinces of the Empire. In Bengal and Bihar, a group of officers, many of them Afghans, seized control. They proclaimed Mirza Muhammad Hakim to be the legitimate Emperor. He was Akbar's half-brother and the Governor of Kabul. This rival claimant promptly invaded the Punjab. Akbar made preparations for a war on two fronts. He sent a large force under his Hindu Finance Minister Raja Todar Mal to reconquer the eastern provinces while assembling his own army at Fatehpur. He left his mother Hamida Banu Begum in charge of the civilian administration while he embarked on a relentless campaign against his enemies. He rallied his huge army outside the walls of Fatehpur, where he erected the huge moving city intended to strike awe into the hearts of all who saw it and to bear visible testimony to his authority and might. His campaign headquarters was established in two great white pavilions. When the army was on the march, he occupied one each night, while the other was carried on ahead for the next day. He selected a few of his principal wives to provide connubial pleasures in the months to come and twenty-eight cannons were always grouped in front of his quarters. They were designed for mobility, to work in concert with the powerful cavalry and were therefore too small for siege work.[22] Next to Akbar's pavilion were the tents occupied by his 12-year-old eldest son Salim and his retinue. To the left were the tents of Murad (his second son) and his retinue, including his tutor Fr Antonio. The most important nobles had their quarters in the second line of tents. Beyond these, the rest of the army was encamped, with the troops billeted close to their officers.

Father Monserrate was deeply impressed by the organisation of the camp. To avoid crowding and confusion, the different sections were divided into messes. Bazaars were established for the King, the princes and the great nobles. They were very large and well-stocked, with all sorts of provisions and merchandise, so that they seemed 'to belong to some wealthy city, instead of to a camp'. Wherever the imperial camp was established, the same ground plan was followed, 'so that anyone who has spent a few days in camp knows his way about the bazaars as well as he does the streets of his own city'. Every night a flaming torch was lit on a tall mast in the middle of the camp to act as a guide for stragglers. Father Antonio estimated that Akbar's army consisted of fifty thousand cavalry, 500 war elephants and 'an almost countless number of infantry', reflecting the diverse character of his vast empire. The lightly-armed and speedy horsemen of the Rajput warrior caste dismounted to fight, while the Turkomens and Persians were at their most dangerous when they appeared to be in headlong flight. He noted that while the Mughal army looked small in camp, it seemed enormous when on the march. It advanced in a crescent formation with Akbar at its head, extending 'over the breadth of a mile and a half, covering the fields and filling the woods'. Akbar eschewed the arid plains and the high mountain passes as places of potential ambush, directing his mighty force through the foothills where streams provided ample supplies of fresh water.

When the army embarked on its campaign, Akbar ordered a great quantity of gold and silver to be loaded onto camels and elephants to purchase provisions *en route*. The astute emperor did not want to alienate the local populace by pillaging. His agents scoured the countryside to purchase supplies and to encourage local traders to sell their wares in the travelling bazaars. Heralds were sent ahead to the rulers of lands beyond the imperial boundary over which the Mughal army had to pass. If they did not oppose its progress, they were not harmed, but amply rewarded when the Emperor returned from certain victory. If they took up arms against him, his wrath would fall upon them. Given such a choice, it is not surprising that, overawed by the vast army and overwhelmed by Akbar's generosity, all obeyed him 'out of self-interest'. Once the army had passed out of the imperial territory, three hundred scouts rode out for eighteen miles in each direction to ensure its safe passage. Sappers and miners went ahead to level roads and build bridges of boats across rivers.

Conversion and Coercion

Akbar leads the Mughal Army during a campaign

Father Antonio was able to follow the Jesuit tradition of annotating the culture and terrain of their missionary territories. He explored the foothills of the Himalayas and drew the first accurate sketch map of that mighty mountain region. Akbar was a firm disciplinarian who was ready to make an example of those who disobeyed orders and Fr Antonio gives an example of this. An officer was ordered to reconnoitre along the banks of the Indus to discover whether the information that the river was fordable by cavalry at a particular place was correct. After travelling for some 25 miles without success, he inquired of its whereabouts from some locals and was told that no such place existed. On hearing this, he abandoned his mission and returned to camp, suggesting that a bridge must be built across the river.

Akbar was furious that his orders had been disobeyed and that the man had believed what could have been deliberate misinformation. He ordered him to be seized and dragged to the place to which he had been told to go. There he was bound to an inflated bag of ox-hide and cast out into the river.

> When report of this was spread through the camp, almost the whole army flocked to the riverside to see this strange sight. The officer was being carried hither and thither in the middle of the river at the mercy of the current. He was weeping, imploring pardon with miserable cries, and trying to move the King to mercy. As he was carried past the royal pavilion, the King gave orders for him to be rescued from the river, entered in the inventories as royal property, exposed for sale in all the bazaars, and finally auctioned as a slave.

Fortunately for the man, one of his friends bought him for eighty pieces of gold and released him, whereupon Akbar pardoned him. Fr Antonio concluded that the Emperor had 'showed by this example how much store he set by military discipline and obedience'.

During the campaign, twelve of Akbar's soldiers who had deserted to the enemy were captured in an ambush and brought before the King. He pronounced that some were to be kept in custody so that their cases might be more thoroughly investigated. Others were convicted of treachery and desertion and handed over for execution. One of them, as he was being hustled off by the executioners, begged for a chance to say something. 'O King,' he said, 'order me not to the gibbet, for nature has bestowed upon me marvellous powers in a certain direction.' 'Well,' said the King, 'in what direction do you thus excel, O miserable wretch?' 'I can sing beautifully.' 'Then sing.' The wretched fellow then began to sing, in a voice so discordant and absurd that everyone began to laugh and murmur, and the King himself could scarcely control his smiles. When the guilty man perceived this, he said, 'Pardon me this poor performance, O King. For these guards of yours dragged me along so roughly and cruelly, on a hot and dusty road, and pummelled me so brutally with their fists, that my throat is full of dust, and my voice so husky that I cannot do myself justice in singing.' The King rewarded this witty saying with such signal grace that for the sake of this one man he pardoned both the fellow himself and his companions.

On 8 March, 1581, Akbar's army reached Machhiwara in the Punjab and soon after the banks of the Indus. The rebels hoped that the swollen river would present an insuperable barrier to Akbar's army, but his cavalry made the crossing. Realising that the game was lost, Mirza Muhammed Hakim fled. Akbar arrived in Kabul on 10 August. Hakim was pardoned by Akbar, who appointed his sister, Bakshi Banu Begum, as nominal ruler of the province before returning to Fatehpur Sikri.

Come Rack, Come Rope

It seems extraordinary that Thomas Stephens was able to maintain contact with events and friends back in England. As well as obvious difficulties of distance, there were political factors (Portugal was technically at war with England for much of Philip II's reign), yet communicate he did. The length of time it took for a letter from Europe to arrive is revealed by a letter sent to him by his brother Richard, who had been appointed a Professor of Philosophy at the University of Paris. The letter was sent from Cahors on 28 May 1581 and reached Thomas Stephens in Goa on 24 October, 1583. Thomas Stephens was glad to hear that 'our esteemed father is well', but curiously he adds that he is 'astonished that he has been spared altogether in this calamity'. It appears that he was involved in the network of those harbouring and protecting Catholic priests. 'It is wonderful', he adds, 'that, after being so harassed by citizens in a peaceful commonwealth, he should have come off safe from a widespread slaughter of citizens.' Whatever the father had been doing, there was an element of risk involved. Richard Stephens appears to have been helping succour Catholic refugees from England. His brother advised him to win 'over the graces of the grandees' to support the work. Unless he did so, 'Christ will not have the wherewithal to feed his own'.

Richard's letter also told him of the martyrdom of Edmund Campion, together with Ralph Sherwin and Alexander Briant. In fact, he had already heard this news from other correspondents. 'Accounts of the persecution in England have informed me of the illustrious martyrdom of Father Campion and his companions', he informed his brother. He must have longed for news from home and greeted every letter with great joy. 'I was exceedingly pleased with the account you gave me of each of our common friends', he wrote. 'It is only natural that I should desire to know something about the state of those whom daily I recommend to God in my prayers.' Doubtless one of these was Thomas Pounde. Edmund Campion had fulfilled an extensive ministry in many parts of the country. He was arrested through treachery at Lyford Grange near Wantage on 17 July 1581. He was brought to London and had a private audience with the Queen and his old mentor Lord Leicester. He was offered a bishopric as an inducement to apostasy. When he refused, he was tortured in the Tower. Under this extremity, he revealed the names of some of those who had harboured him. Thomas Pounde, a fellow prisoner in the Tower, bribed a gaoler to deliver a letter to Campion. The man immediately surrendered it to the authorities, who instructed him to deliver it and obtain Campion's reply. 'It grieveth me much', he wrote, 'to have offended the Catholic cause so highly as to confess the Names of some gentlemen and friends in whose houses I had been entertained. Yet in this I greatly cherish and comfort myself that I never declared any secrets there declared, and that I will not, come Rack, come Rope.'[23] Part of this letter was read out at his trial. It was alleged that the 'secrets' were treasonable plots against the state. Campion replied that they were private confessions that his priestly vow forbade him from revealing.

On 15 November, Lord Vaux, Sir William Catesby, Sir Thomas Tresham and three others appeared before the Star Chamber on charges relating to harbouring Campion. The letter to Pounde was read out by the Clerk, 'wherein he did take notice that by frailty he had confessed of some houses where he had been, which now he repented him, and desired Mr. Pounde to beg him pardon of the Catholics therein.' On 20 November 1581, the trial of Campion, Sherwin, Briant and eleven others opened at Westminster Hall. From the start it was a farce, with flimsy evidence and contradictory witnesses. The verdict was inevitable, but the trial is remarkable for the line that the accused took in their defence. 'The plain reason for our standing here is religion, not treason', protested Ralph Sherwin. Edmund Campion made the same resounding point.

> The only thing we have to say is, that if our religion do make us traitors, we are worthy to be condemned; but otherwise are, and have been, as good subjects as ever the Queen had.

He expressed the same point on the scaffold on 1 December. The message is clear: it is possible to be a good Englishman and a good Catholic. The separation of religion from politics and the supremacy of conscience were making their first manifestations through the Society of Jesus. Campion was seen as a saint and martyr by Catholics from the moment of his death. Robert

Persons in his *Epistle of Comfort to the Priests* saw portents in the very behaviour of England's rivers.

> The wonderful way and standing of the Thames the same day that Campion and his company were martyred, to the great marvel of citizens and mariners, and the like stay of the river Trent about the same time. Which accidents, though some will impute to other causes, yet happening at such special times, when so open and unnatural injustice was done they cannot but be interpreted as tokens of God's indignation.

It may have been Thomas Pounde who composed a poem of some quality from his prison cell in tribute to the Catholic martyrs.[24] He too refers to the river standing still, although inclement weather can hardly have been surprising in early December.

> The scowling clouds did storm and puff apace.
> They could not bear the wrong that malice wrought,
> The sun drew in his shining purple face,
> The moistened clouds shed brinish tears for thought,
> The river Thames awhile astonished stood
> To count the drops of Campion's sacred blood.

Part of the cause of beatification is the general recognition of the person's saintliness. Pounde iterates that the three martyred priests possess such a quality.

> Rejoice, be glad, triumph, sing hymns of joy,
> *Campion, Sherwin, Briant,* live in bliss,
> They sue, they seek the ease of our annoy,
> They pray, they speak, and all effectual is,
> Not like to men on earth as heretofore,
> But like to saints in heaven, and that is more.[25]

Another of those condemned with Campion was Thomas Cottam. Thomas Pounde and Thomas Stephens, his mentors in the faith, had conveyed their enthusiasms to him, for he expressed a desire to join the Indian Mission and would have done so had he not contracted a fever. He was sent to Lyons to recuperate and was ordained priest at Soissons on 28 May, 1580. Eight days later, he left for England with four companions. They were betrayed by an English spy and arrested at Dover, but through a ruse by Dr Ely, one of his fellow-travellers, he was able to reach London safely. Realising that the scheme had placed the doctor in jeopardy, he surrendered himself voluntarily and was committed to the Marshalsea. He was removed to the Tower, where he was severely tortured. After the trial, his execution was deferred until May 30 1582. Before he was hanged and quartered, he shouted 'God bless you all' to the spectators.

Thomas Pounde continued his literary activities from his prison cell. In the year of Campion's martyrdom, he was probably the author of a poem in 85 sestets entitled *A challenge vnto ffox the martirmonger written vpon occasion of this miraculouse martirdom of the foresaide Peter Elcius with a comforte vnto all afflicted Catholyques*. The poem gives an insight into the ferocity of contemporary doctrinal controversies. The first part deals with the martyrdom, in Morocco, of a Spanish priest called Peter Elcius. An account of this had been published in Cologne that year and had come into Pounde's hands. The main thrust of the poem is a riposte to the hugely-influential *Actes and Monuments* of John Foxe (better known as *Foxe's Book of Martyrs*) of 1563. This recounted the histories of Protestants who had died for their faith, particularly during the reign of Queen Mary. Doubt has been cast on the accuracy of many of its accounts, but this is only peripherally the purpose of the author of the poem. Both Protestants and Catholics claimed to have had adherents who had suffered martyrdom. Both sought justification for their claims in St Augustine's statement: *Itaque martyrem non facit poena sed causa*— 'Martyrdom is not made by suffering but by the cause.'[26] As '*A Challenge*' puts it:

> For 'tis not pain that doth a martyr make;
> Ne glorious sort in which he seems to die,
> But faith the cause which thine did them forsake
> When from Christ's spouse they would so fondly fly
> Where truth doth want, to utter wrack they fall.
> Not martyrs made, but most accursed of all.

Pounde launched the full force of his polemic against Foxe in the opening stanza.

> Come forth, fond fox, with all your rabble rout
> Of monstrous monsters in your brainsick book.
> Compare them to this glorious martyr stout
> And thou shalt see how loathly foul they look.

In such controversies, Catholics had two advantages. They could look back to a continuum with the martyrs of past ages (although the Protestants also sought, on occasions, to do so, claiming to represent the authentic spirit of the true Church that had been perverted by Catholic malpractices). Pounde regards such attitudes as chicanery.

> Now where thou sayest thou hast some Saints enrolled
> Which we ourselves likewise do so esteem,
> We say they were not of thy cursed fold,
> But of our flock, which makes us justly deem
> Such monuments are monuments indeed.
> Thee to deface & us to stand in stead.

The other aspect where Catholics had an advantage was that of miracles. For most Protestants, the age of miracles was over, but for Catholics, it was a living part of the process of beatification. Thus Pounde referred to the miracles of Peter Elcius:

> His courage, joy and patience did declare
> The fervour great of constant Xian love.
> The miracles, at martyrdom so rare
> This favour with mighty god doth prove.

Conversion and Coercion 169

The poem, various documents and a covering letter[27] were seized by the authorities. At some time between May 1582 and November 1583, Stephen Rousham, a fellow prisoner in the Tower and future martyr, wrote to Pounde, 'havinge received youre gouden cordiall coumforte', which was presumably his *Challenge*.

A copy of Hakluyt's *Voyages* came into the possession of Thomas Pounde. He must have been delighted to read of his friend's deeds therein. He was released on the accession of James I in 1603, after serving nearly thirty years in prison. He had lost nothing of his rashness, writing to the King six years later, implicitly comparing the pastoral care to foreign visitors to Goa with the treatment of Jesuits in England, and referring to,

> Father Thomas Stephens, these thirty-nine years since, a famous preacher of the Society at Goa, where their colony of St Paul's is, of whose great favours there showed to many of our English Protestants there sometimes arriving, they have in the history of their navigation given good testimony.

In the same year, Pounde wrote to Fr Robert Persons in Rome, expressing his gratitude to Fr William Weston, the fellow student of Thomas Stephens, who had been imprisoned for seventeen years, some of them with Thomas Pounde.

> And next to him to love, my dear brother some time, but many happy spent years since that ten thousand miles hence; I mean my Father Thomas Stephens, was my first messenger for obtaining of my admission into the Society.[28]

Notes

1. A. C. Burnett (ed.), *The Voyage of John Huyghen Van Linschoten to the East Indies*, vol. 1 (New Delhi: Asian Educational Services reprint. 1988), p.164.
2. Ruy Vicente's letter to Claudio Acquaviva. Goa. 8 November, 1581 (Archivum Romanum Societas Iesu: 32, f. 445r).
3. A. Gray and H. C. P. Bell (trans), *The Voyage of François Pyrard de Laval to the East Indies*, vol. II (London: Hakluyt Society, 1887) p. 10.

4. The xerafin was a silver coin current in Portuguese India before the 19th century.
5. I. G. Zupenov, 'Drugs, health, bodies and souls in the tropics', *The Indian Economic and Social History Review*, vol. xxxix, no. 1 (2002), pp. 33,34.
6. Gray and Bell, *The Voyage*, pp. 2, 5–17.
7. J. S. Hoyland (trans), *The Commentary of Father Montserrate S.J.* (Oxford: Oxford University Press, 1922), pp. 196–213.
8. Gray and Bell, *The Voyage*, pp. 97–99.
9. Garcia de Orta, *Colloquies on the simples and drugs of India*, trans. Sir Clements Markham (London: Henry Sotheran and Co., 1895), p. 55.
10. S. K. Pandya, 'Medicine in Goa–a former Portuguese territory', *Journal of Postgraduate Medicine* 28 (1982), p. 123.
11. Sir Wolseley Haig, *The Cambridge History of India*, vol. IV (Cambridge: Cambridge University Press, 1937), p. 88.
12. Hoyland, *The Commentary*, p. 7.
13. J. Horton Riley, *Ralph Fitch, England's Pioneer to India* (<place>: Asian Educational Service, 1998), pp. 98, 99.
14. Hoyland, *The Commentary*, pp.196–213.
15. P. du Jarric, *An Account of the Jesuit Mission to the Court of Akbar*, trans. C. H. Payne (London: Harper & Brothers, 1926), p. 20.
16. 'Arabia Felix' referred to the southern part of the Arabian peninsula now known as Yemen. It was known as 'Happy Arabia' because of its greenness, in contrast to the deserts to the north.
17. Abdu'l-Fazl, *Ain-e-Akbari*, trans H. Blochmann (<place>: Royal Asiatic Society of Bengal, 1927), p. 276.
18. According to James Hough, Akbar gave himself the name 'Cha-Geladiin', meaning 'The Potent King of the Sovereign Lord'. See *The History of Christianity in India, vol I*. Fr Antonio may have been attempting to render this.
19. C. Kutlüturk, 'A Critical Analysis of Akbar's Religious Policy: Din-i-Ilahi', *International Relations and Diplomacy*, vol 4 (June 2016), pp. 407–417.
20. An Islamic Judge who tried offences against *Shari'ah* law.
21. The caliphate or the political successors of Mahomet, representing the focus of unity in the Muslim world.
22. Hoyland, *The Commentary*, pp. 73–90
23. J. V. Holleran, *A Jesuit Challenge* (New York, Fordham University Press, 1999), p. 40.

24. The first person to suggest that Pounde was the author of this poem was the literary scholar, Richard Simpson in *Edmund Campion: a Biography*: (London: Williams and Norgate: 1867) p. 325.
25. *Ibid.*, p. 24.
26. See St Augustine, *Sermo 335*.
27. Richard Simpson also suggested that the covering letter to *A Challenge* was addressed to Francis Tregian, a Cornish recusant imprisoned in the Fleet.
28. H. Foley, *Jesuits in Conflict* (London: Burns & Oates, 1871), p. 59.

5

'Had it not Pleased God'

Mar Abraham

In 1555, Pope Julius III consecrated a monk named Sulaqa as Chaldean Patriarch, recognising his authority over Calicut and the areas of India that were not under Portuguese jurisdiction. In theory, this brought the Thomas Christians within the Roman orbit. In practice, things were not that easy. They had maintained a version of the faith amid centuries of isolation and developed their own ways. By a long and somewhat eccentric custom within the Nestorian tradition, nephews had succeeded their uncles as head vicars of their churches. This practice related to the warrior Nair caste, with which the St Thomas Christians identified, which practiced polyandry. To ensure consanguinity, it was the son of a sister who was regarded as the heir.

It was a firm tradition that St Thomas had selected his clergy from just two families: the Shankcrapun family, which had become extinct, and the Pakalomattam family, which continued to provide the rulers of the Church until 1807. Drawing his authority from afar, the Bishop's function was merely titular. The administration and control of the church was in the hands of a figure bearing the title 'Archdeacon of All India', an office of longstanding traditions with which the St Thomas Christians were entirely happy.

To the Catholics, the faith of the St Thomas Christians was permeated with heresy and error. Their term for the Blessed Virgin was 'Mother of Christ' rather than the Catholic 'Mother of God.' They rejected the use of images. They believed that the souls of the departed did not enter the beatific presence of God until after the Final Judgement. They recognised only three sacraments (baptism, ordination and the Eucharist). In matrimony, there were no formalities other than the consent of the parties and the consummation. Finally, they used sorcery and witchcraft.

The St Thomas Christians of Kerala adhered to the Malankara Church, which took its name from the island where St Thomas was believed to have landed on his first arrival in India. They acknowledged themselves as under the jurisdiction of the East Syrian Patriarch in Mesopotamia. After a schism in 1552, there was a Chaldean Patriarch in full communion with the Catholic Church and a Nestorian one. Around 1563, a monk called Mar[1] Abraham was sent to Malabar by the latter Patriarch, Shem'on [Simeon] VII Isho'yahb, as Archbishop-designate of Angamaly in Malabar. He was greeted joyfully by the St Thomas Christians, but local Catholic missionaries saw him as a representative of the Nestorian heresy. He was arrested in Cochin and sent to Goa, where he was detained for two years before being put on a ship bound for Portugal. He escaped in Mozambique and, by some means, made his way back to Mesopotamia. He had clearly realised that his status would be more acceptable if he was sent by the Chaldean Patriarch Abdisho IV, who was in full communion with Rome, rather than the Nestorian one. Abdisho was prepared to re-consecrate him to his former position, but felt he needed fuller endorsement, sending him to Rome to receive the blessing of Pope Pius IV. There he was received into the Catholic Church and ordained priest by the Patriarch of Venice. In 1567, the Pope ordered Abdisho to re-assign him to his See, but this time as a Bishop in full communion with the Catholic Church. On 27 February, he signed letters to the Archbishop of Goa and the Bishop of Cochin, confirming that 'this beloved brother, Abraham… was appointed Archbishop with our sanction by our venerable brother, Abediessus, Patriarch of the Assyrians'. He is described as going 'to the tombs of the Apostles [i.e. The Vatican] *ad limina*'. This Latin phrase represents a further endorsement. It constitutes the obligation of the members of the hierarchy to be received by the Pope to give an account of their diocese and to receive his counsels.[2]

This papal endorsement did not impress the Portuguese authorities. Indeed, under the agreement known as the *padroado* made with the King of Portugal in 1514, the Pope had surrendered jurisdiction over three Indian dioceses to the civil authorities. Thus on arrival in Goa, Mar Abraham was detained in a convent, but this experienced escapologist soon freed himself. On his return to Malabar, he was again received with great joy by his flock, but faced a great dilemma. He was in full communion with Rome, but the majority of those he led were imbued with doctrines and practices that were anathema to the Catholic Church. As a result, he gained a reputation as a master-equivocator with many in the Catholic hierarchy. He was certainly skilful at playing off different factions against each other, but it must be reckoned that he had been placed in a situation that required him to be 'all things to all men'. He certainly had no reason to be beholden to the Portuguese, who had imprisoned him twice and deported him once and were likely to do so again if the opportunity arose. Thus he ignored a summons to attend the second Provincial Synod at Goa on 12 June, 1575.

Mar Abraham proved an energetic and dedicated Metropolitan. In 1570, he began to build the cathedral of Mar Hormizd at Angamaly. He stressed the necessity of a priesthood versed in the ancient Syriac rite to ensure its retention as the liturgical language of the Malabar Church. In 1574, Everard Mercurian, the fourth Superior-General of the Society of Jesus, appointed Alessandro Valignano as his Visitor to the East. As a great apostle of Inculturation, he must have seemed a welcome arrival to Mar Abraham when he visited his diocese in 1577. It was problematic that the Portuguese viewed the *padroado* as over-riding Papal power in favour of the secular authorities (which, in a sense, it did). They also tended to use religion as a means to extend their political influence.

Fr Valignano was accompanied by the convert priest Pero Luis Bramane, who acted as his interpreter. As a Brahmin himself, Fr Pero had a decided advantage in dealing with the Malabar Christians, who considered themselves to be of a high caste. Mar Abraham assisted the Jesuits in establishing the Vaipikotta Seminary at Chennamangalam north of Cochin in 1577. A priest from Catalonia, Fr Francisco Ros SJ, was appointed as the first Rector. He had been with Fr Stephens at St Paul's College as Professor of Chaldaic and Syriac. One of the functions of the mission was to study the beliefs and customs of the St Thomas Christians so as to determine the best means to bring them within the Catholic fold. By contrast, the attempts of the Portuguese to extend their political influence over the St Thomas Christians by a process of Latinisation were frequently ill-judged and aggressive. It was to counter-balance this that Mar Abraham invited the Jesuits to establish themselves in his diocese. On 3 January 1578, he wrote to the Pope, asking for protection from the Portuguese, who were no more likely to heed any papal admonition than they had previously. His position had been further complicated in 1577, when the Nestorian Patriarch Eliya VI sent a prelate named Mar Simon as a rival Bishop of the St Thomas Christians. The Jesuits saw the opportunity to bring Mar Abraham more thoroughly into the Roman fold and promised him safe conduct with the support of the Pope if he attended the third Provincial Synod in Goa. He did so and was accompanied by Fr Fransisco Ros. The Synod opened on 9 June 1585 and lasted until 24 November. The entire third session dealt with the Malankara Church and produced ten decrees that aimed to bring it into line with Catholic practice and doctrine. Fr Ros was authorised to ensure that the changes were carried out.

In fact, Mar Abraham had already been persuaded by the Jesuits to allow them to purge the Syriac service books of Nestorian heresy and return them to their owners. Where the errors permeated the book to an extent beyond expurgation, it was burnt. Yet, conciliatory as they were, there were clear difficulties. The most immediate of the heresies was the adherence of the St Thomas Christians to the caste system, which explains the reluctance of their leaders to fully embrace the Roman option. Like Hindus, they were born into their status. One of the titles of the Archdeacon in Malayam was *Jathikku Karthavyan*, or 'Leader of the Caste'. The most fertile area for converts to Catholicism was people from the lower castes. Since social intercourse with such people was *outré* for the St Thomas Christians, a parallel church was in danger of developing.

Relations between the Catholic Church and Mar Abraham deteriorated after 1585. He refused to attend the Provincial Council in 1592 and in an intercepted letter to the Nestorian Patriarch, he wrote that the Portuguese were over his head as a hammer over an anvil.

The Union of Crowns

The status of the colony of Goa changed dramatically in 1580 when the Spanish House of Hapsburg became rulers of Portugal. After King Sebastian was killed at the disastrous Battle of Alcácer-Quibir in 1578, he was succeeded by his great-uncle, Henry, Cardinal Archbishop of Braga, who died without issue (he had been seeking a papal revocation of his vow of celibacy) in 1580. Dom Antonio, the illegitimate son of the Duke of Beja, brother of the late King, claimed the throne, but it was seized by Philip II of Spain, who had a genuine dynastic claim. The populace tended to support Dom Antonio but the nobility were overwhelmingly for Philip, who poured wealth into their coffers. Dom Antonio was defeated outside Lisbon by the Spanish after a reign of just twenty days, but he established himself, with French help, in the Azores, where he was still recognised as King. He reigned there for three years before being forced to seek refuge in France, where the ruling House of Medici saw him as a useful tool against Spain, as did the English.

The Union of Crowns was a disaster for Portuguese power and her empire in the east. It meant that Spain's enemies—the important maritime nations of England, the Netherlands and France—also became hers. Previously Portugal's hegemony within the spice trade had been in partnership with the rising maritime power of the Dutch, who shipped the commodities from Lisbon into central Europe. Now the Spaniards declared a trade and fiscal embargo on the rebellious provinces. This meant that the Dutch had lost their main trading partner, whose commerce had financed their war against Spain. Dutch ships harboured in Portuguese ports were repeatedly seized and confiscated by the Spanish. It would only be a matter of time before this confident new nation would challenge Portugal's power in the east, although the new arrangement made little immediate difference in Goa. King Philip II wisely kept his Portuguese administration entirely separate from his Spanish one.

The news of the Union of Crowns reached Akbar the Great. The following year, he sent Fr Antonio Monserrate and Fr Francisco Henriques back to Goa to send congratulations to Philip II, but required Fr Acquaviva to remain at Fatehpur. The anxious Jesuit Provincial in Goa wrote several letters asking for his release and in 1583 the Emperor relented. He had a letter written to the Provincial explaining why he had detained the priest and how much he was missing the Jesuits in his court.

> I have much love for the Father and, considering that he is wise and versed in the laws, I desire to have him every hour in conversation with me, and for this reason I refused him the permission. But as your Paternity asked it of me by letter several times, I did so and gave my permission; and as my intention is that our friendship should go on increasing day by day, it behoves Your Paternity to labour on your side towards preserving it, by sending Father Rodolfo back to me with some other Fathers; and I would like this

to be with the least possible delay, for I desire that the Fathers of this Order be with me, because I am delighted with them.³

A Pressing Need

Even by the exotic standards that permeated Goan society, ten arrivals late in 1582 would have caused a sensation. On 25 February, Alessandro Valignano had departed from Japan with the first official delegation—representing three Christian *Daimyos*—from that country to Europe. Four boys, all Christian converts, were to be taken to Rome as 'the first fruits of the East'. He believed 'there was a pressing need not only to make Japan better known in Europe, but also to make Europe better known in Japan.'⁴ The expedition would also give the young Japanese the chance to see for themselves the universality of the Catholic Church and, hopefully, persuade European princes to underwrite the work of the Jesuits in Japan. Mancio Ito (*Ito Mansho*), the leader of the delegation, was just thirteen. He was representing his relation Otomo Sorin, the *daimyo* of Bungo. Miguel Chijiwa (*Chijiwa Migeru*) was representing the *daimyos* of Arima and Omura. Julião Nakaura (*Nakaura Julian*) and Martinão Hara (*Hara Marachino*) were their companions. All three were all under sixteen. With the group was their interpreter and tutor, Fr Diogo de Mesquita, a Portuguese Jesuit. The journey of two-and-a-half years was vast and daunting.

They reached Goa via Macao and Cochin. At Goa, the party was given an enthusiastic reception by the Viceroy, Archbishop and people. The one reaction that is recorded from the Japanese during their stay in the colony is that they expressed huge admiration for the magnificent Arabian horses that could be seen there. While in Goa, Valignano learnt that he would not be going to Europe. He had been named the Provincial of India by Claudio Acquiviva, the Superior General in Rome, so the expedition proceeded to Lisbon under the leadership of Fr Nuno Rodrigues, Rector of St Paul's College.

The Martyrs of Cuncolim

On his return to Goa in 1583, Fr Rodolfo Acquaviva was appointed as Superior of the Salcete Mission, replacing Fr Alphonso Pacheco. The twelve Jesuits in the mission included Fr Thomas Stephens. Years later it was said of him that, while he was a novice at the Church of San Andrea in Rome, he saw a building that he did not recognise in a dream, which later became his home for the rest of his life. On his arrival at the Jesus House in Salcete, he recognised it as the house he had seen in his dream, but this is not an incident to which Fr Stephens himself refers; nor was the Jesus House to be his home for the rest of his life. The story does indicate, however, that Thomas Stephens was revered and inspired pious legends.

Fr Alfonso Pachêco, a Spaniard, had been sent back to Rome in 1580 to seek support for the Goan mission. 'During this journey he was worn out with care and want of sleep', wrote Thomas Stephens, 'and yet with a spirit undaunted by so many such great dangers and inconveniences, he returned to Goa with thirteen companions who had been greatly wished for.'[5] One of the thirteen was António Francisco, a Portuguese Jesuit, who had been inspired to enter the mission field by the martyrdom of Fr Inácio de Azevedo and forty other Jesuit missionaries who were seized and drowned by Huguenot pirates in 1570 while en route to Brazil. On arrival in Goa, he continued his studies at St Paul's College and was ordained in 1582. He was assigned to serve in the Moluccas, but returned to Goa after his ship was wrecked and was appointed to the mission at Orlim on the Salcete peninsular. It was said that whenever he said Mass, he prayed, at the Elevation, for the grace of martyrdom. This desire for martyrdom was shared by Paolo da Costa, a layman who was an inhabitant of Rachol. He became a friend and confident of

Thomas Stephens. A year before the tragic events of 25 July 1583, he had asked if he could find a way of dying for the Christian faith.

> In order to try him I answered, 'You can easily meet with death, but what fruit do you expect to gather from such a death?' On this he sighed repeatedly and replied: 'Oh, how beautiful it is to lay down one's life for the Faith.'

Francisco Aranha, who was 32 years old, had gone to India with his uncle, Dom Gaspar Jorge de Leão Pereira, the first Archbishop of Goa, and became a Jesuit lay brother. A skilled draftsman and architect, he had built several chapels in the colony, including the church at Cuncolim.

The ideal of martyrdom for the faith was very much part of the Jesuit psyche: indeed in a century of religious conflict in Europe and an expansion overseas into frequently hostile lands, it became a norm of existence in a way that it hardly been since the days of the early church. The text attributed to the early Christian theologian, Tertullian, frequently translated as 'The blood of the martyrs is the seed of the church', reflected the view that current suffering was the key to future strength.[6] At the same time, it was not something to be sought. Hence the priests of the English Mission took every possible precaution to avoid detection.

The Salcete peninsular had a population of around 80,000, scattered over 66 villages. Thomas Stephens described its topography in a letter to his brother.

> On the north and east it is bounded by a broad river, on the west by the Indian Ocean. Moreover to the south it is divided by two small rivers on both sides, and by densely wooded hills. It is six miles in breadth and eighteen in length.

Salcete was renowned for its fertility. 'The ground', wrote Dr John Fryer, an English visitor in the seventeenth century,

> yields as good Cabbage, Coleworts and better Radishes then ever I saw: Besides Garden-Fruit, here are incomparable

Water Melons and Onions as sweet, and as well tasted as an Apple; and for the natural growth of the soil, it is known not only to supply the adjoining islands, but Goa also.[7]

Around a hundred local Christians clustered for protection around the frontier-fortress at Rachol. This formidable military base had been ceded to the Portuguese in 1520 in return for their help in its conquest by the Hindu King Krishnadevaraya of Vijayanagara from Ismail Adil Shah, Sultan of Bijapur. Huge ramparts rose in three tiers above the Zuari River. The garrison was equipped with two hundred pieces of artillery, four hundred cavalry, eight thousand infantry and two hundred elephants.

At the time of the Portuguese first arrival, the population of Salcete was mainly Hindu and it was dominated by high-caste Brahmins. There were scores of temples (or, as they were known locally, pagodas). They were mainly dedicated to Santéry, the cobra-goddess. She was the most popular form of the goddess Durga and was particularly revered in Cuncolim, where a temple dedicated to her was built over an anthill, which was, according to local belief, a sacred place inhabited by reincarnated souls.

Originally, the only chapel attached to the fort at Rachol was dedicated to St John the Baptist in 1521. It was said that Dom Gaspar, the first Archbishop, had shot an arrow into the ground at Raia and ordered that the *Igreja de Nossa Senhora das Neves*— the Church of Our Lady of the Snows—be built there. The Jesuits had been given the spiritual cure of Salcete in 1558 by the ninth Viceroy, Antăo de Noronha, in 1558 as part of the division of the colony into spheres of influence between the Jesuits, Dominicans and Fransiscans. On 3 January 1566, he donated a house at Rachol to the Jesuits and, to support the institution, the boy King Dom Sebastiăo endowed the Society with the lands of destroyed Hindu temples in 1569. It was the policy of the Jesuits that their bases should be in centres of population, so the seminary moved to the Holy Spirit Church in the more populous town of Margão on 17 May 1574.

'Had it not Pleased God'

As well as the seminary and the church, the complex included a small primary school and the *Hospital dos Pobres do Padre Paolo Camerte*, a hospital for poor natives. This had been founded by Fr Paolo Camerte next to St Paul's College in Old Goa in 1551. Fr Camerte was an Italian Jesuit who had arrived in India with Francis Xavier. He was assiduous in overseeing the hospital's development, even raising chickens to provide eggs. At first, it was only for native Christians, but its remit was later extended to all, making it the first institution to cater for patients of all creeds. It had moved to Margão in 1568, so it predated the arrival of the seminary. It was now known as the Hospital of the Holy Spirit. In a letter written on 1 January 1597, the Jesuit father Simão de Sã mentions that the hospital was under the care of the Jesuit brother Pedro Afonso, 'eminent in the art of surgery'. Since 1574, he had been assisted by Br Lázaro Ribeiro, a pharmacist.[8]

Margão was vulnerable to attack. In 1579, the College and church were burnt down by Ibrahim Adil Shah, the Sultan of Bijahur, but the hospital was spared. The following year, the seminary was rebuilt at the more secure location of Rachol. The building was surrounded by the remains of the moat of an old Moslem fort. It lies on a low hill, giving a vast vista of the surrounding paddy-fields. The Royal Arms were engraved over the main gate, with the inscription ARMOS DEL REI SEBASTIAO FUNDADOR DO COLEGIO.

Its official title was the College and Hospital of the Holy Spirit, but it was generally referred to in Jesuit documents as the College of Rachol. A wide variety of subjects was taught, including Portuguese and Latin, rhetoric, history, mathematics, natural sciences, jurisprudence, music, philosophy and theology, with an increasing emphasis on the learning of Indian languages, especially Konkani, which was essential for foreign Jesuits to fulfil their liturgical and pastoral roles locally.

Coat of Arms of the King of Portugal at the entrance to the Rachol Seminary

The province was torn by religious strife. In 1567, Diego Rodriguez, Captain of the fortress at Rachol, demolished the temple of Mahalasa at nearby Mardol with its adjoining house of prostitutes. He proceeded to destroy all of the three hundred or so pagodas in the peninsula. In many cases the administrative control of the *namissi* (temple properties) was transferred to the missionary societies, which was another great cause of resentment. Thomas Stephens' confreres in the Society of Jesus had been highly active in Salcete and had made many converts. 'There were eight churches in this place', he wrote at the time of his arrival, 'and last year three more were added to them. It is only natural to add to them, as the number of Christians is on the increase.'

> There is, however, one part of the peninsular, the one that is nearest the continent, in which there are but a handful of Christians; the pagans of whom there are a great many, are

all of a warlike character and are sworn foes of the Portuguese. They are strongly opposed to Christianity, and have for many years been doing great harm to the Faith, partly by their open attacks and partly by their conspiracies.

Fr Stephens is referring to the great friction between Christians and Hindus in the area around the village of Cuncolim, which was noted for its iron-casting.[9] As Fr Stephens realised, many of the villagers were members of the *Kshatriya* warrior caste. Fr Pero Mascarenhas, the founder of the Salcete Mission, had converted a leading Brahmin from the village. Nineteen families had followed his lead and reprisals ensued. The Portuguese, in defence of the converts, demolished the local temples. By 1569, the village housed a thousand fervent Christians. In 1576, the Viceroy ordered the destruction of all the remaining Hindu temples in the territory. In retaliation, the five southernmost villages in Salcete Province revolted against the Portuguese and burnt down churches and mission stations, including that at Cuncolim. In a further retaliation, Gil Eanes de Mascarenhas, the Captain-Major of the Malabar Coast, invaded Cuncolim through the Sal River, burning and razing all he found before him.

To many a modern eye, the behaviour of the Jesuits will seem aggressive and insensitive. Fr Pachêco accompanied two punitive expeditions by the Portuguese army to Cuncolim. With Pietro Berno, a Lombard from near Lake Maggiore, who had been a novice at Goa with Thomas Stephens and in the party of Jesuits that had sailed to India with him, he was instrumental in demolishing the Hindu temples. As often happens, this destruction was not simply a religious issue. The temple and its religious ceremonies were the centre of the commercial world of bazaars and traditional fairs that brought prosperity to the village. Demolition of the temple meant not only a blow aimed at the local culture, but also at its economic base.

Berno had been the first to set fire to the temple. He also destroyed the sacred ant-heap personifying Santéry, and slaughtered a cow, a sacred beast to the Hindus, and spread its entrails 'upon the altar of the idol so as to clear the place of superstitious people'. He said constantly that no fruit would be gained from Cuncolim until it was bathed in blood shed for the faith. His superiors said that he had converted more pagans than all the other fathers put together, while Thomas Stephens considered that he was hated by 'the infidels' more than any other Jesuit. In protest against such atrocities, the *ganvkars* (chief village councillors) of Cuncolim and the surrounding villages withheld their taxes to the Portuguese authorities and continued to erect temples and celebrate their rituals and ceremonies in defiance of the authorities. In retaliation, their lands were confiscated.

Fr Rodolfo Acquaviva had been Rector of the Rachol seminary for just a week, but had already determined to conduct a mission encompassing all 66 villages in Salcete. It was decided to begin at the most southerly (Cuncolim) and work up the peninsular. The tempestuous hostility of recent times seemed to have been followed by calm, with the villagers even acknowledging the sovereignty of the King of Portugal. Fr António Francisco thought it judicious to write a letter, informing the people of Cuncolim of their impending arrival. The reply was not encouraging. It was not an auspicious time for the Fathers to visit because there was still disagreement in the village about how they should be received. Nevertheless, the Fathers decided to proceed and sent some people ahead to build a shelter of palm leaves since it was the monsoon season.

The five Jesuits spent the night of 24 July 1583 at Fr Antonio's mission at Orlim. Next morning, as he was celebrating Mass at the village church, he had a vision that prefigured his desire for martyrdom. After Mass, the Jesuits headed southwards together with some fifty Christian converts. Their guide was a young convert from Cumcolim, a student from Rachol College, who had been baptised with the name of Domingos. He had accompanied the Fathers on their previous punitive expeditions and pointed out the pagan temples. When they arrived at Cuncolim, they were prevented from entering by a village elder because of the

'Had it not Pleased God'

volatile situation. After waiting several hours and hearing increasingly hostile shouts from the village council, which had been summoned, they decided to plant a cross on the site where they hoped to return to erect a chapel and leave. Unbeknown to them, this was where a Hindu temple had stood until it had been destroyed during the fighting with the Portuguese a year before. Hundreds of heavily armed and outraged villagers surrounded them. The villagers had already deduced that it was the Jesuits' intention to build a church. After a so-called 'Wizard' had worked the people who had been watching the Fathers into a frenzy, they summoned hundreds of heavily armed and outraged villagers who surrounded them. One of the group, Gonçalo Rodrigues, a former soldier, levelled his gun, but Fr Pacheco restrained him, saying, 'come, come, Signor Gonçalo. We are not here to fight.' Then, speaking to the crowd, he said in Konkani, their native language, 'strike me. It is I who have destroyed your idols.'

The villagers fell on them with great ferocity. As one approached Fr Rodolfoo, he said, 'With all my heart, I give my soul and body to God.' His assailant floored him with a single slash of his scimitar to the back of the thighs. To show his readiness for martyrdom, he opened the collar of his cassock and exposed the left side of his neck. He was stabbed twice before a third blow hit his shoulder and nearly severed his arm. 'Forgive them Lord', he exclaimed. 'Francisco Xavier, pray to God for me. Lord Jesus, receive my spirit.' He was killed by an arrow that pierced his breast. Fr Berno was horribly mutilated. Fr Pacheco, wounded with a spear, fell on his knees and spread his arms in the form of a cross. 'Lord, you were pierced with a lance for me. I ask you to pardon those who have wounded me and to send them other missionaries to lead them to heaven.' As he was praying, another lance pierced his throat. He died saying 'Jesus'. Br. Arunha said 'I am neither stupid nor cowardly enough to adore a lump of wood or stone, rather than the true God.' He was stabbed by a scimitar and a lance and fell down a bank into a paddy-field, where he lay until he was discovered. He was then taken before the statue of a

Hindu god and ordered to bow before it. When he refused, he was tied to a tree and, like St Sebastian, shot through with arrows.

Domingos, the local boy, was dispatched by his own uncle. Fr Antonio's head was split open with a scimitar and his body was riddled with arrows. Afonso da Costa, Fr Pacheco's altar boy, had followed him closely, clutching his breviary, which he would not release. His hands were cut off and his knee muscles severed to prevent him escaping. He was killed the following day. At least three other native Christians were massacred (Gonçalo Rodrigues, Francisco Rodrigues and Paolo da Costa) and there were others whose names were unrecorded. The bodies were flung into ditches in the surrounding fields. The bodies of the Jesuits were mutilated. The hatred that the villagers bore towards Peter Berno could be seen 'from the horrible treatment of his body: for they plucked out one of his eyes, cut off the whole of his skull and committed other acts of atrocity of which I am loath to account', wrote Father Stephens. In fact, his genitals had been cut off and stuffed into his mouth.

The bodies of the Jesuits were thrown down a well that was overgrown with thorns. Two days after the massacre, Thomas Stephens recovered the bodies of the others to be buried by their friends and relations. At first, the villagers refused to release the bodies of the Jesuits, but relented on the third day and he recovered them. It was said that they showed no signs of decomposition, although Thomas Stephens does not mention this. 'Such was the end of our Fathers', he wrote, 'who were so eagerly zealous for the salvation of souls as to give rise to the hope that, with their help, the Christian religion would be propagated through the length and the breadth of the land'.

It is difficult to draw a firm conclusion from a single comment in a letter, but it appears that Thomas Stephens was not convinced that the actions of his fellow-Jesuits were all that commendable. Their self-imposed desire for a violent death and their wilful provocation of the villagers to achieve this seems more akin to suicide than martyrdom and their involvement of the young Christian converts, who then died such awful deaths, suggests a lack of care amounting to recklessness. In contrast, the Jesuit missionaries in England took every possible step to ensure self-preservation, although they met death heroically when it became inevitable. Thomas Stephens expresses admiration for their steadfastness and courage, but appears more lukewarm about the martyrs of Cuncolim.

Revenge on the villagers was swift. The Captain-General of the garrison at the Assolna Fort on the banks of the River Sal, raided and destroyed orchards in the village and unleashed atrocities on the population. Seventeen of the *Kshatriya ganvkars* of Cuncolim were invited to parley at the fort under the guise of a safe conduct. In an act of treachery, of which Fr Rodolfo's friend Emperor Akbar would certainly have approved, sixteen were summarily executed and their heads impaled on stakes in the square at Cuncolim: just one escaped by jumping into the river through a latrine.

The Jesuits were buried in the Church of *Nossa Senhora das Neves* at Rachol. In 1597, they were reinterred at St Paul's College to allow easier access for pilgrims who came to venerate their shrine. In 1862 their remains were taken to the Se' Cathedral at Goa, where they remain to this day. The process of canonisation began in 1600, but it was not till 1741 that Pope Benedict XIV declared the martyrdom to be proven. The five priests were beatified in 1893. Their feast day on 26 July is celebrated with great solemnity in Cuncolim, although there is some resentment amongst the Catholics of modern Goa that it was the five European religious who were beatified and not the Goanese converts. Whether it was connected to the martyrdoms or otherwise, in May 1584, the Provincial, Fr, Alessandro Valignano, ordered that the College should be moved back to Margão. There may well have been parties within the Society, some for Margão and some for Rachol. If so, the latter prevailed again in 1588, when at the third Jesuit Provincial Council, almost certainly attended by Fr Thomas Stephens, it was decided to seek permission to transfer the College back to Rachol.

That the Jesuits continued to have a bad reputation amongst at least some of the native peoples is demonstrated in a letter written by the Provincial Francisco Cabral in 1596, in which he describes the efforts of 'Moors and Gentiles' to discredit the Society by charging them unjustly with carrying out conversions by force.

Bernardo

Thomas Stephens sent an account of the deaths at Cuncolim to his brother, Professor of Philosophy at the University of Paris. Much of his letter is taken up by his account of a Brahmin boy known as Bernardo, of 'uncommon character'. The Jesuit Father who he had succeeded at Rachol had baptised him two years before and now entrusted the boy to his care. Bernardo had an elder brother, who also had become a Christian but was 'as far removed from him in a Christian spirit and piety as he was close to him in relationship.' Bernardo's family were also unremitting in their efforts to undermine his new faith. Bernardo expressed a desire to learn Latin and, with the permission of the Father Provincial, was about to leave for Goa where he could study the language. His family expressed great alarm at this and appear to have associated the learning of Latin with a desire to become a priest. 'If he masters the Latin language;', they said, 'it is to be feared that... he will greatly injure us and our sect.' Clearly the destruction of the Hindu temples had not been forgotten. As a ruse, they invited the boy home to say farewell, but really to entreat him to return to them. When this failed and the boat on which he was to leave was about to depart, they seized him so that his brother could plead with him. When this tactic failed, they let him go. He had missed the boat, but decided to proceed on foot. His brother followed him with two companions and demanded to know why he had left without bidding farewell to his family. They threatened him with violence if he didn't return. 'Compelled by necessity, the boy consented.' At home he found his mother and some other relatives who received him with open arms. They set before him food that had been 'so villainously medicated' with the juice of the dutro plant[10] as to make him 'lose instantly his reason and memory, with the result that he knew not where he was or what he was doing.' When he came to, several hours later, they offered him the same 'noxious' food.

> Being out of his senses, he raved in a wonderful manner, embraced shadows which he took for our Fathers and went about, tearing the leaves off the trees, glistening in the moonlight, thinking they were letters that he had received from us, to be delivered to Goa.

After laughing at his plight, his kidnappers poured water over him to bring him round. Then they bound him and flung him into a cave, guarded by 'two ruffians'. When he regained his senses and realised where he was, 'he pitiably lamented his condition, but presently recommended himself and all his affairs to Almighty God'. His mother spared no effort in trying to persuade him to renounce the Christian Faith, as his brother had done and to don, once again, the 'pagan' dress and turban. She promised him mountains of gold if he obeyed and threatened him with no end of torments if he did not. They brought sacred ashes, which, when mixed with food, were believed to have the capacity to change the mind of even the most intransigent. Bernardo, however, made the sign of the cross over the food and swallowed it boldly. When they saw this, they tied his hands. After he had lain in chains for ten days or more, another apostate, a previous acquaintance (the owner of the place where he was being imprisoned), came to see him. Bernardo decided that an economic argument might succeed where others had failed. 'Is it possible, my friend',

> That I am treated in this way in your property and grounds? Do I not know your relations from whom our Fathers buy cloth for baptism every year? How painful will

it be to the Fathers to hear that I am detained in chains in a place belonging to one to whose friends they are so kind.

The point was taken. The apostate went to Bernardo's mother and said,

> I praise your efforts, but beware of being in too great a hurry. You think of trying to change the mind of your son in a single day by resorting to violence. This is simply impossible. He fell away from us gradually and gradually he must be recovered. For we too were once Christians. We were won over to Christianity gradually and gradually did we leave it. This is not to be wondered at, seeing that the Fathers themselves do not prevail upon one on the very first day, but attract people little by little, and, having kept them for some time, wash them at last in the waters of baptism. So shall it be with your boy if you choose to have me as your adviser. First he must be set free. Then we must gently draw him by many allurements, for, if you do him violence, you will only make him all the more obstinate.

The apostate's argument is interesting because it reveals the Jesuits' approach to conversion by creating an entire cultural ambience around the person. This not only accords with the philosophy of Accommodation, but also with Father Stephens's growing realisation that converts potentially could lack a cultural anchor that had to be recognised and replaced. However, it is difficult to reconcile this approach with that of the Martyrs of Cuncolim.

The mother saw the sense in these arguments and ordered that her son be released from his chains and from the cave that had been his prison. He was placed in the care of a 'Guardian' who was to keep watch on him overnight. To keep himself awake, he sang all night and went to sleep at daybreak, when he must have assumed that there were enough people around to keep an eye on the boy. Bernardo observed this process for a couple of days and realised that there was a brief period at sunrise when his overseer slept, leaving no-one to watch over him. He took advantage of this to slip away and conceal himself in a dense plantation nearby. He did not go far because he expected to be overhauled by his pursuers, who would assume that he had headed straight back towards Rachol. In the hue and cry that followed, they scoured the more distant localities, but, as the heat of the day intensified, they returned home, worn out. The boy, who had been watching their movements and listening to their shouts, took the opportunity to flee through the dense hills and hidden valleys until he reached the riverbank, where 'by the disposition of Providence', he found a boat. 'Using a branch of a palm tree for an oar he crossed the river, and was received with joyous surprise by the Fathers who had been praying for him with the utmost solicitude.' The return of Bernardo inspired Thomas Stephens to poetic and apocalyptic prose.

> And these, dear brother, are the storms, these the billows that threaten us as we are sailing on this sea and of which you asked me to inform you. Here are the birds, some of which have been lifted up on high as if on the wings of pious desires and so, as we trust, have gained the regions that they so eagerly longed for, and others are yet on earth though filled with the hope of a like happiness. Here are trees some of which have fallen, not indeed to be burnt but to be transferred to the heavenly mansions and others are bearing fruit of no despicable kind.

In his letter, Richard Stephens expressed concern at the growing force of Calvinism in parts of Western Europe. Given that the brothers kept each other au fait with the happenings of the day, he may be referring specifically to what became known as the *stille beeldenstorm* (quiet images storm) that took place in Antwerp in 1581. A period of iconoclasm occurred after a Calvinist city council was elected and purged the city of Catholic public officials. Images in churches were destroyed in an 'iconoclastic fury' that lasted for several days. In his reply, Thomas Stephens reminds his brother that Calvinism is but the latest (and certainly not the greatest) threat to the Catholic Church that had occurred throughout its history.

> Nor does Calvinism rage so much amongst you as Arianism[11] once did over almost the then known world. Let us pray God, then, that He may grant us to avail ourselves of these calamitous times to make progress in the path of virtue with all patience and longanimity, and the more vigorously to make headway in the face of adversity with our united strength, so that temptation itself may become a means of salvation, and what is the cause of ruin for others may be for us an occasion to acquire glory. May we both receive this grace from Him who has grounded us firmly in the Catholic faith—Farewell.

'Our Troubles have been so Great'

The year 1583 was an eventful one for Thomas Stephens. He must have been astonished when four Englishmen arrived in Goa. Ralph Fitch and John Newbery were merchants and had been sponsored by the Turkey and Levant Company to explore the prospects for English trade along the overland route to the Persian Gulf. They were accompanied at the outset of their journey by John Eldred 'and six or seven other honest merchants'. Tales of the Indian fascination with Western arts and crafts must have filtered back to London, for the two merchants were accompanied by William Leedes, a jeweller and James Storie, a painter. They embarked on the *Tyger*, a ship with which Shakespeare was familiar. 'Her husband's to Aleppo gone', says the First Witch in *Macbeth*, 'Master o' the Tiger', although the Bard's geographical knowledge was a little vague,

Newbery had previously travelled on behalf of the Company as far as Ormuz, the Portuguese outpost at the mouth of the Persian Gulf, in 1581, and presented gifts to the Governor, Matias de Albuquerque. It was now his intention to go well beyond this. He was carrying letters of accreditation from 'the Queenes Majestie' to the two greatest Emperors in Asia (Akbar, and 'the King of

'Had it not Pleased God'

China'). These demonstrate the increasing interest in England in promoting international trade. The first opened as follows:

> To the most invincible, and most mightie prince, lord Zelabia[12] Echebar [Akbar], King of Cambaya, Invincible Emperor &c. The great affection which our subjects have, to visit the most distant places of the world, not without good will and intention to introduce the trade of marchandize of al nations whatsoever they can, by which means the mutual and friendly trafique of marchandize on both sides may come is the cause that the bearer of this letter Iohn Newbery, ioytly with those that be in his company, with a curteous and honeste boldnesse, doe repair to the borders and countreys of your Empire, we doubt not but your imperiall Maiestie through your royal grace, will favourably and friendly accept him.[13]

John Newbery was acquainted with a remarkable young clergyman, whom he addressed as 'right wellbeloved, and my assured good friend'. Richard Hakluyt was around thirty years old at this time. The son of a London merchant, his father died when he was five and his mother soon after. A cousin and namesake who was a lawyer became his guardian. One day, while he was at Westminster School, Hakluyt visited his cousin at his chambers in the Middle Temple. Richard Hakluyt senior had a great interest in Geography. His ward 'found lying open upon his boord certeine bookes of Cosmographie with an universall mappe'.

> From the mappe he brought me to the Bible, and turning to the 107th Psalme, directed mee to the 23 and 24 verses, where I read that they which go downe to the sea in ships, and occupy by the great waters, they see the works of the Lord, and his woonders in the deepe, &c. Which words of the Prophet, together with my cousins discourse (things of high and rare delight to my yong nature) tooke me in so deepe an impression that I constantly resolved, if ever I were preferred to the University, where better time, and more convenient place might be ministred for these

> studies, I would by Gods assistance prosecute that knowledge and kinde of literature, the doores whereof (after a sorte) were so happily opened before me....
>
> ... In continuance of time and by reason principally of my insight in this study, I grew familiarly acquainted with the chiefest Captaines at sea, the greatest Merchants and the best Mariners of our nation by which meanes having gotten more than common knowledge... [14]

At Oxford University, 'his exercises of duty first performed', Hakluyt continued to pursue his interests. He set out to read all the accounts of voyages and discoveries he could find. His education at Westminster would have made him proficient in Latin and Greek, but he learnt Italian, French, Spanish and Portuguese in order to collect and translate exploration narratives. His subsequent career reveals that he probably had some knowledge of Arabic and possibly of certain other Oriental languages. Hakluyt took Holy Orders while at Oxford. Shortly after taking his M.A. in 1575, he began to give public lectures in geography. As a result of his research, he wrote and published a work whose lengthy title indicates its purpose: *Divers Voyages Touching the Discoverie of America and the Ilands Adjacent unto the same, made First of all by our Englishmen and Afterward by the Frenchmen and Britons*. By 'Britons', Richard Hakluyt meant Bretons. The French had been established in Canada for decades, largely through the activities of Breton mariners like Jacques Cartier. Hakluyt's purpose was to demonstrate that the English had rights in North America that preceded those of the French. This call to an imperial destiny was to be the dominant theme of his work.

Amazingly, John Newbery was also familiar with the name of Thomas Stephens and may have even been considering visiting him in India. By some means, Richard Hakluyt had come into the possession of the letter that the Jesuit had sent to his father, describing his voyage to Goa. He lent it to Newbery to copy out and also wrote him a briefing on Francisco Fernandes, the Court

Physician to King Philip II of Spain who is credited with introducing tobacco to Europe.[15] The *Tyger* disembarked the travellers at Tripoli in February, 1583. After staying there a fortnight, they made the nine-day journey over land to Aleppo. The city was a crossroads for East-West trade: the base for 'divers marchants and factours of all nations, as Italians, French men, English men, Armenians, Turks and Moores'. Richard Hakluyt had asked John Newbery to find him a copy of the 'booke of Cosmologie of Abilfada Ismael', the medieval Arab geographer. On 28 May, he wrote to say that his search had been fruitless. 'Some say that possibly it might be had in Persia, but notwithstanding, I will not faile to make inquiries of it, in Babylon, and in Barsara [Basra] and if I can find it in any of these places, I wil send it to you from thence.'

Newbery returned various papers that he had inadvertently packed into his baggage. 'The letter which you delivered me for to copy out, that came from M. Thomas Stevens in Goa, as also the note you gave mee of Francis Fernandas the Portugal I brought thence with me among other writings unawares, the which I have sent to you here enclosed.' While in Aleppo, the little party of Englishmen met the local representatives of the Turkey and Levant Company who asked them to investigate the possibility of opening a factory in Ormuz. Much of their time was spent in acquiring the 'great store of marchandise' that they would take on their journey.

> Such as Clothes, Saffron, all kindes of drinking glasses, and Haberdashers wares, as looking glasses, knives and such like stuffe and... all kinde of small wares that may be devised. And although those wares amounted unto great summes of money, notwithstanding it was but onely a shadow or colour, thereby to give no occasion to be mistrusted, or seen into: for that their principall intent was to buy great quantities of precious stones, as Diamants, Pearles, Rubies, &c to the which end they brought with them a great summe of money and golde, and that very secretly, not to be deceived or robbed thereof, or to runne

into any danger for the same.

Twice a year, a caravan left Aleppo, bound for 'India, Persia, Arabia and all the countreys bordering on the same'. The Englishmen journeyed with it across the desert to Bir on the Euphrates. From thence they went by boat to Fallujah. They had been acquiring goods to trade, in addition to those they may have shipped from England, to the extent that they had to hire a hundred asses to convey their baggage overland to Baghdad on the next stage of their journey. There they stayed for some days, reloading the goods onto boats to travel down the Tigris to Basra. Here, John Eldred and his companions left the party, either by prearrangement, or because he felt he need travel no further to find a commercial opportunity. They made the right decision. When Eldred and 'other honest merchants' departed, it took seventy barges to carry their merchandise, which consisted mainly of spices. They arrived in Baghdad 44 days later from whence they departed for Aleppo with many other merchants in an enormous caravan of four thousand camels. Eldred made Aleppo his headquarters for the next three years. In this time, he travelled extensively throughout the region, not only to further his commercial interests, but also, in his own words, 'as one desirous to see other parts of the country'.

On 22 December 1587, Eldred embarked at Tripoli to return to England and 'arrived in safety here in the river of Thames with divers English merchants, 26 March 1588, in the Hercules of London, which was the richest ship of English merchants' goods that ever was known to come into this realm'. He was now a wealthy man. In 1597 he bought the manor of Great Saxham in Suffolk, and built a mansion that came to be popularly known as Nutmeg Hall, after one of the commodities that had made his fortune. The source of his wealth had been widely noted, with far-reaching consequences. The companions who had parted from Eldred at Basra were not to fare so well. From there, they took a ship to Ormuz, where they rented a shop and began to sell their wares. Amongst their fellow voyagers was Michael Strapone, a Venetian trader. It would not have required a lot of imagination for him to deduce the Englishmen's purpose. The Venetians had long dominated the overland route and had established factories at Ormuz, Goa and Malacca. Strapone and his fellow countrymen viewed the Englishmen as a threat.

> And fearing that those English men finding good vent for their commodities in that place, would be resident therein and so dayly increase; which would be no small loss and hindrance unto them: and to that end they went unto the Captaine of Ormus…

On the very day of their arrival, Strapone denounced the Englishmen as spies sent by the Portuguese Pretender, Dom Antonio. The cry was taken up by the other Venetians who accused them of heresy and demanded that 'they should not be suffered so to depart without being examined and punished as enemies, to the example of others'. The 'Captaine of the Castle', Dom Matias de Albuquerque, was placed in a dilemma. He wanted to help the Englishmen and had a high regard for Newbery. On the other hand, their enemies were accusing them of two capital offences. He could only ignore such charges at his peril, so they were arrested and confined in the castle. He did everything he could to alleviate their condition. To enable them to translate their goods into money, he permitted them to go out of the Castle each morning, escorted by their guards to make their sales, returning at night. Since the Venetians were relentless in their determination to dispose of the Englishmen, Albuquerque consulted the Viceroy of the Indies, Dom Francisco de Mascarenhas. It was decided to send the prisoners to Goa that he could question them on 'what newes there was of Dom Antonio, and whether he were in England, yes or no'. The flimsiness of this ploy is self-evident. In the unlikely event that these London merchants knew anything of the Pretender's whereabouts, by the time the information could be conveyed back to Lisbon, it would be at least two years out of date.

The Portuguese officials made a careful note of what the Englishmen sold each day in Ormuz. When they embarked for Goa, Albuquerque decreed that Newbery should deliver all the money and goods in their possession to the *scrivano* or purser of the ship. He obtained 'a remembrance' (receipt) from him and ordered that the prisoners and their possessions should be delivered to the Aveador-General (Chief Justice) of Goa on their arrival. Before embarking, Newbery wrote to his English colleagues in Basra, requesting that they ask the Levant Company to petition the King of Spain for their release and expressing apprehension about their potential fate.

> God knoweth how we shall be delt withall in Goa and therefore if you can procure our masters to send the King of Spaine his letters for our releasement, you shall doe us great good: for they cannot with justice put us to death. It may be that they will cut our throates, or keep us long in prison: God's will be done.

In his desperation, John Newbery must have recalled that there was one person who might help them in Goa and he must have scrutinised again his copy of Thomas Stephens's letter to his father in an attempt to discern the character of the man on whom their well-being might depend. The ship was carrying 114 horses and around 200 men. The Aveador General of Ormuz, a great friend of Albequerque, who was retiring after his three-year posting, was a fellow passenger. Several days after their departure he summoned Newbery to his cabin and questioned him closely. He reassured him 'that it might be all for the best that I was sent hither, the which I trust in God wil so fall out...' Nevertheless Newbery learnt that they had been overtaken by events beyond their control. The exploits of Sir Francis Drake had not endeared the English to the Portuguese authorities. In the course of his famous circumnavigation of the globe, the English navigator had fired on a Portuguese galleon off the Molucas. 'Perceiving that this did greatly grieve them,' Newbery asked the Aveador General 'if they would be revenged of me for that which M. Drake had done: To the which he answered, No.' With the benefit of hindsight, Newbery added 'although his meaning was to the contrary', but he must have been reassured at the time.

On their arrival in Goa on 20 November, 1583, they were cast into 'a faire strong prison'. Next day they were taken before the Aveador General of Goa, who seems to have been a rare example of an uncorrupted official. He 'would neither meddle with the goods nor the money, for that he could not prove anything against us' so, after being examined, they were returned to the prison. Meanwhile, their goods remained on the ship, which nine days later embarked for Cochin. The Purser, another honest man, allowed the Englishmen's possessions to be carried ashore. Since they were in gaol, there was no-one to claim them, so they remained in store for a day and a night until a third honest (and unnamed) man, who had travelled with them from Ormuz was persuaded to rent a house on Newbery's behalf and transferred the goods there.

This was not the end of the matter. Five days later, the Aveador General decided that the goods and money should be deposited into the keeping of the court official known as the Positor until a decision was made on the case. Despite this, Ralph Fitch revealed that there were depredations made on their baggage.

> While we were in prison, both in Ormuz and here, there was a great deale of our goods pilfered and lost, and we have beene at great charges in gifts and otherwise, so that a great deale of our goods is consumed.

Most likely, the authorities were suspicious of the four Englishmen because they recognised a growing interest in the East India trade amongst other nations and so it might have turned nasty for them 'had it not' in Newbery's words, 'pleased God to put into the minds of the Archbishop and two other padres or Jesuits of St Paul's College to stand our friends.' The Archbishop, was 'a very good man, who hath two yong men to his servantes'.

One was Bernard Borgers, who, according to Ralph Fitch, was from 'Hamborough'; almost certainly he meant Hamburg. The other was a 21-year-old Dutchman, Jan Huygen van Linschoten. The son of a notary in Haarlam, he had joined his brother, Willem, who was a merchant in Seville. After a downturn in trade Willem had introduced him to Vincente de Fonseca, the Dominican who had recently been appointed as Archbishop of Goa. He offered him a position as a bookkeeper in Goa. He embarked on 8 April 1583, so he had only been in the colony for some three months when the English prisoners arrived.[16]

> Also very helpful to the prisoners were the two good fathers of St Paul, who travailed very much for us, the one of them called Padre Marke, who was borne in Bruges in Flanders, and the other was borne in Wiltshire in England and is called Padre Thomas Stevans.

Newbery probably got a message to Thomas Stephens as soon as they arrived in Goa, begging his assistance. Like many Catholic exiles, Fr Stephens was proud to be English and it is as an Englishman that he is most frequently identified by others. It is significant that he mentioned the county of his birth to John Newbery. He must have been thrilled to meet with his compatriots and eager for news of home; yet, had he been there, he would have faced almost certain torture and execution. Since the excommunication of Queen Elizabeth by the Pope in 1579, Jesuits had been regarded as arch-agents of sedition, yet the attitude of these Englishmen to Fr Stephens is one of admiration, gratitude and friendliness. There is no fear of his calling. Since the charge of heresy had been levelled against the Englishmen by the Venetians, the authorities were obliged to deal with this first. Since none of the accused had more than a smattering of Portuguese, this presented some difficulties, but Fitch and Newbery had 'bene certaine yeares in the Low Countreyes' and spoke good Flemish, so Father Mark, who had been thirty years in the Indies, was designated 'to undermine and examine them' and discover 'whether they were good Christians or no': 'They behaved themselves verie Catholikely and devoute, everie day hearing Masse with Beades in their hands, yet still suspected, because they were strangers, and specially English men.'

It is unlikely that all four Englishmen were recusants. Yet it was but a quarter century since England had been a Catholic land—and it was not unlikely that it would be so again. The heir presumptive to the throne was a Catholic, the captive Mary Queen of Scots. Most Englishmen were learning to accommodate themselves to change: the state religion had altered five times in the previous half-century. The world was becoming aware of this flexibility and while the authorities seem prepared to accept the group's professions at face value, they clearly treated them with some circumspection. It seems curious that Thomas Stephens, a native English speaker fluent in Portuguese, was not selected to undertake the cross-examination, but perhaps he was otherwise engaged in the Salcete Mission. The case sheds more light on the Inquisition in Goa. Although the four Englishmen had been accused of heresy, at no point does there appear any threat that they might be referred to the Inquisitors. The Portuguese authorities were clearly less rigorous in their suppression of potential religious dissidence than were their equivalents in England. Nevertheless it appears that the authorities were considering shipping the Englishmen back to Portugal as a way out of their dilemma. This is precisely how they would deal with the case of Charles Dellon nearly a century later. The rumour reached the ears of Fr Mark and Fr Thomas. Clearly the prisoners had impressed with their answers to Fr Mark's catechetics, for they were able to come up with a proposal that would protect the prisoners from their unknown fate. If they were to join the Jesuit Order, they 'could thereby defend them from all trouble'.

This placed the Englishmen in a quandary. The offer was genuine and well-intentioned. It entailed them to find a place of safety, but also meant that they might have to spend the rest of their lives at St Paul's College, which was clearly not their intention.

Nevertheless, they must have discussed the offer and considered it very carefully. Eventually, John Newbery, Ralph Fitch and William Leedes made a tactful response, saying they were 'unfit' for such a vocation. James Storrie, however, decided to take up the offer and the Jesuits were able to obtain his release from the prison where he had languished for thirteen days. This was a fortunate coincidence of interest. Storrie gained his freedom, but because he was a painter, 'whereof there are few in India', he was a godsend to the Society. 'They had great need of him to paint their Church, which otherwise would cost them great charges, to bring one from Portugall.' Life at St Paul's was obviously superior to life in a Portuguese gaol and at first Storrie was highly content. According to Linschoten, the Jesuits gave 'him good store of work to do, and entertaining him with all the favour and friendship they could devise.' He 'is made one of the company', wrote Newbery, 'which life he liketh very well.'

It is evident that Linschoten did not care for the Jesuits and impugned their motives at every opportunity, claiming that their desire to help the Englishmen was born of greed to get hold of their money and the reason for their offer to them to join the Jesuits was to enhance this desire. This may reflect tensions between the Society and the hierarchy, which tended to identify itself more closely with the Portuguese administration. In fact, the process of induction into the Society is long and strenuous— as much an examination of the worthiness of the candidate's credentials as the Society's desire to have him as a member. It is significant that neither Ralph Fitch nor John Newbery show anything but praise and thankfulness for the way the two Jesuits assisted them. 'For if they had not stuck to us', wrote Fitch, 'if we had escaped with our lives, yet we had had a long imprisonment.'

After the release of Storrie, the other three Englishmen remained in prison, 'being in great feare, because they understood no man that came to them, nor any man almost knew what they sayd'. They requested a visit from the Archbishop's two assistants. Linschoten recorded what happened at the meeting.

> They with teares in their eyes made complaint unto us of their hard usage, shewing us from point to point... Why they were come into the countrey, withall desiring us for God's cause, if we might by any meanes, to help them, that they might be set at libertie upon sureties, being ready to endure what justice should ordaine for them, saying, that if it were found contrary,and that they were other than travelling marchants, and sought to finde out by further benefit by their wares, they would be content to be punished. With that we departed from them, promising them to do our best: and in the end we obtained so much of the archbishop, that he went unto the Viceroy to deliver our petition, and persuaded him so well, that he was content to set them at libertie, and that their goods should be delivered unto them againe, upon condition they should put in sureties for two thousand pardawes.

The prisoners had no means of obtaining such sureties, so Fr Thomas and Fr Mark found a man called Andreas Taborer who was prepared to put up the money as a commercial proposition. They obtained their release next day on a bail of 2,150 *pardaus*, on condition that they 'should not depart the country without the license of the Viceroy'. Their release did not please the Venetian traders in Goa. 'It doth spite the Italians', wrote Fitch, 'to see us abroad, and many marvel at our delivery.' Newbery's first task was to recover their money and goods from the Positor. After fourteen days of pleading, he succeeded. This enabled them to go into business as merchants. They were not permitted to leave the colony, but 'otherwise except this, we have as much libertie as any other nation.' To sell their goods, they rented a house in the *Rua Direita* near the Slave Market. Fitch's morale improved instantly and he made a speedy assessment of their commercial prospects. 'There is much of our things which will sell very well and some we shall get nothing for.' Things were going so well that they were able to hire a Dutch boy, recommended by Linschoten and Borgers, as an assistant.

They began to enjoy what Goa had to offer, including its 'marveilous great store of fruits. For all our great troubles, yet we are fat and well liking, for victuals are here plentie and good cheape...' The Viceroy had mounted an expedition to 'Chaul and Diu, they say, to winne a castle of the Moores.' It was thought that he would return around Easter. Fitch was hopeful that 'then we shall get our libertie, and our securities discharged.' Once this was obtained they would return home. 'Then I thinke it will be the best way, either one or both to returne, because our troubles have been so great, and so much of our goods spoiled and lost.' Yet, Fitch had fallen under the spell of the East.

> But if it please God that I come to England, by Gods helpe, I will returne hither againe. It is a brave and pleasant countrey and very fruitfull. The summer is almost all the yere long, but the chiefest at Christmas.

Andreas Taborer proved an avaricious suretor, demanding more and more money to maintain the Englishmen's bail. In order to pre-empt this, they made suit to the Viceroy, who had returned from his expedition, for the return of the surety. The response was, to put it mildly, disappointing: 'The Viceroy made us a very sharp answere and sayd we would be better sifted before it were long, and that they had further matter againste us.' This 'further matter' is unexplained. Whether the Venetians had lobbied further against them; or Andreas Taborer had determined to use the surety as a means of securing a permanent share of the profits of their enterprise; or there was some other reason for the Viceroy to behave as he did, is unknown. There was clearly continuing discussion in vice-regal circles as to what should be done with the Englishmen. According to Linschoten, a member of the Viceroy's Privy Council told them that they were only waiting for a ship that could take them to Portugal. Certainly, the three Englishmen must have felt that they victims of a game of cat and mouse that was permeated with uncertainties. Newbery told Linschoten that 'he knew not what to say or thinke therein, or which way he might be ridde of those troubles.'

The crunch came when another informant told them that they 'should have the *strapado*', a form of torture in which the prisoner's hands are tied behind his back and he is lifted off the ground by a rope tied to his wrists. He is then allowed to drop until his fall is checked with a jerk by the rope. How serious this threat was and who made it is not revealed, but, with no clear prospect of having their surety discharged and with such intimations against their future well-being, the three decided that they had only one choice, 'Whereupon we presently determined rather to seeke our liberties, then to be in danger for ever to be slaves in the countrey'. In preparation for their departure they changed as much money into precious stones as they could afford to outlay without arousing suspicion. Leedes's expertise as a jeweller was invaluable in this. On Whit Sunday morning, 5 April 1584, 'they went abroad to sport themselves', leaving the Dutch boy, who had no knowledge of their plans, in charge of the house. To any passer-by, they were going for a picnic in the country, taking with them 'a good store of meat and drinke. And because they should not be suspected, they left their house and shoppe, with some wares therein unsolde'. They had hired a *Patamar*, or Indian post-boy, who knew the country well. He took them to the frontier of Portuguese territory, which at the time was just three miles from Goa, 'in the mouth of the river in a country called Bardes'. The riverbed was half dried-up, so they crossed it with ease: 'And being set over the river, we wente two dayes on foot not without feare, not knowing the way nor having any guide, for we durst trust none.'

When the news of the Englishmen's flight broke in Goa, 'there was a great stirre and murmuring among the people'. Wild rumours circulated. Some said that they had fled towards Aleppo: others accused Linschoten and Borgers of conniving in their escape. According to the slightly unreliable Linschoten, Fr Mark, who had helped organise their bail, was furious about their departure, calling 'them hereticke's, and spies, with a thousand other railing speeches...' Naturally, James Storrie was not happy that his confreres had left him to his fate. Since he had taken no vows, he was free to leave St Paul's, which is what he did. The Jesuits pleaded with him to remain, but 'he tolde them flatly that he had no desire to stay within the cloister'. He had been told that he could make a good living in Goa and this proved to be the case. He set up shop in a house he rented without the monastery walls 'where he had a good store of worke: and in the end married a mestizos daughter of the towne, so that he made his account to stay there while he lived'. He was happy to tell anyone who would listen about his remarkable journey from Aleppo to Ormuz and his progeny were the first of the many Anglo-Indians.

It would appear that the troubles with the Viceroy suffered by Newbery and his companions were to due to the terms of their bail. Storrie, for whom the Jesuits had vouched, experienced no such difficulties. In fact, the three Englishmen had fulfilled their original intention and fled to the court of Akbar the Great, where they must have presented him with the letter from Queen Elizabeth. They were clearly made welcome, for they stayed in Fatehpur for over a year. Newbery may have been ailing by this time for on 28 September 1585, he set off for Lahore in the hope of returning to England. It was decided that Fitch should continue with the expedition and look into the prospects for trade in Bengal. The assessment that English craftsmen would go down well in India proved entirely correct. Leedes, the jeweller, had become a great favourite of the Emperor, 'who did entertaine him very well, and gave him a house and five slaves, an horse and every day sixe [silver pieces] in money.'

Before he left, Newbery promised Fitch that 'if it pleased God' he would meet him within two years with a ship out of England. It was not to be. He died at Aleppo, his dreams of opening the land route to the east to English merchants unfulfilled. Ralph Fitch was to continue his journey to Siam and Malacca before returning on the overland route via Ceylon. Back home, he found that his executors had assumed he was dead and sold off his property. He had been away eight years.

Notes

1. Mar is a title meaning 'Spiritual Lord' in Syriac.
2. C. G. Herbermann, 'Encyclopaedia of Sects and Religions', vol. 4 (New Delhi: Cosmo Publications: 2005), pp. 1180, 1181.
3. J. Correia-Afonso, *Letters from the Mughal Court* (Anand, India: St. Louis Institute of Jesuit Sources: 1983), pp. 123, 124.
4. M. Cooper, *The Japanese Mission to Europe 1582–1590* (Folkestone, Global Oriental, 2005), p. 9.
5. Biographical details of the Martyrs of Cuncolim are contained in Thomas Stephens's letter to his brother Richard, of 24 October 1583. See J.L. Salanha, *Biographical Note*: (English trans) (Bolar, Mangalore: 1907), pp. xxx-xxxiv. A copy of the original is in the National Library of Brussels, ms 3353–61. f. 6fr-63v.
6. Tertullian, *Apologeticus*, 13.
7. *Travels in India in the Seventeenth Century by Sir Thomas Roe and Dr John Fry*, reprinted from the Calcutta Weekly Englishman, 1873 (London: British Library: 2010), p. 425.
8. J. M. Pacheco de Figuireda, *Goa Dourada nos Séculos xvi e xvii. O. Hospital des Pobres do Padre Paulo Camerte* (Lisbon: Sep. de Studia: 1968), p.117, as quoted by I. Conceição Souza (www.ivosouza.word-press.com>2009/01/13/ evangelization-of-the-village).
9. Eventually the great bell of the Se' Cathedral in Goa would be cast there.
10. Dutro grows wild in Goa. It resembles an aubergine eggplant and bears thorny fruits. This is the sedative that Pyrard de Laval calls 'Deutra' (see Chapter 2), and which describes native woman giving their husbands to make them sleep 'like a dead man', while they took 'their pleasure elsewhere'. It was the sap of the plant rather than the seeds, as he suggests, that was used to cause this effect. 'If anyone takes of it', wrote Thomas Stephens, 'he is out of his mind for twenty four hours, in such a way that you would not be able to tell if he was drunk or utterly abandoned.' The incident with Bernardo confirms that it was mixed with food.
11. Arianism was the Christological error that Jesus, as the Son of God, was created by God. It was proposed early in the fourth century by the Alexandrian presbyter Arius and spread throughout much of the Eastern and Western Roman empires, even after it was denounced as a heresy by the Council of Nicaea (325).
12. Perhaps another attempt to address Akbar by his title of 'Zillulah'.
13. R. Fitch and J. Horton Ryley (ed.), *Ralph Fitch, his Companions and Contemporaries, with his remarkable Narrative told in his own Words*, Book

II (London: T. Fisher Unwin: 1899), p. 44.
14. R. Hakluyt and E. Goldsmidt (ed.), *The Principall Navigations, Traffiques and Discoveries of the English Nation*, vol 1 (Edinburgh: E. and G. Goldsmidt, 1899).
15. R. Hakluy, 'The Relacion of Francisco Fernandes' (BM Additional MS48151:ff 159–60).
16. Fitch, *Remarkable Narrative*, pp. 41–65.

6

Of a very good Talent for Conversions

Matteo Ricci

In Goa, as in the rest of the Catholic world, Wednesday, 4 October, 1582, was followed by Thursday, 15 October, as a result of the switch from the Julian to the Gregorian Calendar, which had been devised by Christopher Clavius.

In 1579, Alessandro Valignano, the Vicar-General of the Jesuit Order in the Indies, summoned Fr Michele Ruggieri to the mission in Macao. The city had been established as a Portuguese outpost in China, at the mouth of the Pearl River, in 1557. True to the principles he had developed in Japan, he ordered him to apply himself wholly to the study of written and spoken Chinese.[1] Three years later, Fr Matteo Ricci departed Goa and joined him, with the aim of fulfilling Francis Xavier's dream of a mission to China. The two men epitomised his prescription for Jesuits in the mission field: 'patience, prudence and a measured approach'. Drawing on this adage, Ricci petitioned the Chinese Imperial Court for permission to enter its territory. This was eventually granted. The Jesuits embarked with a considerable baggage train. As well as personal effects, they brought Venetian prisms, books, paintings and engravings, sundials, clocks and mathematical and astronomical instruments.[2]

At first the Jesuits settled at Chao-ch'ing in Kwantung (Canton) Province, where they continued to learn Chinese and familiarise themselves with the culture. In order to appear part of the society that they had adopted, they wore the garb of Buddhist *bonze* (monks). Their initial aim was not to win converts but to make Christianity acceptable. To this effect, Fr Ruggieri wrote a catechism entitled *T'ien-chu sheng-chiao shih-lu* (*A True Account of God and the Sacred Religion*). This was translated into Chinese in 1584 by Fr Ricci and a Chinese scholar. Around this time, Ricci compiled the first Chinese-Portuguese dictionary.

Fr Matteo Ricci

Like other Jesuits, Ricci was an inveterate cartographer. While in Chao-ch'ing, he produced his map of the world, *The Great Map of Ten Thousand Countries*, which showed China's geographical position on the Globe. He became known in Chinese as *Li-ma-teu* (Ricci Mateo). He became an authority on the Confucian religion, which he realised was entrenched in the Chinese psyche. Indeed, the very name by which Confucius is known in the West is derived from Ricci's Latin translations. He concluded that the Confucian classics were secular in nature and therefore not incompatible with Catholicism. He interpreted references to *shandi* (the Lord-on-High) and *ti'an* (Heaven) as evidence that the Chinese had worshipped God in ancient times. Only during the Ming Dynasty had the original belief in a personal God been subverted. He proposed interpreting this concept of monotheism as a kind of 'natural theology' in the manner of Thomas Aquinas, who had postulated that all men could find a path to God through their reason and instincts.

Ricci was aware that the Chinese, who prized moral principles above all else, could never accept Christianity as a faith system on the promise of rewards in the afterlife alone. He became convinced that the Confucian principles of filial piety, reciprocity and personal virtue were entirely compatible with the tenets of the Catholic Church.

Chinese rituals represented a more complex issue. Heads of families performed rites, which included sacrifices, in honour of their ancestors, while scholars and officials performed them in honour of Confucius. Ricci was aware that the rites were *de rigeur* for the intellectual classes, Renunciation of them would bar any Christian converts from participation in public life. He concluded that the rites were essentially secular in nature, so converts could continue to perform them. A further issue was that of the name of God in Chinese: whether the Confucian name *shangdi* or a generic term *shen* should be adopted by Chinese Christians. Ricci always preferred the title *T'ien chu*, or Lord of Heaven.

Ruggieri, whose knowledge of Chinese was limited, was dispatched back to Rome in 1588 by Valignano to try to persuade the Pope to send an emissary to the Chinese Emperor. This came to naught and he retired to Salerno for the rest of his life. The following year, Fr Ricci moved to Shouguan (Shaozhou), where he became a close friend of the Confucian scholar Ch'u T'ai-su, to whom he taught the mathematics of Christopher Clavius. Ch'u introduced him into the circles of the Mandarins—the high officials of the Chinese Empire—and Confucian scholars. He adopted Ch'u's suggestion that he should don the silk robes worn by Chinese scholars rather than those of a Buddhist monk. This was entirely appropriate: scholars were regarded with deep respect and the robes demonstrated that the Jesuits were their intellectual equals. They let their hair and beards grow long in the manner of Buddhist monks and adopted the title of *daoran*, 'enlightened preacher'.

Fr Ricci was joined in Shouguan by Diego da Pantoja, a twenty-eight-year-old Portuguese Jesuit sent by Valignano to replace Ruggieri. He spoke Chinese fluently and was well-versed in the Confucian classics. Later, they were joined by another Portuguese, Fr João da Rocha, who brought with him a spinet that he taught Fr da Pantoja to play. The Imperial Court was a prime target for Ricci's mission, as that of Akbar had been for Acquavita. He attempted to visit Peking in 1595, but the city was barred to foreigners as a result of a Sino-Japanese war in Korea. He went on to Nan-ch'ang, where he became friendly with two of the royal princes. On their suggestion, he wrote his first book in Chinese, *Jiaoyoulun* (*On Friendship*), which demonstrated the conjunction between the Confucian 'Three Bonds and Five Cardinal Relations' and Catholic doctrine. From February 1599, Ricci lived in Nanjing, where he was chiefly working on his astronomy and geography. He wrote in the third person on the effects of his learning on local scholars:

> The fathers gave such clear and lucid explanations on all these matters which were so new to the Chinese, that many were unable to deny the truth of all that he said, and for this reason, the information on this matter spread among all the scholars of China. From this one can understand how much esteem was given to the Jesuits as well as to our land which thenceforth they did not dare to describe as barbarian, a word they were accustomed to use in describing countries other than China.[3]

This growing reputation ensured that Ricci's second attempt to enter the Imperial capital in 1601 was a success. After their arrival in Peking, the Jesuits were given a difficult time by landlords who, suspicious of their activities, would drive them from their dwellings. They eventually hit upon the idea of renting houses that were supposedly haunted and the problem ceased.

Ricci emulated Acquaviva by bringing gifts for the Emperor Wanli: paintings of the Madonna and of Our Lady with the infants Jesus and John the Baptist; a Roman breviary, a reliquary, two clocks, a copy of his *mappa mundi* and even Fr da Pantoja's spinet, which must have been specially shipped. Yet he still could not gain an audience with the Emperor. An elaborate code ensured that he led a reclusive life, inaccessible even to his own people. He had ascended the Imperial throne in 1572 and his reign of forty-eight years would be the longest in the Ming Dynasty. It was one which witnessed its steady decline. Like Akbar, Wanli was greatly intrigued by these men from afar. A ringing clock was a thing never seen before in China and he summoned Matteo Ricci to enquire about this amazing artefact. Since he could not receive the Jesuits in person, he commissioned an artist to draw full-length portraits of them, so that he could conduct a vicarious interview. He appointed Ricci as Keeper of the Imperial Clocks, a position that included lodgings and a small stipend. Another opportunity was afforded by an eclipse of the sun. The Jesuit's predictions of its time and duration differed considerably from that made by the Court Astronomers. When the Jesuits proved correct, their place was secure.

Contact was made with Imperial officials, who were at first hostile, but who slowly and reluctantly admitted them as they realised that these were no foreign barbarians, but intelligent and cultivated men whose knowledge of the world was in many areas greater than their own. These officials would have gained their positions by demonstrating their intellectual prowess and their mastery of the Confucian classic literature, in which they were amazed to find the Jesuits as well-versed as themselves. Matteo Ricci became a close friend of Xu Guang-qi, who was to become a highly-influential figure in the Imperial Court. The Emperor put him in charge of calendar reform at the *Qintianjian* (the Directorate of Astronomy). He was baptised by Fr Ricci in 1603 and adopted the name Paolo. Together they produced a translation, in 1607, of the first six books of Euclid's *Elements*, based on Clavius's Latin version. Xu built a church on the side of his residence to house the growing gatherings of the faithful.

Other prominent converts to Catholicism were two natives of Hangzhou, Li Zhizao and Yang Tianyun, who invited Fr Lazzaro Cattaneo, Fr Francisco Fortado and other Jesuit missionaries to the city. Li, the Director of Public Works, collaborated with Ricci on numerous scientific essays. He compiled a series of thirty-two books on Catholicism, which he called *Tienxue chuhan* ('Writings on Heavenly Learning'). Yang Tianyun was an eminent neo-Confucian who became a noted Catholic apologist. Together these prominent converts became known as 'the Three Catholic Pillars'. While in Peking, Matteo Ricci published several other books of significance. These included a work of Christian doctrine, *The Secure Treatise on God.* During the last two years of his life, he wrote *Della Entrata della Compagnia di Giesu e Christianita nella Cina*, a history of his mission. Like other Jesuits of the era, he became known as a painter. Fr Diego da Pantoja had become an accomplished musician who may be accredited with introducing Western music to China. He gave concerts at Court on the spinet and taught the Imperial eunuchs how to play the instrument. In 1607, Paulo Xu Guang-qi took Fr Lazzaro Cattaneo with him from Peking to Shanghai, where the priest built a residence and a chapel that are still standing.

Matteo Ricci died on 11 May 1610, but even his death served the cause of assimilation. On the advice of the Chinese officials, Diego da Pantoja petitioned the Emperor for permission to erect a tomb for him, which would enshrine the Jesuit mission on Chinese soil and confer on it the Emperor's blessing. Ricci's funerary inscription, written by the Governor of Peking, described him as 'one who loved righteousness and wrote books'. More than that, he had made aspects of Western learning such as mathematics available in China for the first time. At the time of his death, there were 2,500 Chinese Christians who owed their conversion to him.

After Ricci's death, his assimilative approach to Confucianism was responsible for unleashing one of the longest-running disputes in Catholic history, which became known as the 'Rites Controversy'. The Dominicans contended that the ceremonial rites were idolatrous and represented the worship of demons, while the Jesuits maintained their position that the rites were compatible with Catholic doctrine. The controversy rumbled on for centuries. It was not until Vatican II that the issue was resolved in favour of the Jesuits' view.

The Mirror of Holiness

On hearing of the violent death of his friend Rodolfo Acquaviva, the Emperor Akbar is supposed to have said: 'Alas father, my advice was good that you should not go, but you would not follow it.'[4] Yet his mind may well have been on other things by then. In 1585, he abandoned the spectacular capital he had constructed with such consummate care, moving his seat of government to Lahore. It has been suggested that shortage of water precipitated this action, but it is unlikely that the architects of Fatehpur Sikri would not have understood the nature of aquifers. More likely, the Emperor reverted to the nomadic past of his ancestors, forever pushing towards new frontiers. He had been static too long.

Although Rodolfo Acquaviva must have counted his mission a failure, it certainly made an impact on Indian aesthetics. European visitors to the palaces and tombs of the Mughal Emperors between the 1590s and 1660s were astonished to find them prominently adorned with paintings of Christ, the Blessed Virgin Mary and Christian saints, executed in the style of the late Renaissance. The Mughal artists were also working on miniature paintings, exquisite jewellery and sculptures of the same subjects. Many of them were apparently being used as devotional objects. Once again, the absorptive power of India had asserted itself!

In 1591, a second, briefer Jesuit mission visited Akbar. It consisted of Fathers Duarte Leitão and Christoval de Vega and the lay brother Estavão Riberio. Francis Xavier had said that, even if the Prince failed to convert to Christianity, the mission could still be worthwhile as his patronage could reinforce it. The mission does not seem to have been a success in either of these terms and was withdrawn after a year.[5] A third mission in 1595 was generously subsidised by Akbar and, in some ways, proved highly effective. It was led by Fr Jerónimo Xavier. He was born Jerónimo de Ezpolita y Goñi in Navarre in 1549, but had adopted his name in honour of his great-uncle, Francis Xavier. He entered the Society of Jesus on 7 May 1568 and was ordained priest in 1575, arriving in Goa in 1581. He was appointed Master of Novices, but soon had to give up the position because of his poor health, which was attributed to the 'consequence of the difficult sea voyage and the troubles of acclimatisation'.[6] Many new arrivals must have suffered similarly, including Thomas Stephens two years later. In 1584 he was appointed Rector of the College at Bassein, but ill-health intervened again and, after one year, he was transferred to the healthier climate of Cochin. In 1592, he became the Superior of the Professed House in Goa, a position that placed him second after the Provincial in the Jesuit hierarchy in India. Three years later, when the Emperor Akbar requested another Jesuit mission to his Court, Jerónimo Xavier was selected to lead it. He was accompanied by Fr Emmanuel Pinheiro and Br Bento de Gôis. The missionaries arrived at Akbar's Court on 5 May. On their arrival, Akbar assigned them living quarters in his palace and provided them with a Muslim scholar to teach them Persian.

Akbar had agreed to build a chapel in Lahore for the priests and duly did so, but, despite his warm welcome, Xavier's mission shows many similarities to the first one He became as much a favourite of Akbar as Rodolfo Acquaviva had been. The Emperor would happily engage the Jesuits in dialogue, but hopes of conversion faded. There is no doubt of the high esteem in which he held the Faith, but he was unwilling to accept the doctrines of the Trinity and the Incarnation. He continued to adopt a Universalist approach. 'For the Gentiles regard their law as good, so likewise do the Saracens and Christians. To which then shall we give our consent?'[7] Akbar's many wives must also have been a stumbling block. They represented not only the indulgence of his sensual nature, but the diversity of peoples and faiths within his vast empire. He had already alienated the *Ummah* to the point of rebellion by his inclusive approach to other religions: to have committed himself to any single one would have been politically disastrous.

There is no doubt that Akbar had a great interest in the world of ideas, expressed principally in a fascination with all aspects of religion. Fr Xavier revealed the Emperor's interest in yet another group in a letter written to the Provincial, Fr Francisco Cabral.

> In the month of March [and] at the end of February, I saw a swarm of jogis crowded onto the open space on the opposite bank of the river: all of them gathered in two or three days… and they said that every year they gather together at this same time because the King visits them and gives them alms. He converses with them and, knowing the abilities of all, he chooses those who are most able in sorcery, or the most vivid in appearance, or according

to some other ability and orders that they be given food and a place to live.⁸

Yet Akbar continued to be interested in the learning and rationality of the Jesuits above all other groups. Cultural fusion was the order of the hour. The Jesuits built chapels that architecturally represented an ingenious combination of the Moghul and Catholic Renaissance styles. They capitalised on the Indian love of spectacle by mounting lavish festivals and liturgies. The Emperor commissioned Fr Jerónimo to write a Life of Christ in Persian as the *Dastan-I Masih*, or the *Mir'at-al-Quds*. During his eighteen-year sojourn at the Court, he instilled his writings with the images of the divine light that are of great importance in Sufism. At first he probably wrote in Portuguese, but progressed to Persian as his fluency increased. Given that he did not start to learn the language until he was 46 years old, he produced a remarkable, fluent and voluminous series of writings, including a Life of St Peter, the Lives of the Twelve Apostles and a translation of the Psalms. He even produced a treatise on the Art of Kingship (*Adabu's Saltanus*), which he presented to Akba's son and heir, the Emperor Jahangir, in 1609. In a clever piece of wordplay, he opened his *Mir'at-al-Quds* (The Mirror of Holiness) with the legend of Abgar V, King of Edessa, who was cured of an illness by a miraculous portrait of Christ. The story clearly alludes to Akbar's love of icons, and the similarity of the names would not have gone unnoticed. The work was completed in 1602 and presented to Akbar, who had it read to him. His major work was *Aina-yi-Haqq-Numa* (The Truth-showing Mirror), an extensive dialogue on the very Jesuitical topic of the ways in which reason may be used to discern the nature of true religion. The participants in the discussion are a Catholic priest, representing Xavier himself; a philosopher, representing Akbar; and a Mullah, representing the Court *Uluma*. The book clearly reflects the meetings that took place at Court. Xavier produced an abridged version of the work for Akbar because so much of the Emperor's time was taken up with the business of statecraft.

'A Wonderful Kind'

In a letter to his brother, Thomas Stephens revealed his developing enthusiasm for Indian languages, which he had obviously studied in great depth, acquiring an intimate knowledge of the structure:

> Their pronunciation is not disagreeable, and the linguistic structure is allied to that of Greek and Latin. The phrases and constructions are of a wonderful kind. The letters and syllables have their values and are varied as often as consonants can be combined with vowels...[9]

Thomas Stephens was the first person to identify the similarities between Konkani, Marathi, Latin and Greek. Thus he unknowingly postulated the existence of an Indo-European (or Indo-Aryan) language family. It was not until 1786 that Sir William Jones was to establish the historical relationship between Sanskrit, Latin, Greek and the Germanic languages. The Jesuits realised that knowledge of the languages of India was a key to conversion. Confession is an important part of the work of a Catholic missionary and, since the local Christians could only confess in their own language, it was vital for the Jesuits to have an intimate knowledge of the local languages. None was more aware of this than Thomas Stephens, who played a pioneering role in the codification of the native languages spoken in Goa. He mastered the Konkani language and preached and heard confessions in it.[10]

Thomas Stephens would undoubtedly have played a prominent part in the third Provincial Conference of Christian Missionaries, which took place in Goa in 1585. Among the items discussed was the catechism he had written to instruct the children of new converts in the Christian faith. It appears that he wrote this originally in Portuguese, for the conference requested that it should be translated into Indian languages. Since few of the converts had anything more than a smattering of Portuguese, there were no devotional texts that could be used to instruct them. Fr Stephens expressed this difficulty through the mouth of an Indian in a later work: 'In Portugal there are many devotional alternatives, but we have no knowledge of the Portuguese language.' He wrote his translation in Konkani: probably the first book ever written in that language.

In a letter to the Superior-General Claudio Acquaviva on 6 December 1601, Fr Stephens wrote enthusiastically about his catechism,

> which has been done in the language of the country [and] which the children learn by heart. They do not find themselves at a loss when a superior visits the church and takes a chapter of the doctrine with its questions and answers. I have seen children replying to a whole chapter, small boys and girls who scarcely could speak. One discovers in the confessions that the knowledge of it, however little, is beneficial.[11]

Fr Stephens's zeal for the propagation of the Faith through a knowledge of native languages was reflected in the proceedings of the Fourth Provincial Council of Goa in 1592. It was decreed that 'a compendium of Christian doctrine and instructions should be made and translated into the common languages of the province' and directed that 'churches be assigned to no one but to those priests who are well qualified and know the vernacular of the place.'

One of Fr Stephens's duties was to write an annual report on the progress or otherwise of the Salcete Mission to the Superior General in Rome. His letter of 1601 shows his usual mixture of optimism, pessimism and sensitivity to others that seems to have been his stock-in-trade. He reported that he had been the Rector of the College at Margão for the last six months. Many of the churches in the district had 'vicars who are not fit for their work or have been long in need of a rest'. Some parishes did not possess a priest at all. The 'sad plight of the Christian community stemmed from ignorance and malice'. The populace did not understand 'the things necessary to their salvation', He goes on to list all the good things about the Christians of Salcete. Nuno Rodrigues, the Father Provincial, had created little chapels in remote villages. The Christian population of Margão were all Brahmins and the Church of the *Madre de Deos* at Majorda was extremely lively.

Back in Goa

On 29 May, 1587, the emissaries sent from Japan to meet the Pope returned to Goa. They had arrived in Lisbon in August 1584. From thence they travelled to Madrid, where they were received by King Philip II. He showed them round the newly-built royal monastery of El Escorial. They told him of their admiration of the Arab horses they had seen in Goa and he promised them that they should have one each. The expenditure of 2,000 ducats was part of a total of 7,000 ducats that the King expended on their European journey. This lavish outlay ensured that the generosity towards the Japanese mission that Valignano hoped that the emissaries would engender was not forthcoming: the money had gone elsewhere. Fr Francisco Cabral was to take advantage of Valignano's clear discomfiture at this, writing to Rome to complain about his extravagant behaviour. It was a complaint that had some justification.

When the four young men left on their journey to Rome, Philip II was present to wish them on their way—an unprecedented gesture for a Hapsburg Emperor. In Pisa, the Archduchess of Tuscany insisted on dancing with Mancio. In Rome, they were greeted warmly by the dying Pope Gregory XIII, who showered them with gifts. It must have been gratifying to Alessandro Valignano when he heard that a Papal Bull had been issued, confirming that Japan was the prerogative of the Jesuits. Gregory's successor Pope Sixtus V, whose coronation they attended, treated the emissaries with equal kindness. Mancio Ito was made an honorary citizen of Rome and given the title *Cavaliere di Speron d'Oro* ('Knight of the Golden Spurs'). The young men were greeted throughout northern Italy with pageants and banquets and behaved everywhere with dignity and decorum.[12]

On their return to Lisbon, they indulged their love of horses by riding out frequently as the guests of the Duke of Bragança. Cardinal Alberto told them that they would receive the horses promised by the King when they returned to India. They left Lisbon on 13 April 1586. En route, they wintered in Mozambique. At Goa, the four emissaries were reunited with Alessandro Valignano and their four Arab horses were waiting for them in the shade of the palm trees on the banks of the Mandovi River. The Viceroy, Dom Duarte, told them they could ride freely about the territory. Although the four young men may have thought it, it appears that the horses had not been presented to them at all, but placed at the disposal of the Jesuits, or perhaps Valignano just commandeered them.

In any case, it would be not be easy to convey them to Japan, where the situation had got very difficult for Christians. That very year, the Japanese shogun, Toyotami Hideyoshi, who was seeking to unify the land under his own suzerainty, had conquered Kyushu and banned Christianity as a force that threatened his authoritarian power. Although the edict was not always actively enforced, it made their return difficult. Alessandro Valignano, ever the diplomat, attempted to restore the situation through flattery, conceiving the idea of offering two of the horses as a gift to Toyotami Hideyoshi. When the four emissaries began the next stage of their long journey with Valignano, the two horses went with them, together with a vet, a blacksmith and a riding master. At Macao, where they arrived on 28 July 1588, they had to await Hideyoshi's permission to return to Japan. They spent their time studying Latin and practicing music. 'They are treasures', commented the Jesuit priest Fr Lorenzo Mexia.

The four young men arrived back in Japan on 21 July 1590. One of the Arab horses must have died on the voyage, for only one arrived with them at Nagasaki. The horse seems to have pleased Hideyoshi greatly. The Jesuit Japanese scholar João Rodrigues and Mancio Ito stood close to him, to answer questions. Rodrigues had arrived in Japan as a cabin boy on a Portuguese ship at the age of fifteen in 1577. He spoke Japanese fluently and was nicknamed 'The Interpreter', serving in that role to both Hideyoshi and Tokugawa Iejusu. Three of the young men subsequently became Jesuits and were the first Japanese to be ordained as priests (although Miguel Chijiwa later apostatised from the Catholic faith, married and had four children).

The would-be Jesuit turned merchant Gonsalo Garcia had become a Franciscan tertiary in the Philippines. Knowing that he spoke Japanese, on 26 May 1592 the Spanish Governor of the Philippines sent him on a diplomatic mission to the Imperial Court. He must have reported back to his confreres in Manila, for a year later, and despite the Papal Bull of Jesuit exclusivity, a Franciscan mission led by Fr Peter Baptista arrived in Japan. In contrast to Valignano's pursuit of the powerful as the key to the conversion of the nation, their mission was undertaken amongst the poor. They set up a leper colony and established a friary in Osaka in 1595. Yet, their time in Japan was to be short. The persecution of Christians in Japan began in earnest after a Spanish ship, the *San Felipe*, went aground on the Isle of Tosa in 1596. She was bound for Mexico, but had been blown off-course. One of the passengers was the 20-year-old Franciscan Filipe de las Casas, who was born in Mexico City. He had been serving in the novitiate in the Philippines since 1594 and was returning to his native land to be ordained as a priest. The cargo was confiscated by the Shogun Hideyoshi. The ship's pilot was said to have threatened him with the might of the Spanish King's wrath and it was rumoured that the Franciscans friars, who were all

Castilians, were spies on behalf of their government. Despite their denials, Hideyoshi moved against them. In December, 23 Franciscans (6 friars and 17 tertiaries) and three Japanese Jesuits were arrested. One of the tertiaries was a child of 12; another was 13. Gonzalo Garcia and Felipe de las Casas were among those taken. The prisoners had their ears cropped on 3 January 1597 and the blood-stained tissue was collected with great reverence by local Christians. Toyatomi Hideyoshi was familiar with the Gospel narratives and indeed it is highly unlikely that the Jesuits would not have tried to convert him. In a gruesome re-enactment of Christ's Passion, all 26 were crucified outside Nagasaki on 5 February, including having their sides pierced by lances. In the aftermath of this terrible event, some seventy more Catholics were to perish.

Fr Mancio Ito survived persecution and died in Nagasaki in 1612. Following an edict of 1614 expelling priests from Japan, Fr Martinão Hara went to Macao, where he died in 1639. Fr Julião Nakaura was martyred in Nagasaki in 1633. In 1639, an edict was issued expelling all Westerners from Japan. Only the Dutch, who had taken over much of Portugal's trade with the Orient, were allowed very restricted access to Japanese ports.[13]

One of the 'Professed'

At some point in 1586, Fr Thomas heard of the death of his brother Richard, at Douai, aged 46. In February 1589, he moved nearer the inner heart of the Society of Jesus when he took his vows as a Spiritual Coadjutor. A Jesuit report written around this time describes him as 'of very good wisdom, good judgement and prudence... and of a very good talent for conversions'.[14] This fourth vow bound him to go, without question, delay or distaste, to whatever region or on whatever errand the Pope might send him. Ordination to the priesthood was a parallel induction, fourteen years after he had joined the noviciate.

Soon after, Fr Stephens became one of the 'Professed' and so became a member of the Congregation that chose the Superior-General of the Society. There were several other 'Professed' in Goa. In the 1580s, the Jesuits determined to open a *Casa Professa* in the Old City. A Professed House is one in which the exactitudes of the Rule of St Ignatius are practiced. The site chosen was in a vast square known as the *Terreiro dos Gallos* because cockfights were held there. The project was vehemently opposed by Goa's Senate, the *Santa Casa de Misericordia* and the Franciscans because of its proximity to their institutions.

On the night before they were to be legally restrained from developing the site, two Jesuit fathers and a brother converted a small house there into a temporary church and inscribed the word 'JESUS' on the door. Next morning a bell was rung to call the people to Mass and thereafter that their opponents found it impossible to dislodge the Jesuits.[15] A highly-decorated baroque house was built on the site, completed in 1594. The building of the adjoining Church of Bom Jesus was begun in the same year. The architect was the Portuguese Jesuit Domingo Fernandes, who was assisted by the Chief Government Engineer Julio Simão. It was modelled on the principal Jesuit church in Portugal, the *Espirito Santo* in Lisbon.

Thomas Stephens did not stay long in the Professed House, but it may have been during his short oversight that the impressive stuccoed edifice began to rise in the square. Later he served briefly as *Sosius* or secretary to Nicholao Pimenta, the Father Superior of the Society in India. In 1596, he became Rector of St Paul's College and served as a parish priest in Rachol. He was clearly enthusiastic about furthering the interests of his charge. One João da Cunha complained that the English priest had appropriated the rents of a palm grove and land to the Rachol Seminary that the donor had intended should go the Church of St John the Baptist in Benaulim. If this was the case, there was a certain irony in it, because that was Fr Stephens's next cure.

The lack of priests and Fr Stephens's vow to go wherever he was sent ensured that his ministry was required as a locum parish priest in various Portuguese outposts. He served in at least four parishes in Salcete Province. As a fluent Konkani speaker, he would have been aware of the Hindu legend of how the area came into being. From the Western Ghats, the sixth incarnation of Vishnu, the Lord Parshuram shot an arrow that fell near the sea at Banavli (*ban* means arrow in Konkani) and the land of Konkan arose from the sea. A lake of lotuses called Karmallem Tallem marks the place where the arrow supposedly fell. The Portuguese had distorted the name 'Banavli' into 'Benaulim'. It was a beach town of great beauty surrounded by coconut groves. These were tapped by the *renders* to ferment into the liquor known as *feni*. Many of Fr Stephens's flock would have been *ramponnkars* or fisher-folk. Like Francis Xavier's pearl fishers of the Malabar Coast, they were *Sudras*, the caste of labourers, with whom the Brahmins would have no contact. Their conversion to Catholicism gained them the status of human beings of equal value to others.

Fr Stephens also ministered at the small town of Loutolim (a Konkani name meaning 'the pond where the lush grass grows') in Salcete. After Diego Rodrigues (after whom the island of Rodrigues in the Indian Ocean is named) destroyed all its Hindu temples, one ancient landmark remained. In the spirit of accommodation, Fr Stephens may have used it to illustrate his homilies. The story goes that a wealthy landowner called Mahadar was noted for his acts of charity. His avaricious neighbours took advantage of his generosity and sponged off him until he was destitute. The gods, in recognition of his goodness, granted him a wish. He asked for a small place where he could stand on one foot and pray. He was given it and seeing his devotion, the gods took him into heaven, leaving his footprint behind in the rock. It was said that anyone who prayed there with a pure heart would be blessed.

In 1586, a local Catholic family, the Gaunkors, donated the land to build a church to the Jesuits of St Paul's College. It may be that Fr Stephens went there to supervise the building and consecration of the *Igreja do Salvador do Mundo* (the Church of the Saviour of the World).

The Saviour of the World church at Loutolim

Mormugão was another parish in which Fr Stephens officiated. It lies at the mouth of the Zuari River, which creates a superb natural harbour. Jesuit missionaries had brought Christianity there. On 5 April 1570, St Andrew's Church was consecrated. The following year, Ali Adil Shah of Bijapur invaded South Goa and destroyed its churches. The priests and people fled, but returned after the Portuguese repelled the assault. A temporary structure was erected and thatched with palm leaves, while a new church was being built and in 1594, the Church was re-consecrated. Fr Stephens was probably delegated to prepare the Faithful for this event. The rebuilding of parishes seems to have been a task with which he was frequently entrusted. The Italian traveller Pietro della Valle visited the church in 1624 and described it as 'magnificent, compared with others not only in this region, but even with those in Rome itself'.

Fr Stephens also ministered in the important town of Margão. This area of Salcete was conquered by the Portuguese in 1543. The name is derived from the original 'Mathagrām'—a place with a *matha* or Hindu monastery. Wherever the monastery was, it had been demolished by the Moslems and a mosque built in its stead. Now the Portuguese performed the same service for the town's mosques, building churches in their place. The *Largo de Ingreja* (the Holy Spirit Church), which stands in the Old Market Square, was built by the Jesuits in 1564, but destroyed in a Moslem invasion seven years later. As in Mormugão, the congregation must have worshipped in a temporary structure. It may have been Fr Stephens task to seek to rebuild the church. If this was the case, he failed, as it was not rebuilt till 1645.

Navelim (now a suburb of Margão) is another parish of which Fr Stephens had the brief charge. Today, it has the largest concentration of Catholics in India—over 20,000. The original Church of the Holy Rosary, where Fr Stephens ministered, was built between 1594 and 1598. Its first priest was a French Jesuit, Fr Jean Sena. On the third Wednesday in November, the Feast of our Lady of the Rosary is celebrated. Each year a family is selected to celebrate the feast. They paint the exterior of the church fifteen days before the Feast. The interior is also elaborately decorated and the outside covered with fairy lights. Most of the houses and streets in the village are lit up with colourful lights during the celebrations. At 3am, a beautifully adorned statue of Our Lady is carried in a candlelight procession. The Feast is celebrated for the next two weeks, with novenas, masses, processions, music and dancing. In the evenings, a grand firework display is sponsored by the family selected to celebrate the feast that year. Throughout the day and night, there are Konkani concerts and dances in the evenings. Villagers invite families and friends to celebrate with them in their homes and they visit each other, carrying trays of traditional Goan sweets.[16]

The Synod of Dampier

In 1594, a new Archbishop of Goa was appointed. Dom Frey Aleixo de Menezes was aged just thirty-four. Before his appointment, he had been a Chaplain to King Philip II. An Augustinian monk, he was a man of great austerity, noted for his works of charity. He induced the Confraternity of the *Misericórdia* to establish three houses: one for aged and infirm men, one for widows and one for young girls who, after receiving an education, would be provided with a dowry for their marriages. Each day, the Archbishop invited twelve poor people to dine with him. On 24 November, one of the first events of his cure was the laying of the foundations of the great new church of Bom Jesus. The building was the gift of Dom Jerónimo Mascarenhas, who amassed a vast fortune as Captain of Cochin and then Ormuz, estimated at sixteen million rupees. His family had a particular commitment to the Society of Jesus as his three brothers had all become Jesuits. On his death in 1593, he left all his money towards the establishment of the Professed House in Goa. A priest and a brother from the Society were dispatched by the Provincial from Goa to Ormuz with letters from the Viceroy and a local magistrate urging the authorities to cooperate in realising the legacy. On their arrival, however, they were shocked to discover that most of the Captain's estate had been stolen: only 20% of it was ever recovered.

Soon after his arrival, the Archbishop heard a rumour that Mar Abraham, who had fallen dangerously ill, had applied to the Nestorian Patriarch to appoint his successor. On Menezes's orders the bishop in question was detained at Ormuz and sent back to Mesopotamia. The problem seems to have been caused by Mar Abraham's continuous equivocation. His inability to maintain a consistent doctrinal line as he sought to placate both the Catholic hierarchy and the St Thomas Christians even reached the ears of the Pope in Rome, who wrote to Menezes expressing concern that Mar Abraham had again fallen into

Nestorian error and committed several acts of simony. Mar Abraham was summoned to a Council in Goa to clear his name.[17]

Dom Frey Aleixo de Menezes

Mar Abraham had more sense than to go to Goa without a tenable safe-conduct and ignored all further invitations to attend the Provincial Synod. The Papal brief empowered the Archbishop to take charge of the Angamaly Archdiocese in the event of a vacancy. This occurred on the death of Mar Abraham in 1597.

Menezes attempted to appoint Fr Francisco Ros as the Administrator of the vacant diocese, but Nicholão Pimenta, Superior of the Jesuit Missions in India, regarded the appointment as likely to inflame local feeling. He wrote to Fr Ros, enclosing a letter of appointment that named the Archdeacon, Geevarghese (George) of the Cross, as the Administrator, provided he made a solemn declaration of adhesion to Catholic faith and doctrine. Archdeacon George promised to do so on the first appropriate feast day and his appointment was confirmed by the Pope. At a meeting held at Vaipim, Archdeacon George dropped to his knees as the Declaration of Faith was read solemnly to him in Portuguese, a language of which he spoke not a word. He was then asked to confirm his acceptance and replied in the affirmative in Malayalam *Huva*![18]

Fr Pimenta decided that it was necessary to investigate the situation in Malabar for himself. His journey was fraught with peril. 'I landed at Cochin in bad health', he wrote. This was something of an understatement: during his voyage aboard the Viceroy's carrack, the ship caught fire. The ordnance exploded, 'thundering death and lightning: manifold mischieves to the Rescuers'. From Malabar, he wrote to Claudio Acquaviva, the Superior-General of the Society, attempting to explain the theological and social nuances within the church in Malabar. He had changed his view of Archdeacon George, expressing the fear that, under his tutelage, the St Thomas Christians would relapse into Nestorianism. Nor were there wanting 'persons of ecclesiastical rank possessed of means who proposed to proceed to Babylon and bring from thence another Archbishop'. These misgivings were well-founded. Soon after, Archdeacon George convened a synod at Angamaly at which solemn resolutions were passed to acknowledge no bishops except those sent by the Nestorian hierarchy. Latin priests were refused entry to Syriac-rite churches. The rupture appeared complete. Fr Pimenta urged Memezes to act, declaring that he possessed the right to assume the administration of the Malabar Church *sede vacante*. The

Archbishop resolved to go in person to the Angamaly diocese, threatening to dismiss Archdeacon George and appoint Thomas Kurian, another nephew of Mar Abraham, in his stead. When the Archdeacon heard that he was on his way, he equivocated again, agreeing to give his verbal assent to a profession of faith drawn up for him by the Franciscan fathers.

Menezes remained in Kerala for several months, visiting virtually all the churches of the St Thomas Christians and building a huge stock of goodwill towards himself. On Holy Saturday, at the port of Kadathuruthy (Carturte), his charisma awed the congregation as he celebrated solemn Pontifical High Mass and ordained many priests. Later that evening, Fr Francisco Ros, who had been given the task of translating the *Rituale Romanum* into Syriac, arrived in the town and was amazed. 'Is this Carturte, which I knew so well?' he exclaimed to the Archbishop.

> Only a few months ago, when I came to stay here, they shut the door of the church in my face. I had it opened by the *regador da Rayna* [Governor's watch]. When saying Mass, when I elevated the most Holy Sacrament they all covered their eyes. They thrashed one of my pupils because he named the Pope in the church, and, a few years ago, when I showed them an Image of Our Lady, among the same people many persons covered their eyes, crying out to take away that filth, that they were Christians and did not adore idols or pagodas, which they considered all images to be.

'The visitation through the Serra had often left me exhausted', Menezes wrote, 'but I bear in mind what the Holy Ghost has said: *Adhuc multiplicabuntur in senecta uneri et bene patientes erunt*' (when they call to me, I will answer; in time of trouble, I will be with them; I will deliver and honour them). He came to the conclusion that it was necessary to publicly resolve the contentious theological and organisational issues that were causing confusion and dissent. In many ways, the process must have seemed to him like a reversion over the centuries to the dispute between the

Patriarchs, Cyril of Alexandria and Nestorius of Constantinople. The Council of Ephesus in AD 431 had condemned the error of Nestorius that the Virgin Mary may be called *Chistokolos* ('birth-giver of Christ'), but not *Theolokos* ('birth-giver of God'). This was more than a question of semantics: to Catholics it related to the fundamental doctrine of the Holy Trinity. Twenty years later, the Council of Chalcedon repudiated the monophysite notion of a single nature in Christ, and declared that He has two natures in one person ('one and the same Christ, Son, Lord, only begotten, to be acknowledged in two natures, inconfusedly, unchangeably, indivisibly, inseparably'). Nestorian and monophysite notions were to be found among the tenets of the St Thomas Christians, who, in common with the Orthodox Churches, also rejected the addition of the *Filioque* clause ('the Holy Spirit proceeds from the Father *and the Son*') to the Nicene Creed.

On 30 June 1599, Menezes summoned a Synod in the Catholic church at the village of Udayampoor, which became known as the Synod of Diamper (an alternative name for the village). All priests in Malankara and four laymen elected from each parish were instructed to attend, *sub poena excommunicationis latae sententiae* (on pain of excommunication by force of the law itself). No less than 793 people attended: 133 priests and 660 laity. The Synod lasted for nine days. Doubt was cast on its validity: the Jesuit Fathers, Ros and Campori, who were present, wrote to the Superior-General in Rome, expressing misgivings as to whether the proceedings could be regarded as *in forma*.[19] The resolutions of the Synod were prepared beforehand by Menezes's assistants and it opened with two professions of Faith. The first was by Archbishop Menezes. He was followed by Archdeacon George, who made the declaration in a specially-prepared Malayalam translation. The Archbishop then spoke on the errors of Nestorius, which were duly denounced by the gathering, formally anathematising the Nestorian Patriarch and promising obedience to the Pope. In its nine sessions, the Synod produced 200 decrees endorsed by the participants. A formal union between the St Thomas Christians and Rome was agreed. Syriac was to remain their liturgical language; a further purging of error from the service books was ordered and changes were made to the liturgy to make it conform with Catholic doctrine. The priesthood was to assume the discipline of celibacy. Hindu elements in the marriage rites were to be excised, as were the frequent ablutions that had been incorporated from Hindu worship. Another decree dealt with the 'errors and ignorance' that the St Thomas Christians had absorbed from the Hindu culture by which they were surrounded, including the notion that,

> there is Transmigration of Souls, which after Death go either into the Bodies of Beasts, or of some other Men, which besides which it is a great Ignorance, is also an Error contrary to the Catholik Faith, which teacheth That our souls after Death are carried to Heaven, or Hell, or Purgatory, or *Limbus*, according to every one's Merits, and that there is no such fabulous and false Migration.

Another error was grounded in the fatalism which permeated Hindu society:

> that all things come necessarily to pass, either through fate or fortune, which they call the nativity of men, who, they say are compelled to be what they are... which is a manifest error, and condemned by holy Mother Church foreasmuch as it destroys that liberty of will, with which God created us.[20]

The corollary to such a doctrine is that all men are equal before God, but the St Thomas Christians were obdurate that they would not accept low-caste Christian converts into their churches. The Synod, pragmatically but unworthily, settled for a compromise, acknowledging that their recognition as a high-caste group by Hindu rulers might be put in jeopardy. It was desirable that all Christians worship as one, but, since they were 'subject to heathen princes' who might cause difficulty if caste-lines were blurred, the status quo would be preserved. Until the bishops could establish separate churches for converts from the lower castes, 'let them attend Mass from the Porch', went the instruction.

The Synod also condemned the belief, that would have gone down well in theologically liberal circles in the twentieth century, that all men could be saved by their own laws, all of which are good and lead to Heaven, irrespective of their religion. In the fourteenth Decree of the third session, it was agreed which books would be censored. The Church of the Thomas Christians possessed a rich but highly apocryphal traditional literature, all in manuscript form. After the final Mass all these books were handed to Fr Francisco Ros, who, together with three specially-selected *Cathanars* (priests of St Thomas) would 'correct' them. The purge covered books teaching Nestorian errors; books containing false legends; and books containing sorceries and superstitious practices. Among the books considered in the first category were *The Book of John Barialdan,* which posited the Nestorian doctrine that in Christ that there is disunion between His two persons, the divine and the human; and *The Book of the Procession of the Holy Spirit,* which taught that the Holy Spirit proceeds only from the Father, not from the Son. The *Book of Timothy the Patriarch* claimed that 'the true body of our Lord Christ is not present in the sacraments'; and The 'Sacrifice of the Mass' was attacked in the *Book of Orders,* which stated that 'altars of wood, and not of stone, are to be consecrated'.

Some of the texts were vigorously anti-Roman. The *Margareta Fidel* (*The Jewel*) was attributed to a Nestorian prelate called Abd-isho and claimed that Christianity consisted of three distinct faiths: the Nestorian, the Jacobite and the Roman, of which only the Nestorian faith was true. Some beliefs were alarmingly similar to the growing force of European Protestantism. *An Exposition of the Gospels* claimed that the authority that Christ gave to St Peter over the Church was the same as given to other priests, 'so his successors have no more power or jurisdiction than other bishops'. The virulence of past controversies rebounded down the centuries. The *Life of Abd-isho* claimed that St Cyril of Alexandria, who condemned Nestorius, was a heretic and was in hellfire for having taught that there was only one person in Christ. *The Book of Synods* taught that Roman Catholics were heretics for not celebrating the Eucharist with unleavened bread. Together with the *Margareta Fidel*, it denied that marriage was a sacrament and stated that it could be dissolved. The *Book of Hormisda Raban* declared that images were 'filthy and abominable' and that idols should not be adored. This was consistent with the practices of the Thomas Christians: the elaborate Persian or Thomas Cross (*Mar Thoma Sliba*) was the only ornament permitted in their churches.

In the category of 'false legends', which was reminiscent of some of the apocryphal gospels of early Christianity, *The Infancy of our Saviour* stated that Joseph was a bigamist who had another wife and child at the time he became betrothed to Mary. In the same book, the child Jesus is reproached for naughtiness. The *Parisman or Persian Medicine* contained many spells, including methods whereby one might do mischief to one's enemies and win women. It included the names of many devils, supposing that whomever wrote the names of seven of them on a piece of paper and carried it about his person would be in no danger from any evil. The book contained many exorcisms for the casting out of devils, which mixed Christian words with others that were not intelligible. There were also invocations of the Holy Trinity, often towards the doing of 'lewd things'. The books that were found to be heretical, false or superstitious were handed over to be burnt, but Archbishop Menezes was specific that no book that could be purged of error should be destroyed.

On 25 November 1599, Archdeacon George wrote to the Pope, giving him an account of the proceedings of the Synod and praising the actions of Archbishop Menezes. He requested that Menezes or Fr Francisco Ros be appointed as their bishop, but it is unclear how free he was to write voluntarily; most likely, it was intimated to the Archdeacon that such a letter would be a good idea, but George of the Cross lived until 1640 and never appears to have abrogated the decrees of the Synod, although his relationship with Bishop Ros was, on occasions, fractious.[21] Menezes established a hierarchical structure. On 20 December, Fr Ros was appointed Bishop of Angamaly and the diocese was divided into 75 parishes, with a new priest in each. Four years later, Pope Paul V appointed Francisco Ros to the new see of Cranganore as Archbishop.

Menezes was to come under criticism for his dealings at the Synod from some later commentators, most surprisingly in the *Catholic Encyclopedia* in 1913.

> The only case in which an ancient Eastern rite has been wilfully romanized was that of the Uniat Malabar Christians, where it was not Roman authority but the misguided zeal of Alexius de Menezes, Archbishop of Goa, and his Portuguese advisers at the Synod of Dampier (1599) which spoiled the old Malabar rite.

In fact, Menezes did not 'wilfully Romanise' the Malabar rite. The ancient liturgy traditionally attributed to Saints Addai (believed to be a disciple of St Thomas, the Apostle) and Saint Mari, which had been in continuous use since at least the seventh Century, remained in place. It lacked the words of Institution, however ('This is my body'; 'This is my blood'), of which Pope Eugene IV's *Decree for the Armenians* after the Council of Florence had declared that 'by power of the very words, the substance of the bread is changed into the Body of Christ, and the substance of the wine into the Blood.'

There is no indication that Menezes imposed his will by force on the St Thomas Christians. Indeed, Fr Ros's comments imply that the Malabar Church was brought round by his sheer energy, charisma and commitment. As a Catholic Archbishop, he would believe firmly that there is no salvation outside the Church, whatever interpretation might be placed on that phrase. He perceived the Malabar Church to be permeated with heresy and error and felt it was nothing less than his duty to bring it firmly into the Catholic fold—and yet he was prepared to make compromises that he regarded as necessary to this process. As a prelate who invited the poor regularly to dine with him, it must have pained him to exclude the *Dalits* from the centrality of the liturgy, At least they were now admitted into the church building and the Hindu-style ritual of purification after contact with them had been proscribed. The opportunity was there for a casteless church.[22]

The introduction of a Roman hierarchy under the Portuguese *padroado* must have seemed to many an unbearable loss of independence and tradition. That the old ways died hard was demonstrated on 3 January 1653, when a large number of St Thomas Christians, under the leadership of Mar Thoma I, the successor to Archdeacon George of the Cross, swore the Coonan Cross Oath that they would no longer submit to Portuguese dominance of the life of their church. The dissidents split into a number of factions, the main group re-establishing its links with the Nestorian Patriarchate. In response, in 1661 Pope Alexander VII established an East Syrian Rite hierarchy in communion with Rome—in essence, a Uniate church. By the following year, 84 of the 116 parishes had joined, forming what is now the Syro Malabar Catholic Church.

After the Synod, Archbishop Menezes continued his dynamic diocesan visitation in order to show the St Thomas Christians that they were within his fold, going as far south as Quilon. He considered his mission a success. He wrote to Nicolão Pimenta:

> Had I spent the winter in Goa, those churches would have been lost, nor would I have saved my conscience at a time when that flock was mine and was sadly in need of pastoral care, and Catholic teaching had I abandoned it and had I not rather fed it with healthful doctrine.

The process of the Synod of Diamper sheds more light on the Inquisition in India. Given that it was established to root out the heresy of which the Thomas Christians would have represented a prime example, it was never used as a threat to them and no-one was brought before it, although there is no doubt that

Menezes had imposed his will upon them—at least for that moment.

The Jesuit desire for souls was not slackening. In December,1599, Fr Nicolão Pimenta, the Superior, sent a mission to Bengal and later one to the King of 'Camboia' (Cambodia). He was conscious of the potential political and military value of the outcome of the Synod, writing to Claudio Acquaviva on 21 December 1599 that the St Thomas Christians could place in array 30,000 men in the Portuguese service.

Jan Huygen van Linschoten

A Dutchman in Goa cannot have been all that untoward: despite the revolt of the Spanish Netherlands, they were still technically Philip II's subjects. Dirck Gerritzoon Pomp, who was later nicknamed 'Dirck China', sailed aboard the Portuguese vessel *Santa Cruz*. On arrival in Goa, as later events show, he probably met his countryman Jan Huygen van Linschoten. His ship sailed on to Macao and then to Nagasaki. He was probably the first Netherlander to visit Japan and assiduously collected navigational information en route. Archbishop de Fonseca died in 1587 while on a return visit to Lisbon. When the news reached Goa, Jan Huygen van Linschoten, his bookkeeper, decided to return to Europe. He set sail for Lisbon on 23 November 1588. Calling at the Portuguese outposts of St Helena and Ascension, he utilised his skill as a draughtsman by producing beautiful illustrations of both islands. In the North Atlantic when his ship was attacked by an English privateer, she was forced to run aground in the Azores. He remained on the islands for two years and did not return to Lisbon until 1592. From thence he went back to Holland.[23]

Portrait of Jan Huygen van Linschoten

As a result of his time in India, van Linschoten had amassed a wealth of information about navigation between Portugal and her far-flung outposts. This he now used to good advantage. There was huge interest in Holland in the maritime world. Van Linschoten had interested the Amsterdam publisher Cornelis Claesz, who specialised in travel literature. He renewed his acquaintance with 'Dirck China', who provided him with invaluable information about navigation in the Far East. In 1595 *Reys-gheschrift van de navigation der Portugaloysers in Orienten* (Travel Accounts of Portuguese Navigation in the Orient) was published. and, in the following year, *Itinerario: Voyage ofte schipvaert van Jan Huygen van Linschoten near Oost ofte Portugaels Indien, 1579–1592* (Travel Account of the Voyage of the Sailor Jan Huyghen van Linschoten to the Portuguese East Indies). Van Linschoten's accounts served to further increase the intense Dutch interest in maritime affairs. In 1594, a group of merchants in Amsterdam had formed the *Compagnie van Verre* (the Company for Distant Trade). On 2 April 1595 it sent a flotilla of four ships to the East to explore trade routes to Indonesia. In 1602 the Dutch East India Company (*Verenigde Landsche Ge-Oktroyeerde Oost-Indische Compagnie*) was founded with the specific aim of dominating the spice trade.

The Portuguese military ascendancy over the Malabar coast was challenged as early as 1571, when the Zamorin of Calicut captured the fortress at Chaliyam, the first Portuguese stronghold to fall in India, yet they maintained their dominance of the sea. It was the Dutch who first challenged the Portuguese command of the Indian Ocean. In September 1597, news was brought to Goa of the first two Dutch ships to have ventured into Indian waters. The new Viceroy, Dom Francisco da Gama, grandson of the Navigator, ordered that a squadron of six ships should embark to attack them. The Dutch ships had done a small amount of damage along the Malabar coast before they encountered the Portuguese squadron. A nine-day battle ensued, after which the Dutch ships, severely mauled but still fighting, escaped. Both were later lost, but even as the battle was taking place, the Dutch were fitting out a stronger squadron of six ships, with 800 men and provisions for three years. It sailed from Amsterdam on 13 May 1598 and laid the foundations of Dutch maritime power in the East Indies.

The Dutch attacked most of the Portuguese outposts in the East. Goa was under intermittent blockade from 1603. Awareness of the riches of the East was increasing throughout Europe. 'From Portuguese India came the *Naus*,' declared Cervantes towards the end of the Sixteenth Century, 'loaded with spices and with so much jewels and diamonds that a *Nau* alone was worthy of millions of gold.' In 1592, English privateers captured the great Portuguese carrack *Madre de Dios*, and brought her into Portsmouth. She was laden with jewels, spices, ivory, silk, ebony, porcelain, carpets and many other items. Also found on board was the *Matricola*, the register of the Government and trade of the Portuguese Indies. The point was not missed. In 1599, the Dutch raised the price of pepper from 3/- per pound to 6/. Something had to be done. The Lord Mayor presided over a meeting of the merchants of London at Founders Hall on 20 September and the East India Company (or, to give its precise title, 'The Governor and Company of Merchants of London trading in the East') was mooted. The wording of the petition to the Queen was based on the *Matricola*.

The English move towards the East gathered pace, although it was not without its setbacks. In 1596, Sir Robert Dudley fitted out three ships under the command of Captain Benjamin Wood for the Indian and Chinese trade. None of them was ever heard of again, but interest in these far-off lands was further increased by the publication of an English translation of van Linschloten's *Itinerano* in 1598. The East India Company received its charter on 31 December 1600, although it was not until 1608 that its first ships traversed the Indian Ocean. There can be little doubt that Hakluyt's *Voyages* set the scene for later imperial expansion. In 1601, he was appointed as an advisor to the East India Company, supplying it with maps and briefing its members on potential markets. Portuguese power suffered another setback when four galleons of the Company defeated a squadron of four Portuguese *naus* and 26 barques at the Battle of Swally on 29 and 30 November, 1612.

Ironically, Thomas Stephens may have had a minor influence on the formation of the East India Company. His father must have shown his remarkable letter to his fellow merchants in London and by some process, a copy of it came into the possession of Richard Hakluyt, who in 1598–1600 included it in *The Principal Navigations, Voyages, Traffiques and Discourses of the English Nation*. It has been suggested that Fr Stephens's letter is proof that he was an English spy, briefed to report on Portugal's maritime empire. This is absurd. Hakluyt's *Voyages* is not a compendium of worldwide espionage, but an account of a large number of journeys, some of them apocryphal or even mythical, such as *The Voyages of King Arthur* and *The Long and Wonderful*

Voyage of Friar John of Plano Carpus to the great CAN of Tartaria. Thomas Stephens did send back to England a map of the island of Goa, Salcete and Bardez, but this was a reflection of the great Jesuit interest in cartography and he expressed the hope that he might also send an improved one to the Superior-General in Rome.

It was not only the Dutch and the English who were disrupting Portuguese trade. In 1595, a Moslem adventurer called Puttu Marakkar obtained leave from the Zamorin of Calicut to build a fort at the mouth of the Pudepatam River, some 77 leagues from Goa. From here, he raided the maritime trade of the Malabar Coast, causing much damage to Portuguese commerce. He even made incursions into Portuguese territories and carried off rich spoils. On his death, he was succeeded by his nephew Mohammed Ali, who assumed the title Kunjali Marakkar IV and continued his uncle's depredations. Realising that Portuguese retribution might well be imminent, he strengthened his fortress and the adjacent town, which he renamed after himself. He dubbed himself 'King of the Malabar Moors' and 'Lord of the Indian Sea'. The titles are not as hubristic as they sound: the Marakkars had been in the habit of sharing the spoils with the Zamarin, but Kunjali's overweening arrogance and ambition ensured that he entered into an alliance with the Portuguese for his destruction. The sixteenth Viceroy Dom Francisco da Gama, Count of Vidugeira and great-grandson of Vasco da Gama, sent some light vessels under Fernando de Norhona to blockade the port, pending the arrival of a stronger fleet. Meanwhile, the Zamorin was advancing relentlessly with a force of 20,000 men. Following the arrival of Dom Luis da Gama, brother of the Viceroy, with a powerful fleet, it was resolved to force an entrance into the Pudepatam fort, but the signal for a concerted attack with the forces of the Zamorin was mistimed and the attack was bloodily repulsed. Kunjali held out against further onslaughts and da Gama eventually withdrew, leaving de Norhona's squadron to continue the blockade.

Kunjali was so elated by his success in repelling the Portuguese that he awarded himself the additional titles of 'Defender of the Moslem Faith' and 'Conqueror of the Portuguese'. In the following year, the joint assault was renewed under the command of the greatest Portuguese soldier of his day, André Furtado de Mendoça. The place was stormed with great loss of life on both sides. Kunjali surrendered, on the sole condition that his life should be spared. He was taken on board the fleet with some forty of his followers and they were well-treated, but as soon as they set foot in Goa, several of his followers were torn pieces by the rabble. Kunjali and his nephew were publicly beheaded by order of the Viceroy. In the words of a later commentator, 'The government and the mob went hand in hand to commit murder and a flagrant breach of faith. How can those guilty of such enormities give the name of barbarians to the much more honourable Indians!'[24]

A new landmark appeared in Goa during the Viceroyalty of Dom Francisco da Gama. In 1599, he ordered that an arch of black stone be built in honour of his great-grandfather. The architect was Julio Simão, who had contributed to the design both the Se Cathedral and St Paul's College. It was known as the Arch of the Viceroys (*Arco dos Vice-Reis*). It was a clear symbol of the Portuguese intention to retain their foothold on the Indian sub-continent. It was here that the Senate of Goa would welcome each new Viceroy and hand him the keys of the city. The arch contained two niches. One held a statue of St Catherine: the other one of Vasco da Gama. Dom Francisco da Gama, despite his distinguished lineage, was 'universally disliked by the Portuguese inhabitants' In 1600, he was succeeded as Viceroy by Aires de Soldonha. On the night of 26 December 1600, just before he was due to depart, an officer named Sebastião Tibao applied an acidic solution to the iron bar which held the statue of Vasco da Gama in place. The acid ate through the metal and the statue fell down and shattered. Pieces of it were hung at various points around the city. Before da Gama embarked, a group of armed men went aboard his ship and hung his effigy from the yardarm. When the retiring Viceroy came on board, he saw the effigy and asked what it was. 'It is your Lordship', came the reply, 'whom these men have hung up.' He ordered the figure to be flung overboard and immediately set sail. Two days later, he returned to Goa to take on more live fowls as all those he had taken with him had been poisoned.[25]

Church of Bom Jesus

The Church of Bom Jesus was completed in 1605 and consecrated by the Archbishop, Aleixo de Menezes on 15 May. This must have been a great occasion with a grand liturgy and sumptuous feasting. Thomas Stephens would almost certainly have been present. It was a real milestone in the Society's history in India. The Portuguese were becoming increasingly conscious of the inroads being made into their hegemony of the Indian Ocean by voyagers from other maritime nations. The same step was taken to exclude foreigners from the trade routes that had been taken by the Venetians before them. This too, would be a forlorn gesture. The Viceroy, André Furtado de Mendoça, at the end of the monsoon season in 1609, decreed that all foreigners who arrived in the colony on ships other than Portuguese ones should be imprisoned.

To Agra

By the late 1590s, the Emperor Akbar was pondering the location of his final resting place. It was a Mughul tradition that a man start building his tomb in his lifetime. By 1599, the Emperor had determined that it should be in Agra, so the capital of his empire returned whence it had left 30 years before. Akbar personally supervised the construction of his huge mausoleum. With him went his vast entourage, including his Jesuit friends. In 1600, during fighting in the Deccan, he asked Jerónimo Xavier and Beniot de Gôis to write to the Portuguese authorities at the enclave of Chaul, requesting artillery and munitions. The Jesuits refused to do so, saying that it would contravene their vows and they were briefly alienated from the Emperor, but in 1604, he gave an order under his royal seal to build a church in Agra, known to this day as Akbar's Church.

Akbar died on 27 October 1605. Relations between the Jesuits and his son and heir, Salim, who reigned under the name of Jahangir, were initially good. What appeared a high point in the project to convert the Mughul Empire was reached in 1610 when three of Jahangir's nephews were baptised in the church that bore their grandfather's name, but all three later apostatised. In 1611, the Emperor granted 12 bighas of land to the Society to create a cemetery. Two years later, however, war broke out between the Portuguese and the Mughul Empire. Churches were destroyed and Jerónimo Xavier was sent to Goa to negotiate a peace. He had spent eighteen years at the Mughal Court and accompanying Akbar on his campaigns. He became Rector of St Paul's College, where he died in a fire on 27 June 1617.

Notes

1. Ruggieri's 'greatest achievement' was creating the first complete system of translating Mandarin Chinese sounds using Latin letters. See F. Masini, *The Routledge Handbook of Chinese Applied Linguistics* (London: Routledge, 2019).
2. For sources on Matteo Ricci and the Jesuit mission, see the Bibliography under Brucker, Joseph; Cronin, Vincent; and Gernet, Jacques.
3. See M. Ricci, *History of the Introduction of Christianity in China*.
4. A. Machado Prabhu, *Sarasvah's Children: A History of Mangalorean Christians* (London: I. J. A. Publications, 1999), p. 103.
5. *Ibid.*
6. J. Witts (ed), *Jerome Xavier, letter to Francisco Cabral, S.J.*: 8 September, 1596 (Rome, Documenta Indica, XVII, Vol. 33 of the Monumenta Historical Societis Jesu, 1988), pp. 550–553.
7. Quoted by P. Du Jarric, *Akbar and the Jesuits. An Account of the Jesuit Missions to the Court of Akbar*, tr. C. H. Payne (New York, Hooper & Brothers, 1926).
8. Witts, *Jerome Xavier*.
9. J. L. Saldanha, *Thomas Stephens' letter to his brother, Richard, of 24 October, 1583.* Full text (English trans from the Latin) in *Biographical Note* (Bolar, Magalore 1907), pp. xxx-xxxiv: a copy of the original is in the National Library of Brussels: ms. 3353–61. f. 6fr-63v.
10. Konkani, the main native language of Goa, is a vernacular form derived from Sanskrit roots. It is sometimes referred to as a dialect of Marathi, but it actually predates it. It was a spoken language of many accents and dialects at this time.
11. A. K. Piolkar, 'Two recently published letters of Thomas Stephens', *Journal of the University of Bombay*, vol. xxv, part II (September 1956), p. 121.
12. See J. C. Brown, 'Courtiers and Christians: the first Japanese Emissaries to Europe' in *Renaissance Quarterly* Vol. 47, No. 4 (Winter, 1994), pp. 872–906.
13. For a comprehensive account of the persecution of Christians in Japan see *The Christian Century in Japan, 1549–1650* (Oakland, University of California Press, 1951), pp. 308–361.
14. Saldanha, *Thomas Stephens' Letter*.
15. See www.professed-house.blogspot.com.
16. See *The Goa Herald* (19 November 2014).
17. R. E. Frykenberg, *Christianity in India: From Beginnings to the Present*

(Oxford: University Press, 2008), pp. 134–136.
18. Menezes's account of the Synod of Dampier and the events surrounding it was published by Antonio de Gouveia at Coimbra in 1606 under the title *Jornada do Arcebispo*. An English translation by Dr Pius Malekandathil was published by LRC Publications of Kochi in 2003 as *Jornado of Dom Alexis de Menezes: A Portuguese Account of the Sixteenth Century Malabar.*
19. The Synod of Dampier was regarded as invalid by Bishop Jonas Thaliah, the Syro-Malabar rite Bishop of Rajkot, in his thesis submitted at the Gregorian University in 1952, on the grounds that it was convened without due authority; not conducted according to the canons of the Church; and never properly approved by Rome.
20. The Acts and Decrees of the Synod were fully recorded by Michael Geddes, in his *A Short History of the Church of Malabar* (London: 1694). Reproduced in *Indian Church History Classics*, vol. 1, ed. G. Menarchy (Trichur, South Asia Research Assistance, 1998), pp. 33–112.
21. Dr J. Thekkedath, SDB, *The History of Christianity in India*, vol II (Calcutta, Church History Association of India, 1982), pp. 70–75.
22. At the Catholic Bishops Conference of India, in 2012, the declaration on *The Church's Role for a better India* included the assertion that 'Since one of the major causes of violence is injustice, the Church commits herself to the liberation of the weaker sections like tribals, women and dalits. In particular, she wants to reach out more to unorganized groups like fisherpeople, farmers, migrants, domestic workers, victims of trafficking and so on. She will engage in advocacy and networking with NGOs and other like-minded groups and individuals dedicated to the cause of the poor. She will cooperate with government in its efforts to improve the lot of the poor and help them avail of the benefits and grants set aside in government schemes for them. The Church will be a voice for the voiceless.'
23. J. Wolfe (trans), *John Huighen van Linschoten, His discours of voyages into ye Easte and West Indies:* Book 1 (London 1598), pp. 163–178.
24. R. Kerr, *A General History and Collection of Voyages and Travels*, vol VI, Ch. 4. Section 11 (Edinburgh: William Blackwood, 1824).

7

'An Apostle and a Saint'

Roberto de Nobili

That Thomas Stephens believed strongly in the Jesuit principle of seeking converts by persuasion and example is borne out by a letter he wrote to the Superior-General of the Society in Rome, on 6 December 1601, asking for more missionaries to be sent to India. Had he believed in coercion, he would never have written such a letter.

One such missionary was Roberto de Nobili, born in the Montepulciano region of Tuscany in 1577. He was the eldest son of an Italian nobleman who was a General in the Papal army and a descendant of the Holy Roman Emperor Otto III.[1] At the age of 17, a year after the death of his father, he announced his intention to join the Society of Jesus. His family objected strenuously, although their objection was not to his becoming a priest as such: there was a strong clerical tradition in the family, which had contributed a number of eminent clerics to the Church, including several cardinals and at least two Popes. The objection was to his chosen calling. Within the Society there would be considerably less opportunity for the hierarchical advancement that was part of the family tradition, but Roberto de Nobili stayed firm: 'When God calls, no human consideration should stop us.' He joined the Society in 1596 at the age of 19. He expressed a desire to be employed in the foreign missions. At first it appeared he would be sent to Japan, but a plea for more priests from the Society in India (perhaps that made by Fr Stephens) led to his being diverted to Goa.

Fr Roberto de Nobili

Roberto de Nobili embarked for India in April, 1604. He did not arrive at Goa until 20 May 1605, so he had presumably sojourned at one of the Portuguese outposts en route. Like Fr Stephens before him, he became very ill on arrival. He must have met his fellow Jesuit at this time. He had recovered sufficiently

'An Apostle and a Saint'   253

by the end of the year to voyage to the Jesuit College at Cochin. His new superior was Alberto Laerzio, a fellow Italian who had arrived in India in 1579, at the age of 20. After a short stay in Cochin, Fr Roberto was sent to the 'Fishery Coast' in South India to join a mission to the Paravas, a large tribe of fisher folk. These were the outcasts to whom Francis Xavier had ministered. His first task was to learn Tamil, the ancient Dravidian language of the area (although since their conversion, the Paravas had adopted Portuguese ways in terms of dress and diet).

Fr de Nobili might well have spent the rest of his life labouring amongst the Paravas, but after he had stayed there for seven months, Laerzio decided to send him instead to the city of Madurai, which lay five days' journey inland. There he joined Gonçalo Fernandes, a Portuguese Jesuit, thirty-six years his senior, who had established the mission there in 1596. It was not a great success, being restricted to a few Parava settlers and the occasional Portuguese visitor. No converts had been made from Hinduism. With his newly-acquired fluency in Tamil, de Nobili realised the source of the problem. He had become friendly with the Hindu that Fernandes had placed in charge of the little school he had founded, presumably because of the lack of any Catholic candidates for the job. Over the next few months he was introduced to the complexities of Indian culture, for example, that *Ferengi* (the word by which the Portuguese were referred to) was entirely pejorative. They were despised because they broke every rule in the Brahmin book: to touch or even to be gazed upon by one was contaminating.

Like many other Jesuits, de Nobili realised that, to make any impact on a highly-sophisticated society, he had to adapt himself to the prevailing culture. In order to do this, he had to gain the permission of his superiors. Fr Fernandes was horrified. The contempt of the Brahmins for the Portuguese was entirely reciprocated. The caste system was the antithesis of Christianity, with its belief in the fundamental equality of mankind before God. Customs like *sati*, the immolation of widows on their husband's funeral pyres, were considered criminal and barbaric. To Fr Fernandes, what de Nobili was advocating was not only a repudiation of three generations of missionary work in India, but also involved an acceptance of the very social evils that the mission aimed to eradicate. It would mean turning away from the social outcasts that had embraced the Catholic faith, in favour of those who had shunned and persecuted them.

Roberto de Nobili moved from the missionary compound into a hut in the Brahmin quarter of the city and built a Christian shrine in the Hindu style. He shaved his head, leaving just a small tuft of hair, a *kuDumî*. To indicate that he was a guru, he put a mark of sandalwood paste on his brow. He spoke only Tamil, hired a Brahmin cook and houseboy, and became a vegetarian. According to Brahmin custom, he ate only one meal a day and that was only with Brahmins. He would write psalms on palm leaves like a Brahmin pundit. He was assisted by the fact, simplistically expressed here, that there is no conversion process to Hinduism. All that is necessary is to assume the life-style, as he did. Nevertheless, considering that the Brahmins regarded the Europeans as members of the lowest caste and shunned any contact with them, it was an amazing feat to convince them that he was not only not a *Ferengi*, but also a Brahmin. He ceased to refer to himself as a priest, and adopted the title of *sannyasa*.[2] For a brief period he wore the *Yagnopaveetham* (the Brahmin thread of three strands of cotton cord draped from the shoulder to the waist as a sign of caste) and followed the Brahmin practice of bathing daily and ritually cleansed himself before saying Mass.

Faced with Fr Fernandes's continuing hostility to his project, Fr Roberto decided he had no choice but to appeal over his head to his Superior, Fr Alberto Laerzio. To study his methods, Fr Laerzio spent a month living with him in his mud hut at Madurai. He too was disturbed by the proposal, but agreed to refer it to Archbishop de Menezes. When the reply came, it was equivocal. Somewhat recklessly, Fr de Nobili decided that this gave him *carte-blanche* to press ahead with his scheme. He assumed the role of a Hindu *sadhu* or monk; discovering that he was restricted in that role, he presented himself as a *kshatriya*, one of the castes of holy warriors. In this context, the term means one who surrenders himself to self-sacrifice. Fr de Nobili realised that being a Brahmin mendicant would be the most effective means of acceptance, so he abandoned the black cassock and leather sandals of the Jesuits for the wooden clogs and saffron robes of a *rajasannyas*, or high-caste monk and carried the traditional *kamadulu*, or water jug. As such, he accepted all the restrictions of the caste system and he refused to condemn any Hindu practice or idea, even the despised practice of *sati*. Indeed, he was an eyewitness to the immolation of 400 women following the death of the Nayak ruler of Madurai, praising their extraordinary courage and steadfastness.[3]

On its own terms, de Nobili's strategy achieved some success. The Hindu schoolmaster became his first convert. Roberto de Nobili gave him the baptismal name Alberto in honour of his Superior. Within two years of arriving in Madurai, de Nobili had received another ten young men of high caste into the Church. He became friends with the Brahmin Sanskrit scholar, Shivadharma, from whom he learnt that ancient tongue. He was probably the first European to master the language in which the Vedas and the Upanishads were written. After considerable hesitation, Shivadharma allowed him to study these sacred books of Hinduism. Fr de Nobili persuaded him to read the Bible, which he called the Christian Veda, and later baptised him. By 1609, some sixty converts had been received by de Nobili into the Church. The extent to which these 'converts' realised that they were embracing another faith is not clear. They washed with water from a well, undertook a change of clothing, muttered mantras composed by de Nobili, and ate fruit and sweets, but did not suspect that the new names they were given were the names of Christian saints translated into Tamil. All they were told and knew was that they were being initiated by a Brahmin guru into his own *sampradâya*. Such initiations are a routine matter for most Hindus.

These baptisms raised identical questions to those that the Synod of Dampier had been called to resolve. The converts would retain their caste status and customs, many of which were completely contrary to the spirit of Christianity. The solution favoured by Fr de Nobili was to form a totally Brahmin church, but this was surely the antithesis of the whole purpose of the mission to India. Fr Fernandes certainly thought so. He compiled a detailed denunciation of de Nobili's activities and sent it to the Archbishop. Soon the entire Jesuit mission in South India was debating the merits of de Nobili's approach. His totally Brahmin church, modelled on a Hindu temple, would presumably have excluded his fellow Jesuits as *Ferengi*. Fernandes also submitted a highly-critical report to the hierarchy. As a result, an official censure was issued by Nicolão Pimenta, who had recently been appointed Papal Visitor to the provinces of Goa and Malabar. He declared that the accommodations made by Roberto de Nobili went too far, and were superstitious and schismatic, but he lacked the authority to close the mission; only Claudio Acquaviva, the Jesuit Superior General in Rome could do that. Yet his condemnation would have represented a serious setback for de Nobili's credibility.

Both Pimenta and de Nobili sent detailed reports to the Superior-General in Rome. The fact that it took up to two years for a communication to arrive and be responded to ensured that progress was slow. During that time, around a third of de Nobili's converts lapsed and his sympathetic Superior, Fr Laerzio, was replaced by the less supportive Fr Pero Francisco. The response from the Superior General finally arrived in August 1613. He found de Nobili in error on four counts: the use of the Brahmin personal insignia; the adoption of Hindu rituals; the denial that he was a *Ferengi*; and his wilful separation from his fellow Jesuits. 'You must', he wrote, 'during the day and in the sight of all, deal freely with the Fathers of the other residence, go to their house and talk with them, and they, in their turn, must be allowed to come to your house without any restriction and not by night only.'[4]

Somewhat surprisingly, there was no condemnation of de Nobili's acceptance of the Hindu caste system and customs, although this may have been regarded as implicit. Yet his methods went against the very spirit of the Synod of Dampier, that the Hindu caste system was contrary to the ethos of Christianity. As a result of the Superior General's letter, Fr Pero Francisco issued a prohibition on de Nobili baptising any further converts unless he agreed to submit to the conditions set out. De Nobili seized on a single sentence in Acquaviva's letter as the basis for rejecting the injunctions from Rome: 'No change should be made which would compromise the existence of the mission.' He continued his policy of 'accommodation' for another five years, but it was somewhat negated by the fact that he was not permitted to baptise anyone. He set out the justification for his methods in a letter to Cardinal Bellarmine written on 7 December 1613:

> Before I had learned the Sciences of the Brahmins and read their books, I myself was of opinion that all Indian modes of worship were to be condemned, because I saw that they differed widely from our European ways. I was taxed with superstition practices of which I knew neither the nature nor the purpose. But when by God's mercy I was given though unworthy access to Sanskrit, their learned language, which so far none of ours had learned (for it is unheard of that they should teach it to Europeans), I came to know that all those things which are now being controverted refer to their social customs. Therefore... I changed my mind and rallied to the opposite, though less comfortable, opinion.[5]

After five years in this state of limbo, Pope Paul V ordered the Inquisition at Goa to call a Council to investigate, which met in February 1619. The Primate presided over a team of twenty theologians and priests, including two Papal Inquisitors. De Nobili put up a spirited defence, but the verdict went against him.

Now it was his turn to appeal to the Pope. He pleaded that 'a Christian meaning' be given to the Hindu symbols, since it cannot be shown, still less proved, that they are superstitious.' He never received a reply because the Pope died shortly after the appeal arrived in Rome and it was not until 1623 that Pope Gregory XV resolved the issue in de Nobili's favour.

Fr de Nobili became an authority on the Tamil language. He emulated the achievement of Thomas Stephens by writing no fewer than twenty-one religious works in that language, all written after he had gone blind and under his Tamil name of *Tattuva Pötaker* ('Teacher of Truth'). He died on 16 January 1655.

'A Word from your Fraternity'

In his annual letter in Portuguese to the Superior General in Rome on 5 December, 1608, Thomas Stephens complained that he had received no letters from Rome for three years 'due to the great persecution of the pirates... although I have a feeling that mine have reached you.'[6] His report, while attempting to give an objective account, is, on balance, optimistic. 'In so far as the spiritual is concerned; he writes, 'by the goodness of the Lord, things go on well. The priests live with the fervour expected of them. The Rector is always diligent in his affairs, which is directed to both to the spiritual and the temporal.' Progress on building the new college at Rachol had been good, but the work was hampered by the lack of boats to ship materials up the Zuari River—perhaps the result of the piratical incursions he mentioned ('The help we used to receive ceased and the work remains suspended'). It had been difficult to meet the debts that now totalled two thousand *xerafins*.

The criticism that the Jesuits were over-assiduous in their acquisitions finds an echo. At times the Rector was what Fr Stephens euphemistically describes as 'excessively-diligent' in acquiring the materials needed for the maintenance of the college. Complaints had been looked into by the Father Provincial, who found that everything was in order. The calumniators had been silenced, but the Rector would be more circumspect in his actions in future:

> Generally speaking, Christianity is doing well and progresses in the knowledge of its creator with the doctrine and care of the priests who are in charge. All but one or two [of the priests] know the language.

The Society in Salcete was still having difficulties with the frequently heavy-handed approach of the authorities to the native population:

> We suffered from great grief, caused by overzealous men who are drawn by their own interests and favoured by the captain with undeserved favours, which brought the risk of losing a village of Christians, whose conversion had cost us a lot. But with the help of our own, under the direction of superiors and with all the moderation we could summon, things are improving, and it is hoped they will end.

It is tempting to see a reference to the Cumcolim massacre here and the treachery of the Captain of the Assolna Fort, but that had happened fifteen years before and the Superior General would have been fully aware of it. Thomas Stephens gives no further details of this forgotten, but serious incident, which has set back the efforts of the Jesuits in the cause of Christ, merely adding that 'the times are very troublesome'. Yet, despite such setbacks, the morale of the Jesuits remained high and their commitment to the cause as strong as ever:

> Yet in spite of all these troubles we should not abandon our labours for Christ... If we did that, the blessings of our ministry and edification of the work for conversion we have done in India would cease to exist. Nor should we even think of abandoning our parishes. Although they are large, if we and the orders did so, all that rose up would be confusion and revolt.

Fr Stephens recognises that the task of the missionary, working to bring the Gospel to a people oblivious to the centrality of its message, was far from easy. In fact, he appears to be extremely pessimistic about the apathy of the population towards the mission, which he attributes to the difficulty of surmounting cultural barriers:

> The conversion of the heathen has always been a slow and hard business throughout all the nations of the world it is even slower among these peoples because of their backwardness, their lack of interest in the things of God and things to come.

Nevertheless, his outlook continues to be cheerful and he can even register a poetic note:

> God has always been served well in this Salcete. Our various griefs and labours, though they exhaust us all, including the Provincial, are not always the same. They have their ups and downs, which is the way we prefer to have them. It is the flat road that is tiring.

Fr Stephens's exposition to the Superior General of the difficulties and setbacks faced by the Salcete Mission has been building up to the main point of his letter. He explains how Fr Henrique Henriques, who had come to India in the days of Francis Xavier, had acquired a perfect knowledge of Tamil and written several books in that language. Juan Gonçalves, a skilful Spanish lay brother, had, with the help of Fr Juan de Faria, cut a complete set of type in the Tamil alphabet and a short catechism of sixteen pages had been printed in Quilan in 1578—the first book to be printed in an Asian language. This was followed by a fuller catechism in the following year and then by a vast Tamil *Flos Sanctorum* of 668 pages in 1587.[7]

In his letter, Thomas Stephens alludes to the inspiration given to him by the work of Roberto de Nobili and his ambition to propagate the Gospel in the local vernacular: 'I have strongly desired to see in this Province some books printed in the language and alphabet of this land, as there are in Malabar, with great benefit to Christianity'. However, the issue was complicated. Whereas there were twenty-four letters in the Latin alphabet, to print in an Indian language could require as many as 600 different moulds, although Stephens considered that it might be possible to manage with only 200. Another difficulty was that 'this holy curiosity' could not be accomplished without the 'permission and goodwill' of the Provincial, Fr Francisco Vieira, 'and he has so many things to see to that he can find no time to care for this and much less to take it to heart'. Stephens succeeds in circumventing this difficulty by appealing to the Superior's higher authority: 'A word from your fraternity to the Father Provincial', he tells the General, 'strongly recommending him to do that which he may find to be for the greater glory of God and for the edification and benefit of the Christian community would weigh much and prove an immense boon to us.' Subsequent events demonstrate that the Superior General did indeed take up the issue with the Father Provincial and that any letter he wrote, urging him to give attention to Thomas Stephens's mighty project, avoided the pirates. Had Br Gonçalves and Fr Faria still been alive, things might have been different, but they had died in 1580 and 1582 respectively. Nevertheless, Fr Stephens did not give up on his desire to enable the Gospel to be preached in the Indian vernaculars. He composed a Konkani grammar for circulation amongst his fellow missionaries.

Having mastered Indian languages, Thomas Stephens had absorbed himself in the local culture. He was conscious of the power that the *puranas* had over the Hindu mind, poetic sagas that were sung and passed down through oral traditions. Like the epic poems of the Greeks or Norsemen they are stories of the origin of the world, the coming of the gods and their adventures in love and war, the origin of mankind and the exploits of kings and heroes. Their origin in the distant past is reflected in their very name (*purana* is a Sanskrit word meaning 'ancient'). In the opening chapter of his *purana,* Stephens explained what had motivated him to write the work. After a catechism class, a Brahmin convert approached him and said that the catechism was good, but the converts needed something culturally enhancing for their leisure hours, or they could fall into bad habits, wasting their time in idle talk, even gambling. They needed a Christian literature in their own language, in story form, as they knew from the Hindu *puranas.* Stephens made himself totally familiar with the genre and recognised the need to fill the cultural gap by writing a Christian version of the *puranas.* One of the languages he had acquired was Marathi, the predominant tongue of much of western India. Had he succeeded in his aim, he would have produced the first book in Marathi printed in its own script, Devanagari. He had developed a genuine love of this language and an admiration of its poetic qualities. 'As among the birds, the peacock, as among the trees, the kalpataru, so among languages, Marathi.' He is not only evoking the *Song of Songs* ('As the lily among the thorns, so is my love among the daughters.' Song 2:2), he is dealing with precise superlatives from Hindu mythology and revealing his deep knowledge of the Hindu mindset. The Lotd Krishna wears a peacock feather in his hair as a symbol of his purity and freedom from sexual desire. It was (is!) a popular belief that peacocks did not breed through normal intercourse, but through their tears. The eyes on the peacock tail are thought to protect houses by warding off danger and evil. Not for nothing is it the national bird of India. The kalpataru is the tree of life. It was planted by Indra, the King of the gods, in his abode in Paradise

Pyrard de Laval

Unbeknown to Thomas Pounde, in the very same year that he had written his letters to the two distinguished recipients, Thomas Stephens had been involved in further activity to aid distressed travelers: no less than four Englishmen, a Dutchman and three Frenchmen. The name of the Dutchman is lost to posterity, but three of the four Englishmen are likely to have been Edward Beck, William Hudson and Thomas Davies. The fourth may have perished on the journey back to Europe. They had been serving on the East India Company's ship, *Ascension*, when she was wrecked at the mouth of the Malikha River in East Bengal during the company's third expedition to the Indies in 1609. They had made their way to Surat and from thence to Goa where they were probably arrestedas part of the crackdown on foreign traders. The Frenchmen were led by the famous traveller François Pyrard de Laval. On 2 July, 1602, his ship, *Corbin*, on which he was probably the purser, was wrecked in the Maldive Islands. He was taken prisoner by the Maldivians together with the rest of the crew.[8] A number of them died in captivity in the city of Malé and four were executed for trying to escape.[9] Pyrard realised the futility of such attempts. He learned the local Dhivehi language and became a favourite of Ibrahim Kalaafaan, who he refers to as 'the King'. In fact he was the Regent; the issue is complex. In Pyrard's words:

> About fifty years before this time the King of these Islands, Hassan IX, who was of noble and ancient lineage, seeing that he was but ill-obeyed, and was unable to withstand a formidable rival who wished to depose him, was inspired of God with a resolve to quit all. He departed secretly with his wife and some of his family, without saying a word of his destination to anyone, and went straight to Cochin; where he became a Christian, along with his wife and some of his followers; sending back such as would not be baptised. For this cause his rival, who was his near relative, was at once accepted as King. The name of the latter was Ali ... This former King, when he became a Christian... wrote to all his subjects that they should become Christians and pay him their tribute; otherwise he would come and see to it with a large army of Portuguese, who had promised him their aid. The new King and the Maldive people made answer that they would no longer acknowledge him; that if aught was due to him he might come and get it; and that if he preferred to be a Christian

he should remain where he was—as for them, they would sooner die than change their faith.[10]

Despite the Regent's benevolence, Pyrard longed to get away. One night, in February, 1607, after he had been in captivity for five long years, he had a curious dream.

> I dreamed that I was gone forth of that country, and was in full liberty in a Christian land. I was infinitely overjoyed but at my awakening I was full sorely astonished to find my dream false. Nevertheless, though I was exceeding sad, I arose, and falling on my knees, prayed God with all my heart that He would be pleased out of His grace to deliver me out of the Mahometan servitude and to set me again on Christian soil, where I could resume the free exercise of my religion, which I had been constrained to discontinue for so long a time. Then I made a vow to make a voyage to St James[11] in Galicia, there to render thanks to God.[12]

Two days later, a fleet of sixteen galleys was seen off-shore. The King of Bengal had sent his Armada to conquer the Maldives. The King of the Islands ordered his fleet to put to sea to meet the invader, but when he realised it was too late, resolved to flee to one of the other islands. In the confusion and panic, Pyrard and his companions were forgotten. He recalled his dream and wondered if his hour of deliverance had come, but realised that he was playing a risky game. If he failed to join the royal party, he would be doomed if the King returned to Malé and found him still there. On the other hand, not to attempt to flee would doom him to a living death of subservience and exile.

To avoid embarking with the King, Pyrard hid in a wood for four hours with his three companions and some 'poor folk', who had also been left behind. When they emerged, he wandered about the royal palace, which was entirely deserted. 'There were all sorts of things, gold, silver and jewellery, lying about, but I never dreamed of touching any'. Although his honesty appears commendable, there was no point in him taking anything. If the

King returned and he was found in possession of items stolen from the palace, his fate would be sealed. On the other hand, if the Bengalis landed, they would be bound to take any treasures from him. This is indeed what occurred. As soon as the Captain of the Armada realised that the King had fled, he ordered eight of his galleys to go off in pursuit, while the other eight landed. Pyrard threw himself on their mercy. The Bengalis assumed that he was a Portuguese and stripped him of all he had as a prelude to killing him.

> But when they found out that I was not a Portuguese, they treated me more humanely, and conducted me to their Captain, who took me under his protection, assuring me that I should suffer no evil; then he had me clad in other garments, and bade me remain in his galleys for my safety, at least for that day and night. Afterwards I was allowed to go where I liked throughout the island, without anyone saying a word.

The King had made the mistake of fleeing in a sailing vessel, which was rapidly overtaken by the oar-propelled galleys. A pitched-battle took place, during which the King was stabbed to death by pike and sword thrusts. Pyrard felt no regrets when he heard of his demise. 'His ill fortune cast him into this fate', he wrote, 'which he fully merited for the great cruelties he had used.'

Because he had knowledge of the working and stowing of a cannon that had been taken from the wreck of his ship, Pyrard was treated well by the Bengalis. 'The cannon in question', he wrote, 'was the most beautiful example to be seen anywhere, and had great renown in the Indies, many kings and princes having been continually on the point of coming to see it.' Indeed, he believed that the sole purpose of the King of Bengal in invading the Maldives was to capture this cannon. After ten days, having thoroughly ransacked the island, the Bengalis resolved to leave, allowing Pyrard and his three companions to embark with them. A month later, they arrived at Chittagong, at the mouth of the

Ganges, in the Kingdom of Bengal. There was great rejoicing at their arrival. The Subahdar ('King') received Pyrard warmly and gave him both his liberty and subsistence, 'saying that if I would remain with him, he would do great things for me.'[13] After a month, however, he met the Master of a ship that was bound for Calicut, who said that if the four companions voyaged there with him, they might well pick up a Dutch ship that was bound for Europe. They arrived there after an eventful journey. Pyrard must have possessed qualities that appealed to the native princes, for the local ruler, the Zamorin, warmly welcomed him, providing with a house and servants.[14] He discovered that the Dutch fleet on which he had hoped to embark, had been there a month before and would not return for many months. After waiting for eight months, he began to despair of ever returning to Europe. There were two Jesuits who were running a mission in Calicot, Fr Hilaire, a Portuguese and Fr Jacomo Fenicio, an Italian.[15] Pyrard claimed that Fenicio behaved 'very roughly' towards him, but this belies his character as it has come down to us. He had been parish priest of Arthunkal, a small nearby seaside town, since 1584. In that year, the Jesuit catalogue, *Provinciae Indiae Orientalis* had described him as 'learned in philosophy and theology, of good disposition and intellect'.

After seven years at Arthunkel, Fr Fenicio was transferred to Calicut, where he met Pyrard. He returned to Arthunkal in 1619. In the following year, he rebuilt the church. He was much loved and called *Athunkal Veluthachan*, or 'white-skinned father'. He was revered as a saint and was said to have performed many miracles even while he was still alive. Even the Hindus believed in the power of his prayers and approached him for his blessings. He established the tradition of receiving Hindus returning from a pilgrimage to the shrine of the Lord Ayyappa at the nearby Sabarimala Temple. They wore a *malu* (string of beads) to mark their devotion to a period of *vrata*—the renunciation of worldly pleasures. At the Basilica they removed the beads and took a bath in large tank that had been provided or went for a dip in the sea. The church provided meals and accommodation for those pilgrims that desired it.¹⁶ Fr Fenicio was known as the second Apostle of the East (Francis Xavier being the first). When he died in 1632, vast crowds attended his funeral. Whatever Pyrard thought of him, he took his advice. Seeing that no Dutch ship had arrived, the two fathers suggested that the companions might go to Cochin to seek a Portuguese ship. A Dutch Protestant told them that he had previously had a bad experience at the hands of the Portuguese and one Frenchman decided to stay in Calicut.

The two Jesuits gave the others letters of commendation to help them on their journey. They arranged with some Moslem boatmen to take them to Calicut. They were told that they had to embark at night, to catch the high tide, and to meet outside the Portuguese trading post, a little further down the coast. The Dutchman was intending to see them off, but was taken ill so he did not do so.¹⁷ What followed is somewhat confused. On arrival at the rendezvous point, the companions were fallen upon by twenty or thirty Portuguese, Metifs and Indian Christians, shouting 'matar, matar' ('Kill, Kill'). After raining blows on them, they bound their hands and threatened to kill them if they uttered a word. They held their swords to the prisoners' throats for an hour. Pyrard thought that it was the two Jesuits who had betrayed them, but later doubted whether this was so. It later transpired that the gang was seeking to kidnap the Dutchman, with the intention of exploiting his gunnery skills. Eventually the captors bound the companions and threw them aboard their ship, which Pyrard called the *Almedie*.

The captain was a Metif called Joan Furtado, 'a cruel and wicked man'. When she put to sea, she proved to be not entirely watertight and the scuppers, into which they had been flung, were so full of water that they thought the ship was about to sink. They hugged the coast until they reached the territory of the Zamarin of Calicut, who was a friend of the Portuguese. They landed on a deserted shore at night, bound their captives even more strongly, marched them across country and locked them in a shed during the hours of daylight. Spies were sent to Calicut to find out the reaction to the kidnapping. They returned next day to say that the Zamarin of Calicut was furious at their actions and had sent a party to destroy the ship. The captors brought their prisoners Portuguese clothing 'so that none might recognise us' and, at nightfall, marched them along the road to Tanur by the light of the moon. They hauled up during daylight for two days before reaching their destination. They concealed themselves in a wood and sent a boy into town to tell the priest of the Jesuit church and the factor who handled their commercial affairs of their arrival. The boy returned with a letter. When they read it, the captors looked disconcerted. It transpired that Fr Hilaire had arrived to brief his fellow Jesuit on the Sabahdar's wrath at the treatment of his friends. The kidnappers realised that their captives were becoming a liability; indeed, they may well have wondered why they had ever kidnapped them. They resolved to send them to the Portuguese outpost of Cochin, which was twelve leagues away. They stripped them of the Portuguese clothing, leaving them dressed in flimsy shrouds and they were put aboard a large fishing boat manned by 'Mouchois', the fishermen of the Malabar coast, which was bound for Cochin. They told the released captives that they had sent letters of introduction on their behalf to the Governor of the enclave and also to the Jesuit fathers. In fact the letters, in the hope of a reward, denounced them as captured pirates, who were in league with the dreaded Malabar pirate chieftain 'Kunhi Ali'. When they arrived at Cochin, they were kept on board while the letters were delivered to the Governor. An hour and a half later, a Portuguese *merigne* or sergeant arrived to arrest them with a party of eight slaves, Christian *Caffres* (Kaffirs) of Mozambique, armed with halyards. Word had got about of their arrival and their alleged offences and a great crowd had assembled to watch their progress through the city, telling them that they were about to be hanged. In the main square they were shown the gallows where some Dutchmen had recently been executed. 'All this gave us but a poor hope for our future', recorded Pyrard, with considerable understatement.

They were taken before the *Capitão de Cidade* (Governor) Dom Francisco de Menezes, a great nobleman. He asked them many diverse questions. His wife and daughters had expressed a desire to see them, so they were taken to their chambers. The daughters were *metifs* and very pretty. They showed great interest in the companions and Pyrard thought that they would have helped them had they the means to do so. Instead the Governor ordered that they should be taken to appear before the *Ouvidore de Cidade* (the city magistrate). Again, they were followed through the streets by a vast crowd. Some were sympathetic, telling them to have no fear, but to put their trust in God, while others called them Lutheran robbers that should be hanged. After examining them, the magistrate sent them back to the Governor, declaring that he dealt with criminals and these were prisoners-of-war that did not come under his jurisdiction. Obviously, their presence was viewed as having the potential for a diplomatic incident, so no-one wanted to take responsibility for them. The Governor decided that the best way out of the dilemma was to refer the case upwards, so he commanded the *merigne* to take them to the Tronco or city gaol, there to await being shipped to Goa to be judged by the Viceroy.

The Tronco was a high tower. Prisoners who bribed the gaoler occupied an upper chamber, but remained in chains. Those less fortunate were lowered through a trapdoor in the floor on a platform on pulleys, into the lower chamber. There was only one window, 'of an arm and a half's length in thickness'. It was barred with iron grills, through which the gaoler would pass food to the prisoners.

Every day, the Portuguese and *Metif* prisoners were given a single coin, a silver Goanese tanga, which seems to have come from a charitable fund. The companions received this, despite being in neither category, The other prisoners received, once a day, some cooked rice with badly prepared fish, about enough food for just one meal. Water was provided to drink and for washing and bathing. Pyrard described the prison as 'truly the most frightful and cruel that existed anywhere in the world'. Some people had been incarcerated in these terrible conditions for as long as six years. The small chamber housed around 120 men of 'all sorts and conditions'. A great iron chain stretched along its entire length, to which was fastened the foot of anyone imprisoned for a crime. Fortunately, the companions were not subjected to this treatment. The chamber was the 'most filthy, stinking and noisome place imaginable,

> For the prisoners perform all their necessities one after another in vessels which are only voided in the evening. This engenders such an infection and an atmosphere so stinking and stifling, that one can hardly breathe. For at night the grill is shut, with a trapdoor from above, so that the heat of the climate, added to that of the place where so many people are huddled up pell-mell, engenders a close and stifling atmosphere, wherein it is impossible to survive long without becoming sick.

The lamp that was lit in the chamber at nights frequently went out for lack of air. Every night the prisoners were subjected to a body search by the gaolers. Because of the great heat, most of them were stark naked and some slaves and paupers were employed in ceaselessly working a large fan. The place was so overcrowded that it was only possible to lie down sideways. Pyrard felt that, without the fan, life would be impossible. The heat was insufferable and the rancid atmosphere caused the companions to break out in huge boils. After nine days in this condition, Pyrard realised they had no hope of survival. Fortunately, their deliverance was at hand—and from an unexpected source. Some of the Portuguese prisoners advised them to write to the Jesuit Fathers of Cochin College. They did so, despite believing, erroneously, that it was the Jesuits who were responsible for their plight. The Superior came to visit them, recognised that they were French Catholics and pleaded with the Governor for their release. The Governor replied that he had no authority to do this, but he would grant them parole for the period while they were waiting to embark for Goa.

After the companions had endured this regime for two months, the *Armada do Sud* arrived at Cochin to victual in preparation for the return journey of a hundred leagues to Goa. The Governor had clearly forgotten about them and the companions had to ask the Jesuits to remind him of their existence. They were delivered into the hands of the *Capitão Mór da Costa Malavar,* the Admiral of the Fleet of the Malabar Coast. In order that the proper form should be observed, they were flung back in the Tronco to await the fleet's departure. To their horror, irons weighing thirty to forty pounds were attached to their legs. They were still wearing these when, two days later, they were escorted to a galley by two *merignes* and eight *pions*. Such was the weight of the irons that they could hardly walk and the metal cut into their legs. On arrival at the harbour, they were presented to the Admiral, who assigned them to a galliot. Their ill-fortune continued: Pedroso de Poderoso, the Captain, was described by Pyrard as 'the cruelest fellow in the world'. He had previously been taken prisoner and been very badly treated by the Dutch and, for some reason, he thought that the companions were of that nationality. Their irons were not removed and the galliot was very small, with lots of people on board, so Pyrard was compelled to lie down, unable to move, with everyone stepping on him as they moved around the ship. The crew were most unpleasant, continuously telling them that all three of them would be hanged when they got to Goa.

On the first evening at sea, the galliot met a large merchantman from the Malabar Coast. The Captain and crew were anxious to take her as a prize, 'as well for the profit as for the honour'. As they sought to board her, their prow struck the other vessel with such force that the huge spritsail boom snapped in two. The cable that supported it sprang free and landed on

Pyrard's back as he lay on the deck with his feet in irons. He passed out. Such was the weight of the cable that it took ten men to lift it off him. Water was thrown over him to bring him round, but the only medical help available was from a 'miserable barber', whose knowledge was restricted to bleeding and dressing slight wounds. He bled Pyrard and slapped some kind of plaster on his back, which rapidly became inflamed. The Captain, seeing his plight, immediately had him put in the forecastle. This was where everyone did their 'necessities', so they were constantly stepping over him. Such were his injuries that he could not turn over. He was convinced that his spine was broken. The Captain would quite happily have seen him dead, so that he could be flung overboard. Fortunately, Pyrard received a great deal of assistance from a Dominican friar called Brother Manuel de Christ, who obtained clean clothing and a mattress and bedding. Brother Manuel secretly brought Pyrard food and even persuaded the Captain to remove one of his leg irons. The forecastle was also where the cooking took place, so Pyrard was 'tormented' by the heat and smells. The cook, however, 'a Canarin of Goa and a Christian' was also as helpful as he could be to him.

This ordeal was not helped by the weather. Under normal circumstances, a voyage from Cochin to Goa might take as little as two or three days, but they encountered strong contrary winds and driving rain such that it took twenty. The waves swept over the fo'c'sle, drenching Pyrard. The excessive length of the voyage meant that water had to be rationed, so he suffered an extreme thirst to add to his tribulations. When the ship stopped to take on supplies at the port of Kannanŭr on the Malabar coast, where there was a Jesuit mission, the friar tried to persuade the Captain to allow Pyrard to go into the hospital there, but he was obdurate in his refusal.

The Captain waited four days for a favourable wind. When the ship arrived in Goa, Pyrard described himself as looking like 'a very mummy, or like a corpse dried in the sun'. In his account of the voyage, he never mentioned the fate of his companions, but

'An Apostle and a Saint' 273

as soon as the ship anchored, all three were carried to the Royal Hospital. One of his companions was afflicted with an ulcer. There was nothing physically wrong with the other, except that he was suffering from acute exhaustion. Here they were so well treated and cured of their ailments that they forgot that they were still technically under arrest.[18]

So these were the three Frenchmen that were aided by Thomas Stephens, in addition to the Dutchman and the four Englishmen. Pyrard de Laval recorded what transpired.

> The Jesuit fathers spared no trouble to set us free. Five of them: the Procurator of the Christians, Gaspar Alemán, Father Thomas Stephens, an Englishman, Father Jean de Cenes, a Lotharingian from Verdun, Father Nicholas Trigault, a Walloon from Douay and good Father Estienne de la Croix, a Frenchman from Rouen, joined forces for this purpose and got us out of jail in three weeks. Undoubtedly, these good fathers would have gladly helped us all the way home in spite of the trouble we caused them. They could not have done more for us had we been their own brothers.[19]

The Jesuits and, in particular Thomas Stephens, appear to have persuaded the authorities to send the Englishmen to Lisbon. They voyaged on the same carrack as Archbishop Menezes, who was travelling back to Portugal to be installed as Archbishop of Braga. They were still under arrest on arrival. The diplomatic corps got onto the case. On 14 February 1611, Hugh Lee, the English agent in Lisbon, wrote to Thomas Wilson that 'the release of the prisoners from the East Indies has not come from court, so neither Bucke nor the rest may yet depart'. The issue was causing interest at the highest levels, possibly because there was concern that the Portuguese might regard being employed in the East India Company as an offence in itself. On 16 April, Francis Collingham, an English agent in Madrid, wrote to no less a person than Robert Cecil, the 1st Earl of Salisbury and the Lord High Treasurer, informing him that the English prisoners held in Lisbon had been set free. On 26 June, Hugh Lee reported to Salisbury that the men were embarking for England. 'They seem to be very malicious fellows', he reported. This appears to have been the case. At some point they must have encountered the 'very famous' Sir Robert Shirley, who had been in the military service of Shah Abbas of Persia and was returning to England on a diplomatic mission to King James I and other European powers on behalf of the Shah to seek an alliance against the Ottoman Empire. For some reason they had spread 'slanderous report of Sherley since his departure towards England', which had clearly shocked Lee. They had claimed that Shirley 'uses his commission without the privity or consent of the King of Persia, whose ambassador he pretends to be; also that she who [he] accepts for his lady and bedfellow, is known as a common woman.' In fact, on his journey across Europe, Sir Thomas had been honoured by both the Holy Roman Emperor and the Pope. His wife was a member of the ruling house, the Safavids, and an Orthodox Christian.[20]

When Beck landed in Lisbon, he told Lee that he could 'say something to the purpose if he be dealt with accordingly'. What this was never revealed, but may have concerned his dealings with the Jesuits in Goa. He would have been aware that the English authorities saw the Society as an enemy and might be eager for information about them. Perhaps he had done the same as James Storie a quarter century before, and professed his interest in joining the Society in order to improve his position. This is corroborated by Lee, who reported that 'Beck gave out that he was recommended by Thomas Stevens, an English Jesuit in Goa, to Henry Fludd, the Jesuit in Lisbon'. Perhaps Thomas Stephens knew Fludd from his days at San Andrea in Rome and was commending Beck as a candidate for the novitiate. If so, Beck's scheme rebounded. In his letter to Salisbury, Lee describes Beck as 'a Jesuit', not the best possible supposed calling in which to be embarking for England and mentioned in a letter to the King's Chief Minister. It would almost certainly have ensured that he would have been apprehended on his return and interrogated. Lee may have regarded it as his duty to pass on information about Beck to the authorities, a man they might have regarded as a danger to the state. Had this been his main motivation, though, he would surely have gone into more detail. More likely, Beck had so exasperated him with his churlish behaviour and groundless accusations against Sir Thomas that he was seeking to cause him a great deal of trouble. Beck would have been able to offer explanations of his conduct that, while not casting him in the best possible light, would have saved him from the rigours of the law and Lee would have known this too.

Perhaps Pyrard was able to make the acquaintance of members of the Maldivian royal family during his stay in Goa. In Cochin, Hassan IX had assumed the title and name of King Dom Manuel after his conversion. Under threat from the Portuguese, it was agreed that he would continue to receive tribute from his former subjects. On his death in 1584, he was succeeded as titular King by his eldest son, Dom João Sri Kathiri Maha Radun. The new King had committed an offence regarded by King Philip I and II as 'so outrageous and scandalous that it were better not to speak of it'. For this, he had been sentenced to death by the *Rellação* (court). However, he was useful to the Portuguese and to execute him would constitute something of a diplomatic disaster. He was kept at Goa under the surveillance of the Viceroy from 1591, under house arrest in a mansion opposite St Paul's College. With him was his Queen, Dona Francisca de Vasconelles, a well-connected Portuguese lady. She had arrived in India with the 'Orphans of the King' as part of the annual fleet in 1584. She married the King around 1587 and bore him a son and a daughter. On his death around 1603, he was succeeded by his son, Dom Felipe de Malvidas, who was then aged around 18. The new King spent a great deal of time trying to persuade the Portuguese authorities to recover his realm. Doubtless he was interested in speaking with Pyrard, who had recent experience of his lost kingdom.[21]

Bassein

In 1611, Thomas Stephens was sent to teach Marathi at Bassein near Bombay for a year, probably to enable him to work on his Christian *Purāna*. He is described in the Society's records as *Mestre de Lingua* (Master of Languages). It is the only place in India in which he is recorded as ministering outside Goa. In 1508, the Portuguese navigator Francisco de Almeida had sailed into the deep natural harbour his countrymen came to call *Bom Bahia* ('the good bay'). At the time, the area was under the rule of the Gujerat Sultan. On 20 January 1533, Nuno da Cunha captured Bassein, which is twenty-eight miles north of the city that later became known as Bombay. On 23 December, Bassein and the seven islands of Bombay were ceded to the Portuguese by a treaty of peace and commerce between the Gujerat Sultan, Qutb-ud-Din Bahadur Shah, and Nuno da Cunha.

Bassein (in Portuguese, Baçaim; today, Vasai) became an important Portuguese outpost. It was the site of the Fort of San Sebastian, commemorating the fact that it was on the feast day of that saint that Nuno da Cunha achieved his great victory. With the establishment of Portuguese rule, Bassein's natural beauty, pleasant climate and prosperity attracted a number of rich *Fidelgos*. They built castle-like palaces in the vicinity of the fortress, so that the place had the appearance of a European city. It became known as 'Dom Baçaim' through the number of people bearing that aristocratic title who lived there. Within sixteen years of its secession, the Franciscans had built twelve churches, as well as the Cathedral of St Joseph, built by the Royal Decree of João III.

Francis Xavier visited the city in 1544 and paid two further visits during 1548. The permanent Jesuit presence in the city dates from 1549 when Fr Melchior Gonçalves arrived to distribute a royal grant to the Franciscan Recollects, the French reform branch of the Order, whose strict observance of the monastic vows did not permit them to handle money. Three years later, Xavier sent Fr

'An Apostle and a Saint'   277

Belchior dos Anjos and Br Manoel Teixeira to Bassein to found a church dedicated to the Mother of God. Its associated educational institution gained collegiate status in 1560. It received a huge boost in 1564 when Isabel de Aguiar, a widow originally from Ormuz, donated the income from three villages in the Provincia de Norte to the Society. Its dedication was changed to that of the Holy Name of Jesus in 1568. The church, built in laterite and basalt, was modelled on the Church of the Gezu, the Jesuit mother church in Rome. It had a single nave and chapel, both barrel vaulted. The adjacent college was arranged around a two-storey cloister with colonnaded arcades. In the chancel stood the sepulchre of the great benefactress, Isabel de Aguiar, who died in 1591. Across the square from the church was an orphanage for forty boys and a shelter for the needy, which had a chapel dedicated .to Our Lady of Help.

The prosperity of Bassein increased so abundantly that it was considered the richest city in the Portuguese overseas empire at the time. As Portuguese domination of the area increased, it became the capital of the Portuguese Province of North India, Goa being the capital of the Province of the South. In the year of Fr Stephens's arrival in the city, such was its importance that a mint (*Casa de Moeda*) was established there. During his time there, at the College there were in residence eleven Fathers, thirteen Scholastics and numerous Brothers.

'The Highest Efforts of the Poet's Genius'

Thomas Stephens completed the *Christian Purāna* in 1614 and returned to Rachol College. To achieve publication, the work had to pass through various processes of censorship under what seems to have been a different working title than that under which it would eventually be published. It would appear that Fr Stephens had written the first draft in Portuguese and then translated it into Marathi. On 3 April, Paulo Mascerenhas, who had been appointed to the task by 'the Very Reverend the Inquisitor', confirmed that he had examined the two texts of 'The Treatise on the coming of the Redeemer into the World' and found them compatible, 'as far as the language permits'. On 2 June in the following year, the work received a three-fold endorsement. The Inquisition Council, which had the power to suppress it, merely requested a copy. 'It may be printed', wrote the Archbishop of Goa succinctly. Fr Stephens's tactic of seeking the approval of Rome over the head of the Provincial also paid off, with Fr Francisco endorsing the work 'by the special authority I have received from the Very Revd Father Claudio Acquaviva, General of the same society'.[22]

Thomas Stephens's dedication, written in Portuguese at Rachol on 29 April, 1616, is to 'The Most Illustrious and Most Reverend Lord, Dom Frey Christovão de Lisboa, Archbishop of Goa, Primate of India', who had expressed enthusiasm for the work and a desire to see it published. 'For to whom else', he asks rhetorically:

> Could I more reasonably dedicate a Treatise composed for the welfare of this new Christian rock than to him who above all has its interests at heart; through whose hands could better pass this food for those sheep, than those of their lawful and most vigilant Pastor; to whom else could be submitted a work prepared for the instruction and edification of this mystical body than to its head? Were even these reasons to fail, the particular love and benevolence, with which Your Lordship, as Ordinary, approved this book, and the wish you have manifested to see it printed, would not only encourage me but compel me to urge this humble and earnest offering of my work on your Lordship's acceptance.[23]

Traditionally, the *Puranas* dealt with the origins of the universe and the role of the gods, taking the form of a didactic dialogue between questioner and respondent. In the *Christian Purana*, the author cleverly introduces a flavour of Jesuitical disputation between a Brahmin who has difficulties with aspects of Christian doctrine whose questions are answered by a *Pâdri*. The work is written in a mixture of Konkani and Marathi. It is in two sections.

'An Apostle and a Saint' 279

The *Pailem* (first) *Purana* tells the story of the Old Testament, from Creation to the prophecies of the coming of Christ, while the *Dusarem* (second) *Purana* narrates the life of Christ. It would appear that Thomas Stephens began the second part first, using the Devanagari script that was the most usual text for writing in Sanskrit. However, he had to concede the practical impossibility of printing anything in an Indian script, so it was published in Marathi in Roman type on the printing press at St Paul's.

It was immediately considered a literary masterpiece. It became a liturgical document, with Indian Catholics insisting on having readings from it after Mass on Sundays and on feast days. In the words of Cyril Veliath, SJ:

> Despite having had to start from scratch Stephens yet succeeded in gaining a peerless grasp of the grammar, philosophy, and symbolism of the Puranas, and besides, while writing the Christian Purana, he took great care to do so in a manner that enthralled both the refined and common class of citizens. He avoided archaic and convoluted words and phrases, and at each stage of the writing he took care to accentuate the basic Christian message of love.[24]

Thomas Stephens's roots also emerge in the Christian Purāna. He uses such English phrases, translated into Marathi, as 'Rome was not built in a day'. The poem is written on an epic scale. It opens with an invocation to the Almighty: '*Vo namo visuabharita*'. The principal characters and episodes of the Old Testament are interwoven with those of the New. The epic builds towards its crowning events: the Passion, Death and Resurrection of Jesus Christ. As Pascal Roque Lopes expresses it, this represents 'the highest efforts of the poet's genius..., bringing home to his readers a lesson in love, self-sacrifice and forgiveness'.

> The divinity of Christ and the realities of His humanity, His joys and sorrows, His gentleness and tenderness of heart, His self-sacrificing love for man, His purity of life

and the universality of his personality are brought out with power and force.[25]

The first part follows closely the events of the Old Testament with few digressions, although in the concluding section on the prophecies of the coming of the Saviour, he includes the prophecies of the Sibyls (oracular seers of antiquity). In his fourth eclogue (published around 38BC), Virgil cites the Cumaean Sibyl as having foretold that an offspring of the gods will be born of a virgin and will free the world from its wickedness and fear. Thus, for the Church, the Sibyls signified the supremacy of Natural Law—that the ways of God may be perceived, however dimly, by all men of good will. Fallen human nature is capable of right thinking about God and of a pious expectation of divine help. They also highlight the universality of Christ's mission, which is precisely why Thomas Stephens included them in this section.

The *Dusarem Purana* opens with the poet's invocation to the Blessed Virgin, the Apostles and the Saints. The second *Auasuaru* (section) incorporates a cosmic dimension: the Holy Souls in Limbo desiring their release. God is working his purpose out. To further the Salvation History, Thomas Stephens drew upon the *Protoevangelium of James*, a 'gospel' dating from the mid-second century AD. It tells the story of St Anne, the mother of the Blessed Virgin and her husband, St Joachim. Although it was regarded as apocryphal in the Western Church, it was greatly venerated in the Eastern churches. The *Dusare Purana* also discusses the nature of piety and on Christian doctrine. There is a clear distinction between the true meditation of holy men and the mere play of the imagination. Baptism and the Holy Eucharist are the true springs of the soul's nourishment.

Like Roberto de Nobili, Matteo Ricci, Jeronimo Xavier and others, Thomas Stephens faced the dilemma of how purely Christian concepts could be translated into the indigenous vernacular. There were three choices: they could attempt to adopt the western word into the local vernacular; they could use the nearest word in the language in which they were working to the concept they were seeking to express; or they could devise new words. All of these men did all three. Thomas Stephens devised new words, mainly based on formulating compound nouns out of existing concepts. There were, of course, difficulties involved in transposing a word associated with Christian concepts from a European language into an Indian one. He presented Jesus Christ to his readers in the traditional forms with which they were familiar, using Hindi titles of holiness, including the term *swami*, an ascetic or yogi who has been initiated into a Hindu monastic order founded by a religious teacher; *tarak*, a Hindi boy's name meaning 'star' or 'protector'; *parameshvara*, a compound of three words (*param* meaning supreme; *isha* meaning ruler or master; and *vara* meaning Excellent) that literally means 'the Excellent Supreme Ruler'; *jagatguru*, a guru, or teacher or guide of the World, a title traditionally bestowed on *ācāryas*[26] belonging to the *Vedanta*[27] school; *moksharaj* is a compound of two words (*moksha* meaning the death and rebirth cycle in Hinduism; and *raj* meaning king), thus styling Jesus as king over the ultimate goal of existence; and finally *jhana-snana*, 'the bath of knowledge or enlightenment (the term which he used for baptism) seems to have been borrowed by Roberto de Nobili and is still in use amongst the Tamil Christian community.

Christian concepts like Heaven, Holy Spirit, Satan and Hell could not be readily understood by local people. Thomas Stephens therefore used familiar concepts like *Vaikuntha*, the eternal home of the Supreme Lord Vishnu; and *Yamapuri* where human souls go after death, a place which is presided over by the deity called *Yama*, who keeps records of human actions and decides on the fate of the soul. *Devchar* were spirits or ghosts, a term particularly used in Goa. For the idea of 'salvation', he used several Marathi words. Two of the most prominent are *mokṣa* and *mukti*, which, on the surface mean emancipation, liberation or release, but also possess a mystical sense in Hinduism, meaning an escape from *samsāra*, the cycle of death and rebirth, a concept alien to the Christian tradition. Yet the taking of words and the recharging of them with Christian meaning is very much part of that tradition. One of the words used by St Paul to denote 'Salvation' is *Soteria* (Σωτηρία), which means rescue or safety, deliver, heal or save. Yet it also has connections with the name of the Greek goddess of safety, deliverance and preservation from harm. The word passed into Latin as *salvatio* and so into the Catholic vernacular. So successful was Paul's attempt to infuse the word with a Christian doctrinal meaning that it would be fair to say this is now the main way that it is understood. Thomas Stephens attempts such a Pauline technique in his poetic description of the Ascension. Jesus sits at the right hand of God the Father. All the Holy Souls from Limbo are assigned to their respective places. The work of Salvation is complete! Of course, Thomas Stephens's hope was that the terms he used would take on an indigenous Christian meaning. There was strong precedent for this. The early Church had adopted secular words such as *salvatio* to its own usage. Other examples include 'apostle' from the Greek, ἀπόστολος (apóstolos), meaning 'someone sent out' or a delegate. The word 'Gospel' derives from the Old English, *gōd-spell*, meaning 'Good News'. In each of these and many other cases, the Christian meaning of the word has superseded all others.

The work achieved rapid recognition. In 1615, the year after Fr Stephens had completed the *Christian Purāna*, Francisco Vieira, the Provincial for the Society of Jesus, gave it his *Nihil Obstat*, enabling it to be read in churches throughout Goa. This was a precursor to its publication in Rachol in 1616. It was the first work to have been published in Marathi and established it as a literary language. It would be another two hundred years before a book in Marathi was published in the Devanagari script. Joseph L. Saldanha gave a measure of Fr Stephens' achievement:

> When the history of the entire Marathi language comes to be written, there will be found space for depicting the grandeur and solemnity of the first great and noble Song of Christ, in fact the only song of Christ, written in

> Marathi by an Englishman, and containing the outpourings of the exotic spirit that burnt with luminous ardour when it lived for the true welfare of the people of this part of India.[28]

According to Fr Henry Hosten, SJ, the work was so appealing that 'not only do the Christians derive much profit from it, but even the gentoos [gentiles: i.e. Hindus] take pride in speaking of it.'[29] It is certain that Thomas Stephens must have written a great deal more than can now be attributed to him. Given his grounding in poetic appreciation at Winchester College, it is highly likely that, like his fellow Jesuits, Edmund Campion and Robert Southwell, he wrote poetry in English, but such efforts would surely have predated his journey to India. The Central Library in Panjim contains a bound volume of the *Kristapurana* bearing the date, 1767. As well as the great poem itself, it contains three poems on the *Paixão de Cristi* (the Passion of Christ), or, in Marathi, the *Christi Vilāpikā*. Dr S. M. Tadkodkar, Head of the Department of Postgraduate Instruction and Research in Marathi at Goa University, has attributed the authorship of two of these to Thomas Stephens.[30] The author of the second poem in the series, is identified within the text as Fr Manoel Jacques de Noronha, who was ministering in the Azossim district of Goa. It is likely that he was a fellow Jesuit of St Paul's. Four stanzas of the *Kristapurana* were incorporated into the third poem. The Portuguese scholar and politician, Joaquim Heliodoro da Cunha Rivara, wrote of it:'

> There is no doubt that the poet ... was well conversant with Stephens' classic writing. One cannot avoid the possibility that Stephens himself wrote the *Vilāpikā*, since that writing is included in the same bound [volume].

Rivera wrote two versions of his O *Ensaio Historico da Lingua Concani* (History of the Konkani Language). In both, published in Nova Goa in 1857 and in 1857, he edited versions of Thomas Stephens's *Arte da Lingoa Canarim*.[31]

At the age of 70, Fr Stephens's formerly robust health was waning. Stomach troubles turned every attempt to take food or drink into an act of torture. The faithful of Salcete prayed for his recovery, but he died peacefully at the Professed House in Goa. In the year after his death, the Governor of Goa Fernâo de Albuquerque wrote to King Philip III on 14 February 1620.

> It is not convenient for the service of Your Majesty to have foreign prelates here, nor for the foreign members of the Society of Jesus to come to these missions. This is so true that an English priest of holy life while on his death bed in the professed house of the Society in the city said an hour before he died that the Portuguese had insufficient suspicion in admitting foreigners into the State. From the quality of the priest and the hour he was in, one paid more attention to what he said. He did not say whether his words were applicable to the religious alone, but I believe that he meant both the ecclesiastics and the laymen.[32]

De Albuquerque's words have to be taken with some circumspection. Initially, he states that Stephens's objections to foreign settlers were restricted to 'foreign prelates' and foreign Jesuits. It is unlikely that Fr Stephens, as a foreign Jesuit himself, would have made such a remark, particularly when, according to the Governor, he had but an hour to live. One of the cornerstones of the Society was its transcending of national identities and boundaries. It is extremely unlikely that Thomas Stephens could have suggested that the work of the Society in India should be restricted to Jesuits who were Portuguese in origin, especially since the permanent lack of sufficient human resource ensured that the Society was always desperate for any eligible recruits it could get, whatever their country of origin.

Later in his letter, the Governor expands his focus to include foreign laymen, Again, it is unlikely that Thomas Stephens, who had built a memorable reputation for his assistance of and sympathy for foreigners in trouble in the colony, should make such a statement. Most likely, de Albuquerque is invoking the memory of Thomas Stephens to add substance to his own concerns about the decline of Portuguese power in the East. Portugal would lose her century-old rule over Ormuz during his governorship. Yet the letter reveals that Fr Stephens was regarded as 'a priest of holy life'. Despite his 40 years in Goa, during which he can have spoken his native language but rarely, it is significant that it was as an Englishman that he was remembered. Although his burial place is unknown, the revelation that he died in the Professed House makes it virtually certain that he was laid to rest in the adjacent Basilica of Bom Jesus, near where the shrine of St Francisco Xavier would be created five years later.

Thomas Stephens's Konkani Catechism was published in 1622 under the title *Doutrina Christam em Lingoa Bramana Canarim*. His Konkani Grammar, which must have been circulating in manuscript as a source book for his fellow missionaries, was published in Rachol in 1640 under the title *Arte da Lingua Canarum composta pelo Padre Thomaz Estavaō da Capanhia de Jesus*. It may have been the inspiration of Thomas Stephens' work that led to the writing of another *Purāna* within two decades of his death. The French Jesuit Fr Etienne de la Croix (1579–1643) had arrived in India in 1602. His *Discourso sobre a Vida do Apostolo Sam Pedro*, published in 1634, is much more confrontational than the work of Thomas Stephens. He makes St Peter his mouthpiece to refute and ridicule Hinduism. A further work, written in Marathi verse and set in Latin type, was published in 1655. The *Sancto Antonichy Zivitus Catha*, or *Life of St Anthony of Padua*, was written by another Jesuit, Antônio de Soldanha. This was followed, in 1667, by the first translation of parts of the Bible into Konkani by Ignazio Arcamone, an Italian Jesuit with the Salcete mission. His *Segllia Verunsache Vanjel* was printed in Roman script at the Rachol Seminary.

The decline of Goa from a major trading hub to an interesting backwater led to a parallel decline of St Paul's College. By the middle of the eighteenth century it had closed. By 1827, when a French cleric, the Abbe Cotttineau, visited the site, it was completely overgrown and 'la retraite des serpents'. The walls stood starkly in a ruined state. Two years later, most of the building was demolished. Today, the only vestige of the original college is its gate. By contrast, the *Christian Purāna* proved to have enduring popularity. It was reprinted in 1649 (when it was first described as a *Purāna*) and 1654, but the epic mainly reached its readership in handwritten copies, which expresses the devotion in which it was received. When the fearsome Tippu Sahib, Sultan of Mysore, carried off 60,000 Konkani Christians from Mangalore to Srirangapatna in 1784, their faith and hope were sustained by the *Christian Purāna* and they met in secret to read it. In 1801, when the Scottish surgeon Francis Buchanan visited the Catholic hamlets of Kanara, he noted how prayer combined with musical renderings of the Christian *Purāna* consecrated every family gathering.[33]

However, the work had its difficulties. The Portuguese authorities occasionally sought to impose their language on the populace in a policy that was the reverse of the Jesuit policy of *Accommadatio*. This had obvious consequences for the dissemination if the *Christian Purāna*. In 1648, the Viceroy, Francis Távora, decreed that local languages should cease to be used in public proceedings, which included religious worship. It was ordered that books written in Marathi should be confiscated. This would have included the *Kristapurana*. Fortunately, many hand-written copies had been made and circulated. The work also continued to flourish amongst Christians in areas beyond the Portuguese jurisdiction. In 1750, Sebastião José de Carvalho e Melo became Secretary of State (Prime Minister) of Portugal. He was a reformer who abolished slavery in Portugal and its Indian territories, reorganised the armed forces, abolished *Autos-de-fé*, the *Limpeza de Sangue*[34] and the statutes and legal distinctions between Old and New Christians and the resultant discrimination. Having lived in London and Vienna, he was familiar with the anti-Jesuit traditions in both Britain and Austria. He regarded the dominance of the Society in education and science as a barrier to the spirit of the Enlightenment. He took advantage of an attempt on the King's life in 1758 to accuse it of treason. As a result the Jesuits were expelled from Portugal and its colonies in the following year. Their property and assets were seized by the state: thus ended their 200-year contribution to Goan life.

The Jesuits in India were not caught unawares, as their impending suppression had been rumoured for some time. When the purge came, the authorities sought to extend it even to those Jesuits who were beyond their jurisdiction. The Father Provincial, Luis Lopes, was ordered to recall them to Goa. Not all obeyed the summons. Fr Albert Zarth of the Kittur Mission was one of several who considered themselves under no obligation to obey an order given under duress to return to the Jesuit houses at Goa and into the arms of the Portuguese law. In all, 127 Jesuits were expelled from Goa, returning to Portugal aboard two ships. Of these, twenty-four died on the voyage, sixteen quit the order and forty-five were repatriated to Italy. The remaining forty-two were incarcerated in prison. The loss of this considerable force for education and welfare must have contributed to the further decline of the colony.

Other regimes noted what had happened in Portugal. A number of countries followed suit, including France, Spain, the Kingdoms of Sicily and Naples and the Duchy of Parma. Pope Clement XIV came under intense secular pressure to suppress the Jesuits and promulgated the necessary decree in July 1773. Although in theory this meant its end of the Society, this was not quite so. The Russian Orthodox Empress Catherine the Great and the Lutheran King Frederick William III of Prussia refused to acknowledge Papal decrees. Both countries had large numbers of Catholics in their recently-annexed Polish territories, so the Society maintained its presence there. During his exile in France during the Napoleonic Wars, Pope Pius VII resolved to restore the Society. He did so when he returned to Rome in 1814. By 1838 the Jesuits were active in India again. They were no longer confined to the provinces of Goa and Malabar as in the past.

In 1873, Henry D'Abroa wrote to Gerson da Cunha that the *Christian Purāna* was read in church during Lent and Holy Week. It was received with such reverence that an amazing silence set in once the recitation began. Some two and a half centuries after the publication of the third edition, Joseph Saldhana published a fourth in Mangalore in 1907. He based it on manuscript copies, notably one in the possession of King's College, London. The manuscripts had belonged to the library of William Marsden, a prominent Orientalist and First Secretary to the Admiralty. He had made an extensive collection of coins, books and manuscripts when based in the Far East. Many of the manuscripts were been obtained from archives in Goa. The library was donated by Marsden to King's College, London, in 1853, but in 1916 it came into the possession of the School of Oriental Studies.

In 1926, W. F. Sequisa compiled a list of churches where the singing of the *Christian Purāna* still prevailed. He noted that it was not only chanted in churches, but in the home and at work in the fields. Perhaps the greatest compliment to the power of the *Christian Purāna* came in 1935 when a Dr Hivale produced a Protestant version in Poona, the Christian *Katha* (or 'Christian Story'). The 'Romish' passages were, of course, omitted. In 1957, the *Kristapurana* was finally transliterated into Devanagari script by Prasad Parkashan, nearly two and a half centuries after it was first written.

In February, 2011, a two-day seminar on the *Kristapurana* took place at Goa University. Appropriately, the proceedings were conducted in Marathi and the University Hall was filled to capacity. Amongst the contributors was the Salesian priest, the Revd Dr Nelson Falcao, who had completed a translation of the work into modern Marathi. His presentation covered aspects of the principles of Inculturation contained in the *Kristapurana*. He stated that the basis and foundation of inter-religious dialogue is the fact that no religion and no person have the monopoly of the knowledge and experience of God, stating, 'God is beyond all knowledge. He is a mystery. We have to keep seeking, finding, recognizing and experiencing God in every person and in every religion. In trying to do that we have to love one another since we are in God and God is in us.'[35]

Thomas Stephens' devotion to the people of Goa and beyond has never been forgotten. He is commemorated by the Father Thomas Stephens Educational Trust, which was founded in the Vasai (Bassein) District in 1994 to run the Father Stephens Academy School. The building was blessed by the Rt Revd Thomas Dabre, Bishop of Vasai on 4 January 1998. The proposal to found the Thomas Stephens Konknni Kendr (TSKK) in Goa was first brought before the Jesuit Provincial Congregation in 1978. In 1982 it was registered as a society and it became operational in January 1986 at Loyola Hall in nearby Miramar. The Institute is devoted to issues related to the Konkani language, literature, culture and education.[36] It is now based in Alto Porvorim, across the Mandovi River from Panaji, the state capital. The TSKK produces a research bulletin, publishes works in the Konkani language and runs language courses. In 2006, the current Director of the Institute, Pratap Naik, was involved a campaign to get official recognition for the Latin script of Konkani (Romi Konkani). This is the written form of the language on which Thomas Stephens had a great impact with his writing and printing. Around 500,000 of the estimated seven million Konkani speakers use this script. A rich literary tradition has developed and the liturgical literature of the large Catholic minority is printed in it. It is overwhelmingly the means of choice for Internet communications in Konkani. It is also the medium for *Tiatr*, the form of traditional musical theatre that is popular in Goa.

Despite the Sahitya Akadedemi, India's National Academy of Letters, recognising Romi Konkani as a literary language, only the Devanagari script is officially recognised as the means for written communication in Konkani in Goa. It was argued that the recognition of an alternative script would be divisive. The campaign for Romi Konkani has made some progress, but has not yet achieved all its objectives. In September 2008, the Advisory Board of the Official Language Cell of the Government of Goa recommended the use of Konkani in Roman script in government offices. Three state-level Literary and Cultural conventions of Konkani in the Roman Script (*Romi Lipi Konkani Sahitya ani Sonvskrutik Sommelan*) were held in Goa in 2008, 2010 and 2011. On 29 August 2012, *The Times of India* reported that Goa's Chief Minister, Manohar Parrikar, had promised government support for the development of Konkani written in the Latin script. It is surely only a matter of time before this is achieved.

Fr Pratap Naik has built up a collection of over three hundred trees and plants in the grounds of the Institute. He believes that the culture of a place is reflected not only in its language, but in many other aspects, including flora. His aim is to plant a specimen of every fruit-bearing tree that grows in Goa. The collection reflects the province's past as a crossroads of trade, with plants coming from many parts of the world. Each is neatly labelled with its name in Konkani and English and its botanical name. Many of the plants must be those that Thomas Stephens failed to recognise on his first arrival in Goa. He had been particularly impressed by the versatile uses of the palm. The 1913 Catholic Encyclopaedia expressed the view that Stephens, 'at the time of his death, was held in general repute as an apostle and a saint.'[37] Hopefully this work has illustrated his saintly apostolic work in the colourful context of his times.

Notes

1. Details of the life of Roberto de Nobili may be found in *A Pearl in India, The Life of Roberto de Nobili* by V. Cronin (New York: Dutton, 1959) and *Preaching Wisdom to the Wise, three Treatises by Robert de Nobili*, .J (Boston College: Institute of Jesuit Studies, 2000).
2. From the Sanskrit, a religious ascetic who has abandoned all claims to

'An Apostle and a Saint'

religious or social status.

3. J. Kamat, *Roman Catholic Brahmin! Biography of Roberto De Nobili*. Available at www.kamat.com/kalranga/people/pioneers/nobili.htm.
4. *Roberto de Nobili; a Case Study in Accommodation*, available at www.home.snu.edu/~hculbert/nobili.htm.
5. A. Sauliere, *The Life of Father Robert de Nobili, S.J. (1577–1656)*, as quoted by R. De Smet, *Journal of Hindu-Christian Dialogue*, vol 4 (1991), pp. 359–360.
6. A. K. Priolkar, 'Two Recently Discovered Letters of Fr Thomas Stephens', *The Journal of the University of Bombay* 25/2 (September 1956), pp. 114–123.
7. A hagiography of fourteenth-century origin, which was regularly updated.
8. Pyrard de Laval, F., *The Voyage of Pyrard de Laval to the East Indies, the Moluccas and Brazil*, 3rd edition (Paris 1611). Gray, A. (trans), assisted by Bell, H. C. P.: vol. 1, (Hakluyt Society, London, 1887), p. 76.
9. *Ibid.*, p. 82.
10. *Ibid.*, p. 242.
11. The shrine of the Apostle at Santiago de Compostela. Pyrard was to fulfil this pledge.
12. Pyrard, *The Voyage*, pp. 309–320.
13. *Ibid.*, p. 426.
14. *Ibid.*, p. 381.
15. *Ibid.*, pp. 405, 406.
16. The custom continues to this day, but its future is in doubt, supposedly because of a lack of interest amongst the younger generation.
17. Pyrard, *The Voyage*, pp. 439–443.
18. *Ibid.*, pp. 2–6.
19. Pyrard is referring to Nicolas Trigault, SJ, who was appointed Procurator to the China Mission in 1612. He travelled back to Europe to recruit missionaries, raise money and publicise the work of the mission. In Antwerp, his portrait was painted by Peter Paul Rubens. He translated and edited Matteo Ricci's China Journal and devised one of the first systems to Romanise Chinese writing. He became deeply distressed by a dispute about religious terminology and committed suicide in 1628
20. R. Raiswell, *Sherley, Sir Thomas (1564–1633/4)*: *Oxford Dictionary of National Biography* (Oxford: OUP, 2004).

21. Pyrard, *the Voyage,* pp. 244–247.
22. J. L. Saldanha (trans. and ed.), *The Christian Puranna of Thomas Stephens, S.J.* (Mangalore, Simon Alvares, 1907), p. LXXXVIII.
23. *Ibid.,* p. LXXXIX.
24. C. Veliath, S.J., 'Thomas Stephens: A Human Monument of Inculturation in India', *Bulletin of the Faculty of Foreign Studies,* 9 (Tokyo, Sophia University: No 46, 2011), p. 21.
25. www.pascallopes.blogspot.com.
26. A preceptor or instructor in religious matters: the founder or leader of a sect.
27. One of the six orthodox schools of Hindu philosophy.
28. Saldanha, *The Christian Puranna,* pp. LXXXIV-LXXXV.
29. Quoted by N. Falcao, *Kristapurana: A Christian-Hindu Encounter: A Study of Inculturation in the Kristapurana of Thomas Stephens, SJ (1549–1619)* (Pune: Snehasadan / Anand: Gujarat Sahitya Prakash, 2003).
30. S. Tadkodkar, *Goan Christian Marathi Vilapika during the 17th Century* (Delhi: B.R. Publishing Corporation, 2009).
31. J. H. da Cunha Rivera, *Ensaio Historico da Lingua Concani* (Nova Goa, Impensa Naciona, 1857), p. 124.
32. Saldanha, *The Christian Puranna,* p. XXXVII.
33. F. Buchanan, *A Journey from Madras through the Countries of Mysore, Canara and Malabar* (London: Black, Parry & Kingsbury, 1807).
34. Literally 'cleanliness of blood': it referred to those considered to be 'Old Christians' without Muslim or Jewish ancestry.
35. Bosco Information Service, Bis. 2304 (Mumbai, Feb. 2011). Available at www.bismumbai.blogspot.com/2011_02_01_archive.html.
36. See https://www.tskk.org/. Konkani is an Indo-Aryan language spoken in the Indian states of Goa, Karnataka, Kerala and Maharashtra. It is the official language in Goa, and one of the known languages of India. According to the 2001 census of India there are just under 2.5 million Konkani speakers in India.
37. D. O. Hunter Blair, 'Buston, Thomas Stephen' in C. B. Herbermann; E. A. Pace; C. E. Pallen, *The Catholic Encyclopedia* vol. 3 (New York: Robert Appleton Company, 1907), p. 89. Thomas Stephens was also know as Thomas Stephen Buston, the son of Thomas Stephens of Bushton. See J. L. Saldanha, 'Stephens, Thomas' in *The Catholic Encyclopedia* vol. 14, p. 292.

Bibliography

Manuscripts

Stephens, T. *The Christian Purana of Father Thomas Stephens: A Work of the 17th Century. Reproduced from Manuscript copies and edited with a Biographical Note, an Introduction, an English Synopsis of Contents and Vocabulary.* 4th ed. Ed. Joseph L. Saldanha. Mangalore: St Aloysius' College, 1907. Pp. xci + 597. XB.

Stephens, T. Two unpublished letters of Stephens, his obituary notice and the Catalogues of the Goan Province in the Roman Archives of the Society of Jesus; the Codes Novitiorum 1565–1586 in the Archives of the Novitiate of the Roman Province.

Letters and Papers

David, R. (ed.). *A Letter written from Goa, the principal city of all the East Indies by one Thomas Stephens, an Englishman, and sent to his father, Master Thomas Stephens, anno 1579* from *Hakluyt's Voyages, a Selection by Richard David.* London: Chatto and Windus, 1981.

Priolkar, A. K. 'Two Recently Discovered Letters of Fr. Thomas Stephens', *Journal of the University of Bombay*, 25, part 2 (25 September, 1956), pp. 114–123.

Vincente, Fr R. *To Fr Claudius Acquaviva*, Goa, 8 Nov., 1581. Mumbai: Seth Gordhandas Sunderdas Medical College and King Edward Memorial Hospital, 1982.

Jesuit Sources

St Ignatius de Loyola. *The Constitution of the Society of Jesus*, translated with a commentary by Ganss, G. E., S.J. St Louis: Institute of Jesuit Sources, 1970.

Bibliography

Coelho, I. Thomas Stephens, SJ (1549–1619), an updated bibliography at http://indianchristianwritings.blogspot.com/2009/10/thomas-stephens-sj-1549-1619-updated.html.

Books

Alden, D. *The Making of an Enterprise; The Society of Jesus in Portugal, its Empire and Beyond, 1540–1750*. Stanford, CA: Stanford University Press, 1996.

Borges, C. J. *The Economics of the Goa Jesuits, 1542–1759*. New Delhi: Concept Publishing, 1994.

Borges, C. J. 'Stephens, Thomas (1549–1619)' in *Oxford Dictionary of National Biography*. Oxford: Oxford University Press, 2004, pp. 482–483.

Borges, C. J. and Feldman, H. (eds). *Goa and Portugal, their Cultural Links*. New Delhi: Concept Publishing Company, 1997.

Boxer, C. R. *The Portuguese Seaborne Empire, 1415–1825*. London: Penguin Books, 1969.

Da Silva Gracias, F. *Health and Hygiene in Colonial Goa, 1510–1961*. New Delhi: Concept Publishing Company, 1994.

Dellon, C. *An Account of the Inquisition at Goa*. Pittsburg: R. Patterson & Lamdin, 1819.

De Souza, T. R. and Borges, C. J. (eds). *Jesuits in India: in Historical Perspective*. Goa: Xavier Center of Historical Research, 1992.

Donnelly, J. P. (ed. and trans.). *Jesuit Writings of the Early Modern World, 1540–1640*. Indianapolis and Cambdridge: Hackett Publishing Company, 2006.

Du Jarric, P., SJ. *An Account of the Jesuit Mission to the Court of Akbar*, trans by C. H. Payne. New York and London: Harper & Brothers, 1926.

Falcao, N. M. *Kristapurāna, a Christian-Hindu Encounter. A Study of Inculturation in the Kristapurāna of Thomas Stephens, S.J. (1549–1619)*. Gujarat: Gujarat Sahitya Prakash, 2003.

Ferroli, D., SJ. *The Jesuits in Malabar, Vol. I.* Bangalore: Bangalore Press, 1939.

Foley, H., SJ. *Jesuits in Conflict.* London: Burns and Oates, 1873.

Foley, H., SJ. *Records of the English Province of the Society of Jesus, Vol. 3.* London: Burns & Oates, 1878.

da Fonseca, J. N. *An Historical and Archaeological Sketch of the City of Goa.* Bombay: Thatcher & Co. Ltd., 1878.

Gauvin, A. B. *Art on the Jesuit Missions in Asia and Latin America, 1542–1773.* Toronto: University of Toronto Press, 2001.

Hakluyt, R., *The Principal Navigations, Voyages, Traffiques and Discoveries of the English Nation.* Glasgow: Thomas Davison, 1914.

Harris, J. G. *Tales of the First Firangis, Part III.* New Delhi: Aleph Book Company, 2015.

Henn, A. *Hindu-Catholic Encounters in Goa. Religion, Colonialism and Modernity.* Bloomington: Indiana University Press, 2014.

Hough, Revd J. *The History of Christianity in India.* London: B. B. Seeley and W. Burnside, 1839.

Leach, A. F. *A History of Winchester College.* London: Duckworth & Co, 1899.

van Linschotten, J. Huyghen. *The Voyage of John Huyghen van Linschoten*, transcription of the 1598 English translation, ed. Burnett, A, C. London: Hakluyt Society, 1885.

Maclagan, Sir E. *The Jesuits and the Great Mogul.* London: Burns, Oates and Washbourne, 1932.

Newitt, M. *The First Portuguese Colonial Empire.* Exeter: University of Exeter Press, 1986.

Poliath, P. *The Catholic Church in India.* Changanacherry: HIRS Publications, 2019.

Poliath, P. *The Liturgical Heritage of the Syro-Malabar Church: Shadows and Realities:* Changanacherry, HIRS Publications, 2019.

Pyrard de Laval, F. *The Voyage of Pyrard de Laval to the East Indies, the Moluccas and Brazil*, trans Gray, A., assisted by Bell, H. C. P. London: Hakluyt Society, 1887.

Rodrigues, L.A. *Souls, Spices and Sex: The Struggle for European Ascendency in Portuguese Trade, 1510–1961.* Margao, Goa: Cinnamon Teal Publishing, 2018.

Saldanha, J. L. (trans. and ed.). *The Christian Puranna of Thomas Stephens, SJ.* Mangalore: Simon Alvares, 1907.

Tadkodkar, S. M. *Goan Christian Marathi Vilapika:during the 17th Century.* New Delhi: B. R. Publications, 2010.

Waugh, E. *Edmund Campion.* London: Hollis and Carter, 1935.

Worcester, T. (ed). *The Cambridge Companion to the Jesuits.* Cambridge: Cambridge University Press, 2008.

Županov, I. G. *Part Four: South Asia.* Po-Chia Hsia, R. (series ed.), *A Companion to Early Modern Catholic Global Missions.* Leiden and Boston: Brill, 2017.

Županov, I. G. and Xavier, A. B. *Catholic Orientalism: Portuguese Empire, Indian Knowledge (16th-$18^{th}c$).* New Delhi: Oxford University Press, 2015.

Županov, I.G. *Intercultural Encounter and the Jesuit Mission in South Asia (16th–18th Centuries),* co-edited with Anand Amaladass. Bangalore: Asian Trading Corporation, 2014.

Županov, I. G. *Missionary Topics: The Catholic Frontier in India.* Ann Arbor: University of Michigan Press, 2005.

Articles and Essays

Anonymous. 'John Fryer, M.D., F.R.C.S., British Traveller of the 17th Century and his Impressions of Modern Medicine in India', *Osmania University, Hyderabad, Bulletin of the Department of the History of Medicine,* Issue 2 (1964), pp. 241–250.

Aranha, P. 'Early Modern Catholicism and European Colonialism: Dominance, Hegemony and Native Agency in the Portuguese Estado da India', paper at the Freising Conference on World Christianity, Weisbaden, Harrassowitz, 2014.

De Almeida Teles e Cunha, J. M. *Confluence and Divergence: The Thomas Christians and the Padrado, c. 1500–1617* in Journal of Eastern Christian Studies 63/1–2(2011), pp. 45–71.

De Silva, T. R. 'The Council of Trent (1545–1563): Its Reception in Portuguese India', *Transcontinental Links in the History of Non-Western Christianity*, ed. Klaus Koschorke, Wiesbaden, Harrasowitz Verlag, 2002, pp. 189–201.

Eliasson, Pär. 'Kristapurāṇa: Reshaping Divine Space', *Journal of Hindu-Christian Studies*, 30/9 (2017).

Falcao, Revd. Dr. N., SDB. *The Kristaparana of Thomas Stephens (1549–1619), An Overview*. Oxford: Blackfriars, 2014.

Pandija, S.K. 'Medicine in Goa, a former Portuguese Territory', *Journal of Postgraduate. Medicine*, 28 (1982), p. 123.

Roe, Sir Thomas and Fryer, Dr. John. *Travels in India in the Seventeenth Century* London: Trübner, 1873.

Robinson, R., 'Cuncolim–Weaving a Tale of Resistance', Mumbai, *Economic and Political Weekly*, Vol. 32, No. 7, (Feb, 15–21, 1997); pp. 334–340.

Sharma, S. K. 'Revisiting Portuguese Colonization in India', *Madya Bharti: Research Journal of Humanities and Social Sciences* 72 (January–June, 2017), pp. 135–156.

Veliath, C. 'Thomas Stephens – A Human Monument of Inculturation in India', *Tokyo, Bulletin of the Faculty of Foreign Studies*, No. 46, (2011), pp.153–178.

Walker, T. 'Stocking Colonial Pharmacies: Commerce in South Asian Indigenous Medicines from their Native Sources in the Portuguese Estado da India'. In *Networks in the First Global Age (1400–1800)*, ed. Mukherjee, R. New Delhi: Primus Press, 2011, pp.141–170.

Woods, D., 'Racial Exclusion in the Mendicant Orders from Spain to the Philippines', *UCLA Historical Journal*, vol. 11(0) (1991), pp. 69–92.

Xavier, A. B. 'Power, Religion and Violence in Sixteenth Century Goa', *Portuguese Literary and Cultural Studies*, 17/18 (2010), pp. 27–50.

Županov, I. G. 'Drugs, health, bodies and souls in the tropics: medical experiments in sixteenth-century Portuguese India', *The Indian Economic and Social History Review*, vol. xxxix, No 1 (January-March, 2002), pp. 1–45.

Župonov, I. G. 'One Civility; But Multiple Religions: Jesuit Mission among the St. Thomas Christians in India (16th-17th Centuries)', *Journal of Early Modern History*, Vol. 9 (3) (2005), pp. 284–325.

Župonov, I. G. 'Conversion, Illness and Possession: Catholic Missionary Healing in Early Modern South India', *Purushartha*, 27 (2008), pp 263–300.

Županov, I. G. 'The Wheels of Torments; Mobility and Redemption in Portuguese Colonial India (sixteenth century)' in *Cultural Mobility, a Manifesto* ed., Stephen Greenblatt et al. Cambridge: Cambridge University Press, 2009, pp.24–74.

Theses

Correja-Afonso, J., *Jesuit Letters and Indian History*, Bombay, Indian Research Institute, St. Xavier's College, 1955.

Eliasson, Par, *How Thomas Stephens, S.J. (1549–1619) conveys a Christian message of salvation in words with Hindu connections.* University of Gothenburg, 2005.

Eliason, Par, *Mukti in Kristapurāna*, University of Gothenburg, 2015.

Index of Persons

Page numbers in italics refer to illustrations.

Abbas I ('The Great'), Shah of Persia, 273, 274
Abd al-Malik I, Sultan of Fez, 36
Abdisho IV, Chaldean Catholic Patriarch, sends Mar Abraham to Rome, 174
Addai (Thaddaeus), St, disciple of St Thomas, 239: Malabar liturgy attributed to, 239
Agbar V, King of Edessa, 220
Abraham, Mar, Archbishop, appointed Metropolitan of Angamaly by Nestorian Patriarch, 174: arrested and sent to Goa, 174: seeks Catholic endorsement, 174: ordained Catholic priest and consecrated bishop, 174: reputation as equivocator, 175: builds Cathedral of Mar Hormizd, 175: asks Pope for protection from Portuguese, 176: assists in establishment of Vaipikotta Seminary, 176: attends provincial synod, 176: allows purging of Syriac service books, 176, 177: position threatened by appointment of Mar Simon, 176: requests Nestorian Patriarch to appoint his successor, 231: equivocation of, 231; alleged error and simony, 231, 232: refuses to attend Council in Goa, 232: death, 232
Abroa, Henry d', on *Christian Purâna*, 287
Abul Fazl, Grand Vizier, 141: critical of Akbar's attitude to licentiousness, 154
Acquaviva, Alberto, 10th Duke of Atri, father of Bl. Rodolfo, 46
Acquaviva, Claudio, SJ: Superior General, 80(9), 222, 233, 235, 245, 259, 260: Chamberlain to Pope Pius V, 46: Provincial Superior, 20: considers running Royal Hospital in Goa to be against Society's constitution, 133: expresses disquiet at Jesuit mercantile activities in Japan, 51: appoints Alessandro Valignano as Visitor to the East, 175, 179: finds Roberto de Nobili in error, 256, 257: supports Thomas Stephens, 261, 278
Acquaviva, Bl. Rodolfo, SJ, 46, 136, 187, 215, 218, 219: teaches at St Paul's College, 138: leads mission to Akbar, 142: reproves Akbar for

licentiousness, 154, 155: kept at his Court by Akbar, 178: appointed Superior of Salcete mission, 180: challenge to Cuncolim and martyrdom, 186, 187, Akbar on, 217
Adil Shah, Sabaio Ali I, Sultan of Bijapur, 114:
   lays siege to Goa, 120, 126: destroys churches in South Goa, 229
Adil Shah, Sabaio Ibrahim, Sultan of Bijapur, burns down College and Church at Margão, 183
Adil Shah, Sabaio Ismael, Sultan of Bijapur, 181
Adil Shah, Sabaio Yusif, Sultan of Bijapur, 83.96, 114
Aethelstan, Anglo-Saxon courtier, 1
Afonso, Pedro, SJ, surgeon, 133: at Hospital of the Holy Spirit, Margão, 183
Aguiar, Isobel de,
   endows church in Bassein, 276: death, 277: sepulchre of, 277
Akbar, Abu'l Fath Jalah ud din Muhammad, ('Zeldanus') Mughal Emperor, xvi, 45, 188, 194, 214:
   as administrator, 141, 142, 149–155: repeals law on apostasy, 157: appoints Fr Antonio as tutor to his son, 156: arranges discussions between religious groups, 148: gives audiences, 145: Court of, 144, 145, 148–152: description of, 145, 146: founds *Din-i-Ilâhi* (the Faith of the Divine), 157: *fatwa* against, 158: accused of heresy, 157, 158: interest in figurative art, 157: visits Shaykh Salim Chishti, 142: invites Jesuit Mission, 45, 141: founds Fatehpur Sikri, 142–144: esteem for Jesuits, 156, 178, 179: abolishes *jizyah* tax, 158: declares himself *khalifa* (caliph), 158: attitude to licentiousness, 154, 155: patron of learning, 153: messianic beliefs, 157: succeeds father, 141: congratulates Philip II on ascending to Portuguese throne, 178: Queen Elizabeth letter to, 194, 195, 208: massacre of Rajputs, 141: and religion, 142–144, 146–148, 156: revolt against, 158, 159: abolishes *saki* and child marriage, 157: opposes *Shariah* law, 156–158: upbringing, 141: at war, 150, 159–163, *161*: wives and concubines, 142, 144, 155, 159, 219; on death of Rodolfo Acquaviva, 217: moves capital to Lahore, 217, 218: subsidies Jesuit mission, 218: builds chapel in Lahore, 219: commissions Jerónimo Xavier to write Life of Christ, 220: supervises building of his mausoleum, 248: moves capital to Agra, 248: asks Jesuits to seek Portuguese military assistance, 248: gives

Index of Persons

church to Jesuits, 248: death, 248
Albuquerque, Afonso de, soldier: captures Goa, 83, 84: founds Royal Hospital, 132: abolishes *sati*, 85
Albuquerque, Fernão de, Viceroy, writes to King about death of Thomas Stephens, 283, 284
Albuquerque, Matias de, Viceroy,
orders Jesuits to administer Royal Hospital, 133; Governor of Ormuz, 194
Aleman, Gaspar, SJ, Procurator, aids distressed travellers, 273
Alexander VII, Pope, endorses East Syriac Rite hierarchy, 240
Alfred, King of Wessex, 1
Allen, Mark, xix
Allen, Dr William, 16, 17: founds Douai Seminary, 17; founds English College in Rome, 30, 32
Almeida, Francisco de, navigator, 275
Alvarez, Balthazar, SJ, Spiritual Director of Teresa of Avilla, 25, 26
Alvarez, Henry, SJ, tells Pounde and Stephens about Jesuits, 14, 15
Anjos, Belchieor dos, SJ, founds Collegiate Church of the Mother of God in Bassein, 276

António, Dom, Portuguese pretender, 199:
reigns for 20 days, 177: defeated by Spanish, 177: reigns in the Azores, 177: seeks refuge in France, 178
Aquinas, St Thomas, OP, and Natural Law, 213: on slavery, 115
Aranha, Bl. Francisco, SJ, architect, builds church at Cuncolim, 181; martyred at Cuncolim, 187
Arcamone, Ignazio, SJ, translates Bible into Konkani, 285
Ataide, Luis de, Count of Atouguia, Viceroy, 114
Aubrey, John, chronicler, 13
Augustine, St, on martyrdom, 167
Avila, St Teresa of, mystic, 25, 26
Aylmer, John, Bishop of London, 43
Azevedo, Bl. Inácio de, SJ, martyred by Huguenot pirates, 180

Baertz, Gaspar, SJ, Rector of St. Paul's College, 94–96
Bahadur Shah, Sultan of Gujerat, 276:
concludes alliance with Portuguese, 139: takes cannabis, 139: appoints Garcia de Orta as his consultant physician, 139

Bakshi Banu Begum, appointed Governor of Kabul by Akbar, 163

Baptista, St Peter, SSF, leads mission to Japan, 225

'Barbudo, Lançarote', English mercenary soldier, 1

Barrera, Antonia Moniz, Governor of Goa, bans Brahmins from the city, 98

Barreto, Francisco, Governor of Goa, bans Brahmins from public office, 97

Beaugé, Zenon de, Capuchin, attempts to intercede with Inquisition, 108, 109

Beck, Edward, traveller helped by Thomas Stephens, 262:
in Lisbon, 273: slanders Sir Robert Shirley, 274: described as Jesuit, 274, 275

Becket, St Thomas à, 99

Bellarmine, St Roberto, Cardinal, letter from Roberto de Nobili, 257

'Bernado', Brahmin boy, converts to Christianity, 190:
desire to learn Latin, 190: seized by family, 190–192: escape, 192, 193

Bernier, François, physician, on Indian physicians and their lack of understanding of anatomy, 123

Bernini, Gian Lorenzo, architect, 18

Berno, Bl. Pietro, SJ, 46, 47, 60, 136:
demolishes Hindu temples, 185: martyred at Cuncolim, 187: mutilation of body, 187

Boullaye-le-Gouz, François de la, 101:
on Inquisition, 104

Borba, Diogo de, SSF, 94: establishes Confraternity of the Holy Faith, 84

Borgers, Bernard, helps English travellers, 201, 202, 205, 207

Borja, St Francisco de, SJ, 3rd Vicar-General, 18, 58: co-founds Roman College, 27, 28

Borromeo, St Carlo, Cardinal Archbishop of Milan, 55, 56: assassination attempt, 56: Evelyn Waugh on, 55

Braganza, Constantino de, Viceroy, banishes Brahmins from Goa, 98

Bramane, Pero Luis, SJ, linguist, only Indian to be received into the Society before its suppression, 138: interpreter for Alessandro Valignano, 176

Briant, St Alexander, SJ, trial and execution 164–166: regarded as saint, 166

Bristow, Richard, translator of Bible, 17

Brooksby, Edward, helps Robert Persons, 41

Broukner, Sir William, High Sheriff of Wiltshire, sends copy of Pounde's *Six Reasons* to London, 43

Browne, Anthony, 1st Viscount Montague, 14

Buchanan, Francis, on *Kristapurana*, 286

Cabral, Francisco, SJ, Provincial, 47–50, 189, 219:
  complains about extravagance of Alessandro Valignano, 223

Cambaut de Coislin, Mlle du, Charles Dellon dedicates book to, 106

Camerte, Paulo, SJ, founds hospital in Old Goa, 133, 182

Camôes, Luis Vas de, author of the *Luciados*, 77:
  on corruption in Goa, 116: lover of Luisa Barbara, 77: writes sonnet to Garcia da Orta, 140

Campion, St Edmund, SJ, xv, xvi, 4, 5, *11*, 16–18, 21, 24, 46, 55, 283:
  writes *Brag*, 43: with English Mission, 43: attends trial of John Storey, 10: scholar of Christ's Hospital, 5: becomes Jesuit, 11: deacon of Church of England, 9: joins seminary at Douai, 9: arrest, torture, trial and execution, 164, 165, 189: Latin Orator of Oxford University, 4, 5: Fellow of St. John's College, 5; speech from dock after condemnation, 6, 165: welcomes Queen Elizabeth to Oxford, 5: audience with Queen Elizabeth, 164: in Tower of London, 164: regarded as saint, 165, 166

Campori, John, SJ, questions validity of Synod of Dampier, 235

Carletti, Francisco, merchant, on colic 129(52)

Carré, Abbé Barthélemy, 102, 103, 111: *Le Courrier du Roi en Orient*, 111.

Carvalho e Mello, Sebastião José de, Prime Minister of Portugal, abolishes slavery, *Autos da Fé* and legal distinctions between Old and New Christians in Portugal and India, 286: expels Jesuits from Portugal and its colonies, 286

Casas, St Felipe de las, OFM, (St Philip of Jesus) 225

Catesby, Sir William, accused of harbouring Edmund Campion, 165

Catherine II ('the Great'), Empress of Russia, refuses to acknowledge Papal decrees, 287

Cattaneo, Lazzaro, SJ,
  first missionary in Shanghai, 136, 216: builds chapel in Shanghai, 217

Cecil, Robert, 1st Earl of Salisbury, 273

Cecil, William, 1st Baron Burghley, admires Edmund Campion, 5

Cenes, Jean de, SJ, aids distressed travellers, 273

Cervantes, Miguel de, on spice trade, 243

Chijiko, Miguel (Chijiwa Migera),
in Japanese delegation to Europe, 179: ordained priest, 225: apostatises, 225

Chishti, Moinuddin, Sufi mystic, founder of Chistiyya Order in India, 142, 143: doctrine of *Wahlat-al-Wujud (Unity of Being)*, 143

Chishti, Shaykh Salim,
Sufi mystic, 155: visited by the Emperor Akbar, 142: tomb of, 143, 144

Christ, Br Manuel de, OP, aids Laval on board ship, 272

Ch'u T'ai-su, Confusian scholar, 214

Claesz, Cornelis, publishes van Linschotten's works, 242

Claver, St Pedro, SJ, and slavery, 115

Clavius, Christopher, SJ,
astronomer and mathematician, 28, 29, 29.57, 58, 138, 214: reform of calendar, 29, 211: edition of Euclid's *Elements*, 216

Clement V, Pope, suppresses Knights Templars, 59

Clement VIII, Pope, 231–233, 238

Clement XIV, Pope, suppresses Society of Jesus, 287

Clynnog, Dr Morys, Warden of English College, 31, 32

Collingham, Francis, English Agent in Madrid, 273

Columbus, Christopher, xix, 62, 83

Costa, Afonso da, altar boy, martyred at Cuncolim, 187

Costa, Alvaro da, priest and patrician, 117

Da Costa, Paolo, Jesuit layman, desire for martyrdom, 180, 181: killed at Cuncolim, 187

Da Costa, Ventura, domestic servant, bridegroom, 117

Cottam, John, schoolmaster, 13

Cottam, Thomas, SJ,
schoolmaster, xv, 13: at Douai, 13; becomes Jesuit novice, 13: ordained at Soissons, 167: desire to join Indian mission, 166: trial, 166

Cotton, George, arrested by orders of Bishop of Winchester, 15

Cottineau de Kloguen, Abbé Denis Louis, visits ruins of St Paul's College, 285

Coutinho, Francisco, Viceroy, 98: bans Indian physicians, 122

Coutinho, Miguel Vaz, SJ, Vicar General: founds Seminary of the Holy Faith, 84, 85

Criminale, Ven Antonio, SJ, first Jesuit martyr in India, 95

Croce, Andrea, Bishop of Tivoli, donates *Sant'Andrea a Montecavallo* to Jesuits, 17, 18

Croix, Etienne de la, SJ, assists distressed travellers, 273:

Index of Persons 305

writes *Discorso sobre a Vida de Apostolo Sam Pedro*, 285

Crowley, Rev Richard, Puritan, response to Pounde's *Sixe Reasons*, 43

Cunha, José Gerson da, physician and linguist, 288

Da Cunha, João, accuses Thomas Stephens of appropriating rents, 237

Da Cunha, Nuno, Admiral, captures Bassein, 276

Cunha Rivera, Joaquim Helidoro, edits *Arte de Lingoa Canarim*, 283

Cyril, St, Patriarch of Alexandria, 237: dispute with Nestorius, 235, 237, 238

Dabre, Thomas, Bishop of Vasai, blesses Father Stephens Academy School, 289

Dalrymple, William, xiii

Da Sâ, Simão, SJ, 183

Davanzati, Bernardo, scholar, 110

Davies, Thomas, traveller helped by Thomas Stephens, 262

Della Valle, Pietro, traveller, xiii, 68, 84:
   on class system in Goa, 116, 117: attends Goan wedding, 117, 118: visits church at Mormugão, 229, 230

Dellon, Charles Gabriel, physician, 102, 107, 109, 111: arrested at Damão, 102, 103: before the Inquisition, 104–106, 108: imprisoned in Goa, 103–105, 108: imprisoned in Portugal, 106: comments on 'pandites' (Indian hereditary doctors), 124, 125 and on bleeding, 125: *Relacion de l'Inquisition de Goa*, 106, 107

Dias, Fr Peter, SJ, honesty of impresses Akbar, 45

Domingos, Brahmin convert, 186;
   martyrdom of, 188

Donatus, Latin scholar. *Ars Grammatica* of, 3.4

Don John of Austria, victor of Lepanto, 35

Drake, Sir Francis, 36:
   fires on Portuguese ship, 200, 201

Dudley, Robert, Earl of Leicester, 9:
   interrogates Edmund Campion, 164

Dudley, Sir Robert, fits out ships for voyage to the East Indies, 244

Edward VI, King of England, 6

Elcius, Peter, Priest and Martyr, subject of Thomas Pounde's poem, *A challenge unto ffox*. 167

Eldred, John, merchant, 194:
   amasses fortune in Aleppo, 198

Eliya VI, Nestorian Patriarch, sends Mar Simon to Kerela as

rival Bishop to Mar Abraham, 176
Elizabeth I, Queen of England, xiii, 7–10, 12, 17, 23, 24, 33, 35, 53, 99, 194, 244:
excommunication by Pope, 202: interrogates Edmund Campion, 164
Ematas, Francisco Delgado, Grand Inquisitor, 104
Euclid, mathematician, 28, 29: *Elements*, 138, 216
Eugene IV, Pope, *Decree for the Armenians*, 239

Fabii, Fabio de, Jesuit novice master, 18
Falcão, Alexei Dias, OP, inquisitor, sent to Goa, 96
Falcao, Nelson, SDB, translates *Kristapurana* into contemporary Marathi, 288
Faria, Juan de, SJ,
assists in printing first books in an Asian language, 260: death, 261
Federici, Cesare, horse dealer, 120
Felton, John, St, tried and executed for treason, 9
Fenicio, Jacomo, SJ, 'Second Apostle to the East', mission in Calicut with Fr Hilaire, 266:
parish priest in Arthunkal, 266: revered as saint, 266: established tradition of receiving Hindus returning from pilgrimage, 266: funeral, 266
Fernandes, Domingo, SJ, architect of Church of Bom Jesus, 227
Fernandes, Francisco, Court physician to Philip II, 196, 197
Fernandes, Gonçalo, SJ,
founds Madurai mission, 253: in conflict with Roberto de Nobili, 254, 256
Fitch, Ralph,
merchant, xviii, 87, 202, 206: description of Fatehpur Sikri, 143: arrives in Goa, 194: imprisoned in Goa, 204, 205: escape from Goa, 207: flees to Court of Akbar, 208: further journeys, 208: assumed to be dead, 208
Fitzgerald, James Fitzmaurice, seeks to invade Ireland, 35
Fitzgerald, Sir William, Lord Deputy of Ireland, 35
Fludd, Henry, SJ, 274
Fogg, Martha, xix
Fonseca, João Vicente da, OP, Archbishop of Goa, 60, 201:
offers position to Jan Hughen van Linschotten, 202: obtains release of English prisoners, 205: death, 239
Fortado, Francisco, SJ, in China, 216
Foster, Suzanne, xix
Foxe, John, polemicist, *Foxe's Book of Martyrs*, 167
Francisco, Bl. Antonio, SJ, 44, 46;

Index of Persons

in Salcete Mission, 180, 186: desire for martyrdom, 180, 186
Francisco, Pero, SJ, prohibits Roberto de Nobili from baptising converts, 257
Frederick William. King of Prussia, refuses to acknowledge Papal decrees, 287
Fryer, John, surgeon, 105:
    admires Garcia da Orta's garden, 140: on Indian physicians, their reluctance to undertake surgery or phlebotomy and their overuse of leeches, 124: shortcomings of Indian apothecaries, 124:
    describes Salcete, 181
Furtado, Joan, pirate, 267
Furtado, Manuel de Mendonça, Governor of Damão, 102, 103

Galileo, Galileo, astronomer, 28
Gama, Estâvão da, Governor General of Goa, 84
Gama, Francisco da, Viceroy of the Indies, 114, 243, 245, 246: builds Arch of the Viceroys, 246: dislike of populace for, 246: hung in effigy, 246, 247
Gama, Luis da, Admiral, besieges Cuneale Fort, 245
Gama, Vasco da,
    Navigator, 58, 83, 84, 114, 245, 246: statue vandalised, 246, 247

Garcia, St Gonsalo, OFM, 51: crucified by Toyotami Hideyoshi, 226
Garnet, Henry, SJ, Head of English Mission, 27
Gascoigne, George, masque writer, 9
Geevarghese (George) of the Cross, appointment as Administrator of Angamaly diocese, 233:
    makes declaration of loyalty to Catholic faith, 233: disavows declaration, 233: threatened with dismissal by Archbishop Menezes, 234: equivocation of, 234: and Synod of Diamper, 235, 237–239: death, 238: successor, 240
Gerard, Fr John, SJ, 52
Gilbert, George, SJ, 42, 43: founds Catholic Association, 16
Gilbert, Sir Humphrey, 36
Gôis, Br. Bento de, SJ:
    selected for mission to Akbar, 219: refuses Akbar's request to seek military assistance from Portuguese, 248
Gomez, Antonio, SJ:
    Rector of St Paul's College, 94: clashes with Francis Xavier, 94–96
Gonçalves, Juan, SJ:
    prints first book in Asian language, 260: death, 261
Gonçalves, Melchior, SJ, establishes Jesuit presence in Bassein, 276

Gonsalves, Sebastian, SJ, 51
Good, Fr William, SJ, 44
Gracias, Fátima da Silva, author, *Health and Hygiene in Colonial Goa*, 112
Gregory XIII, Pope, 23, 28–33, 36, 214:
  and Inquisition, 99: clarifies *Regnam in Excelsis*, 23: death of, 223, 224
Gregory XV, Pope, resolves issues in Roberto de Nobili's favour, 258

Haffner, Revd Dr Paul, xix
Hakim, Mirza Muhammed, Governor of Kabul:
  revolts against his half-brother, Akbar, 159: defeated and pardoned by Akbar, 163
Hakluyt, Richard, author, xviii, 4, 195:
  obtains Thomas Stephens' letter to his father, 196, 244: advisor to East India Company, 244: *The Principal Navigations, Voiages, Traffiques...* xviii, xix, 169, 196, 244, 255
Hamida Banu Begum, mother of Akbar, placed in charge of civil administration, 159
Hamilton, Kathy, xix
Hara, Martinão (Hara Marachino):
  in Japanese delegation to Europe, 179: ordained priest, 225: death of. 226

Hartley, L. P., author, *The Go-Between*, xv, 290
Hassan IX ('King Dom Manoel'), Sultan of Maldives, 275:
  becomes Christian, 263: deposed, 263: death, 275
Hatton, Sir Christopher, Privy Councillor, helps Thomas Pounde, 15, 43
Henrique, Cardinal, Regent of Portugal, later King, authorises Inquisition in Goa, 96
Henriques, Francisco, SJ:
  interpreter on mission to Akbar, 142: creates chapel at Fatehpur Sikri, 147: returns to Goa, 178
Henriques, Henrique, SJ, writes and prints books in Tamil, 260
Henry, Cardinal and King of Portugal, succeeds to the throne, 177
Henry II, King of England, contention with Thomas a Becket, 99
Henry the Navigator, Prince, 59:
  discovers *Voto de Mar* ('Turn of the Sea'), 59
Hideyoshi, Toyotami, Shogun, 225:
  conquers Kyushu, 224: bans Christianity, 224: confiscates cargo of *San Filipe*, 225: arrests and crucifies 26 Christians, 226
Hosten, Henry, SJ, on *Kristapurana*, 282

Index of Persons 309

Howard, St Philip, 13th Earl of Arundel, tutored by Edmund Campion, 9
Howard, Thomas, 4th Duke of Norfolk, 9
Hudson, William, traveller helped by Thomas Stephens, 262
Humayun, Mughal Emperor, 139, 141
Hunt, Simon, SJ, schoolmaster, teaches William Shakespeare, 27
Hyacinth, Fr, OP, dissolute priest, before Inquisition, 106, 107

Ismael, Abilfada, Arab geographer, 197

Jahangir, Mughal Emperor, see Salim
Jahangir Quli Beg, Subahdar ('King') of Bengal, send fleet to attack Maldives, 264
James I and VI, King of England and Scotland, 274: accession, 169
Jarric, Pierre du, SJ, 148
Jewell, John, Bishop of Salisbury, Richard Stephens secretary to, 11
João III, King of Portugal, 56, 59, 94, 96, 276:
 frees slaves of non-Christians who converted, 76: grants charter to St Paul's College, 137: letter from Francis Xavier, 88, 89: agrees *padroado* with Pope, 175
João Sri Kathari Maha Radun, titular King of the Maldives, sentenced to death, 275: under house arrest, 275: marriage, 275: death, 275
Johnson, Christopher, schoolmaster and poet, 4
Jones, Sir William, philologist, postulates existence of Indo-European family of languages, 221
Julius III, Pope, appoints Chaldean Patriarch, 173

Kalaafaan, Ibrahim, Sultan ('King') of the Maldives, takes Pyrard de Laval captive, 263: attacked by Subahdar of Bengal, 264: flees and killed, 264, 265

Laerzio, Alberto, SJ, Head of Jesuit College of Cochin, 253, 254
Lainez, Diego, SJ, Superior General, 138
Laval, François Pyrard de; traveller, xviii, 71, 72, 98, 116, 262:
 on Brahmins, 90, 91: on class system in Goa, 116, 117: on dress in Goa, 119: on Hindus, 92, 93: on Inquisition, 110, 111: on sex and drugs, 75, 76, 81(38): on Royal Hospital, 134–136: on St Paul's

College, 137, 138: on *Sati*, 119: on slavery, 76–78: on syphilis, 75, 76: shipwrecked and made captive on Maldive Islands, 263: learns Dhevhi language, 263: dreams of freedom, 263, 264: vows to make pilgrimage to Compostela, 264: captured by Bengalis, 264.265: voyages to Calicut, 264, 265: befriended by Zamarin, 265: kidnapped by pirates, 267, 268: arrested and imprisoned at Cochin, 268, 269: description of conditions in prison, 269, 270: horrific voyage to Goa, 271, 272: in Royal Hospital, Goa, 272: helped by Jesuit Fathers, 273

Lee, Hugh, English Agent in Lisbon, 273, 274

Leedes, William, jeweller, arrives in Goa, 194;
    imprisoned in Goa, 204: escapes from Goa, 207: becomes favourite of Akbar, 208

Leitào, Duarte, SJ, report on cholera epidemic of 1570, 125: on 2nd mission to Akbar, 218

Leo X, Pope, agrees *padroado* with Portugal, 175

Lewis, Dr. Owen, Regius Professor, 16

Linschoten, Jan Huyghen van; adventurer: *242:*
    xviii, 60–62, 71–74, 92, 117, 119, 201, 202, 204–207, 241: dislike of Jesuits, 131, 132, 204:

on bubonic plague, 126: on corruption in Goa, 116: on dress in Goa, 119: helps English captives, 204, 205: on Hindus, 92: on Indian physicians, 122, 123: on life at sea, 62, 121: offered position in Goa: on sex and sensuality, 73–75: on sickness and disease, 121: returns to Portugal, 241: knowledge of Portuguese maritime secrets, 242

Publications: *Reys-geschrift...*, 242: *Itinerario:...*, 242: English translation of, 244

Linschoten, Willem Huyghen van; merchant, 202

Lopes, Luis, SJ, Provincial Superior, ordered to recall Jesuits to Goa, 287

Lopes, Pascal Roque, on the *Kristapurana*, 279

'Lopez, Estevan', English mercenary soldier, 1

Lisboa, Christovão de Sà e, Archbishop of Goa,
    calls commission to investigate Roberto de Nobili, 257: endorses *Kristapurana*, 277: work dedicated to, 278

Li Zhizao, Director of Public Works, converts to Catholicism: writes *Tian Xue*, 216

Louis XIV, King of France, 111

Loyola, St Ignatius de, SJ: 57, 94, 99:
    founds Jesuits, 24: appoints Xavier as Provincial of India,

Index of Persons

95: co-founds Roman College, 27, 28: *Spiritual Exercises*, 24, 25, 227
Luisa Barbara, slave, romance with Luis Vas de Camôes, 77

Maffei, Giovanni Pietro, SJ: description of life at sea, 61
Mal, Raja Todar, Finance Minister (*Wazir*) and soldier, sent by Akbar to crush rebellion, 159
Malmesbury, William of, 1
Mana Vikrama, Zamarin (Samoothiri) of Calicut,
  captures Chaliyam from Portuguese, 243: permits Pate Marcar to build fort, 245: allies with Portuguese, 245: besieges Cuneale Fort, 245: befriends Pyrard de Laval, 266
Mancio Ito (Ito Mansho), SJ:
  leads Japanese delegation to Europe, 179, 223: made honorary citizen of Rome, 224: returns to Japan, 225: ordained priest, 225: death of, 226
Manucci, Niccolao, Venetian merchant, 108,
  account of Emphrem Nevers before the Inquisition, 108: *Storia do Mogor*, 108
Manuel I, King of Portugal, endows Jesuit College at Coimbra, 57
Mari, St, Malabar liturgy attributed to, 239

Marakkar, Putti, pirate, builds fort on Pudepatam peninsular, 245:
  raids Malabar coast, 245: death, 245
Marracar, Mahomet Cuneale (Kunjali Marrakar), Moslem chieftain:
  renames fort and town after himself, 245: under siege, 245, 246: agrees to surrender if life spared, 246: treacherously betrayed and killed, 246
Mascarenhas, Gil Eanes de, Captain of Malabar, commits atrocities in Salcete, 185
Marscarenhas, Francisco de, Viceroy, 199, 206, 208:
  releases English prisoners, 205
Mascarenhas, Jerónimo de, Captain of Cochin:
  amasses fortune, 231: endows Church of Bom Jesus, 231: estate stolen, 231
Marscarenhas, Manuel de, Captain-General of Mylapore, 107
Mascarenhas, Revd Paulo, censors *Kristapurana*, 277
Marscarenhas, Pedro de, Viceroy, 96, 97;
  grants property to Garcia de Orta, 140
Mascarenhas, Fr Pero, SJ, founds Salcete Mission, 184
Marques, Francisco, OP, Inquisitor, sent to Goa, 96

Marsden, William, orientalist, donates library to King's College, London, 288

Martin, Gregory, scholar and linguist, 5, 9, 17, 18: translator of Bible, 17

Mary, Queen of Scots, 9, 15, 203

Mary Tudor, Queen, 5, 10, 17, 167

Maryam Zamani, wife of Akbar the Great, gives birth to future Emperor Jahangir, 142

Mendoça, André Furtado de, soldier and Viceroy: storms Cumeale Fort, 246: promulgates decrees against foreign merchants, 247, 248

Menezes, Duarte de, Viceroy, 224

Menezes, Francisco de, Governor of Cochin, 268–272

Menezes, Frey Aleixo de, *232*: appointed Archbishop of Goa, 231: Chaplain to Philip II, 231: austerity and charitable works of, 231, 240: expels Nestorian Bishop, 231: empowered to take charge of Amgamaly archdiocese, 233: visitation to the St Thomas Christians, 234–236, 240: and Synod of Diamper, 235–241: establishes church hierarchy in Kerela, 239, 240: criticism of, 239: consecrate Church of Bom Jesus, 247: case of Roberto de Nobili referred to, 254, 256: created Archbishop of Braga, 273

Mercurian, Everard, SJ: Superior General, 18, *19*, 25, 26, 175: writes to Thomas Pounde in prison, 21–23, 42

Mesquita, Diogo de, SJ, with Japanese delegation to Europe, 179

Mexia, Lorenzo, SJ, on Japanese emissaries, 225

Monserrate, Antonio, SJ, 152: writes journal of mission to Akbar, 142: on Akbar, 145–156: on justice and punishments, 151, 152: on Islamic marriage, 155: appointed tutor to Akbar's son, 156: on campaign with Akbar, 159–163: returns to Goa, 178

Montaigne, Michel de, essayist, 18

Muiz-ul-Mulk, Chief *Qazi* of Bengal, drowned by Akbar, 158

Munday, Anthony, writer and spy, 41: on life at English College, 32–35

Murad Mirza, Prince, tutored by Fr Antonio Montserrate, 156, 159

Murtaza Nazim Shah, Sultan of Ahmednagar, lays siege to Goa, 126

Naik, Pratap, SJ, Director of Thomas Stephens Konkanni Kendr, 289: campaigns for

Index of Persons 313

Konkani Roman script, 289: creates botanical garden, 290
Naique, Polpotto, sailor, sentenced by Inquisition, 113
Nakaura, Julião, SJ:
    in Japanese delegation to Europe, 179: ordained priest, 225: martyred in Nagasaki, 226
Nami, Abdul, Chief Imperial *Qadi*, sentences Brahmin to death, 157
Nebrija, Antonio de, botanist, Garcia de Orta studies under, 139
Neri, St Philip, 33
Nestorius, Archbishop of Constantinople, dispute with Cyril of Alexandria, 235
Nevers, Ephrem de, Capuchin friar, ministers in Madras, 107:
    complaint to Captain General, 107: arrested and tried by Inquisition, 108, 109, 111
Newbery, John, merchant, 195:
    has Thomas Stephens' letter to his father, 196, 200: travels to Ormuz, 198: opens shop in Ormuz, 198–200: denounced as spy and heretic, 199: sent to Goa, 194, 199, 200: asks Turkey and Levant Company to petition Philip II on his behalf, 200: imprisoned in Goa, 201–205: helped by Thomas Stephens, 201–204: escapes from Goa, 207: flees to Court of Akbar, 208: attempts to return to England, 208: death of, 208

Nobili, Roberto de, SJ, *252*
    birth and background, 251: becomes Jesuit, 251: travels to India, 252: and caste system, 253–257: in conflict with Gonçalo Fernandes, 254: adopts Brahmin lifestyle, 254: assumes role of Hindu monk, 255: approach to conversion, 255, 256: witnesses *sati*, 255: first European to master Sanskrit, 255: seeks to form 'Brahmin' Church, 255: methods denounced by Gonçalo Fernandes and Nicolão Pimenta, 256: found in error by Claudio Acquiviva, 257: prohibited from baptising converts, 257: investigated by Inquisition, 257, 258; writes works in Tamil, 258: blindness and death, 258: seeks to convert Christian concepts into indigenous vernacular, 280

Noranha, Dom Antão da, Viceroy:
    divides spiritual care of Goa between Dominicans, Franciscans and Jesuits, 182: donates house at Rachol to Jesuits, 182

Norhana, Fernando de, Admiral, besieges Cuneale Fort, 245
Norhana, Manoel Jacques de, SJ, *Paixão de Cristo* attributed to, 283
Nunez, Melchior, SJ, 96

O'Neill, Hugh, Earl of Tyrone, gains pardon for Sir Thomas Stukeley, 35

Orta, Garcia de, physician, 75; on drugs, 75, 140: education, 139: accompanies Martim de Sousa to India, 139: performs first autopsy for cholera in India, 130: consultant physician to Bahadur Shah, 139: garden in Bombay, 140: studies effects of cannabis, 139- 141: marriage, 140: settles in Goa, 139: publication: *Colóquios dos Simples e Drogas da India*, 140

Otomo Sorin, *Daimyo* of Bungo, 179

Otto III, Holy Roman Emperor, 251

Pacheco, Bl. Alphonso, SJ, 47: seeks support for Goan Mission in Rome, 180: with mission in Salcete and martyrdom, 185–187

Paleotti, Gabriele, Cardinal Bishop of Bologna, 54, 55

Pantoja, Diego da, SJ, in China, 214, 215: introduces western music to China, 216, 217; petitions Emperor for permission to build monument to Matheo Ricci, 217

Parkashan, Prasad, publisher, transliterates *Kristapurana* into Devanagari script, 288

Parker, Geoffrey, historian, on the Inquisition, 101

Parker, Matthew, Archbishop of Canterbury, Richard Stephens secretary to, 11, 12

Paterson, James, xix

Paul III, Pope, 24, 84, 85: pronouncements against slavery, 115

Felipe Sri Kathari Maha Redun, titular King of the Maldives, 275

Parrikar, Manohar, Goan Chief Minister, promises support for Konkani written in Roman script, 289, 290

Paul V, Pope, 239: orders Council to investigate methods of Roberto de Nobili, 257: death, 258

Paul, St, apostle, 281, 282

Pereira, Gaspar Jorge de Leão, Archbishop of Goa, 181: determines site of Chapel of Our Lady of the Snows, 182

Pereira, Gil Eanes, SJ, Vicar General of Bengal, suggests Akbar invite Jesuit mission, 45

Pereira de Meneses, Joseph, naval commander, expedition to Diu, 106: accused of cowardice, 106: accused of sodomy before Inquisition, 106: acquitted, 106

Index of Persons 315

Persons, Robert, SJ, xvi, 4, 5, 11, 21, 27, 30, *30,* 33, 39(34), 44–46, 55, 169;
  with English Mission, 42, 43: *Epistle of Comfort to the Priests,* 165, 166
Peter, St, 237
Philip II, King of Spain (Philip 1 of Portugal), 35, 36, 152, 163, 241, 275:
  founds university at Doual, 9: assumes throne of Portugal as Philip I, 177: keeps administration of Spain and Portugal separate, 178: pays for Japanese delegation, receives them and presents them with horses, 223: Aleixo de Menezes chaplain to, 231
Philip III, King of Spain (Philip II of Portugal), 283, 284
Pimenta, Nicolāu, SJ, Father Superior, 240:
  Thomas Stephens becomes secretary to, 237: appoints Archdeacon George as Angamaly administrator, 233: journey to Malabar, 233: expresses fear that St Thomas Christians would relapse into Nestorianism, 233: sends missions to Bengal and Cambodia, 241: censures Roberto de Nobili, 256: appointed Papal Visitor, 256
Pinheiro, Emmanuel, SJ, selected for mission to Akbar, 219
Pius IV, Pope, 55, 174
Pius V, Pope, 10, 23, 45, 46: *Regnams in Excelsis,* 9, 10

Pius VII, Pope, restores Society of Jesus, 287
Plantijn, Christoffel, printer, 45
Plautus, Latin playwright, 4
Pliny, mathematician, *Natural History,* 2
Poderoso, Pedrosa de, sea captain, cruelty to Laval, 271, 272
Pomp, Dirck Gerritzoon ('Dirck China'), 242: voyages to Goa, China and Japan, 241
Pounde, Ellen, mother of Thomas, 15
Pounde, Thomas, SJ, xv–xvii, 12, 52, 53, 164, 189:
  betrayed and imprisoned, 15: imprisoned in Bishop's Stortford Castle, 43, 44: 'Esquire of the Body' to Queen, 12: fall and humiliation while dancing at Court, 12: inherits Belmont House, 12: letter to Edmund Campion intercepted, 164, 165: interrogated, 52–54: obtains *Hakluyt's Voyages,* 169: at Lincoln's Inn, 12: imprisoned at Ludlow, 9: in Marshalsea Prison, 15, 16, 21–23, 42–44: performs in royal masque, 12: received into Society of Jesus, 20–23: writes *Six Reasons,* 43, 44: associated with Thomas Stephens, 12–16, 19, 20, 164, 169: tortured, 52: in Tower of London, 164: composes poem to Catholic martyrs, 166: *A Challenge unto ffox,* 167–169:

released from prison, 169: writes to James I, 169, 262
Pythagarus, 92, 93

Raleigh, Sir Walter, 36
Ramponi, Plăcido Francesco, artist, description of Goa, 70, 71
Raya, Krishna Deva, King of Vijayanagora, cedes Rachol fort to Portuguese, 181
Redfern, Helen, xix
Ribeiro, Br Estavão, SJ, on 2nd mission to Akbar, 218
Ribeiro, Br. Lázaro, SJ, pharmacist, at Hospital of the Holy Spirit, Margão, 183
Ricci, Mateo, SJ, 46, *212*, 280: mission to China, 136, 211–217: and adoptionism, 211, 212, 217: studies at St Paul's College, 138: composes first Chinese/Portuguese dictionary, 212: as cartographer, 213: dons robes of Buddhist monk, 214: audience with Emperor Wanli, 215: appointed Keeper of Imperial Clocks, 214: predicts eclipse of the sun, 214, 215: baptises Xu Guang-qi, 216: translates Euclid into Chinese, 216: as painter, 216: death, 217: monument to, 217: seeks to express Christian concepts in indigenous vernacular, 280
Writings *On Friendship (Jiaoyoulun)*, 214: *The Secure Treatise on God*, 216: *Della Entrata della Compagnia di Giesu e Christianita nella Cina* (History of his Mission), 216

Richmond, William, buys Bushton Manor, 3
Rocha, João da, SJ, arrival in China, 214
Rodrigues, Diego, Captain of Fortress at Rachol, discovers island of Rodrigues, 228: destroys pagodas in Salcete, 184, 228
Rodrigues, Gonçalo, former soldier, with Salcete Mission, 186: martyred at Cuncolim, 187
Rodrigues, João, SJ, interpretor, 225
Rodrigues, Nuno, SJ, Rector of St Paul's College, 223: leads Japanese delegation to Europe, 180
Rodrigues, Simon, SJ, Provincial of Portugal, 57, 94–96
Ros, Francisco, SJ, Professor at St Paul's College, 176: Rector of Vaipikotta Seminary, 176: attends provincial synod in Goa, 176: Archbishop Menezes attempts to appoint as Administrator of Angamaly diocese, 233: translates Roman rite into Syriac, 234: and Synod of Diamper, 235, 238: purges literature of St Thomas Christina, 237: appointed

Index of Persons

Bishop of Angamaly, 239: appointed Archbishop of Cranganore, 239
Rousham, St Stephen, prisoner in Tower of London, 169
Ruggieri, Michele, SJ, 136, 214: joins mission to China, 211 studies Chinese, 211: writes Chinese catechism, 212: linguistic achievements, 249(1)

Sacrobosco, Johannes de, (John Hollywood), mathematician, 28, 29
Salim, Nur-ud-din-Muhammad (Emperor Jahangir), 142, 159, 220:
succeeds to throne, 248: initial good relations with Jesuits, 248; three nephews baptised, but later apostatised, 248: grants land to Jesuits foe cemetery, 248: war with Portuguese, 248
Saluqa, Shimon VIII Yohannan, Chaldean Patriarch, 173
Sandys, Edwin, Bishop of London, 10, 15
Sarrava, A.J., on Portuguese Inquisition, 128(39)
Sassetti, Fillippo, on Jews, Brahmins, Portuguese, Hindus and Muslims, 91: on 'absolute Rule' in Goa, 110
Sebastião I, King of Portugal, 36, 37, 97, 114:
arms of, *183:* decree banning non-Christians, 98, 99:
donates land in Goa to Jesuits, 182: killed at Battle of Alcácer-Quibir, 177
Sebastian, St, 187
Sequisa, W. F., on Christian Purâna, 287
Seymour, Edward, Duke of Somerset, Lord Protector, *3*
Seymour, Thomas, Lord Sudeley:
executed on orders of brother, 3: ownership of Bushton Manor transferred to, 3
Shakespeare, William, xv, xviii, 13, 14, 27: *Macbeth,* 194: *The Tempest,* xviii
Sherwin, St Ralph, SJ, 30, 32, 55: trial and execution, 164, 165: regarded as saint, 166
Shirley, Sir Robert, diplomat, soldier and traveller, 273: slandered by Edward Beck, 274
Shirley, Lady Teresia (neé Sampsonia), Safavid noblewoman, marries Sir Robert Shirley, 274
Shivadharma, Sanskrit scholar, 255
Sighelm, Bishop of Sherbourne, possible mission to India, 1
Silveira, Francisco Rodrigues da, soldier, 68:
on corruption in Goa, 116
Simão, Julio, engineer and architect, work on Se Cathedral, 227, 246:

work on St Paul's College, 246:
designs Arch of the Viceroys, 246
Simon, Mar, Bishop, appointed to St Thomas Christians by Nestorian Patriarch, 176
Sixtus V, Pope, 224
Smith, Dr. Richard, first Chancellor of Douai University, 16
Soame, Sir Stephen, presides at inaugural meeting of East India Company, 244
Soares, Lopo, Governor of Goa, abolishes child-killing, 85
Soldanha, Aires de, Viceroy, betrays Cuneale, 246
Soldanha, Antônio de, SJ, writes Life of St Anthony of Padua in Konkani, 285
Soldanha, João de, Admiral, 58
Soldanha, Joseph L, SJ:
on the *Kristapurana*, 282: publishes 4th edition, 287
Somers, Admiral Sir George, xviii
Sousa, Martim Afonso de, Viceroy, founder of Brazil, 139, 140:
appoints Garcia de Orta as his Chief Physician, 139: concludes alliance with Sultan of Gujerat,
Souza, Francisco de, SJ, chronicler, on St Paul's College, 137

Southwell, St Robert, SJ, poet, xv, xvi, 27: on religious life, 19, 20, 26
Stephens, Jane, neé Prator, mother of Thomas Stephens, 2
Stephens, Richard, fl. 1533, 44, 56:
granted lease to Bushton Manor, 2: harbours Catholic priests, 164: letters from son, Thomas, xviii, 44, 46, 61–64: sheltering Catholic priests, 190
Stephens, Richard,
birth, 3: Secretary to Bishop of Salisbury, 11 and Archbishop of Canterbury, 11, 12: Professor of Theology at Douai, 12, 16, 17: Professor of Philosophy at University of Paris, 164, 189: correspondence with brother, Thomas, 163, 164, 181, 189, 190, 193, 194: helps Catholic refugees from England, 164, 190: on Calvinism, 193: death of, 226
Stephens, Thomas, SJ, ('Padre Estevan,' 'Stephen de Buston'), xv–xix, 9, 37, 45, 56, 58, 59, 62, 68, 84, 114, 115, 121, 122, 131, 132, 136, 142, 194, 218, 247, 252:
on policy of Accommodation, 51, 228: birth, 2; on Calvinism, 193, 194: recognition that converts needed cultural foundation, 192: correspondence with brother,

Index of Persons

Richard, 163, 164, 181, 189, 190, 193: account of massacre at Cuncolim, 187–189, 259: recovers bodies from Cuncolim massacre, 187, 188: enters Society of Jesus, 4, 17, 18; first Englishman to sail round Cape of Good Hope, xviii, 62, 65, 66:: on flora in India, 78, 81(38), 122, 209(10), 290: on friction between Christians and Hindus, 184: letter included in Hakluyt's *Voyages*, 169: helps English prisoners, 202, 203: imprisoned in Ludlow, 9: mentioned in letter to James I, 169: leaves England, 15: letters to father, xviii, 44, 46, 61–67, 72, 196, 244: on martyrdom, 181: on people of Goa, 72: journey to Lisbon, 54: mission with Thomas Pounde, 12–16, 19: joins Jesuit Province of India, 27, 44–46: ordination, 136, 227: supports Pounde's entry into Society of Jesus, 20, 21, 23: in Rome, 17–21, 25–29, 33, 36, 44, 46: studies at St Paul's College, 136, 138: describes Salcete, 181: supposed vision as novice, 180: voyage to Goa, 60–67: propounds existence of Indo-European group of languages, 221: linguistic abilities, 221, 228, 276: on wildlife, 63–67: writes annual report to Rome, 222, 223, 258, 259, 260; takes vows as Spiritual Coadjutor, 226: Jesuit report on, 226: one of the 'Professed', 227: accused of appropriating rents for Rachol Seminary, 237: creates map of Goa, 245: belief in conversion by persuasion, 251: plea to Superior General for more missionaries in India, 251: expresses admiration for work of Roberto de Nobili, 260: desire to express Christian concepts in local vernacular, 260, 261, 280: and *puranas*, 261, 262: helps distressed travellers, 262, 273: death, 283–285: remembered as an Englishman, 284: *Catholic Encyclopedia* on, 290

Writings: *Arte de lingoa Canarim* (Konkani grammar) 261, 283, 285: *Christi Vilâpika* (*Paixão de Cristo*), 283: *Doutrina Christam em Lingoa Bramana Canarim* (Konkani catechism), 221, 285: *Kristapurana*, xvii, 262, 276–283, 285–288: becomes liturgical document, 279: receives *Nihil Obstat*, 282: first work to be published in Marathi, 1616, 283: reprinted 1649, 1654: gives hope to exiled Konkani Christians, 286: prohibited by Viceroy, 286: 4th edition published by Joseph Soldanha, 287: transliterated into Davanagari script, 288

Ministry: Secretary to Father Superior, 237: Rector of Margão College, 222: Rector of St. Paul's College, 227: **Salcete Mission**, 180, 181,

185, 203, 222, 228, 259, 260: **Bassein,** Holy Spirit College, 276: **Parish Priest at: Benaulim,** Church of St John the Baptist, 227: **Loutolim,** Saviour of the World Church, 228, 229: **Margão,** Holy Spirit Church, 230: **Mormugão,** St Andrew's Church, 229: **Navelim,** 230: **Rachol,** Our Lady of the Snows, 237, 277:

Stephens, Thomas, grandfather of Thomas Stephens, 9, 14

Storey, St John, Regius Professor, 10:
    kidnapped and tortured, 10: trial and execution, 10, 11: trial and execution, 10, 11

Storie, John, painter, arrives in Goa, 94:
    imprisoned in Goa, 204: associate of Jesuits, 204: remains in Goa, 207, 208: opens shop, 208: marries, 208: begets first Anglo-Indians, 208

Strapone, Michael, Venetian merchant, 199:
    denounces Newbery's party in Ormuz as spies and heetics, 199:

Stukeley, Sir Thomas, 35, 36:
    becomes English folk-hero, 36, 37

Sumitada, Daimya of Omura:
    converts to Christianity, 50: cedes Nagasaki to Jesuits, 50

Summers, Admiral Sir George, wrecked off Bermuda, xvi

Taborer, Andreas, provides surety for English prisoners, 205, 206

Tadkodkar, Dr S, M, , on *Paixão de Cristo*, 283

Tavernier, Jean-Baptiste, merchant, account of Inquisition, 108

Távora e Brito, Henrique de, Bishop of Cochin, 45

Távora, Francisco, Viceroy, prohibits local languages, 286

Teodôsiô II, Duke of Braganza, 224

Teixera, Manoel, SJ, founds Collegiate Church of the Mother of God in Bassein, 276

Thaliah, Bishop Jonas, CMI, questions validity of Synod of Dampier, 250(19)

Thoma I, Mar, Archdeacon, breaks with Rome, swears Coonan Cross Oath, 240

Thomas, Apostle and Saint, 2, 239:
    martyrdom of, 2: founds Malankara Church, 173, 174

Thompson, Flora: *Lark Rise to Candleford*, 8

Thynne, Sir John, Receiver of the Crown, surveys Bushton Manor, 2

Tibão, Sebastião, vandalises statue of Vasco da Gama, 246

Index of Persons 321

Timoji, Hindu chieftain, aids Albuquerque to capture Goa, 83
Tippu Sahib, Sultan of Mysore, carries off 60, 000 Konkani Christians, 285, 286
Tokugawa Iejusu, Shogun, 225
Topcliffe, Richard, torturer, Thomas Pounde interrogated by, 52, 53
Tresham, Sir Thomas, accused of harbouring Edmund Campion, 165
Trigault, Nicolas, SJ, assists distressed travellers, 273
Tripp, Rev Henry, Chaplain to Marshalsea Prison, 43

Valignano, Fr Alessandro, SJ: Vicar-General in the Indies, 46–48; *48*, 54, 55, 118, 189, 211, 214, 225: on corruption in Goa, 116: formulates policy of Accommodation, 48–50, 175: and Japanese delegation to Pope, 179, 223–225: builds trade of Nagasaki, 50, 51: appointed Visitor to the East, 175, 179: Accord with Mar Abraham, 175, 176: establishes Vaipikotta Seminary, 176
Vasconelles, Francisca de, titular Queen of Maldives, marries King João, 275
Vaux, William, 3rd Baron, accused of harbouring Edmund Campion, 165

Vaz, Fr Antonio, SJ, honesty of impresses Akbar, 45
Vega, Christoval de, SJ, on 2nd mission to Akbar, 218
Veliath, Cyril, SJ, on *Kristapurana*, 279
Vicente, Ruy, SJ, Provincial, 142: accepts administration of Royal Hospital on temporary basis, 133: requests Akbar for return of Rodolfo Acquaviva, 178: Akbar's reply, 178, 179
Victoria, Queen, 100
Vidal, Mme, 102, 103
Vieira, Francisco, Father Provincial, indifference to Fr. Stephens' project, 261: endorses it, 277, 278: gives it *Nihil Obstat*, 282
Vilela, Fr Gaspar, SJ: pursues policy of Adoptionism, 49
Volk, Rebecca, xix
Vossenkuhl, Prof. Wilhelm, xix

Walsingham, Sir Francis, Principal Secretary, 52
Wanli (Zhu Yizhun), Chinese Emperor, 215–217
Watson, John, Bishop of Winchester, 15, 43
Waugh, Evelyn, author, on Carlo Borromeo, 55
Weston, William, SJ, Head of English Mission, 27, 169
White, Dr. Richard, Professor of Civil Law, 16
White, Sir Thomas, Founder of St. John's College, Oxford, 5

William of Wykeham, Bishop of Winchester, founds Winchester College, 3

Wilson, Sir Thomas, Keeper of State Papers, 273:
describes Edward Beck as a Jesuit, 274, 275

Wood, Anthony à, 30

Wood, Captain Benjamin, commands flotilla lost at sea, 244

Wriothesley, Henry, 2nd Earl of Southampton, 12, 14, 15

Wriothesley, Henry, 3rd Earl of Southampton, xv, 14

Wriothesley, Thomas, 1st Earl of Southampton, 12

Xavier, St Francis, SJ, ('Goencho Saib'), xvii, xix, 49, 57, 93, 182, 187, 228, 253, 266:
and Adoptionism, xvii, xix, 49, 89: dislike of Brahmins, 89, 90: mission to China, 96, 211: death, 96: mission to the East, 94: in Goa, 88, 94–96: dispute with Antonio Gomez, 94–96: on Hinduism, 87: requests Inquisition, 96, 97, 112: in Japan, 95, 96: founder member of Jesuits, 24: in India, 27; appointed Provincial of India, 95: writes to King, 88, 89: mausoleum of, 70: mission to Paravas, 89: and St.Paul's College, 94–96: on mission, 218: founds Collegiate Church of the Holy Name, Bassein, 276

Xavier, Jerónimo, SJ, birth and background, 218:
on the Emperor Akbar, 157: at Bassein College, 218: at Cochin, 218: Superior of Professed House, 218: leads mission to Akbar, 219: becomes favourite of Akbar, 219: commissioned by Akbar to write Life of Christ, 220: other writings, 220, 221: refuses Akbar's request to seek military assistance from Portuguese, 248: sent by Emperor Jahangir to Goa to negotiate peace with Portugal, 248: Rector of St Paul's College, 248: death, 248: seeks to translate Christian concepts into indigenous vernacular, 289

Xu Guang-qi (Xu, Paulo),
in charge of Chinese calendar reform, 216: baptised by Mateo Ricci with the name Paulo, 216: builds church, 216: translates Euclid, 216:

Yang Tianyun, converts to Catholicism, 216

Yazdi, Mullah Muhammed, *Qazi* of Jaunpur, pronounces *fatwa* against Akbar: drowned by Akbar, 158

Young, Richard, Government Agent, 52–54

Zarth, Albert, SJ, refuses summons to return to Goa, 287

Index of Places

Abyssinia, 137
Afghanistan, 141
Africa, 59, 64, 72, 106, 107
Agra, 142, 143:
    Akbar returns capital to, 248;
    'Akbar's Church', 248
Ajmer, home of Moinuddin
    Chishti, 143
Ahmednagar Sultanate, 126
Alcalá de Henares, University,
    47, 139
Aleppo, 194, 198: caravan to
    India from, 198
Alicante, 56
Alto Porvorum, Thomas
    Stephens Konkanni Kendr,
    289
Amsterdam, 107, 242
Angamaly, 174, 175:
    diocese of, 232, 239: Archdeacon
    George convenes synod at,
    233
Antmodar, Mount, 2
Antwerp, 10, 44: Calvinism in,
    193: iconoclasm in, 193
'Arabia Felix' (Yemen) , 152,
    170(16)
Arima, 179
Arthunkal,
    Jocomo Fenecio parish priest,
    266: St Andrew's Basilica,
    266: Sabarimala Temple near,
    266
Ascension Island, 241
Ascona, Switzerland, 47
Atlantic Ocean, 59
Assolna, fort, 187, 259
Azossim, 283
Azores, 59, 177, 241
Babylon, 233
Baghdad, 198
Bahrein, 70
Bardez, 207, 245: annexed by
    Portugal, 1543, 88
Basra, 200: River Euphrates at,
    198
Bassein (Baçaim, Vasai), 51, 96,
    142, 275:
    captured by Nuno da Cunha,
    275: Fort of São Sebastião,
    276: St Joseph's Cathedral,
    276: Collegiate Church of the
    Mother of God (later
    rededicated to the Holy
    Name of Jesus) founded by
    Francis Xavier. 218, 276, 277,
    Thomas Stephens teaches
    Marathi at, 276: mint (Casa
    de Moeda), 276: Father
    Stephens Academy School,
    288, 289
Bélem, 58:
    Monastery of Our Lady of Beth-
    lehem (Jerónimos

Monastery), 58, 59: Bélem Tower, 60
Benaulim (Banavli),
  Church of St John the Baptist, 237, Thomas Stephens accused of appropriating rents from, 237: Thomas Stephens as parish priest, 237: *ramponnkars* (fisher-folk) at, 228
Bengal, Sultanate and Mughul fiefdom, 45, 134, 158, 208, 241, 264, 265:
  Malikha River, 262
Bergen-op-Zoom, 10
Bermuda, xviii
Bihar, 158
Bijapur, 83, 96, 114, 120, 126, 181
Bir Mahali, Syria, River Euphrates at, 198
Bishop's Stortford, Thomas Pounde imprisoned at Castle, 43, 44
Bologna, 54:
  University, 23
Bombay (Mumbai):
  Garcia da Orta's garden in, 140: ceded to Portuguese, 276
Braga, 177
Brazil, 70, 180:
  founded by Martim Afonso de Sousa, 139
Bruges, 202
Bungo, Japan, 179
Bushton, Wiltshire, 2, 3, 14, 136:
  Bushton Manor in, 2: lease of manor granted to Richard Stephens, 2: ownership transferred to Thomas Seymour, 3

Cadiz, 36
Cahors, 164
Calais, 10
Calicut, 173, 265.267:
  Zamarin of, 243, 245, 266: Jesuit Mission in, 266
Cambay (Khambat), 114
Cambodia, Jesuit mission to King, 241
Cambridge, visit of Queen Elizabeth to University, 8
Canary Isles, 62, 66
Cambrai, 13
Canton (Guangdong), 211
Cape Bojador, 59
Cape Comerin, 115
Cape of Good Hope, xviii, 1, 27, 62, 65, 66, 84, 116
Castelo de Vide, birthplace of Garcia de Orta, 139
Catalonia, 176
Ceylon (Sri Lanka), 113, 131, 208
Chaliyam, 267:
  fortress captured from Portuguese by Zamarin of Calicut, 243
Chennamangalam, Vaipikotta Seminary at, 176
Chao-ch'ing (Zhaoqing), Jesuit mission at, 211
Chaul, 206
China, xvi, 70, 102, 136, 140, 211:

Index of Places 325

Jesuit mission, 96, 211–215:
Queen Elizabeth writes to
Emperor, 194, 195; Ming
Dynasty, 213, 215:
Mandarins, 214: war with
Japan, 214
Chittagong, 265:
River Ganges at, 265
Civitavecchia, 36
Clyffe Pypard, Wiltshire, 2, 3
Cochin (Kochi), 95, 174, 176,
179, 201, 218, 231, 233, 263,
266, 268, 275:
Jesuit College, 253, 270, 271: city
jail (*Tronco*), 269–271
Coimbra: Jesuit College, 46, 57:
University, 94
Cologne, 107
Cork, 35
Cranganore (Kodungallur),
Archdiocese, 239
Cuncolim, 113, 181, 186, 259:
friction between Hindus and
Christians, 184–187:
ganvkars massacred by Portuguese treachery, 187:
'Martyrs of Cuncolim, 188,
189, 192

Damão, 102, 103, 106, 111:
Inquisition in, 102, 103, 106,
107: prison, 103
Deccan, 248
Devizes, Wiltshire, 3
Diamper (Udayamperoor),
Synod at, 235–241, 250(19),
256, 257
Diu, 96, 106, 114, 206:

bulwark of St. John, 1: ceded to
Portuguese, 139: siege of, 1
Douai, 16–18, 226:
English Seminary, 11, 12, 16, 17,
30: University, 16, 17
Dover, 167
Dublin, 9, 10

East Ham, Essex, 43
East Timor, 113, 131
Edessa, 220
El Escorial, San Lorenzo de.
Royal monastery of, 223
England, 61, 107, 143, 164:
at war with Portugal, 163
Ethiopia, 72
Eton, College, 30

Fallujah, River Euphrates at, 198
Farlington, Hampshire, Belmont
House in, 12
Fatehpur Sikri, 141, 142, 148,
159, 163:
architecture, 144: building, 143,
144, 149: Court of Akbar the
Great, 41, 142, 144, 145, 148–
154, 208: foundation by
Akbar, 142: Akbar deserts,
217, 218
Buildings: *Diwan-I-Am* (Hall of
Public Audience), 144:
Ibadat Khana, ('House of
Worship'), 141: *Jama Masjid*
('the Friday Mosque'), 144:
palace of *Jodha Bai,* 144):
Naubat Khana (Drum
House), 145: *Parcheesi* Court,
145: tomb (*dargah*) of

Shaykh Salim Chishti, 143, 144
Fishery Coast, 89, 95, 253
Flanders, 202
Florence, 54, 91, 109
Florida, 35
France, 7, 16, 87, 177, 287

Galicia, 264
Genoa, 5
Goa, xviii, 37, 44–47, 51, 60, 61, 66, 68, 69, 83, 84, 93–95, 98, 102, 110, 113, 114, 122, 131, 136, 139, 141, 142, 146, 164, 169, 174, 175, 178, 179, 185, 190, 194, 199, 211, 218, 223, 224, 240, 241, 244–248, 256, 269, 270, 274–276, 283, 287: attacked by Ali Adil Shah I, 120, 126: captured by Afonso de Albuquerque, 83, 84: Bangany Spring, 78: Carambolim Lake, 125: Charles Dellon at, 102, 103: Aveador General (Chief Justice), 200, 201: class system, 116, 117: corruption, 116: dress, 119: epidemics, 125: flora of, 78, 79: Franciscans in, 227: gambling, 72: Hindus in, 110: Inquisition, xvii, 6, 97, 100, 101, 103–110, 112, 113, 203, 257, 258: Japanese delegation in, 179: languages, 221: Mandovi River, 83, 114, 132, 224, 289: Mint, 112: *Monte do Rosario*, 126: Municipal Council (*Officials de Camara*), 114: Feast days, 118, 119, 134, 137: Church Councils, 75, 77.97, 98, 99, 221, 222, 232: ban on Indian physicians treating Christians, 122: Mausoleum of St Francis Xavier, 70: medicine, 122, 123, 132, 133: Dutch blockade of, 243: Provincial Councils, 175, 176, 189: Royal Dockyards: 99: *sati*, 119: Senate, 113, 114, 227, 246: sex and sensuality, 73–76, 100: sickness and disease, 121, 125: under siege, 126: slavery in, 76–78, 115, 205, 286: syphilis, 75, 76: Supreme Court, 78: trade, 70–72, 120, 121: measures against foreign traders, 262: Ward of the Potters, 125: decline of, 285: Jesuits expelled from, 286, 287

Buildings: Arch of the Viceroys, 114, 246, vandalised, 246, 247: Gunpowder Factory (*Casa de Polvora*), 102, 105, 113: prison, 103, 104, 201: Professed House (*Casa Professa*), , 218, 227, 231, 283, 284: Viceregal Palace, 70, 97, 118, 119

Churches: Bom Jesus, *247*: 138, 227, 284, foundation, 231, consecration, 247: shrine of St Francis Xavier, 285: St Francis of Assisi, 105: Se' Cathedral of Santa Catarina, 68.84, 108, 132:, 188, 246: Collegiate Church of St Paul, 137

educational institutions: Goa University, 283, 288: **St Paul's College**, 47, 94, 96, 97,

Index of Places 327

97, 126, 132–138, 180.182, 188, 201–204, 228, 246, 248, 275, 283: curriculum, 137, foundation, 136, annual penitential procession, 137, first printing press in Asia, 137, 279 Thomas Stephens studies at, 136, becomes Rector, 227, decline and demolition of, 285: Seminary of the Holy Faith, 84, 85, 94, placed under authority of Francis Xavier, 94, becomes St Paul's College, 94: College of São Roque, 126
medical and welfare institutions: Padre Camerte Hospital, 133, 182: **Royal Hospital,** 132–138, 272, annual timetable, 134: daily routine, 133–136, Jesuit reluctance to administer, 133: prescription of cow's urine, 135, 136: regulations, 136, staffing, 134: **St Lazarus Leper Hospital,** 88: Confraternity of the *Misericorda,* 132, 133, 227, 231, Archbishop Menezes establishes three charitable houses for, 231
streets: Market Place, *74*, 85: Rua Direita, 76, 205: Terreiro dos Galos, 227
Gran Canaria, 62
Great Saxham, 198
Guinea, 63
Gwalior, 142: prison, 151

Haarlam, 202
Hamburg, 202

Hangzhou, 216
Hoxton, Essex, 43

India, xviii, 9, 58, 64, 66, 67, 76, 86, 87, 102, 121, 123, 132, 136, 141–143, 173, 218, 224: languages of, 221: Catholic Bishops Conference of, 250en22
Indian Ocean, xix, 131, 228: Dutch challenge Portuguese naval dominance of, 243, 247
Indonesia, 243
Indus River, 163
Ireland, 35, 36

Japan, xvi, xvii, 44, 46–50, 95, 132, 179, 211, 224, 251: culture of, 49, 50: emissaries to Europe, 179, 223–225: war with China, 214: Imperial Court, 225: persecution of Christians in, 225, 226: Europeans expelled from, 226
Jaunpur, 158
Java, 140
Jerusalem, 24

Kabul, 9, 163
Kannanur, 272
Kenilworth, Royal Pageant at, 9
Kennington, Surrey, 15
Kerala, 138, 174, 234
Kittur, Jesuit Mission, 287
Korea, 214
Kyushu, conquered by Toyotami Hideyoshi, 224

Lake Maggiore, 47, 185
Lahore, 152, 206:
   Akbar moves capital to, 217: builds chapel in, 219
Lisbon, 36, 47, 56–58, 60, 66, 67, 70, 71, 113, 177, 178, 180, 199, 223, 224, 241, 273:
   College of Santo Antão, 57: Hospital Real de Todos-os-Santos, 57: plague in, 57: *Santa Casa da Misericorda*, 132: Church of São Roque, 57: River Tagus, 50, 68, 83: University, 139: Church of *Espirito Santo*, 227
London, 14, 32, 34, 42, 43, 68, 107, 164, 167, 194, 195, 286:
   Founders Hall, 244: Lincoln's Inn, 12, 52: Middle Temple, 195: River Thames, 155, 198: St. Lawrence Jewry, 43: St. Paul's Churchyard, 10: Tyburn, 52; Westminster Hall, 165, Star Chamber in, 165:
   Educational institutions: Christ's Hospital School, 5: King's College, 287, 288: School of Oriental Studies, 288: Westminster School, 195
   Prisons: Marshalsea, 15, 21, 42, 43: Newgate, 52: Tower of London, 10, 164, 169
Loutolim,
   Diego Rodrigues destroys temples, 228: Thomas Stephens ministers at, 228: legend of Mahadar, 228: Gaunkor family donates land to build church, 228: Church of the Saviour of the World (*Igreja do Salvador do Mundo*), 229, *229*: Thomas Stephens parish priest at, 230
Louvain, University, 16
Ludlow, Thomas Pounde and Thomas Stephens imprisoned in, 9
Lyneham, Wiltshire, 3
Lyons, 107, 166

Macao, 50, 51, 84, 113, 132, 134, 179, 224, 226, 241:
   established as Portuguese outpost, 211: Pearl River, 211
Machhiwara, 163
Madagascar (Isle of St Laurence), 66
Madeira, 59.62, 84
Madras (Chennai), Fort St George, 107:
   St Andrew's Church, 107
Madrid, 56, 223, 274
Madurai, 253, 255
Majorda, Church of Madre de Deos (Mãe de Deus), 223
Malabar Coast and Region, 2, , 93, 114, 174–176, 185, 228, 233, 243, 256, 261, 268, 271, 287:
   pirates, 115, 245, 246, 268
Malacca, 94, 95, 113, 131, 134, 199, 208
Maldive Islands:
   Pyrard de Laval wrecked upon, 263: invaded by Subahdar of Bengal, 264, 265

Index of Places

Malé, 264:
  crew of *Corbin* kept prisoner in, 263
Mangalore, 286, 287
Marcourt, Luxembourg, 25
Margão, 223:
  attacked by Ibrahim Adil Shah, 183: Church of Holy Spirit, 182: Hospital of the Holy Spirit (Padre Camerte Hospital), 182: Old Market Square, 230: school, 182: seminary, 182, 183: Thomas Stephens parish priest at, 230
Maryland, 115
Mecca, 147, 156
Mesopotamia, 8, 174, 231
Mexico, 225
Midhurst, Sussex, 14:
  Cowdray House, 14, 60
Milan, 54–56
Miranmar, Loyola Hall, 289
Miyako, Japan, 49
Modena, 54
Moluccas, 94, 131, 180, 200
Montepulciano, 251
Montmartre, 24
Mormugão, 229:
  St Andrew's Church, 229, picture of, 229: visited by Pietro della Valle, 229, 230: Zuari River, 229
Morocco, 36, 167
Mozambique, 66, 67, 76, 113, 131, 174, 224, 268
Munster, 35
Mylapore, 2, 108:
  shrine of St. Thomas, 1, 2

Nagasaki, 47, 113, 225, 241:
  given to Jesuits, 50, 51: 26 Christians crucified at by Toyotami Hideyoshi, 226
Nan-ch'ang, 214
Nanjing (Nanking), 214
Naples, Kingdom of, 46, 47
Navarre, 218
Navelim, Church of the Holy Rosary. 230:
  Thomas Stephens parish priest at, 230: patronal festival, 230
Netherlands, The, 241, 242:
  trading partner with Portugal, 178: at war with Spain, 178: allowed restricted access to Japanese ports, 226
'New Kingdom of Granada' (Colombia), 115

Omura, Japan, 50, 179
Orlim, 180, 186
Ormuz, 95, 113, 131, 142, 194, 198, 199, 201, 231: lost by Portuguese, 284
Osaka, Franciscan Friary, 225
Ottoman Empire, 24, 35
Oxford, University, 5, 9, 10, 16, 28, 196:
  colleges: Balliol, 5: Exeter, 30: Merton, 16: New, 4, 6, 16: Oriel, 17:
St. John's, 5

Padua, University, 47
Pamplona, Castle of Xavier, 24
Panjim (Panaji), 289:

Central Library, 283
Paris, 107:
    University of, 24, 164
Peking (Beijing), 214–217
Persia, 143, 273
Persian Gulf, 194
Philippines, 51, 94, 225
Picenza, 54
Pisa, 223
Pittsburgh, 107
Poland, large population of Catholics, 287
Ponda, prison, 113
Porto Santo, 62
Portugal, 35, 46, 58, 59, 76, 94, 96, 105, 106, 134, 139, 174, 206;
    creates first maritime empire, xix: Inquisition in, 96, 100: *patriado* with Pope, 175: Union of Crowns with Spain, 37, 177, 178: at war with England, 163, 178
Pudepatam, river and peninsular, 245, 246: fort, under siege, 245

Punjab, 159, 163

Quilon (Kollam), 240, 260

Rachol, 180, 193, 276, 277, 282, 285:
    Chapel of St John the Baptist, 182: Church of Our Lady of the Snows (*Nossa Senhora das Neves*), 188, Thomas Stephens parish priest at, 237: fortress, 181, 182: Jesus House, 180, 182: main gate, *183:* Moslem fort, 183: seminary (College of the Holy Spirit), 113, 184, 186, 190, Thomas Stephens accused of appropriating rents for, 237: curriculum, 184: moves to Margão, 182, 189, returns to Rachol, 183, 189, 277: Zuari River, 181, 258: seminary, building of, 258, debts, 258
Raia, Church of Our Lady of the Snows, 113, 182
Red Sea, 67
Reims, English Seminary, 17
River Trent, 166
Rodrigues, island discovered by Diego Rodrigues, 228
Rome, 1, 4, 5, 11, 15, 17, 18, 24, 25, 28, 35, 36, 45, 47, 56, 60, 89, 99, 141, 174, 175, 179, 214, 224, 235, 287:
    Flaminian Gate, 54: Inquisition, 99: Quirinal Hill, 17: Vatican, 175
    Churches, Chiesa del Gesú, 277: Sant'Andrea a Montecavallo, 13, 17, 19, 47, 180, 274: S. Girolamo della Carita, 33: Santa Maria Maggiore, 45
    Colleges: English College, 30–35, 42: German College (Collegio Teutonico), 47: Roman College (Gregorian University), 27–29, 250(19): Sapienza University, 9
Rother, River, 14
Rotterdam, 107

Index of Places

Saint Helena, 241
Salcete, 180, 186, 222, 224:
   annexed by Portugal, 1543, 88, 230: descriptions, 181: Hinduism in, 182, 186: Jesuit Mission, 180–186, 203: myth of origin, 228; revolt against Portuguese rule, 185: Sal River, 185
Salamanca, University, 139
Salerno, 214
Santiago de Compostela, Shrine of St James, 291(11)
Scotland, 107
Seville, 202
Shanghai, 136
Shaoguan (Shaozhou), 214
Siam, 208
Siena, 54
Socotra, 67
Soissons, 167
Southampton Water, 14
Spain, 35, 56:
   Union of Crowns with Portugal, 37.176, 177
Spanish Netherlands, 16, 241
Srirangapatna, Konkani Christians exiled to, 286
Stratford-upon-Avon, 13
Surat, 106, 107, 142, 262

Tanur, 267:
   Jesuit church, 268
Tenerife, 62
Titchfield, Hampshire, 15:
   Place House, 14

Tosa, Isle of, Japan:
   San Filipe runs aground on, 225
Tripoli, Lebanon, 197, 198
Tuscany, 251

Udayamperoor, see Diamper

Vaipim, 233
Varca, Church of Our Lady of Gloria, 113
Vasai—see Bassein
Venice, 18, 24, 120:
   dominance of eastern trade routes, 199, 247
Verdun, 273
Vienna, 286
Vimeiro, Portugal, 35
Viterbo, Italy, 54

Wales, 31
Wantage, Lyford Grange, 164
Waterford, 38
Western Ghats, 228
Wiltshire, 202
Winchester, Prison, 15:
   St Stephen's Priory, 2: Winchester College, 3, 4, 12, 28, 283

Index of Subjects

Adoptionism, policy of (*Accommodacio,* Accommodation, or Inculturation), xvii, xviii, xix, 48, 49, 131, 175, 192, 286: Francis Xavier and, 89, 95: Mateo Ricci and, 211, 212, 217: Roberto de Nobili and, 253, 257: Thomas Stephens and, 51, 228

Acts of Parliament,
Supremacy, Act of, 1559, 5, 6, 8, 9: Uniformity, Act of, 1559, 6

Anglo-Saxon Chronicle, 1

Arabs, 87, 106

Archbishopric of Goa and Damão, 84

Arianism, 194, 209(11)

Armenians, 109

Augustinians, 231

Battles:
Alcácer Quibir, 1578: 36, 177:
Lepanto, 1571, 35, 36:
Swally, 1612, 244

Bible,
Authorised version, 17, 255:'Books of Daniel, Esdras and Esther, 152: Douay translation, 16, 17: Psalms. 195: Song of Songs, 262

Brahmins, 72, 86, 87, 89–93, 97.98, 109, 138, 155, 182, 184, 190, 223, 228, 262:
attitude to Portuguese, 87, 253; banished from Goa, 98: Pyrard de Laval on, 120: *nagar* sub-division: Thomas Christians and, 93: distaste of Francis Xavier for, 89, 90: Portuguese attitude to, 253: Roberto de Nobili adopts lifestyle of, 254–257

Buddhism, 158:
monks (*bonze*), 212, 214

Calendars,
Julian, 29, 211: Gregorian, 29, 211

Calvinism, 108, 193, 194:
Huguenot pirates, 180

Capuchins, 107, 108

Castes (*Varnas*), 85, 86, 87,
Brahmins, see separate entry: Dalits, 86, 87, 93, 240: *jogi,* 219, 220: Kshatriya, 86, 87, 184, 255: Nair, 173: Sudra, 86, 228: Valśhya, 86, 87

Caste System, xvii, 85–87, 253:
Portuguese and, 86.87, 240, 253: St Thomas Christians and, 3, 173, 177, 236, 237, 240: Roberto de Nobili and, 253–257

Catholic Association, 16

Chaldean Catholic Church,
Pope appoints Saluqa as Patriarch, 173: in Communion with Rome, 174

Church of England, 108:
    Book of Common Prayer, 6:
    Commissioners for Causes Ecclesiastical, 43
Consistory Courts, 100
Company for Distant Trade (*Compagnie van Verre*), 243
Confraternity of Christian Doctrine, 56
Confraternity of São Roque, 57
Confucianism, Mario Ricci and, 213–216
Congregation of the Oratory, 33
Counter-Reformation, 55
Crusades, the, Arab name for Crusaders, 87

Dhivehi, language, 263
Dissolution of the Monasteries, 2, 7
Divine Right of Kings, 7
Dominicans, 84, 99, 103, 106, 202:
    and Rites Controversy, 217
Dutch East India Company (*Verenigde Landsche Ge-Oktroyeerde Oost-Indische Compagnie*), 243:
    challenges Portuguese naval dominance of Indian Ocean, 243

East India Company, 107, 111, 273:
    foundation, 244: victory at Battle of Swally, 244: third expedition to Indies, 262
East Syrian Patriarchate, 174

Ecumenical Councils,
    Ephesus (431), 235: Chalcedon (451), 235: Florence (1431–49), 239: Nicaea (325), 209(11): Trent (1545–63), 17, 54, 55, 85, 98, 235: Vatican II (1962–65), 217
'Elizabethan Settlement', 7, 17, 100

French East India Company (*Compagnie des Indes orientale*), 102, 111
Franciscans, 84, 99, 227, 276:
    mission to Japan, 225: 23 missionaries crucified by Toyotami Hideyoshi, 226: Franciscan Recollects, 276

Greek language, 221:
    epic poetry, 261: words recharged with Christian meaning, 281, 282
Gujaratis, 109, 143

Hapsburg, House of, 223:
    become rulers of Portugal, 177
Hieronymites (Order of St Jerome), 58
Hinduism and Hindus ('Gentiles'), 71, 72, 76, 83, 85–92, 97–99, 109, 110, 142, 144, 149, 156, 158, 177, 181, 184–187, 228, 236, 255, 256, 266:
    Brahmins, see separate entry: âcâryas, 281, castes—see separate entry: friction with Christians, 184–187: Lord Ayyappa, 266: Durga,

Index of Subjects

goddess, 182: food laws, 91: infanticide, 85, 97, 98: *jagatguru*, 281: *karma*, 85: *kalpataru* (the tree of life), 262: *matha* (monastery), 230: *manusmriti* (law). 85, 86: *mala* beads, 266 medicine, 112: *moksa*, 281: *mukti*, 281: orphans, 97: physicians (*vaidyas*), 140: *puranas*, 261, 262, 278 reincarnation, 85, 93: Santéry, the cobra goddess, 182, 185: *sdti*, 85, 98, 119, 157, 253, 254: in Salcete, 181, 184–187: Lord Parshuram, 6th incarnation of Vishnu, 228: *vrata* (austerity), 266: lack of conversion process, 254: Roberto de Nobili and, 253–257: sacred books—*Vedas* and *Upanishads*, 255: *swami*, an ascetic or *yogi*, 281: *Vaikuntha*, 281: *Vedânta* School of Hindu Philosophy, 281: Supreme Lord, Vishnu, 281: Yama, God of Death, 281: Yamapuri, 281: ridiculed by Etienne de la Croix, 285

Indo-European Language Family, 221

Inquisition, The, xvii, xviii, 99–107, 111, 127, 128, 203: abolition, 112: *auto-da-fé*, 104, 109: and bigamy, 106, 107: 'Black Legend' of, 107: in Damão, 102, 103, 106, 107: in Goa, 96, 97, 99–101, 103–106, 112: cases cited by Fatima da

Silva Gracias, 112:
and Jesuits, 111: and New Christians, 110–112: in Portugal, 96: Pyrard de Laval on, 110: punishments, 100.101, 105–107, 112: in Rome, 99: secrecy of, 109, 110: and sodomy. 106, 107: investigates Roberto de Nobili, 256, 257: and the *Kristapurana*, 277

People appearing before the Tribunals:
Felicitana de Azavdo, widow, 112: Catherine Boteli, midwife, 112:
Charles Dellon, physician before, 104–106, 203:
Miguel de Souza, 113:
Joseph de Pereira de Meneses, naval commander, 106:
Polpotto Naique, sailor, 113:
Ephrem Nevers, friar, 108, 109:
Anno Pinto, midwife, 112, 113

Islam, 45, 71, 72, 76, 83, 95, 97, 142, 144, 245, 246, 264:
caliphate, 158: *Chistiyya* Order, 142, 144, 146, 148: *dhimmi* (people of the book), 158: *fatwas*, 158: *hadj*. 157: *hadiths* (sayings of the Prophet), 157:: *kâfir* (infidels), 158: Muslim physicians (*hakims*), 140: polygamy, 155: *Qu'ran*, 146, 154: *Shari'ah* (Islamic laws), 91, 148, 152, 154, 156–158: Shi'ites, 156, 158: *shirk* (polytheistic heresy), 157: Sufism, 142, 157, 220: Sunnis, 156, 157: *ulema* (scholars),

156–158: *ummah* (Islamic community), 219: doctrine of *Wahlat-al-Wuyud* (Unity of Being), 143

Jacobite Syrian Church, 237
Jainism, 144, 156
Jews, 91.97, 109, 114, 139, 158
Jesuits—see Society of Jesus

Knights Templars, 59
Konkani ('Canarin'), language and people, 71, 85, 117–119, 138.183, 186, 221, 222, 228, 249, 272, 278, 292(35):
 dress, 119: myth of origin, 228: Thomas Stephens grammar of, 261, 285: Cunha Rivara writes history of, 283: Thomas Stephens catechism in, 285: Bible translated into, 285: Thomas Stephens Konkanni Kendr (Konkani Language Institute), 289: campaign for Konkani Roman script (Romi Konkani), 289: *Tiatr*, Konkani musical theatre, 289

Latin, language, 190, 221, 224, 282

Malayalam language, 138, 177, 233, 235
Marathi language, 249, 262, 276–279, 282, 278, 281, 282, 285: Devanagari script, 262, 278, 282, 288: *Kristapurana* first work to be published in, 283: *Paixão de Cristo* written in, 283: books written in prohibited by Viceroy, 286
Medici, Royal House, sees Dom Antonio as useful tool against Spain, 177
Medicine, sickness and disease, 121:
 ague, 121: Asiatic cholera, 125, 126, 140: bubonic plague, 121, 126, believed to be brought on Portuguese ships, 126: circulation of the blood, 123: cholera, 125: colic ('mordexijn'), 121, 129(52): diarrhoea, 125: dysentery, 76: epidemics, 125: fever, 125: gallstones, 122: Garcia da Orta, 139, 140: in Goa, 122, 123, 132–136: health and hygiene, 72, 75: Muslim physicians (*hakims*), 140: piles, 121: rupture, 122: syphilis, 75, 76, believed to originate from the Portuguese, 76
 Drugs and medicinal herbs: effects of cannabis (*bhang*), 75, 139–141: datura, (deutria), 75, 81(38), 191, 209(10): galangal, 140: opium, 75: tamarind, 140
 Hindu physicians (*vaidyas*), 122, 123: lack of understanding of anatomy, 123; use of bleeding, 125: banned from treating Christian patients, 122: overuse of leeches, 124: reluctance to undertake surgery or phlebotomy, 123, 124:

Index of Subjects 337

shortcomings of Indian apothecaries, 124

Military Order of Christ, 59:
Moors, 59, 72, 83, 109, 120, 219
Mughals, 139, 141, 142, 160, 248: art and artists, 218

Napoleonic Wars, 287
Natural Law, 115, 213
Nestorianism, 2, 173, 174, 231–233, 235, 237, 240
New Christians, 71, 91, 97, 98, 123:
and Inquisition, 110–113: adopt Portuguese names, 98

Oratorians, 113
Order of the Humiliati, 56
Orphans: of Hindus, 97, 98:
'Father of Christians' ('*Pai de Cristâos*'): 97, 98: 'Orphans of the King' ('*Ortas do Rei*'), 60, 84

Papacy, 18, 23
Paravars, 89: adopt Portuguese dress and diet, 253
Persian, language and people, 160, 219, 220
Portuguese Empire, 56, 59, 60, 63, 85, 111, 113, 131, 178, 194, 247
Privy Council, 15
Protestantism, 110, 115, 169, 173, 237, 266, 269
Puritanism, 7, 43

Rajputs, 142, 160
St Thomas Christians (Malankara Church), 1, 2, 4, 5, 93, 174–176, 231–237:
administration, 173: and caste system, 93, 173, 177, 236, 237: Catholic view of as heretic, 173, 174: system of succession, 173: and Catholic doctrine, 176: purging of literature, 176, 177: attempts to align with Catholic Church, 176: visitation of Archbishop Menezes to, 234: Nestorian and Monophysite doctrines of, 235: and Synod of Diamper, 236, 239–241: union with Rome agreed, 236: and Hinduism, 236, 240: literature of, 237, 238: hostility to images, 238: superstitions, 238: liturgy of Addai and Mari, 239: Coonan Cross Oath and split with Rome, 240: military capacity, 241
Salesian Order, 288
Sanskrit, 221, 249, 255, 257, 261, 278
Sex and Sensuality, 73–75
Ships and Shipping,
'*Almedie*,' pirate ship, 267: '*Armada do Norte*,' 114: '*Armada do Sud*,' 114, 115, 270, 271: **Ascension,** East India Company ship, wrecked in East Bengal: **Corbin,** wrecked in Maldive Islands, 263: **Hercules,** 198:

Madre de Dios, Portuguese treasure ship, captured by English privateers, 243, *Matricola* found on board, 243, 244: *São Lourenço,* carrack (*nau*), xviii, 136, voyage to Goa, 60–67, 84: *San Filipe,* runs aground in Japan, 225, cargo confiscated by Toyotami Hideyoshi: *Santa Cruz,* Dirck Pomp sails aboard: *Sea Venturer,* wrecked off Bermuda, xviii: *Tyger,* mentioned in *Macbeth,* 194

Sino-Japanese War, 1592, 214

Slavery, 72, 76–78, 115, 116, 145: abolished in Portugal and India, 286

Society of Jesus, 4, 5, 11, 14, 18, 32, 34, 46, 47, 50, 54–58, 62, 85, 89, 94, 97, 231, 283, 284: policy of Accomodation, 48, 49, 89, 95, 175, 192, 211, 212: and agriculture, 131: and cartography, 245: 1st mission to Emperor Akbar, xviii, 141–157: 2nd mission to Akbar, 218: 3rd mission to Akbar, 157, 218–220, 248: accused of avarice, 131, 132: approach to conversion, 192: mission to China, 211–217; response to cholera epidemic of 1570, 125: Cuncolim Martyrs, 180, 181: and education, 27, 131, 132: English Mission, xvi, 27, 42, 43: esteem of Emperor Akbar for, 156, 178, 179: expulsion from Goa, 113: foundation of Society, 24, 26, 93, 94: Indian Province, 27, 44–46, 95, 247, 251, 256: only one Indian admitted, 138, and Inquisition, 111: mission to Japan, 46–50, 95, 223, 224: Jesuit formation, 18–23, 27, 44, 47, 204: reputation, 189, 202, 204: Royal Hospital, Goa, 133: Salcete Mission, 182–190, 222, 223: separation of religion and politics, 165: and slavery, 115: *Spiritual Exercises,* 24–26: suppression of Society, 138: vows and constitution, 24, 26, 132: welfare facilities in the *Estado da India,* 131, 132; and Rites Controversy, 217: crucifixion of Japanese Jesuits, 226: missions to Bengal and Cambodia, 241: print first books in non-European language, 260: mission in Calicut, 266: Cochin College, 263, 270, 271: transcends national identities, 285: expelled from Portugal and its colonies, 286, 287: expelled from France, Spain, Kingdom of Naples and Sicily and the Duchy of Parma, 287: restored by Pope Pius XIV, 287: returns to India, 287

Spice trade, 83, 178, 198, 243, 244:
Cervantes on, 243

Synod of Diamper, 235–241, 250(19), 256, 257

Syriac, language and liturgy, 175, 176, 233, 250(19):

Index of Subjects

Roman rite translated into, 234: remains liturgical language of St Thomas Christians, 236, 239

Tamil, language and people, 138, 253, 255:
Parava pearl fishermen, 89: first books in non-European language printed by Jesuits, 260
Times of India, 289.290
Turkey and Levant Company, 194:
John Newbury asks to petition Philip II on his behalf, 200
Turkomen, 160

Wiltshire Life, magazine, xv

Zen Buddhism, hierarchy of Japanese Mission modelled on grades of, 50

www.ingramcontent.com/pod-product-compliance
Lightning Source LLC
Chambersburg PA
CBHW032016230426
43671CB00005B/104